# THE DIGITAL SILK ROAD

# THE
# DIGITAL
# SILK ROAD

## China's Quest to Wire the World
## and Win the Future

# JONATHAN E. HILLMAN

HARPER
BUSINESS
*An Imprint of* HarperCollins*Publishers*

HarperCollins books may be purchased for educational, business, or sales promotional use. For information, please email the Special Markets Department at SPsales@harpercollins.com.

FIRST EDITION

*Designed by Kyle O'Brien*

Library of Congress Cataloging-in-Publication Data
Names: Hillman, Jonathan E., author.
Title: The digital Silk Road: China's quest to wire the world and win the future / Jonathan E. Hillman.
Description: New York: Harper Business, 2021. | Includes bibliographical references and index. | Identifiers: LCCN 2021027591 (print) | LCCN 2021027592 (ebook) | ISBN 9780063046283 (hardcover) | ISBN 9780063046290 (ebook)
Subjects: LCSH: China—Foreign economic relations—21st century. | Information services industry—Economic aspects—China. | Silk Road—History—Electronic information resources. | International economic integration—Strategic aspects.
Classification: LCC HF1604 .H55  2021 (print) | LCC HF1604 (ebook) | DDC 337.51—dc23
LC record available at https://lccn.loc.gov/2021027591.
LC ebook record available at https://lccn.loc.gov/2021027592.

21 22 23 24 25   LSC   10 9 8 7 6 5 4 3 2 1

# CSIS | CENTER FOR STRATEGIC & INTERNATIONAL STUDIES

The Center for Strategic and International Studies (CSIS) is a bipartisan, nonprofit policy research organization dedicated to advancing practical ideas to address the world's greatest challenges.

CSIS does not take specific policy positions; accordingly, all views expressed herein should be understood to be solely those of the author's.

Center for Strategic and International Studies
1616 Rhode Island Avenue, NW
Washington, DC 20036
202.887.0200
www.csis.org

For Liz

# CONTENTS

# INTRODUCTION

This book was born at 195 Broadway, a twenty-nine-story building wrapped with Roman columns in New York City's bustling financial district. Long before my U.S. publisher, HarperCollins, moved in, it was the headquarters of American Telephone and Telegraph, better known as AT&T, and the site of several historic transmissions: the first sustained transatlantic radio communication in 1923, the first transatlantic phone call in 1927, and the first two-way videophone call in 1930. During the Cold War, AT&T adopted the slogan "Communications is the foundation of democracy," and for most of the twentieth century, 195 Broadway stood at the center of an expanding communications empire.

As this century unfolds, communications are racing faster, reaching further, carrying more—and increasingly coming from China. In 2017, Chinese engineers used a special satellite to hold the first intercontinental, quantum-encrypted video conference, a major step toward constructing an unhackable network. In 2018, Huawei and Vodafone demonstrated one of the first 5G wireless calls. The same year, Hengtong Group celebrated foreign sales of 10,000 kilometers of subsea fiber-optic cable, the systems that carry the vast majority of international data. Communications, the Chinese Communist Party (CCP) is proving, does not have a political preference. It is a powerful tool, for liberation or repression, depending on who controls it.

Just three decades ago, China was completely dependent on foreign companies for all these capabilities. Huawei was a middling reseller. China's most advanced communications satellites were made in the United States. The world's subsea fiber-optic cable providers were exclusively from the United States, Europe, and Japan. Lacking these systems, let alone the ability to produce them, China's first connection to the global internet came through a Sprint satellite network in 1994. Since then, China has leapt from customer to supplier, from copycat to innovator, from network offshoot to operator.

China's rapid rise is overshadowed only by its global ambitions for the next three decades. Chinese leader Xi Jinping has called for his country to dominate advanced technology manufacturing by 2025, to lead standard setting by 2035, and to become a global superpower by 2050. Xi is mobilizing companies to pour resources into developing digital infrastructure at home and sell more of their products overseas through his Belt and Road Initiative. The Digital Silk Road, part of that initiative and the focus of this book, connects China's bid for technological independence at home and its quest to dominate tomorrow's markets.

History cautions that much more than sales figures are at stake. AT&T applied its expertise to help develop nuclear weapons, a missile warning system, and a secret communications network for Air Force One, among other national security projects. "The blessing of the state, implicit or explicit, has been crucial to every twentieth-century information empire," observes Tim Wu, a Columbia Law professor who joined President Biden's National Economic Council, in *The Master Switch*. Now a new information empire is emerging with vast support from the Chinese state. These pages describe its contours and grapple with its consequences.

While I was writing this book, the stakes became even starker as the COVID-19 pandemic paralyzed the physical world. The streets of New York and so many other cities became quiet, and during the darkest of those days, everything seemed dangerously brittle if not already broken: health systems, supply chains, and financial markets. Digital infrastructure, normally out of sight and out of mind, suddenly felt like the one system that did not fail. It provided a lifeline to family, friends, work, school, food, entertainment, and more. The digital world roared ahead.

Out of necessity, my journey to understand digital infrastructure became even more virtual. Instead of flying to Los Angeles to tour one of the world's busiest internet exchanges, and the gateway for massive data flows to and from Asia, I took an online tour of the facility and then continued onward to Cape Town to visit one of Africa's largest data centers—all while eating lunch from my desk. I enrolled in online courses on surveillance systems offered by China's largest camera manufacturer, gaining access that would have been difficult, if not impossible, in person. I became a beta user of Starlink, Elon Musk's mega-constellation of satellites that aims to deliver broadband to the farthest reaches of the Earth.

These virtual excursions had their limits. I couldn't wander, as I had grown accustomed to doing while visiting Chinese infrastructure projects around the world before the pandemic. I couldn't bump into fellow classmates between lessons and learn about them and why they were taking the course. Even the most high-definition video can't capture the smell of a place or the feel of rain, sun, and wind. Yet the opportunities were still amazing—the information I accessed, the places I saw, the people I met, all safely amid a global pandemic.

But life did not migrate online for everyone, nor in the same way for those privileged to have access. Roughly half of humanity still lacks internet access. In China, nearly a billion people have access, but foreign connections are so restricted that most people are essentially using a separate internet. The pandemic also opened the floodgates for more pervasive and sophisticated forms of surveillance. Chinese surveillance cameras landed everywhere, from the European Parliament to Alabama's public schools, armed with thermal imaging to detect fevers.

With its reach expanding rapidly, China may seem destined to host the headquarters of the next information empire. Huawei's sprawling

European-style campus in Dongguan, an hour outside Shenzhen, already makes AT&T's Roman touches look modest. But the United States still occupies a position of strength. Among its many advantages are world-leading research universities, innovative companies, deep pools of private capital, openness to immigrants, and a global network of partners and allies. The question is whether the United States can rise to the challenge, rebuilding at home while leading a coalition of countries that offers real benefits to the developing world.

After a year of remote work, the very idea of a physical headquarters feels outdated. But this journey has taught me that the digital world is becoming even more heavily dependent upon physical systems. Nearly every device, and every network node, still falls within the physical or legal boundaries of a sovereign state. As more of daily life depends on digital infrastructure, and more physical objects are connected, it is not merely different versions of the internet that are emerging but different worlds. Communications has a foundation, and the competition to control it is underway.

# THE DIGITAL SILK ROAD

# CHAPTER ONE

# THE NETWORK WARS

If history is written by the victors, so are fantasies of the future. Among the most alluring and dangerous of these tales, born in the blinding glow of Cold War victory, was the idea that communications technology would inevitably promote liberty. As former U.S. president Ronald Reagan told a London audience in 1989, "More than armies, more than diplomacy, more than the best intentions of democratic nations, the communications revolution will be the greatest force for the advancement of human freedom the world has ever seen."[1]

Having recently left office, Reagan was triumphant. America was ascendant, its archrival gasping. The Soviet Union led the world in steel, oil, and nuclear weapons production, but Soviet computers were two decades behind their U.S. counterparts. Heavy industry, Soviet leaders were discovering, matters less in the information age. "The biggest of big brothers is increasingly helpless against communications technology," Reagan boasted.

Democracy was on the march in Hungary and Poland, and Reagan even saw it sprouting in China, where authorities had brutally suppressed demonstrations in Beijing and other cities weeks earlier. Nicholas Kristof, then Beijing bureau chief for the *New York Times*, witnessed the violence in Tiananmen Square and later wrote, "The Communist Party signed its own death warrant that night."[2] Foreign correspondents and diplomats debated whether the Party could last weeks, months, or a year.[3]

Even as the CCP defied those expectations, predictions that technology would bring about its demise only became more popular. By 1993, illegal satellite dishes were popping up faster than the government could tear them down. "The information revolution is coming to China, and in the long run it threatens to supplant the Communist revolution," Kristof wrote.[4] Satellites failed to deliver that change, but then came the internet, and bloggers were cast as the new freedom fighters.

Few were as courageous and inspiring as Li Xinde, author of *Chinese Public Opinion Surveillance Net*. Li was investigating reports of government corruption, posting his findings online, and then moving on before local authorities could arrest him. "It's the Chinese leadership itself that is digging the Communist Party's grave, by giving the Chinese people broadband," Kristof wrote in a 2005 profile of Li titled "Death by a Thousand Blogs."[5]

But the fantasy that connectivity favors liberty has long faded. In its place, a much darker reality is unfolding. Democracy is retreating, and digital authoritarianism is on the march.

The CCP is harnessing communications technology to cement its control at home and expand its influence abroad. Like a medieval castle, China's domestic internet has only a handful of entry points, giving Beijing an unrivaled ability to monitor, censor, and cut off network traffic. Surveillance cameras armed with artificial intelligence (AI) have blanketed public spaces, logging faces, automating ethnic profiling, and contributing to the imprisonment of over a million Muslim minorities.

China has become not only the biggest of big brothers but also the world's largest provider of communications technology. Huawei has operations in more than 170 countries, but it is hardly China's only digital giant. Two Chinese companies, Hikvision and Dahua, churn out nearly 40 percent of the world's surveillance cameras. Hengtong Group supplies 15 percent of the world's fiber optics and is one of the world's four suppliers of submarine cables, which carry 95 percent of international data. China's global navigation satellite system, Beidou, provides more extensive coverage over 165 of the world's capital cities than does America's GPS.[6]

From outer space to the ocean floor, these connections are all part of China's Digital Silk Road, or DSR. Amorphous by design, the DSR sits at the intersection of Chinese leader Xi Jinping's signature policy efforts. It was first mentioned in 2015 as a component of China's Belt and Road Initiative, Xi's vision for moving China closer to the center of everything through infrastructure projects, trade deals, people-to-people ties, and policy coordination. Dangling promises of investment and speaking to the aspirations of the developing world, China has convinced 140 countries to sign onto the Belt and Road.[7]

Like the Belt and Road, the DSR is a China-centric concept wrapped in warm and fuzzy rhetoric about cooperation and mutual benefits. There are no formal criteria for what qualifies as a project, but as Chinese technology companies encounter greater scrutiny abroad, the concept has proved a savvy marketing tool. The "Silk Road" imagery evokes a romanticized version of ancient times: camel caravans on the move, cultures mingling, ideas flowing. In reality, it advances "Made in China 2025," another of Xi's signature initiatives, which aims to capture market shares in high-tech industries that amount to global domination.

Before the DSR was formally unveiled, China's digital reach extended quietly into American communities. Rural carriers in a dozen U.S. states purchased Huawei equipment.[8] China Telecom and China Unicom, the country's two largest state-owned telecommunications companies, won licenses to carry international calls within the United States. Along with China Mobile, they connect with other networks in nearly twenty U.S. cities. Hikvision cameras watch over apartment buildings in New York City, a public school in Minnesota, hotels in Los Angeles, and countless homes.

Having awoken to the dangers of allowing its chief competitor's technology in U.S. networks, Washington has started severing these connections. The U.S. Congress banned carriers that receive federal funding from purchasing Huawei equipment, and the Commerce Department prohibited U.S. companies from selling components to Huawei. The New York Stock Exchange delisted China Telecom, China Unicom, and China Mobile. The Federal Communications Commission (FCC) is revoking China Telecom and China Unicom's licenses.[9] After struggling to identify Hikvision cameras, the U.S. government has removed them from its facilities. All five companies, and hundreds more Chinese entities, have been sanctioned by the United States for offenses ranging from supporting the Chinese military to committing human rights abuses.[10]

The United States has also been playing defense abroad. The global reach of U.S. sanctions prevents any company, U.S. or foreign, from selling components to Huawei that rely on U.S. intellectual property. Publicly and privately, U.S. officials have lobbied foreign leaders and companies to avoid using Chinese suppliers. The State Department's "Clean Network" Initiative, launched in the Trump administration's final year, aimed to limit Chinese suppliers of 5G equipment, Chinese carriers, Chinese cloud providers, Chinese apps, and Chinese involvement in underseas cables.[11]

Convinced it cannot rely on access to U.S. technology, China is pushing ahead with major investments at home. Xi has called for $1.4 trillion in spending through 2025 on "new infrastructure," which includes 5G systems, smart cities, cloud computing, and other digital projects.[12] In March 2021, China approved its Fourteenth Five-Year Plan, a blueprint for the country's development, which for the first time declared technological self-reliance a "strategic pillar."[13] Xi has also called for China to follow an economic model of "dual circulation," a concept that aims to continue China's exports to foreign markets while reducing its reliance on foreign technology domestically.[14] As China bolsters its capabilities at home, it will have more to offer overseas.

The DSR is already accelerating in the wake of the COVID-19

pandemic. While exposing the risks of physical connectivity, the pandemic also raised the costs of being on the losing side of the digital divide. Better-connected economies were able to handle massive transitions to the virtual world. The roughly half of humanity that remains unconnected to the internet had fewer options. The pandemic's financial shock has left developing countries cash-strapped with even less room to borrow. Compared to the large transport and energy projects that characterized the Belt and Road's early years, digital projects are often cheaper and faster to complete.

With these lines drawn, the stage is set for competition between the United States and China to intensify in third markets. Warnings from U.S. officials about the risks of Chinese communications technology are now echoed in Australia, Japan, South Korea, and large parts of Western Europe. But the United States has been less effective in offering affordable alternatives. China is exploiting that opening by pushing deeper into developing and emerging markets, where affordability trumps security. A world of competing digital ecosystems, each with its own equipment and standards, is taking shape. Practically everyone is caught in the middle.

Despite extolling the importance of networks for years, leading thinkers largely failed to consider the possibility of a world in which the United States is not the dominant hub. China's rise and reach beyond its borders is now eviscerating long-held assumptions about technology and liberty, Western primacy, and the very nature of power. Journalists and academics have been grasping for the right words to describe this contest. Is it a trade war? A new Cold War? The reality is more complex, and the stakes fundamentally higher. The United States and China are fighting for control over the networks of tomorrow.[15]

The Network Wars have begun. This book shows how we arrived at this point, provides a tour of the battlefield, and explains what the United States must do to win.

## THE RECKONING

The story of how we arrived here is uncomfortable, which is why there have been few honest accountings. Rather than probe how the United States contributed to China's technological rise, Washington and Silicon Valley mostly prefer to tell stories that minimize their failures. There are many variations, but a common theme is that China cheated its way to the top. This sense of unfairness is easy on the American psyche, letting everyone off the hook, but it raises the risk of repeating past mistakes. Complaining offers no strategic insights for competing.

There was plenty of lying, cheating, and stealing. But as the following chapter recounts, what is even more shocking is the myriad of legal opportunities that China exploited. Chinese officials masterfully dangled the prospect of access to China's market, maximizing concessions as foreign companies willingly undercut each other to hand over their intellectual property and enter into partnerships with Chinese firms. With generous state support, those partners eventually became their competitors. Everything was for sale, including the management practices that transformed Huawei from a disorganized copycat into a global juggernaut.

What made these mistakes possible was not merely foreign greed and Chinese savvy but also a powerful and genuinely held belief in the liberalizing effects of communications technology. The collapse of the Soviet Union appeared to prove that communications technology shifted power from governments to individuals, allowing them to speak freely, organize, and hold officials accountable. Every new type of connection, from the fax machine to the internet to the cell phone, was hyped as offering an express lane for carrying liberty around the world.

Few ideas have been as powerful, persistent, and wrong in recent history. It was powerful because it brought a wide range of political philosophies into alignment with the commercial interests of U.S. companies on the vanguard of developing communications technologies. Despite a few powerful warnings, such as those offered by scholars Rebecca MacKinnon and Evgeny Morozov, this view persisted because of this alignment of interests and the allure of believing that the United States could do good by doing well around the world, regardless of local context.[16] And it was wrong because it confused means and ends, overlooking how these tools could be used differently.

Among the faithful were not only Reagan and Kristof, a conservative and liberal, but also John Perry Barlow, a libertarian who captured the feeling of America's internet pioneers in what he titled famously "A Declaration of the Independence of Cyberspace." "Governments of the Industrial World, you weary giants of flesh and steel, I come from Cyberspace, the new home of Mind," he began. "On behalf of the future, I ask you of the past to leave us alone. You are not welcome among us. You have no sovereignty where we gather."[17]

Barlow was not merely saying that governments lacked legitimacy in the information age, but writing his ode to internet freedom in 1996, he pointed out that they also lacked the capabilities to rule cyberspace. "You have no moral right to rule us nor do you possess any methods of enforcement we have true reason to fear," he explained. "Cyberspace does not lie within your borders. Do not think that you can build it, as though it were a public construction project. You cannot. It is an act of nature and it grows itself through our collective actions."

But Chinese strategists knew better. Where Reagan, Kristof, and Barlow saw the unstoppable march of freedom, Chinese officials saw a struggle for power. Shen Weiguang, one of China's founding fathers of information warfare, explained in a lecture to the Chinese National Defense University in 1988, "Countries with advanced networking technology rely on networks to expand their 'information territory' to many other countries and threaten the latter's 'information sovereignty.'"[18] As the Cold War was ending, the battle for information territory was just beginning.

The CCP took predictions of its death by communications technology all too seriously. "The Western world's information strategy is composed of a public opinion offensive and ideological infiltration, the cultivation of forces within the socialist countries to act as agents to whip up hostilities, the practice of economic coercion, and the practice of outright subversion and creation of all manner of division," Shen cautioned in 1989.[19] But unlike their Western counterparts, Chinese officials did not view these outcomes as inevitable. They set out to build networks that served their own goals.

The Party began asserting its absolute authority over online activities in 1994, a year before the internet was commercially available to the public.[20] These restrictions grew over the years, and in 2005 the Chinese government released what Reporters Without Borders dubbed the "11 Commandments of the Internet." The list banned information that "endangers national security," "subverts the government," "undermines national unity," "disseminates rumors," or "undermines social stability."[21] The rules were wide-ranging and intentionally vague, giving authorities ample room for interpretation. This was Barlow's declaration turned upside down, a vision of cyberspace with the state at its core.

Having publicly articulated different plans for the internet, Chinese authorities faced the colossal technical challenge of building it and enforcing these edicts. Many observers thought that was impossible. "In the new century, liberty will spread by cell phone and cable modem . . . Imagine how much it could change China," U.S. president Bill Clinton said in 2000 while advocating for China's admission to the World Trade Organization. "Now, there's no question China has been trying to crack down on the Internet. Good luck! That's sort of like trying to nail Jell-O to the wall," he said to laughter and applause.[22]

But foreign companies provided the hammer, trading control over their technology for access to China's domestic market. When Chinese state security services sponsored an expo in Beijing called "Security China 2000," more than 300 foreign companies, including many U.S. companies, rushed to pitch their wares.[23] Publicly, foreign technology companies cast their offerings as essential for opening Chinese society. Executives proclaimed they were exporting not just goods but also values. But as they fought for a slice of China's market, they were jeopardizing both their profits and principles.

As optimism was peaking, Chinese authorities were busy modifying foreign technology for their own ends. Li's main blog was taken down weeks after Kristof's profile, but they both remained undaunted. "I have more than 50 different sites set up. I regularly maintain about three at a time. If they shut one down, I replace one," Li explained.[24] Kristof still believed that technology was weakening the Communist Party. "This is a cat-and-mouse game . . . But the larger truth is that the mice are winning this game, not the cats," he wrote in 2008.[25]

But at that point, China was moving from copycat to innovator and winning a much bigger game. The global telecom competition had become a war of attrition, and overextended Western companies were retreating from the network hardware business. Chinese firms had graduated from being entirely dependent on foreign companies to eating their market share. The epic collapse of the Canadian telecom giant Nortel, examined in the following chapter, overlapped not coincidentally with Huawei's meteoric rise. Huawei scooped up Nortel's brightest minds and tapped them to develop next-generation wireless networks.

While American leaders were busy singing the praises of connectivity, the United States was not investing enough in actually connecting the world, including rural and lower-income communities at home. Shunning big government and industrial policy, Washington assumed market forces would succeed. But as Western firms raced to roll out high-speed internet, they focused primarily on larger, richer markets, creating digital divides. Connectivity disparities arose between developed and developing countries, between urban and rural areas, and between rich and poor. China turned these fault lines into runways for its tech giants. Now they are cleared for takeoff.

## NAVIGATING THE BATTLEFIELD

The battlefield is vast and filled with places that are unfamiliar to national security experts. Competition is playing out in industry committees and working groups where standards for emerging technologies are being decided. It is playing out in city halls across the developing world as leaders work to attract foreign investment and technology to develop their economies without becoming digitally dependent. And it is playing out in the sum of billions of decisions as individuals vote with their wallets. The implications for security are wide-ranging, but it is first and foremost an economic and technological competition.

To help navigate this terrain, the following chapters provide a tour of China's expanding digital infrastructure footprint across four layers: wireless networks, internet-connected devices, internet backbone, and satellites. While not exhaustive of China's digital activities, these areas enable AI, big data applications, and other strategic technologies. In every layer, China is gaining globally and positioning itself to reap economic and strategic rewards.

This is a journey in the truest sense because global networks have a physical footprint. Barlow was too quick to dismiss the notion that cyberspace could be a "construction project" and that states could exercise sovereignty within it. Even the "cloud" is tangible, consisting of data centers and fiber-optic cables. And even companies operating satellites in space must answer to national authorities. The construction of networks, as Shen realized, opens avenues for accumulating and exercising power. By focusing on hardware, this book helps reveal the connections between our physical and digital worlds and the competition to control them.

Project by project, China is strengthening its position in global networks. For five years, I have tracked China's global infrastructure push, assembling one of the largest open-source databases of Chinese projects and studying them on the ground. Among other treks, I have driven a freshly paved road to the China-Pakistan border, climbed aboard a Chinese-made railway that runs from Ethiopia to Djibouti, and stepped onto Chinese docks in Piraeus, Greece. These are just a few of the flagship projects in China's Belt and Road Initiative.

But don't be fooled, as I was initially. China is not merely forging new transport networks. Its grandest ambitions run underground, underseas, and through the airwaves. Each of the three projects above has a less visible digital dimension. Chinese fiber-optic cables span the China-Pakistan and Ethiopia-Djibouti borders. A Chinese subsea cable is slated to connect Pakistan and Djibouti and includes a branch that will extend to Europe. In Piraeus, Huawei has installed routers and switches, overhauling the port's network and providing free Wi-Fi for cruise ships and other visitors to the port. China has been packaging digital infrastructure with traditional infrastructure, and the world desperately needs both.

The allure of China's sales pitch can be seen even in rural Montana, as chapter 3 describes. When I visited Glasgow, Montana, one of the most isolated towns in the United States, I expected residents would be alarmed that Huawei equipment was carrying their calls. But as I learned, Maslow's digital hierarchy of needs is different. The risk of losing access can feel more immediate and threatening than the presence of foreign equipment. Most users, whether in rural America or developing Asia, are less concerned about foreign espionage than simply avoiding a giant bill. Without offering affordable alternatives, a task that will require rediscovering industrial policy, U.S. officials are fighting a nearly impossible battle.

Fear alone will not stop China's DSR. Far from being appalled by China's repressive use of surveillance technology at home, a distressing number of foreign leaders are intrigued. They see an opportunity to acquire tools that could not only strengthen their own rule but also reduce crime and spur growth in their cities, as chapter 4 explains. Chinese surveillance technology is being used in more than eighty countries, on every continent except Australia and Antarctica, according to Sheena Chestnut Greitens, a professor at the University of Texas at Austin.[26] Like other connected devices, from smart appliances to fitness bands, these systems often favor cost over security, making them vulnerable to error and attack.

A new map of the internet, with contours that reflect China's interests, is taking shape. China's "Big Three" state-owned telecommunications firms—China Telecom, China Unicom, and China Mobile—are expanding into emerging markets in Asia, Africa, and Latin America. In just a decade, China has graduated from being dependent on foreign companies for subsea cables to controlling the world's fourth major provider of these systems and laying enough cable to circle the earth. These moves, detailed in chapter 5, are part of an asymmetric strategy: Beijing wants to carry, store, and mine more of the world's data while keeping its own networks out of reach.

Space is "the new commanding heights," according to Chinese military leaders. Completed in 2020, China's Beidou satellite network guides not only Chinese missiles, fighter jets, and naval vessels but also cars, tractors, and cell phones. China offers a starter kit for countries with space ambitions, complete with satellites that China launches and even controls until its partners can take over. The competition is moving to low earth orbit, as chapter 6 describes. Elon Musk's SpaceX, Amazon, and several other companies are rolling out massive constellations of satellites to provide global broadband. China, of course, has its own plans.

China stands to gain exponentially more if it can integrate its activities within and across these layers. Network effects occur when a service or product becomes more valuable with wider use. As Theodore Vail, who created a telecommunications empire as president of AT&T, explained in 1908: "A telephone—without a connection at the other end of the line—is not even a toy or a scientific instrument. It is one of the most useless things in the world. Its value depends on the connection with the other telephone—and increases with the number of connections."[27] Clearly, network effects are not new, but they are more important than ever.

Through the DSR, China is moving itself toward the center of global information networks at a time when information has never been more valuable. As Tom Wheeler, the former chairman of the FCC, explains in *From Gutenberg to Google*: "The capital asset of the nineteenth and twentieth centuries was industrial production facilitated by networks. The capital asset of the twenty-first century is information created by networks."[28] James Currier, a Silicon Valley investor, estimates that network effects are responsible for 70 percent of the value created by tech companies since 1994. The most powerful and defensible network effects stem from physical nodes and links because they require massive up-front investment.[29]

China is making those investments and piecing together cutting-edge systems. In 2017, Chinese engineers held the world's first quantum-encrypted video conference. Doing so required utilizing a $100 million purpose-built satellite, fiber-optic networks on the ground, and advanced algorithms. Even though the system was not perfect, it was a major step toward building an ultra-secure network. "They've demonstrated a full infrastructure," Caleb Christensen, the chief scientist at MagiQ Technologies, which makes quantum cryptography systems, told Sophia Chen at *Wired*. "They've connected all the links. Nobody's done that."[30]

China's focus on emerging markets could supercharge its network effects. More than half of global population growth until 2050 is expected in Africa, where Huawei has built 70 percent of the 4G networks.[31] The Chinese subsea cable connecting Pakistan and Djibouti will become the shortest internet link between Asia and Africa, the two regions where international bandwidth has been growing most rapidly in recent years.[32] China has even positioned itself as the central node between Nigeria and Belarus, which own Chinese satellites and, with Beijing's encouragement, signed a contract to provide backup services for each other. As China develops next-generation technology, it is also making a bid for next-generation markets.

That two-punch combination could position China to set global standards for the next wave of communications technologies, further magnifying its network effects. Widely accepted standards, such as USB, a standard for cables, allow equipment to work together across countries and manufacturers.[33] Set the global standards, and your products become more universal. Understanding this, Chinese officials have long said that third-rate countries build things, second-rate countries design things, and first-rate countries set standards. They are investing heavily in existing standards organizations and have proposed creating a Belt and Road Standards Forum, a parallel structure with Beijing at the center.[34]

If China becomes the world's chief network operator, it could reap a commercial and strategic windfall. It could reshape global flows of data, finance, and communications to reflect its interests. Insulated from the reach of U.S. sanctions and espionage, it could possess an unrivaled understanding of market movements, the deliberations of foreign competitors, and the lives of countless individuals enmeshed in its networks.

The African Union (AU) headquarters, which China financed and built, is a cautionary monument to these digital dangers. In 2018, *Le Monde* reported that data was being secretly sent from the AU's servers in Ethiopia to China every night for five years.[35] But the AU would not risk offending Beijing, its largest patron. Instead of switching to a non-Chinese network provider, it signed a new partnership agreement with Huawei.[36] In 2020, the AU discovered that the building's surveillance footage was being exfiltrated—again to China.[37] This is perhaps the sunniest forecast for a world wired by China. Beijing, after all, views the AU as a partner.

Given China's persistent attacks on U.S. networks, there is little doubt it would use even greater network power to target Americans. In recent years, China has stolen the personnel files of twenty-three million U.S. government employees, eighty million health records, and credit card and passport information for hundreds of millions of Americans.[38] With access to this data and more, the Chinese state already "knows" more about many Americans than those people can remember about themselves. It has used this information to give Chinese companies an edge and to crush U.S. intelligence operations overseas, as Zach Dorfman reported for *Foreign Policy*.[39] That is what information advantage looks like: China sees more and more, while its competitors go blind.

The stakes extend far beyond commerce and intelligence. In October 2020, four months after Chinese and Indian troops clashed over contested territory in the Himalayas, Mumbai lost power. Trains ground to a halt. Hospitals, already overwhelmed by COVID-19 cases, switched to emergency generators. It all might have been a warning sent from Beijing, according to a report by Recorded Future, a cybersecurity firm. For weeks, Chinese hackers had been targeting India's critical infrastructure with malware.[40] They may have had an inside track: nearly all India's power plants built over the last decade use Chinese equipment.[41]

These are just previews of the power that China could wield if it succeeds in becoming the world's indispensable hub and gatekeeper. It could attract supporters and reward compliance by granting access and privileges. It could penalize dissenters and destroy competitors by denying services and imposing sanctions. Dominating networks could allow China to exercise power far from its borders, as great powers have done throughout history, but with a much smaller global military footprint. The DSR could chart a course toward a new kind of empire.

## LOSING CONTROL

On October 1, 2019, three decades after Reagan saw democracy emerging in China, tanks rolled through Tiananmen Square again. With 15,000 soldiers marching, the parade to mark the seventieth anniversary of the founding of the People's Republic of China left no question about who was in control. Chinese leader Xi Jinping, clad in a Mao-style suit, rode in an open-top limousine and reviewed missiles, drones, and hundreds of other pieces of military equipment. "There is no force that can shake the foundation of this great nation," he told a flag-waving audience.[42]

Chinese surveillance cameras, armed with the latest AI, watched over the crowds. Internet access slowed to a trickle for local customers, while China's Big Three focused on serving their main client, their networks carrying ultra-high-definition video of the parade and even coordinating the timing of the fireworks display.[43] Chinese state media broadcast the parade in multiple languages to every region of the world via satellite, cable, and internet. China's Beidou satellite system guided hundreds of military vehicles in the parade in near-perfect synchronization.

Long gone is the optimism about China's democratic transformation and the positive role that technology would play. Communications technology appears to be a force for authoritarianism, a cudgel instead of an open microphone. And as China's DSR stretches further, it often appears from the outside to be highly centralized, a regiment of Chinese companies marching in lockstep, like soldiers in the parade. This, of course, is the image that Chinese leaders want the world to see.

These images are alarming, and yet the Network Wars are just getting started. Communications technology is not good or evil, but merely a tool. But missing that lesson, beliefs about technology in Washington have swung from optimism to pessimism, and threaten to tip even further, toward paranoia. China appears to be everywhere, united, and always in control. In this overdue but panicked reassessment, both China's vulnerabilities and America's strengths are being overlooked.

In reality, the militarized ceremony concealed deep fears among Chinese officials. In advance of the celebration, internet access was so heavily restricted that even the editor of the state-owned nationalist *Global Times*, Hu Xijin, complained, "The country isn't fragile, I suggest we should leave a narrow opening to foreign websites."[44] Hu later deleted his comment. While Beijing celebrated, Hong Kong was consumed with protests, which Chinese officials accused the United States of fomenting, echoing the assessment of Shen Weiguang, the information warfare strategist, from years earlier.[45]

Paradoxically, while China's technological capabilities have advanced, the fear of contagion has only grown larger in Chinese officials' thinking about networks. "The internet has increasingly become the source, conductor, and amplifier of all kinds of risks," cautions Chen Yixin, a protégé of Xi Jinping and leader of the CCP's powerful Central Political and Legal Affairs Commission. "Any small thing can become a public opinion whirlpool; a few rumors [spread] through incitement and hype can easily produce a 'storm in a teacup' and abruptly produce a real-life 'tornado' in society."[46] Chen calls this the "magnifier effect."

Three weeks after the parade, Li Xinde, the courageous citizen-journalist, was taken into custody. Technology had tipped the cat-and-mouse game further in favor of his enemies, and Li was dodging hackers as well as censors and changing his website domain name up to sixty times a year.[47] Li's most recent investigative report, on corruption involving a public security bureau in Tianjin, was immediately deleted, as were numerous reprints published across WeChat and other websites.[48] In January 2021, Li was sentenced to five years in prison. But authorities weren't done. They also sentenced Li's son to one year in prison.[49]

These actions are chilling, yet they also reveal cracks in China's digital authoritarianism. As powerful as the state's toolkit has become, it did not erase every instance of Li's report, which was reproduced on other blogs. Nor were these digital tools powerful enough to assuage the fear of authorities, who resorted to old-fashioned physical detention and intimidation. Most telling of all, the reaction was entirely disproportionate to the threat. "I'm not out to overthrow the government," Li has explained. "I'm not out [to] subvert the rule of the Communist Party."[50] Indeed, Li's work actually assists the CCP's avowed anti-corruption goals.

The CCP's response to threats has been severe but haphazard. Its rush to monitor everything has outpaced its ability to make sense of what it sees. The race to deploy surveillance equipment has created a thicket of fragmented local systems rather than a unified national system, wasting resources and raising concerns among Chinese citizens about personal data security. In the chaos, a surveillance-industrial complex is thriving. While their technology is becoming more sophisticated, these companies often promise more than they can deliver, especially in foreign markets.

Coordination challenges are even greater overseas, where Chinese companies operate with less oversight and foreign governments have their own priorities. China's government elevates issues but does not usually provide detailed marching orders. Through the Belt and Road, for example, Xi has called for building "smart cities," an expansive term for enhancing urban areas with digital infrastructure. But the Chinese government does not appear to have provided even top-level guidance to companies pursuing these projects abroad, according to a study by James Mulvenon, a leading expert on Chinese technology, and his colleagues for the U.S.-China Economic and Security Review Commission.[51]

The lack of coordination and supervision can be seen on the ground. In the Pakistani capital of Islamabad, half of the Chinese surveillance cameras installed as part of a flagship Huawei project malfunctioned.[52] In Kenya, Chinese companies are helping to build a multibillion-dollar high-tech hub outside Nairobi that few companies appear eager to occupy.[53] A Chinese subsea cable stretching 6,000 kilometers from Cameroon to Brazil remains severely underused, adding little but debt to Cameroon's development prospects. Instead of creating network effects, these and other disjointed projects may prove to be digital white elephants.

The CCP's paranoia presents perhaps the greatest challenge to

China's global network ambitions. China's fortress-style internet is designed for isolation from the world, which harms innovation and constrains China's ability to connect with foreign networks. Mainland Chinese cities are absent among the rankings of the world's most connected hubs, which all have open internet exchanges, a model that remains anathema to Party leaders. Their conundrum is that greater international connectivity requires giving up some control.

The United States' openness to foreign connections, in contrast, has provided it with massive commercial and strategic advantages. Almost a quarter of the world's internet traffic flows through the United States, including 63 percent of international traffic destined for China,[54] a commanding position that U.S. intelligence officials describe as a "tremendous home-field advantage."[55] Access to the world's largest network of underseas cables powers U.S. financial centers and U.S. tech companies, three of which control over half of the global market for cloud services.[56] These advantages are often taken for granted because the United States has been the incumbent network power since the internet was invented.

The United States could harness its strengths with a strategy that goes on the offensive in tomorrow's markets. The U.S. private sector is pioneering technologies that could disrupt China's advantages in developing markets, including low earth orbit satellites that provide global broadband. Leading a coalition of partners and allies, the United States could offset China's scale with a critical mass that develops and protects sensitive technology while offering more to the developing world.[57] Success will not be cheap, or easy, and will require building bridges to the European Union and India, partners with common interests but also their own aspirations.

The United States is threatened not only by China's rise but also by the risk of overreaction. Washington is adopting a more defensive posture, bringing greater scrutiny to domestic networks, internet exchanges, and submarine cables. The desire for greater protection is well warranted given China's expanding activities and track record of cyberattacks, espionage, and cooperation between Chinese companies and the People's Liberation Army (PLA). But the United States must also consider how each decision could impact its position within global networks. The consequences are not as straightforward as they might initially appear. Getting the balance right starts with understanding how we got here.

# CHAPTER TWO

# CTRL + C

At the end of 1994, Northern Telecom was preparing to celebrate its one hundredth anniversary. From its humble beginnings selling fire alarms and telephone supplies in Montreal, the company had grown into one of the world's leading telecommunications suppliers. With $8.87 billion in annual revenue, 57,000 employees worldwide, and thousands of patents, its future looked even more promising. To mark the occasion, it unveiled a sleeker name and a bold, all-caps logo: NORTEL. The *O* was a stylized globe wrapped with a planetary ring—fit for "a corporation that knows no boundaries," its advertisements explained.[1]

History was accelerating, Nortel executives believed, and strongly in their favor. "No period in recent history has seen such a far-reaching shift in global dynamics," CEO Paul Stern observed a year earlier. "It is not only the scope of change, but the speed with which it is happening. As the speed quickens, a new civilization unfolds: an information society."[2] His successor, Jean Monty, told shareholders: "As this century ends, two great currents are running through the world economy: globalization and the information revolution. They are creating spectacular new growth opportunities for companies like our own."

Nortel's captains of industry fashioned themselves as agents of empire. They were architects and builders, if not rulers, of the information society they saw emerging. In the early 1990s, the company declared its intention to become the world's leading supplier of telecommunications equipment by 2000. Its logic was as straightforward as any plan for world dominance: first Canada, then the rest of North America, then the world. Executives posed for full-page photos with world maps and ancient artifacts in the company's annual reports. Invoking Cicero, the Roman philosopher-statesman, Stern asked, "Will we remain the same when the same is no longer fitting?"[3]

Two decades later, little remained of Nortel, which marked its 115th anniversary in bankruptcy court. Its path to failure was shrouded in what appeared to be success. It was an early mover into China's alluring market. It invented core technologies for wireless and internet networks, semiconductors, and even a touch-screen phone a decade before the iPhone.[4] It became the most valuable company in Canadian history.

Nortel's downfall stemmed from mistakes in everything from accounting to management. But its executives also made the strategic blunder of helping their Chinese partners become their fiercest competitors. It was an error all too common among the Western companies that raced into China's market, believing their values and bottom lines were neatly aligned.

Using China's massive market as bait, Chinese firms copied and gained control over Western technology. They broke agreements and filed for patents using confidential information. They benefited from generous government subsidies. They stole secrets from their competitors' labs, showrooms, and computers, contributing to what General Keith Alexander, former head of the U.S. National Security Agency, once called "the single greatest transfer of wealth in history."[5]

But even more shocking is how many of China's shortcuts were legal and overt. Chinese firms imported Western technology, partnered with Western firms through joint ventures in China, adopted their management practices, and hired their brightest minds. For decades, Nortel and other leading Western telecommunications companies were complicit in their own demise. Even as warning signs mounted that Chinese authorities had a different information revolution in mind, essential technology, processes, and even people remained for sale. Few played the game as well as Huawei.

## "A WORLD OF NETWORKS"

Like explorers eyeing the New World, Nortel executives saw opportunity everywhere in 1994. What was good for Nortel's bottom line, they strongly believed, was good for the world.

To celebrate its past and lay claim to the future, the company hired six leading thinkers to write short essays on "A World of Networks," the company's vision for telecommunications in the twenty-first century. "For more than a century now, Northern Telecom and its employees have shared the conviction that information technologies should exist to better the human condition," Jean Monty explained in a preface to the series. "As we enter our second century, we carry forward that spirit—people reaching out to meet the challenge of bringing the world together through communications."[6]

Authors offered different bumper stickers for the massive changes underway: "information surge," "information age," and "information society." But for the most part, this was window dressing on a common vision: power shifting to individuals, democracy thriving, markets expanding. Bridges would replace walls, and freedom would flow. A world of networks was a world unchained.

Boundaries were indeed disappearing, and new markets beckoned, none more strongly than China. To attract foreign technology and upgrade their telecommunications sector, Chinese authorities were relaxing some restrictions on foreign investment. On March 31, 1994, the United States and its NATO allies abolished the Cold War–era system that had prevented most telecommunications exports to China and other communist economies (especially the Soviet Union, until its collapse). Three weeks later, China connected to the global internet. The race to connect the world's most populous country was on.

China's sheer size and needs were impossible to ignore. During 1994 alone, China added ten million telephone mainlines and 930,000 new mobile telephone subscribers, an annual growth rate of over 50 percent and nearly 150 percent, respectively.[7] But a year later, China still had less than three lines for every one hundred people, underscoring a massive demand that would be met in the following years. Western firms viewed this opportunity with a gold rush mentality. The timid would miss the opportunity of several lifetimes. The brave would make fortunes and cement legacies.

Nortel was already there. It had been working in China since 1972 and launched its first joint venture with a Chinese company in 1988 to produce private business exchanges, phone networks often installed in hotels and government agencies.[8] Four years later, the venture was selling more than 100,000 lines annually and planning to triple production. Four Canadian managers supervised two hundred Chinese employees. In less than three years, the plant graduated from essentially importing machines from Canada to importing parts and performing complete assembly. The company began looking for ways to use local materials to reduce costs.[9] Instead of creating a competitor, Nortel executives believed they were strengthening their company's bottom line.

But Chinese authorities shrewdly played foreign companies off each other. China's domestic switching network was criticized as consisting of "seven countries, eight systems," meaning that all the equipment came from eight companies in seven countries. These companies were Nortel of Canada, Ericsson of Sweden, AT&T of the United States, Siemens of Germany, Alcatel of France, BTM of Belgium, and NEC and Fujitsu of Japan. Allies that held the line against exporting technologies to communist states during the Cold War were now commercial competitors. Executives understood there were risks in forming joint ventures in China, but with their competitors moving in, the cost of missing out loomed even larger. Every deal was a battle, and winning required giving more concessions to the Chinese government.[10]

When Nortel and AT&T squared off over a joint venture with the Chinese government in 1994, they pulled out all the stops. Nortel hosted Chinese vice-premier Zou Jiahua in Canada, taking him for a tour of Niagara Falls as well as Nortel's factory. They even served him fish stew prepared by a chef from Zou's hometown. But Zou's time with AT&T, which he visited only for a day during the same trip, was more memorable. He and his entourage were ferried around in armored limos with Secret Service protection and a police escort.[11] Nortel executives felt the deal slipping away.

Believing that billions in future revenue were at stake, Nortel sweetened its offer and called in the Canadian government to help. It agreed to set up an R&D facility in Beijing, becoming the first foreign supplier to do so, as well as a semiconductor plant in Shanghai.[12] The Canadian government, having only recently patched up relations with China after the Tiananmen Square protests, agreed to finance Chinese purchases of Nortel equipment.[13] Negotiations dragged on until just hours before the deal was scheduled to be signed during Canadian prime minister Jean Chrétien's visit to Beijing in November 1994. In a final concession, Nortel agreed to allow the Chinese to appoint the joint venture's chief financial officer.

The deal was done, and Nortel's leaders were candid about the trade they were making with Chinese authorities. As Nortel chairman Arthur MacDonald explained: "The Chinese are trading market access and share for technology transfer. We are committed to helping them with that. Our goal is to extend advanced telecommunications services throughout China. In time we want to develop technology in China for the global market."[14] What Nortel executives did not yet appreciate is that technology transfer cannot be undone, while market access can shift like the wind.

Restrictions were so loose that one U.S. company even partnered with the Chinese military to sell advanced networking equipment in China. Adlai Stevenson III, a former U.S. senator and son of a former U.N. ambassador and presidential candidate, headed the U.S. partner company SCM/Brooks Telecommunications. The Chinese partner was Galaxy New Technology, which was controlled by a Chinese military agency. The joint venture, which was called HuaMei ("China-America"), included military officers and others with direct ties to the PLA on its board of directors and purchased networking equipment from AT&T ostensibly for use in Chinese hotels. The same technology, a U.S. government review later noted, could have been used to improve the Chinese military's command and control capabilities.[15]

The sale would have been unthinkable several years earlier. Since 1949, the United States and its NATO allies had limited sensitive exports to the Soviet Union, Warsaw Pact countries, and China through the Coordinating Committee for Multilateral Export Controls (CoCom). The group was far from perfect, but it helped limit the Soviet Union's ability to import strategically important technology. CoCom's resolve stemmed from shared perceptions of the Soviet threat, and action was catalyzed by effective U.S. leadership. The group ran on consensus, and enforcement was left to individual members.

The collapse of the Soviet Union threw CoCom's future into question, and by the time it was disbanded in March 1994, restrictions on China had already been significantly loosened. In 1991, CoCom had adopted a "core list" that effectively cut restrictions in half.[16] Two years later, U.S. officials had proposed lifting more restrictions on fiber optics, switches, cellular systems, and other telecommunications equipment. Explaining the policy change, a confidential U.S. government memo noted that China was preparing to invest up to $17 billion in its telecommunications infrastructure in the next decade.[17] That could be a windfall for U.S. exporters, proponents of lifting the restrictions argued, or a gift to their foreign competitors if nothing was done.

The view from the White House looked remarkably similar to the view from Nortel's headquarters. "Change is upon us," President Clinton told a gathering of Asia-Pacific economies in 1993. "The pole stars that guided our affairs in the past years have disappeared. The

Soviet Union is gone. Communist expansionism has ended. At the same time, a new global economy of constant innovation and instant communication is cutting through our world like a new river, providing both power and disruption to the people and nations who live along its course."[18]

The West saw massive commercial opportunities in China and manageable risks.[19] The future of export controls, NATO members believed, should focus more narrowly on limiting nuclear, biological, and chemical weapons and their missile delivery systems to "rogue states," such as North Korea, Libya, and Iran, as well as nonstate actors. China's cooperation would be key. In August 1993, the United States discovered that China had transferred missile technology to Pakistan.[20] Yet by the following January, U.S. officials were suggesting that China might eventually join the new export control regime they anticipated replacing CoCom.[21] With democracy and open markets ascendant, anything seemed possible.

The export of telecommunications equipment fit perfectly into the Clinton administration's first U.S. national security strategy of "Engagement and Enlargement." The strategy aimed to expand the "community of market democracies" while deterring threats. More democracy, and more open markets around the world, it reasoned, would translate into greater security and prosperity for the United States. The strategy had three components: maintaining defense capabilities, opening markets and spurring growth, and promoting democracy.[22] U.S. officials believed that exporting telecommunications equipment could serve all three of these objectives.

A critical mass of senior U.S. officials viewed strong exports as essential to maintaining America's technological edge. The private sector was moving faster than the government and producing more advanced technology. William Perry, an academic and technology executive who was appointed as Deputy Secretary of Defense and later elevated to Secretary of Defense, recognized this shift and increased procurement from the private sector. But Perry also realized that U.S.

government procurement would only amount to a fraction of private sector sales. Exports were needed to keep U.S. companies successful, allowing them to invest more in R&D and develop the next generation of technology. William Reinsch, who served as Under Secretary of Commerce, neatly summarized the administration's logic: "exports = healthy high-tech companies = strong defense." Instead of slowing its rivals down, as export controls sought to do, the United States resolved to "run faster."[23]

More U.S. exports meant growth and jobs, as President Clinton was fond of reminding American audiences. "Some of our export controls, rules and regulations, are a function of the realities of the Cold War which aren't there anymore . . . We want to move this much more quickly, and we'll try to slash a lot of the time delays where we ought to be doing these things," Clinton told a tech company during his first visit to Silicon Valley after taking office in 1993.[24]

Communications technology would also help promote democracy abroad. In its "Engagement and Enlargement" strategy, the administration did not shrink from declaring that "China maintains an authoritative regime even as that country assumes a more important economic and political role in global affairs."[25] But history appeared to be turning in the West's favor. Standing in Moscow, the center of the former Soviet Union, Clinton told an audience of Russian citizens in 1994: "Revolutions in information and communications and technology and production, all these things make democracy more likely. They make isolated, state-controlled economies even more dysfunctional. They make opportunities for those able to seize them more numerous and richer than ever before."[26]

As a result of these changes, by 1994, the U.S. government did not require a review of the HuaMei venture.[27] "This joint venture dramatizes the economic opportunities for the United States as a result of the astonishing changes in China,"[28] Stevenson told the *Chicago Tribune*. But the bigger change was within the United States. In April, the U.S. government created a general license that allowed U.S.

companies to export high-speed computers, machine tools, and tele-com equipment—items that previously required government approval but were judged to be no longer state of the art. Export licenses de-clined by more than half between 1993 and 1994 while U.S. exports to China climbed. By 1995, U.S. companies were exporting nearly $2 billion annually in goods that would have required licenses under the old rules.[29]

This lighter touch made commercial sense, but it also carried se-curity risks. U.S. companies were required to conduct due diligence to ensure the end user was civilian, a task that ranged from difficult to impossible in China's economy. In the late 1970s, the Chinese military had been given a wider mandate to engage in commercial activities, which the government hoped would make up for shrinking military budgets.[30] By the early 1990s, the PLA oversaw a multibillion-dollar empire with stakes in hotels, farms, and international corporations. Without licenses, which created a centralized record of sales, U.S. gov-ernment oversight of individual transactions and trends was limited. Commercial agility came at the cost of intelligence.

Nortel and the U.S. government's views reflected widely held op-timism that open societies and open markets were not only gaining momentum but were unstoppable. But this belief was anchored too solidly in recent events and assumed that the future would be a more intense version of the recent past. Less time was spent probing the risks of engagement. Instead of cautiously viewing technology as a double-edged sword, government and industry leaders touted it as a magic wand for good.

Among the six thinkers who contributed to Nortel's "A World of Networks" series, only John Polanyi, a Nobel Prize–winning chemist and son of the polymath Michael Polanyi, sounded a cautious note. "If ever the sources of information, destined to impact with ever-increasing force, fall into the hands of those who reject human values, the technology that can come to the aid of democracy will instead destroy it," he wrote.[31] I asked Polanyi, who fled Germany for Great

Britain with his family in 1933, why he was the lone dissenting voice. "Hitler and Stalin both bowed to science before embracing barbarism," he replied.[32]

Ignoring these risks, Nortel's vision was a global projection of its ambitions reframed as universal. A full page in its 1994 annual report was titled "Northern Telecom's Vision for Enriching Human Potential through Communications" and included highlights from the company's work in North America, Europe, and Asia. At the top of the list, it quoted Cheng Weigao, Communist Party secretary of China's Hebei province, which had spent millions buying Nortel's telephone switching equipment: "The old wisdom in China was, 'To get rich, you built highways and then telecommunications.' The new wisdom is you build telecommunications networks, then highways."[33] Nortel's vision and China's vision, this assumed, were one and the same.

## "TO SERVE THE COUNTRY"

As Jean Monty surveyed the globe in 1994, Ren Zhengfei was fighting to survive at home. Ren was struggling to transform Huawei, the company he founded in 1987, from a reseller of foreign products to a developer of its own technology—and teetering on the edge of bankruptcy. Foreign suppliers were dominating China's market with advanced products and financing offers. The Chinese government was funneling resources toward its own state-owned enterprises. Huawei was being crushed, and yet by 2007, it would surpass Nortel in annual revenue.[34]

Like any good origin story, Huawei's official history plays up its humble beginnings. According to company lore, Ren had no political connections, and Huawei had to prove itself abroad before receiving significant state support. Exaggerating Huawei's weaknesses makes its success appear purely the result of hard work rather than any special treatment. In this telling, Ren is the visionary general directing an outnumbered force of industrious employees, making sacrifice after sacrifice on their way to victory over foreign companies. By concealing its connections with the state, the Huawei "miracle" becomes even more a tale of national pride.

But earlier versions of Huawei's origin story read much differently. Before Western governments put the company under greater scrutiny, Huawei's own statements credited the Chinese state with a greater role. "If there had been no government policy to protect [nationally owned firms], Huawei would no longer exist," Ren said in 2000.[35] In the "updated" version of Huawei's origin story, its early connections with the Chinese military are omitted entirely.

While serving in the military, Ren joined the CCP. In 1982, he was one of 1,545 delegates elected to attend the Party's Twelfth National Congress. Held every five years, these gatherings are the central events for announcing leadership transitions. Sitting in the Great Hall of the People in Beijing, Ren listened to Deng Xiaoping encourage his comrades to "blaze a path of our own" while learning from the outside world. "Both in revolution and in construction we should also learn from foreign countries and draw on their experience, but mechanical application of foreign experience and copying of foreign models will get us nowhere,"[36] Deng cautioned.

By June 1994, Ren was well-connected enough to meet with Jiang Zemin, China's president and general secretary of the CCP. During that encounter, Ren recalls planting an idea: "I said that switching equipment technology was related to national security, and that a nation that did not have its own switching equipment was like one that lacked its own military. General Secretary Jiang replied clearly: 'Well said.'" Ren mentioned that China's only shot at producing a leading piece of equipment was the telephone switch.[37] Huawei, of course, was only two months away from releasing a major upgrade of its first switch.[38]

Ren realized that Chinese authorities viewed the new world of networks with great caution. They were walking two tightropes, both of

which threatened their grip on power. The first tightrope was international: a delicate balancing act between development and dependency
on foreign companies. They wanted the cutting-edge technology that
only foreign companies could provide, but they were understand-
ably suspicious of Western motives. In the late nineteenth and early
twentieth centuries, Western companies had extended railways and
telegraph lines into Chinese territory, growing their dominant market shares and saddling China's government with massive debt. This
humiliation could not be repeated.

The second tightrope was domestic: balancing economic growth
and social stability. Chinese authorities wanted the economic growth
that new communications technologies could provide. They were also
attracted by applications that enhanced the state's control. But they
were wary of allowing these technologies to spread too widely. "It
must be recognized that only the Communist Party can lead China,
otherwise it will fall into anarchy," Ren wrote in a document for new
employees. "A rapidly-developing economic society, without stability,
without strong leadership, that falls into an anarchic state would be
unimaginable."[39]

Ren's suggestion that China develop its own telephone switch was
not a novel idea. He knew it was already a strategic government goal
and may have participated in the PLA's efforts to produce its own
switching system. Ren's experience before Huawei remains a matter
of debate, with some accounts suggesting that he worked as a director
at the Information Engineering Academy (IEA), a research institute
under the PLA's General Staff Department that developed telecommunications technology for the military.[40] One of their top priorities
was to produce a digital telephone switch based on foreign technology.

Ren tapped his military connections to help Huawei grow. In 1992,
Huawei won a major contract with the PLA, which was desperate
to find equipment for its first national telecommunications network.
Huawei lacked the technical expertise to deliver, and the PLA sent a
team of twenty-five senior researchers from its affiliated universities

and institutes to assist. With state support, Huawei acquired critical knowledge to develop its first products.[41]

The following year, Huawei launched its first product developed in-house, the C&C08 telephone switch, having previously imported and resold technology. To make that leap, Huawei had recruited engineers from the state-owned enterprise that worked with IEA to reverse-engineer foreign equipment and produce China's first indigenous digital switch.[42] Huawei followed this up by developing a higher-capacity switch that could handle five times as many lines, which it released in 1994, after Ren's conversation with Jiang, setting the company up for more lucrative government contracts.

Ren got his wish in 1995, when the Chinese government launched a series of policies to assist Huawei and other producers of domestic switches. The government restricted foreign investment in the types of switches that Huawei produced, forcing foreign companies to enter into joint ventures with an emphasis on sharing technology, and placed tariffs on imports of foreign telecommunications equipment. China's Ninth Five-Year Plan, spanning 1996 to 2000, doubled telecommunications investment.[43]

Huawei was becoming a national champion. Between 1994 and 1996, eight of China's most senior leaders visited Huawei, and they liked what they saw. Each visit was "an inspection" that brought publicity to Huawei and allowed Chinese leaders to showcase the nation's technological progress. When Vice-Premier Zhu Rongji of the State Council visited in June 1996, he brought the presidents of China's four major banks along with him. Zhu encouraged Huawei to compete with foreign companies not only at home but also abroad and promised financial support.[44] Several months later, Liu Huaqing, vice chairman of the Central Military Commission, also made a visit.[45]

More state support followed. The Chinese government played matchmaker, encouraging provincial and city-level government bureaus to purchase from domestic manufacturers. During two conferences, held in 1997 and 1998, twenty-five million lines of digital switching equipment were sold. Huawei won 40 percent of the orders.[46] Just a few years earlier, Nortel had bragged in its annual report that its joint venture had sold 500,000 lines of digital switching equipment in China, the most of any foreign equipment manufacturer.

State banks got the message as well. Huawei gained access to zero-interest loans, had restrictions waived on loans under $3 million, and received two $1 billion lines of credit in 2000.[47] Between 1998 and 2019, Chinese state banks provided Huawei with $15.7 billion in loans, exports credits, and other forms of financing, according to a *Wall Street Journal* investigation.[48] Huawei paid them back on time, strengthening a relationship that benefited both sides.

Huawei's identity as a private company, once a matter of pride, has become a matter of survival. The company insists that it is independent of the Chinese state. "Huawei is an independent business, we are committed to be on the side of our customers when it comes to cyber security and protecting privacy. We will never harm any nation or individual," Ren told the *Financial Times* in 2019.[49] To be sure, Huawei's early connections with the Chinese state were weaker than those of ZTE, among other competitors. But Ren carefully cultivated ties, and the Chinese state supported every critical technology that Huawei developed.[50]

Huawei's core guiding document emphasizes its contributions to the Chinese state. The company's charter, which Ren spent two and a half years fine-tuning before its adoption in 1998, notes: "Huawei considers its mission to be serving the country through industry and rejuvenating the country through science and education, and through its development, the company will make contributions toward the communities where it is situated. Work tirelessly for the prosperity of the motherland, for the revitalization of the Chinese nation, and for the happiness of one's family and oneself."[51] Huawei's mission has always been a national mission.

This is hardly surprising given Ren's service in the PLA, his forays into CCP politics, and the critical support that the Chinese government provided to his company. Nor does acknowledging Huawei's assistance from the Chinese government negate the strategic acumen and human toil behind its success. Ren's business strategy and the dedication of his employees were critical, especially in connecting overlooked markets, as chapter 3 explains. But from Huawei's earliest days, Ren cultivated financial support and protection from foreign competition. Becoming a national champion, in a country that favored state-owned enterprises, was essential to Huawei's survival.

## "WE MUST PUT ON OUR AMERICAN SHOES"

Where Huawei's experience appears more extraordinary is the single-mindedness with which it emulated its foreign competitors, using all tools at its disposal to catch up. Huawei learned by copying foreign equipment, through joint ventures with Western companies, and by spending heavily on Western management consultants. It developed a network of research efforts in Western tech hubs. It hired away talent from its competitors.

Ren even established an R&D team dedicated to "copinism," the legal copying of foreign technologies, an idea that Deng Xiaoping had popularized.[52] In 2002, Ren told a reporter that Huawei had no advanced technology, explaining that there were many technologies already available in the world. Huawei did not need to develop it; the company could just "take" it, he said, referring to the "copinism" concept.[53] Of course, Huawei's path to overtaking Nortel and its other Western competitors is also littered with allegations of illegal copying.

Ren's trip to the United States in 1997 was a formative moment in the company's development. He and his colleagues visited IBM, Bell Labs, Hewlett Packard, and Hughes, the aerospace company. At the end of their trip, they barricaded themselves in a hotel room, worked through Christmas Day, and emerged with a one-hundred-page document summarizing their takeaways. Upon returning to China, Ren spent two days briefing senior management and circulated the notes among the staff.[54]

Ren was especially taken with Western thinking about product development. An IBM vice president, Arleta Chen, gave him a copy of *Setting the PACE in Product Development,* a book that was popular among management consultants at the time.[55] Companies using this system, it promised, could cut the time required to take a product to market in half. "The product development process is the battleground of the 1990s and beyond," the book claims.[56] These sentences surely resonated with Ren, whose speeches are heavy with military metaphors. Ren ordered hundreds of copies for his staff, and even more consequentially, he hired IBM.

When IBM began advising Huawei in 1997, the Chinese company was in chaos.[57] IBM's initial review found that Huawei's sales representatives took orders without confirming whether Huawei's plants could produce the products in time. Staff struggled to predict demand. Some parts were understocked, while others were overstocked. Huawei was delivering only half its orders on time, an abysmal performance compared to the 94 percent average for telecom manufacturers worldwide.[58] Huawei was so dysfunctional that it struggled to calculate with any precision how much profit it made—or lost—each year.[59]

Ren poured resources into the effort and demanded that his employees precisely follow IBM's instructions. "Huawei's most basic goal is survival, and of course we will try to catch up with our Western counterparts in the long run. To achieve this goal, we must put on our American shoes," Ren told his staff.[60]

The IBM transformation was like a religious conversion at Huawei, and Ren had little patience for nonbelievers. He expected strict adherence rather than adaptation. "We want every one of you to wear a pair of American shoes, and we will have our American advisors tell us what American shoes are like," he explained. "You may wonder whether those American shoes can be adapted a bit after they come to China. Well, we have no right to change anything; that is at the discretion of our advisors . . . We must humbly learn from the best if we are ever going to beat them."[61] After one senior executive expressed skepticism during a staff meeting, Ren pulled out a utility knife. "If you think the IBM shoes pinch your feet, then cut your feet off," he demanded.[62]

No expense was spared. To ensure that IBM was just as invested in the process, Ren even decided to replace Huawei's services and application software with IBM products.[63] When someone asked about IBM's rates, Ren replied, "Don't be foolish. You are paying $680 an hour, but you're getting the knowledge they've developed over 30 years. If you ask for a discount, they'll only hand over knowledge from the past three months. Which one is a better deal?"[64] Between 1997 and 2012, Huawei spent at least $1.6 billion on consulting services and transformation projects aimed at adopting the best practices of Western firms, a staggering 1 percent of its sales every year.[65]

What IBM thought would take nine months stretched into a seventeen-year endeavor to transform Huawei. In management consulting terms, IBM sent a small army to Huawei, which hosted anywhere from a dozen to a hundred consultants at one time.[66] The IBM consultants provided hands-on training for basic business operations, even showing Huawei employees how to run more effective meetings.[67] After spending four years overhauling Huawei's product development processes, IBM helped Huawei redesign its financial services, which became one of the most powerful tools in Huawei's arsenal for closing deals.

Huawei's internal transformation opened lucrative doors abroad. When Huawei approached British Telecom (BT) about qualifying as a vendor, no Chinese company had ever met BT's minimum standards. It was a long shot, but IBM consultants coached Huawei through the process. Huawei qualified, made its pitch with rock-bottom prices, and won a contract in 2005, marching into the U.K.'s networks for the first time.

The West's most underappreciated export to China might be

corporate management practices. Management consulting does not have the cloak-and-dagger aura of acquiring expertise and technology by illicit means. Yet it transformed Huawei. IBM was Huawei's most important partner, but Ren also hired Accenture, Mercer, and other consultancies.[68] Their services allowed Huawei to rewire itself and win new business abroad. From the chaos of the early 1990s, Huawei emerged as a globally competitive company.[69]

## "A NEW IDEOLOGICAL AND POLITICAL BATTLEGROUND"

Praise for technology's liberalizing effects reached a crescendo in the spring of 2000, when the United States backed China's entrance into the World Trade Organization (WTO). U.S. government officials and corporate leaders argued that China's membership was not only a commercial imperative for opening its market but also a moral imperative for opening its society. But as they raced to stake claims in China, Western companies were risking both their commercial futures and the values they espoused.

The U.S. government again paved the way for deeper commercial engagement. "China has chosen reform despite the risks. It has chosen to overcome a great wall of suspicion and insecurity, and to engage the rest of the world," President Clinton explained at the Johns Hopkins School of Advanced International Studies in Washington, D.C., on March 9. "The question for the United States, therefore, is, do we want to support that choice or reject it, becoming bystanders as the rest of the world rushes in. That would be a mistake of truly historic proportions."[70]

Clinton needed Congress to grant China permanent normal trading status, and U.S. companies descended upon Capitol Hill to lobby lawmakers. Technology companies played a major role because they were poised to increase their exports, supporting U.S. jobs at home and, it was hoped, delivering social benefits abroad. During a Senate

Foreign Relations Committee hearing in April 2000, senior leaders from the U.S. government, Nortel, and Motorola described a windfall that would follow China's WTO entrance and warned against missing such a historic opportunity.[71]

Techno-optimism approached techno-evangelism. "I have worked in China for 10 years now, and I believe in my heart and in my head that Motorola, through its commercial engagement with China, has been a powerful and positive force for change," Richard Younts, a senior executive and advisor to Motorola's CEO, explained. "We have contributed in no small way to the process of reforming and transforming China. We do not only export American goods to China; we export American values."[72]

Nortel chairman Frank Carlucci was among the most powerful voices for admitting China into the WTO. Before entering the private sector, Carlucci had a long and distinguished career in government, beginning as a foreign service officer in the State Department and rising to become President Reagan's national security advisor and his last secretary of defense. The Cold Warrior argued that "China's WTO accession will help the Chinese people gain increased access to communications tools like the Internet. These tools cannot be controlled and they will help connect the Chinese people to the rest of the world like never before."[73]

Carlucci had just returned from a trip to Beijing, where he met with Chinese leader Jiang Zemin. WTO entry, Carlucci explained, was the "single-most discussed topic in China." Jiang, he recounted, "said they were going to enter into the new economy. They see it as their opening to the world. They see it as their opportunity to develop their country much faster, and they see it as an opportunity to deal with some of the complicated issues that they face." "It's an open and shut case," Carlucci told Congress. "Granting [permanent normal trading status] to China will guarantee U.S. companies access to China on our terms; denying [it] will place the terms of our access in China's hands." Congress ultimately agreed, and six months after the hearing, the United States normalized trade relations with China.

But a month before Carlucci's hearing, Jiang had presented a dramatically different vision to senior Party officials. "Information networks have already become a new arena of thought and culture and a new ideological and political battleground," he declared. "In sum, the basic policy concerning information networks is to actively develop them, strengthen supervision over them, seek their advantages while avoiding their disadvantages, use them for our own purposes, and strive for a position where we always hold the initiative in the global development of information networks."[74] Jiang recognized that battle was intensifying rather than concluding. And he intended to keep China's networks firmly within the Communist Party's hands.

Jiang's views on technology were shaped by his experience leading China's Ministry of Electronics Industry in the 1980s. In 1983, he led a Chinese delegation to visit technology companies in Canada and the United States. Jiang's report to the State Council, the country's top administrative body, reads like a playbook for China's rise during the following decades. "Our country's electronics industry lags behind in science and technology," he underscored.[75] To catch up, Jiang called for importing U.S. and Canadian technology, setting up joint ventures, and increasing academic exchanges.

Jiang's thoughts on setting up R&D in the United States foreshadowed China's most controversial activities in the decades ahead. "There are a lot of Chinese-American experts in Silicon Valley, and they have many small companies of their own," he observed. "We need to look into setting up an R&D company in this area with either a foreign company or a Chinese-American owned company, and send personnel there to undertake design and development work. This would be very helpful for making full use of favorable conditions to import technology and secure market information." On its face, this was a recipe not for innovating within the United States but rather extracting information from it.

Jiang also believed that China's tech industry should serve its military first and foremost. Two months after returning from Canada and the United States, Jiang argued in a piece for *People's Daily*, "The development of electronic military equipment has a bearing on national security and therefore must be our top priority."[76] The following year, Jiang reiterated that one of the "most fundamental" responsibilities of the electronics industry was to "provide advanced military electronic equipment to modernize national defense."[77] "The ideology guiding the electronics industry is to ensure the production of military products and find civilian applications for military technology," he explained in 1985.[78]

During the 1990s, the first Gulf War and NATO's bombing of Yugoslavia cemented Jiang's views about the importance of new technology for military power. China was only an observer to these conflicts, but as Jiang watched the U.S. military launch precision-guided missiles and destroy Russian equipment that closely resembled the Chinese military's inventory, he began to think more about communications technology and combat. By 2000, he viewed information as part of the battlefield. "In a high-tech war, an army cannot exercise sovereignty over its territorial waters and airspace without sovereignty over its information," he told a meeting of China's Central Military Commission. "One can foresee that informationized warfare will be the main form of war in the 21st century."[79]

To Western ears in 2000, however, Jiang sounded as if he were welcoming an open internet. In August, he addressed the World Computer Congress, which had gathered in Beijing. "The fact that information can be transmitted rapidly and widely is turning the world into a borderless information space. Information crosses rivers and mountains effortlessly and spreads throughout the whole world," Jiang told the audience.[80] But the Chinese leader's main message was to ask developed countries to assist with China's technological development, and he was not hesitant to use some of their rhetoric to warm them up for that pitch.

Jiang also cited the challenges that increased connectivity posed and proposed a big idea that got relatively little attention. "To promote sound development of the Internet, we advocate adopting an international Internet treaty to bring countries together to work to strengthen supervision of information security in order for us to be able to fully enjoy the positive aspects of the Internet." This was a call for protecting the state against the very forces that the West hoped technology would unleash. But compared to Jiang's flowery language about information movement, it barely registered. "Jiang appeared to accept the inevitability of free information flows," the *New York Times* reported.[81]

## THE GOLDEN SHIELD RUSH

While the West focused on the commercial aspects of selling technology, China was fixated on its military and national security implications. Instead of clashing, these views became reinforcing as Western firms openly supported, and profited from, China's security agenda.

A major trade expo held in Beijing highlighted the disconnect between the West's claims that it was exporting its values and the reality that the Communist Party was importing tools to maintain its hold on power. "Security China 2000" attracted hundreds of foreign companies, including Cisco Systems, Motorola, and Nortel, among others. As Greg Walton, an independent researcher, documented in a major report, one of the organizers was the CCP Central Committee's Commission for the Comprehensive Management of Social Security. Western companies were pitching their wares to China's security services.[82]

The centerpiece of the event was China's "Golden Shield." According to one of its chief architects, Golden Shield had six goals: a network connecting public security forces, a centralized database for Chinese police, standards to promote interagency information sharing, network safety and data integrity, capabilities to improve network performance, and, finally, mechanisms for monitoring real-time traffic and blocking undesirable content.[83] The last goal received the most attention from Western observers, who called it the "Great Firewall," missing that the project had much larger ambitions, and that it was focused more on domestic surveillance than external vigilance.[84]

The "Golden Shield" name anchored the project in a tradition of state-backed networks. During the 1990s, the Chinese government had backed a series of "Golden Projects." Golden Customs would collect customs and trade data. Golden Card would connect banks, businesses, and consumers to a public credit card system. Most ambitious of all, Golden Bridge would connect China's government agencies, state enterprises, and the public, essentially serving as a national intranet. Other projects were launched to monitor tax data, agriculture, and health care,[85] collectively forming what Zhu Rongji, then a vice-premier of the State Council, called "the national public economic information network."[86]

The central aim of the Golden Projects was not to connect China with the world, but to connect China with the CCP.[87] By making itself the administrator and central node in all these networks, the CCP was positioning itself to benefit from increased information flows so that it could better monitor, and ultimately manage, the state and the economy. As the Soviet Union's demise so vividly highlighted, bureaucrats struggle to set prices, allocate resources, and make other decisions with the efficiency of markets. The Golden Projects appeared to offer a solution to one of Communism's greatest challenges. The Party viewed connectivity as a means for enhancing its coordination and control.

Chinese officials still needed foreign technology to make Golden Shield a reality. After securing support for China's WTO membership, the Chinese government was perhaps less concerned about human rights criticisms limiting their access to Western technology. Instead of minimizing the scope of what they had in mind, if anything, Chinese officials played up Golden Shield's intended reach. By late 2000, Chinese officials were claiming they had spent $70 million on the project and planned to spend much more in the years ahead, according to Walton.[88] Western companies should have been alarmed by what amounted to blueprints for a digital panopticon. Instead, they scrambled for a piece of the action.

At the Security China 2000 exhibition, Nortel was promoting JungleMUX, a digital networking product that was initially developed for electric and power utility companies.[89] By replacing their wire cables with fiber optics and using JungleMUX, companies were able to transmit more data, faster, over longer distances. When GE acquired these technologies from Nortel in 2001, it noted, "They are ideal for use in telecommunication applications for industrial and commercial customers with large, geographically dispersed sites such as petrochemical plants, airports and transportation corridors."[90] But it was the product's secondary use that was of greater interest to Chinese authorities: it was also capable of carrying large amounts of surveillance video, over great distances, to a central control center.[91]

Nortel's joint ventures in China were already helping to build some pieces of the surveillance apparatus. As Walton reports, Nortel was partnering with Tsinghua University to develop speech recognition technology.[92] The potential applications were broad, ranging from automating customer service hotlines to government surveillance of telephone conversations. One of Nortel's Chinese joint ventures produced the first switch compliant with U.S. and European laws that required telecom equipment to be capable of allowing the government to intercept communications.[93] Those capabilities were designed in countries where the rule of law regulated and constrained governmental use. In China, however, the Party is the law.

Nortel's OPTera Metro series, also on display at the expo, underscores the dual-use nature of the technology that Western firms were marketing. The product managed network traffic to improve network performance. Doing that, however, required an ability to inspect the traffic itself and establish administrative controls that could easily be used for other purposes. For example, administrators could configure silent alarms, which report events without alerting the user, transfer files to and from computers on the network, and reroute traffic.[94] A product developed to maximize information flows was well-designed to also enhance state control.

Nortel included the OPTera products in its "Personal Internet Strategy," a big idea that resonated in Western boardrooms and Chinese government bureaus.[95] The goal was to deliver more customized content to internet users and to do so more efficiently. But it required tracking user behavior, device characteristics, and even location. "Imagine a network that knows who you are, where you are, and can reach you whether you're on your mobile phone or at your desktop," Nortel's ads proclaimed. "Even better, imagine instead of finding your Web content, it finds you. Sounds personal. Exactly."[96]

Exactly, indeed. Three months after the expo, Nortel won what was the single largest optical contract in China's history.[97] The one-year $101 million deal with China Telecom, China's largest state-owned telecom company, included delivering and installing 15,000 kilometers of long-haul fiber network with a raft of OPTera products. "This next-generation optical network will span key regions of north, south, and southwest China, providing China Telecom with massive bandwidth, unparalleled levels of intelligence, and the industry's lowest cost per managed bit," an industry publication declared."[98] Speed, intelligence, and efficiency. Sounds perilous.

The dual-use challenge is traditionally more, well, challenging. Sellers worry about buyers setting up front organizations to mask their identities and the products' destination and use. But Golden Shield was largely advertised and outsourced in plain view. Western companies descended on Beijing to attend a security expo that gave them an audience with China's security services. Golden Shield's key components were highlighted in the annual reports of the companies that won the contest to supply them.

Nortel saw bigger prizes over the horizon. The deal with China Telecom strengthened its position as China's leading supplier of optical infrastructure, and more sales followed, appearing to vindicate Nortel's strategy. It also sold OPTera systems to Shanghai Telecom, creating China's first high-speed citywide optical network,[99] and to China Unicom.[100] But the rush would be shorter-lived than Western executives realized. Their Chinese partners were about to become their direct competitors. Unbeknownst to Nortel, a clandestine battle had already begun.

## "HUAWEI'S ACHIEVEMENTS MAKE US ALL PROUD"

A mysterious visitor arrived at Nortel's U.S. headquarters around 2000. The two-building complex, with nearly as much space as Buckingham Palace, towered over a highway in Richardson, a suburb of Dallas, Texas. Nortel built the office in 1991, joining a growing roster of U.S. tech firms that were attracted to the Dallas–Fort Worth area's tax breaks and educated workforce. Given the dense ecosystem of telecom companies, there was a steady stream of people passing through the Nortel complex in those days.

But this encounter was so bizarre that former Nortel employees still remember the incident two decades later. The visitor was returning a fiber card used in Nortel switches and asking for a refund. The product, however, was in pieces. It had been disassembled, likely as part of a reverse-engineering effort. The visitor worked for Huawei, or a front company, former Nortel employees later told Tom Blackwell, a journalist at the *National Post*.[101]

The incident looks brazen in retrospect. The fiber card might have been expensive for a hobbyist, but it would have been a drop in the bucket for Huawei. By asking for a refund, the visitor risked drawing attention to reverse engineering. But the decision may have reflected a cold calculation that the consequences of detection were outweighed by the potential benefits of this intelligence. Returning the equipment gave the visitor an opportunity to ask questions, squeezing as much information from the process as possible.

Nortel might have responded differently had it known that Cisco, just six minutes down the road, was also under attack. Around the same time, Huawei was allegedly collecting the intelligence it needed to copy Cisco's routers, according to court documents from Cisco's lawsuit in 2003, and subsequent filings from the U.S. Department of Justice.[102] An independent expert concluded that Huawei copied Cisco's source code and replicated it verbatim in its own routers.[103]

The similarities were striking on the surface as well. The Huawei router product, Quidway, even used similar model numbers. The user interface was similar. Huawei's user manuals plagiarized entire sections of Cisco user manuals, including typos.[104] In 2001, Huawei's U.S. advertising campaign included images of San Francisco's Golden Gate Bridge, on which Cisco's logo is based. Subtlety was not the goal. "The only difference between us and them is price," the ads said.[105]

Huawei may have been emboldened by the experience. Having gained valuable information and marketed similar products, it suffered only negative headlines and legal fees in foreign markets. Meanwhile, Ren's "copinism" was working within China. In 1999, Cisco had 80 percent of the Chinese market for routers. By the time it settled its lawsuit with Huawei in 2004, Cisco had only 56 percent of the Chinese market for routers and Huawei had 31 percent.[106]

The Cisco case briefly reemerged in 2012 after Huawei's senior vice president Charles Ding falsely claimed that Huawei had been vindicated by an independent review. In response, Cisco disclosed new details about the misappropriated code. But Cisco's general counsel Mark Chandler was careful to point out, "It's not about the US or China and we respect the efforts the Chinese government is making to increase intellectual property protection."[107] Cisco appeared weak and worried about losing access to China's market.

Nortel's reaction to the suspicious visitor was even more restrained.

It considered suing, former employees told the *Globe and Mail*, but decided to leave the matter alone. Huawei was not about to leave Nortel alone, however. It had much bigger plans for the United States, beginning in Texas.

On Valentine's Day in 2001, Huawei opened up its North American headquarters in Plano, Texas, off the President George Bush Turnpike and just a ten minute drive down Route 75 from Nortel's office. The subsidiary, which it called Futurewei, started with a relatively small staff of thirty, but it had plans to expand and rented 24,000 square feet.[108] For Huawei, the office was a way to parachute into one of telecom's most vital hubs—just as Jiang Zemin had proposed after his 1983 visit to the United States and Canada.

Texas state and local officials bent over backward to help Huawei expand. They were eager to attract new investment, especially after the dot-com bubble burst, taking a toll on tech companies in the area. In 2009, the city of Plano approved a $712,800 grant for Huawei to invest in a new marketing and advertising office.[109] To bring home the deal, Texas governor Rick Perry personally lobbied Ren during a trip to Beijing.[110]

Perry was eager to showcase Huawei's investment as an example of Texas's thriving economy. At an opening ceremony in October 2010, he piled on the praise. "This is a company with a really strong worldwide reputation. Innovators of quality telecommunications technology," he said.[111] "The ripple effect of this company is going to be quite substantial," Perry noted, suggesting positive economic impacts with no thought of the political fallout that would follow.

Perry must have known that Huawei craved public affirmation from U.S. officials, and he was happy to praise Ren personally. "What a really interesting man he is. Rather straight spoken. If you didn't know any better, you'd say he grew up out in West Texas," he chuckled from behind the podium. "He truly is a very powerful chief executive officer, and a very focused and hard-driven individual, which, in the world that we live in today, is a great attribute."[112]

But Huawei's hard-driving culture has also left a trail of alleged misdeeds, including targeting employees for their access to trade secrets and confidential information.[113] This challenge is widespread in the tech sector, where careers are fluid, competition is fierce, and intellectual property is highly prized. Ambitious employees see opportunities to rise faster when moving from one company to another, and some have been willing to betray their former employers and break the law. But even in this hypercompetitive environment, the scope and duration of Huawei's activities stand out.

Huawei promoted these practices from the very top, according to the U.S. Department of Justice. In 2001, it allegedly recruited Shaowei Pan, a senior engineer at Motorola's headquarters in Schaumburg, Illinois. Pan, in collaboration with several Motorola engineers, developed products for Huawei while remaining employed at Motorola, and ostensibly under the cover of that firm, he made several trips to Huawei's office in Beijing and its Futurewei office in Texas between 2001 and 2004. His work, which used proprietary technology from Motorola, was important enough that he had direct access to Ren, who met with him in Beijing and exchanged emails.[114]

Many of the details about Pan's correspondence with Huawei were destroyed. After an Illinois court ordered Pan to hand over his computer, Pan ran a program called "Eraser" that makes data irrecoverable by deleting and writing over it. He also changed the computer's clocks, ostensibly to frustrate investigators from piecing together a timeline. Asking an engineer to hand over a computer that could lead to his conviction was like expecting John Dillinger to politely hand over his guns. Huawei may have gotten lucky.

But not all was lost, and in the data fragments that were recovered, investigators found what they believed was a smoking gun. "Attached please find those document [sic] about SC300 (CDMA 2000 1X) specification you asked," Pan wrote to Ren and another senior executive at Huawei in March 2003.[115] Pan was handing over the specifications for one of Motorola's most advanced 3G wireless base stations to the CEO of a chief rival. Moreover, Motorola lawyers argued, he was doing so not simply on his own accord, but in response to Ren's requests.

Ironically, it was during this period that Huawei nearly became American. Not long after Pan's specifications email, Ren also received a game-changing offer from Motorola. In December 2003, Motorola COO Mike Zafirovski traveled to China's Hainan Island and joined Ren for a walk along the beach to discuss the future of their two companies. Weeks later, they agreed that Motorola would buy Huawei for $7.5 billion.[116] But unconvinced of Huawei's value, Motorola's board ultimately decided to pass.

By 2004, Nortel's world of networks was starting to look more dangerous. After more than a decade of underscoring the opportunities that China's market offered, the company's annual report acknowledged that it faced "newer competitors, particularly from China" in the global market.[117] In response, its strategy was to double down in Asia, particularly in India, China, and South Korea, and expand its focus into information security. "Nortel is working to provide next generation solutions for seamless defense against a variety of threats from the core of the network through the desktop, making it possible for service providers and enterprises to eliminate specific threats before they have the opportunity to spread," it announced.[118]

While emphasizing its focus on security, Nortel did not mention that it was being hacked from China. In 2004, Nortel security advisor Brian Shields was alerted to unusual behavior within the company's network. A senior executive appeared to be downloading documents that were highly technical and unrelated to his area of the business.[119] When asked, he had no recollection of the files. Reviewing the activity, Shields discovered a massive breach. Since at least 2000, hackers had been operating within Nortel's internal network.

"Once you were on the inside of the network, it was soft and gooey," Shields later told the *Wall Street Journal*.[120] The hackers gained access to the email accounts of seven senior executives, including CEO

Frank Dunn, and extracted a treasure trove of documents. During the six-month period that Shields tracked their activities, the hackers accessed more than 1,400 documents, including technical papers, product development plans, and even sales proposals with pricing information. Nortel reset passwords, but otherwise did little to strengthen its defenses. Shields wrote a report that was filed away and essentially ignored. The hackers changed their tactics, and six months after the initial breach was discovered, the hacking resumed in full.[121]

Shields had tracked the data trail to Shanghai, home to Unit 61398, one of the PLA's major cyber units.[122] Although he could not conclusively prove the source of the hack, the Shanghai connection was significant in another respect. Just years earlier, Nortel had built the city's first fiber-optic network with its OPTera products. Nortel's secrets were being plucked from its computers in North America, and en route to their final destination, they were literally flowing through the network it had built in Shanghai.

## THE FALL

During Nortel's final years, Huawei was circling the Canadian tech giant. First as a dove, then as a hawk, and finally as a vulture.

A peace offering began to take shape in 2005, when Mike Zafirovski left Motorola to become Nortel's CEO. The global telecom landscape was shifting. As Huawei and ZTE began undercutting the competition on pricing, Western companies were consolidating. Greater scale promised to help underwrite the increasingly expensive R&D they needed to remain competitive. In the following years, Lucent would merge with Alcatel, Ericsson would acquire Marconi, and Nokia and Siemens would combine their telecom businesses.

In February 2006, Huawei and Nortel announced their intention to form a joint venture to offer higher-speed broadband.[123] The new company would be based in Ottawa, with Nortel as the majority owner. Although the partnership was not yet finalized, Nortel had already begun marketing Huawei gear to carriers and jointly developing products. Nortel and Huawei hoped these announcements would help secure contracts from carriers.

The rivals' interests appeared aligned, but their partnership revealed a fundamental reversal in roles. Nortel once had the technology that Huawei craved. Now it wanted to sell Huawei's broadband products. Huawei once had the market access that Nortel craved in China. Now it wanted Nortel's access to North American markets. It was clear which company had the momentum. Huawei was ascendant, and Nortel was about to fall faster than anyone realized.

When the carrier contracts failed to materialize, the venture was no longer attractive.[124] The partnership folded in June 2006, only four months after being announced and before officially becoming operational. "Huawei has not done a successful joint venture with anyone," Zafirovski told the *Vancouver Sun* several years later.[125] But perhaps it was a successful joint venture for Huawei after all. In Nortel's rush to begin product development and marketing before completing the joint venture, it may have handed over additional information.

Huawei surpassed Nortel's annual revenue in 2007, and the Canadian firm spiraled downward. Without a doubt, the company faced several major challenges, and Chinese competition was just one among them.[126] In the words of one former senior executive, Nortel confronted "a perfect storm of rapid expansion, a tech bubble, industry consolidation, and the global collapse of customer capital investment."[127] The last of those forces, the 2008 financial crisis, pushed Nortel beyond the brink of recovery. Its stock, valued at roughly eighty-four dollars a share at its peak in 2000, plummeted to cents on the dollar. On January 14, 2009, the tech giant filed for bankruptcy and became the largest corporate failure in Canadian history.[128]

Despite championing Nortel's rise over the years, the Canadian government was unwilling to step in and stop its fall.[129] Former Nortel executives argued that the company was strategically important and must be salvaged. They proposed using the company's roughly $1 billion Canadian dollars in tax credits, which it had earned by spending on R&D over the years, to build a national high-speed network.[130] But Canadian officials viewed Nortel's decline as a crisis of the company's own making.

The same decision would have been unthinkable in Beijing. After providing political and financial support for Huawei, the Chinese government would never allow it to go bankrupt without a national champion to take its place. "Other nations saw the industry as strategic and they fought to protect and promote their own companies within this sector," explains Robert D. Atkinson, a Canadian-American economist and president of the Information Technology and Innovation Foundation. "Nowhere is this more true than in China."[131]

In a final attempt to save Nortel, a group of former executives approached Huawei in May 2009. They planned to form a new company that would acquire Nortel's assets, and they pitched Huawei on making a minority investment. The two sides hammered out a deal and moved it forward for approval. But in a reversal of Motorola's decision to reject the deal that Zafirovski had arranged in 2003, this time it was Huawei's board that rejected the deal.[132]

Nortel was dead, but Huawei was far from done with it. When Nortel announced its plans to liquidate, Huawei was the highest bidder. That prospect set off alarms in Washington, D.C., because Nortel's customers included Verizon and Sprint, which carry U.S. government data. Perhaps realizing that the U.S. government might carve those customers out of a deal with Nortel, Huawei dropped its bid.[133] Nortel sold off its assets to other companies, eventually raising $7.3 billion for its creditors—less than 3 percent of its $250 billion peak value, and $200 million less than Motorola's missed opportunity to buy Huawei.[134]

Even if Huawei could not have Nortel's market access, it still wanted the Canadian company's knowledge. In 2011, it remained outside the fray when Nortel's patents went up for auction. A coalition of Western companies paid $4.5 billion for 6,000 patents, a deal of unprecedented size and scope.[135] But Huawei had been scooping up an asset that was even more valuable: Nortel's employees. "When Nortel collapsed, 3G had just started developing in the world," Ren told the *Globe and Mail.* "As the industry evolved from 3G to 4G, and then to 5G, [Nortel employees] also improved themselves during the process. What they have contributed to Huawei is what they had in their minds. It's definitely not about intellectual property theft."[136]

Huawei reached into Nortel's most senior ranks. It hired Nortel's former chief technology officer, John Roese, to lead its North American R&D efforts and set up facilities in Silicon Valley and other tech hubs.[137] Nortel veterans were looking for their next paycheck and excited about the opportunity to join a growing company that was pouring money into R&D. "We opened a big facility in San Diego . . . We did the same thing up at Ottawa. When Nortel kind of disappeared, one of the things that happened very quickly, en masse, some of the top technical experts in Nortel just kind of walked across the street," Roese explained in 2011.[138]

Nortel's collapse seemed primarily a Canadian problem in 2011, but its downfall, along with Lucent, the primary U.S. supplier of telecom equipment, has reverberated worldwide. "The conversation about 5G was really lost a decade ago, when Western nations decided that they weren't going to invest in the underpinning infrastructures . . . and the result was we just didn't have the choices," Jeremy Fleming, the head of Britain's Government Communications Headquarters (GCHQ), an intelligence agency, said in 2021.[139]

Blinded by ambition and greed, Western companies and governments helped create their own biggest competitor in a sector that would become even more strategically important in the years ahead. Executives pushed to steer their companies deeper into China's markets. Elected officials craved their support and wanted to assist their growth. Even state and local officials participated by offering Huawei incentives to open offices in Texas. Employees at rival firms jumped at opportunities for greater responsibility and reward, some of them crossing legal lines in the process. After being cast out, Nortel's employees had even fewer choices.

Nortel's world of networks was wide open. Huawei strolled in through the front door. Its rise left a trail of allegations, including being a mastermind of theft as well as the beneficiary of Chinese industrial espionage. It sucked up generous subsidies, loans, tax incentives, and other forms of often opaque state support. But its biggest moves happened in plain sight. It had gained access to Western technology through reverse-engineering, joint ventures, and R&D labs. It spent heavily on IBM and other consultants to adopt Western management and finance practices. It even plucked the top employees from its competitors. Copying technology, processes, and people, the capture was complete.

Like all fallen empires, Nortel left behind a trail of artifacts. Its computers were auctioned off to companies that had no idea the equipment had been hacked. When the Canadian defense department purchased Nortel's headquarters at a discount in 2010, it discovered that the $200 million building was riddled with listening devices.[140] The government spent $790 million on renovations but determined the building could not meet the top security requirements for intelligence sharing. In 2011, Nortel's U.S. headquarters in Texas was sold, and the logo with the global *O*, created to celebrate its centennial, was removed.[141]

But even after Nortel had ceased operations, its hardware continued to run, oblivious to the company's fate. Nortel routers were still directing data flows around the world. Nortel cell towers and switches were still connecting calls. At its peak in 2000, Nortel estimated that 75 percent of North America's internet traffic was running through its equipment.[142] When it came time to replace their systems, Nortel customers would need to find a new supplier. The world of networks was more vulnerable than ever, including in America's own backyard.

# CHAPTER THREE

# "WHEREVER THERE ARE PEOPLE"

The hum of hundreds of small fans filled the basement of the Nemont Telephone Cooperative's office in Glasgow, Montana. Walking past rows of metal towers, under bunches of wires snaking across the ceiling, I noticed an aging brown metal cabinet with a familiar name: Nortel. Before the Canadian telecom giant went bust, it was the primary supplier for Nemont, which provides service for customers scattered across 14,000 square miles, roughly the size of New Jersey and Connecticut combined.

Huawei's flower-shaped logo was everywhere. It was printed on metal cabinets that housed the room's newest equipment. It marked the base stations sitting inside those cabinets, their green lights flashing as data flowed through. In a service closet attached to the main room, stocked with parts and tools, there was a reddish-brown plastic box mounted on the wall. Across its Huawei label, a technician had jokingly written "Nortel" with a black marker.

Getting to Glasgow wasn't easy. Of all U.S. towns with at least a thousand residents, it is the farthest away from any major city.[1] Residents have embraced this distinction as a badge of honor. For ten dollars, you can buy a "Middle of Nowhere" T-shirt from the local sporting goods store. Hotels are few, and the one I chose had a charmingly modest sales pitch, advertising itself as "somewhere in the middle of nowhere."

That Nemont and rural wireless carriers in a dozen U.S. states turned to Huawei reveals a central failure of U.S. policy.[2] Because the town's population numbered in the thousands rather than the tens of thousands, larger U.S. carriers were not interested in making adequate investments. Even with access to U.S. government funds, Nemont found that equipment from Ericsson, Nokia, or Samsung was too expensive.

Echoing Mao's strategy of "encircling cities from the countryside," Ren Zhengfei directed Huawei to focus on markets that Western providers overlooked.[3] "Go to the countryside, go to the countryside, a vast world and many achievements await," an early brochure instructed employees.[4] Huawei gained traction in rural China, expanded internationally into developing countries, and arrived in rural America with a long track record of bringing connectivity to forgotten markets.

Glasgow's experience is not so different from that of developing and emerging markets around the world. With precious few resources for cell phone towers, high-speed internet switches, and fiber-optic cables, smaller markets from rural America to Africa have few viable options. They also know that failing to join global networks is a death sentence. Huawei has not been their first choice, but often it has been their only affordable choice.

Around the world, Chinese firms have thrived in the digital divide that Western firms left in their wake. Few viewed these projects as anything more than scattered opportunism. But as China's champions ventured abroad, they gained critical experience and positioned themselves to dominate tomorrow's fastest-growing markets.

## THE EMPIRE BUILDER

When I traveled to Glasgow in August 2019, I followed the route that created it. Like many northwestern American towns, Glasgow is the product of network technology from an earlier era. During the 1880s, the railroad tycoon James Hill built lines through the Great Plains and into the Pacific Northwest. He was hardly the first to dream of connecting the continent with iron, but his approach was more methodical. Instead of racing toward the coast, Hill saw an opportunity to settle the land and create new markets for freight traffic.

Little stood in the way of Hill's expanding empire. The government encouraged the railways' expansion, providing land grants and loans to build new track, ignoring the social and environmental toll the railway companies left in their wake. Railway executives bribed public officials with free transportation and stock options. Several states tried and failed to regulate the railways, which stretched across their borders.

Beginning the journey in Chicago, I boarded a double-decker train and settled in for the night, falling asleep in Minnesota and waking up the next morning in North Dakota. Out the window, yellow-brown plains rolled on and on.

As the sun rose, the train pushed further north, climbing to the top of the United States. Over the next six hours, it passed through towns with names reminiscent of a time when the train was cutting-edge technology: Devils Lake, Minot, Williston, Wolf Point. So many communities sprang up along these routes that Hill, who was known as the Empire Builder, did not have time to name them himself.

When it came time to name a patch of northeast Montana, one of Hill's engineers spun a globe and landed on Glasgow, Scotland. The town was officially established in 1887 and grew as ranchers and farmers were attracted by cheap train fares and the prospect of a new life. For ten dollars, a family could fill a boxcar with its possessions and head west. "Pin your faith in Glasgow and you shall wear diamonds," one advertisement beckoned.[5]

But Hill and the other railway tycoons would not continue entirely unchecked. In 1887, the same year Glasgow was founded, Congress created the Interstate Commerce Commission (ICC) to set maximum shipping rates for the railways and later expanded its mandate to cover telephones, telegraphs, and wireless companies. As the first independent U.S. agency, the ICC served as a model for subsequent regulatory bodies, including the FCC, which assumed the ICC's communications authorities upon its creation in 1934.

Glasgow remains a railway town, but it has become a waypoint rather than an origin and destination. Twice a day, passenger trains crossing between the coasts pause for a few moments in town. My train arrived relatively full, but I was the only passenger to disembark. Climbing down the metal stairs, I stepped out of the train's lunchtime bustle and into relative calm.

Across the tracks, a brick building with a row of watering holes beckoned: Montana Tavern, Alley's Palace, and Stockmans Bar. A nearby sign advertised reunion celebrations for the local high school. The railway engineer's spin of the globe cast a long shadow. The local high school's mascot is the Scottie, short for Scottish Terrier.

Vacant buildings and shrinking classrooms tell a story of decline. When a nearby air force base began shutting down in the late 1960s, some 16,000 people left the area. The exodus continued through the 1980s and 1990s, as train stops across the Great Plains were consolidated. Although Glasgow's station remained open, the closure of nearby stops devastated its neighbors.

Gregg Hunter, a Glasgow native, has lived through these changes, juggling different jobs along the way, often several at once. When Hunter finished high school in 1977, his graduating class had 158 students. He initially went into the auto business, towing damaged cars and selling parts at local dealerships. Agriculture is the lifeblood of the local economy, and Hunter eventually switched to selling farm equipment, which he did for twenty-five years.

Hunter is the guy you call when something goes wrong. On the weekends, he moonlights as an emergency medical technician. He's also a certified locksmith and serves on the boards of his church and the local chamber of commerce.

Hunter's enthusiasm for his hometown remains undiminished. He loves the outdoors, and when the workday ends, there's running, hunting, and fishing, all at his front door.

But the 2008 financial crisis forced Hunter to reevaluate his plans. "I had turned fifty, didn't have any money in my 401(k), and I needed to figure out retirement and health insurance," he told me.

Nemont was hiring and offering attractive benefits. Hunter landed a job as a public relations and marketing specialist, and for the last dozen years has helped Nemont grow even as Glasgow's population shrinks.

In 2020, the local high school, Hunter's alma mater, graduated just fifty-two students. It's a small but significant figure for the region—in 2007, only one student graduated in the neighboring town of Froid. She got to choose the class motto, colors, and keynote speaker: the governor of Montana.

In most of the world, the movement of people from rural to urban areas is usually a positive trend associated with development. But the decline of rural American communities often looks more like decay: deindustrialization, declining incomes, and worsening health outcomes.

Technology contributed to this vicious cycle. "Digital inequality in America is on a dismal trajectory," explains Susan Crawford in *Fiber: The Coming Tech Revolution and Why America Might Miss It.* "Poorer, rural, disabled, and minority Americans are far less likely to have wired high-speed internet access at home than rich people in urban areas, just as, a hundred years ago, they were far less likely to have electricity."[6]

Faster broadband networks were rolled out in urban areas, widening the gap with rural American towns such as Glasgow. Businesses closed and relocated to areas with better connectivity. The brightest among Glasgow's rising generation shipped out for college, and after graduating, there were fewer and fewer jobs waiting at home. When Glasgow residents met to brainstorm for the city's economic plan in 2013, their wish list included: "Stronger economy," "Industry beyond agriculture," and "Keep [our] kids here, come back after education."[7]

Glasgow occupies a new frontier. The city was born out of an adventurous westward migration and a network of iron that made it possible. Its first residents took great risks in pursuit of something bigger and better than what was immediately available to them. As networks of fiber and radio race ahead, the community they created must fight to avoid being left behind.

## DIGITAL DIVIDES

Like a storm moving across the plains, the digital divide between urban and rural America arrived swiftly, but not without warning. Surveying America's communications landscape in 1999, the FCC's first report on broadband deployment saw mostly blue skies ahead: "We are encouraged that deployment of advanced telecommunications generally appears, at present, reasonable and timely."[8] Just a year later, the storm clouds were gathering: "We reach the troubling conclusion that, in all likelihood, market forces alone will not guarantee that many rural Americans will have access to advanced services."[9] Since then, the question has been not whether there is a divide but how wide it is.

Debates about how to bridge the digital divide often begin with disagreement over how to measure it. The FCC's early reporting examined broadband availability by zip code. If there was a single subscriber in a given zip code, this implied the entire zip code could get access.[10] This is like assuming that because one person drives a Mercedes, everyone else in that zip code can buy one as well. Even in Detroit, Cleveland, and other densely populated urban areas, some providers skipped low-income neighborhoods when deploying faster networks, a practice critics call "digital redlining."[11] While acknowledging some gaps in access, these approaches systematically underestimated the challenge.

The most heated debates are about minimum standards. These debates are technical, but they often stem from philosophical differences about the roles of government and the private sector. In 2004, the FCC considered 200 kilobits per second (Kbps) adequate broadband. Four years later, it increased the baseline to 4 megabits per second (Mbps) for downloading and 1 megabit per second for uploading, or 4 Mbps/1 Mbps for short. As long as speeds increase, resolutions about minimum speeds will remain temporary. While the government tries to bridge yesterday's digital divide, new gaps are emerging.

Tom Wheeler, who chaired the FCC from 2013 to 2017, made rural broadband access impossible to ignore. In 2015, the FCC concluded that more than half of all rural Americans lacked access to a new benchmark of 25 Mbps/3 Mbps.[12] "The standard recognized how Americans were actually using the internet at home," Wheeler told me. "I said at the time, however, that it was table stakes, the minimum required for use of the internet, and that it would have to increase over time."[13]

Not everyone agreed. The FCC allows its commissioners to voice dissenting opinions, and Ajit Pai wrote a withering critique. He started with a nod to literature: "Before Humpty Dumpty had a great fall in *Through the Looking-Glass*, he told Alice, 'When I use a word, . . . it means just what I choose it to mean—neither more nor less.' So too, apparently, at the FCC. For today's report declares that 10 Mbps Internet access service is no longer broadband. Only 25 Mbps or more counts." The government was only raising the benchmark, Pai argued, so that it could extend its own regulatory power.[14]

In 2017, President Trump appointed Pai to succeed Wheeler as the chairman of the FCC. In his first speech as chairman, Pai laid out his priorities and put closing the digital divide at the top of the list. "There is a digital divide in this country," he said, addressing his colleagues. "I believe one of our core priorities going forward should be to close that divide—to do what's necessary to help the private sector build networks, send signals, and distribute information to American consumers . . . We must work to bring the benefits of the digital age to all Americans."[15]

Wheeler and Pai have remarkably similar goals. Both believe that broadband access is a necessity for communities to thrive. Both want to improve access, especially in rural areas. Pai is intimately familiar with rural America, having grown up in Parsons, Kansas, a railway town with about 9,000 residents. Both believe that Huawei equipment is too risky to include in American networks.

Listen closely, though, and you'll hear Wheeler talk more about the positive role that government can play. Pai waxes on about the virtues of free markets and warns against the dangers of regulation. It is a debate that runs through American history, through the railway industry and the founding of the ICC, and all the way back to the competing visions offered by Alexander Hamilton and Thomas Jefferson. It is the divide behind America's digital divide.

## "PEOPLE'S LIVES ARE AT STAKE"

To understand how these challenges were playing out locally, I joined Hunter, his colleague Leif Handran, and a third Nemont employee, a technician, for a day of service calls.

I expected that Glasgow residents would be alarmed to discover Chinese equipment in their midst. Two months earlier, President Trump had declared a national emergency. Almost 70 percent of Glasgow's county voted for Trump in 2016, and American views of China had soured nationally. U.S. officials were issuing daily warnings, creating a steady stream of headlines about the risks that Huawei posed. CNN pointed out that Huawei equipment was serving local cell phone networks near central Montana's Malmstrom Air Force Base, home to more than one hundred intercontinental ballistic missiles capable of carrying nuclear warheads.[16]

But as I listened to Glasgow residents, a different story emerged, one that reveals an uphill battle for U.S. officials warning against security risks without offering affordable alternatives.

I arrived at Nemont's service office at 8:00 a.m. on a Monday, and technicians were already reviewing and triaging outstanding requests. In one case, an elderly customer's screen reader, a device that reads content aloud, was not working. They knew her. They knew her husband had died recently. And they knew that the incoming calls and emails were probably overwhelming. From the call, they could hear that the house was full of extended family and friends. Practically everyone in the house had an opinion about what was wrong with the screen reader, but no one had fixed it. The technicians moved her to the top of the service list, asked her to refrain from making any adjustments to the device, and five minutes later, a technician was en route.

As this unfolded, I realized that I've never physically met anyone on the other end of a customer service call. I began to question the well-known platitudes. If a company is putting all "customers first," doesn't that create a mob of people waiting for help? And if "the customer is always right," how do you break the news when they're wrong? There was something refreshingly honest about Nemont's approach.

Nemont's relationships are different. The company's owners are also its customers. In 1950, a group of residents, mainly farmers, banded together to create Montana's first telephone cooperative, and Nemont, which stands for Northeastern Montana, was born. Small-town life provides additional incentives. As Hunter explained, "We're part of these communities. We see our customers at the gym, at church, at high school football games, everywhere."

The next service call was the City of Glasgow office. Its internet connection had stopped working overnight, and because calls were carried through the same connection, the office was essentially paralyzed. When we arrived, staff were doing their best to focus on nondigital tasks, but even in rural America, most "paperwork" is electronic.

Down the hall, the Glasgow City Council convenes twice a month in meetings that would make America's founders proud. Every meeting begins with the Pledge of Allegiance, and members of the public can comment on any agenda items. Afterward, the Council moves through its agenda, typically in half an hour, and there's another opportunity for public comment before the meeting adjourns.

The technician opened a closet, ran a few tests, and replaced a router. After fifteen minutes, which included some friendly banter about the past weekend's activities and the coming week's weather, the city's office was back up and running.

The next customer was a retired farmer who had lost internet access. After a twenty-minute drive away from the town center, we took a turn off the highway and onto a dirt road for three miles. An American flag hung from a pole on the side of the driveway, and a small white house sat at the end. "He's not a big fan of visitors," the technician advised. I stayed outside and took in the landscape.

Extending in all directions, gentle hills and wheat fields disguised high-tech connections. Agriculture drives Glasgow's economy, and modern farm equipment is highly networked. Tractors use wireless networks to process satellite images, fine-tune seeding, and increase crop yields. The local John Deere dealership is more Apple Store than ACE Hardware. Its equipment uses cellular connections to transmit data to a virtual "operations center" that helps customers track and optimize output.[17]

Outside the house, a wooden telephone pole held a white, dish-shaped radio antenna thirty feet in the air. From that perch, the antenna could reach a tower several miles away. A wire ran from the top of the pole to the roof of the house. The system can handle wind speeds up to 125 miles per hour and temperatures from negative 40 degrees to 130 degrees Fahrenheit. These dedicated antennas provide speeds of up to 30 Mbps/30 Mbps at fifty dollars a month.[18] Instead of laying three miles of fiber-optic cable, which could have cost nearly $100,000, Nemont only needed to install the dish and run a wire to the house.[19]

Everywhere we went, it seemed the national emergency had not yet arrived. Most residents were unaware that their phone calls and emails ran through Chinese equipment. Until recently, they did not have a reason to ask who made their network hardware. After all, do you know what brand of equipment your cell phone is pinging right now?

Most people I spoke with did not have a strong opinion about China, and those who did were more likely to view it positively as a customer for local crops. There was anxiety about the trade war that had resulted in higher tariffs and lower agricultural exports. But the technology war behind the trade war remained, for most, invisible. The local paper had not published any articles mentioning Huawei. "For most of us, China is what you set the dinner table with on Thanksgiving," Hunter joked.

Their biggest fear was dropping off the grid altogether. Emergency services were dependent on Huawei equipment, as was much of daily life. Hunting, fishing, and other outdoor activities are popular among residents and a draw for tourists. All rely on wireless communications. "It's not just Jim-Bob calling his buddy," another Glasgow resident explained. "People's lives are at stake."

These priorities are entirely rational, and yet they stand at odds with U.S. official warnings about Huawei and other Chinese technology companies. In Maslow's hierarchy, physiological needs for air, water, food, and shelter are the most fundamental. The second tier includes personal security, employment, and other safety needs. The third tier includes the need to connect with others. At first glance, the government's demands seem like a reasonable request. U.S. officials are essentially asking people to prioritize the security threat that Huawei poses over their need to connect.

But Maslow's digital hierarchy of needs is different. Digital connectivity meets not only higher-level needs, such as connecting with friends and family, but also basic needs, such as bringing access to critical emergency services. For people using networks with Huawei equipment, the risk of losing access to existing services can feel more immediate and threatening than the more abstract fear of surveillance or foreign disruption of services. Most users, whether in rural America or countries around the world, are less concerned about foreign threats than they are about simply avoiding a giant bill. Without offering affordable alternatives, U.S. officials are fighting an impossible battle.

Nemont executives were not naive when deciding to use Huawei equipment. They knew the Chinese firm's reputation was suffering in Washington. In October 2012, the House Permanent Select Committee on Intelligence released a damning investigation into national security risks posed by Huawei and ZTE. "China has the means, opportunity, and motive to use telecommunications companies for malicious purposes," it observed.[20]

Unbeknownst to the congressional investigators, one of the Netherlands' largest mobile networks, KPN, had launched its own investigation in 2010 and discovered even more specific risks stemming from its decision to contract with Huawei. The company's internal report found that Huawei staff in the Netherlands and China were able to eavesdrop on all numbers within the network, including those of the Dutch prime minister and Chinese dissidents living in the Netherlands, and could see which numbers Dutch police and intelligence services were monitoring. KPN worried the report would significantly harm the company's reputation, and it was only made public in 2021, after the Dutch newspaper *De Volkskrant* obtained a copy.[21]

The Congressional investigation's verdict was about as bad as it could have been for Huawei and ZTE. The committee faulted Huawei for not cooperating and adequately answering questions. Its recommendation was clear: "U.S. network providers and systems developers are strongly encouraged to seek other vendors for their projects. Based on available classified and unclassified information, Huawei and ZTE cannot be trusted to be free of foreign state influence and thus pose a security threat to the United States and to our systems."

Congress greatly raised awareness about these risks, but it was less imaginative when considering solutions. The investigation noted that Huawei's products were being sold below market value. To address these challenges, it recommended investigating China's unfair trade practices, improving private sector information sharing, and expanding the role of the Committee on Foreign Investment in the United States, which screens foreign investments for national security risks.

What it did not recommend, however, was government support to make better alternatives available.

As a result, Nemont had few attractive options. "We're a small regional carrier and don't have the resources of the larger national carriers," Hunter explained. In late 2009 and early 2010, when Nemont was deciding how to upgrade its wireless networks to 3G, Huawei quoted prices that undercut the competition by 20 to 30 percent.[22] Rather than requiring Nemont to buy a standard package, Huawei was also willing to customize their order at a lower cost.

The U.S. government provides funding to rural areas to help defray internet and phone costs, and wanting to avoid jeopardizing that support, Mike Kilgore, Nemont's CEO, wrote to U.S. officials before installing Huawei equipment in 2011. "I was begging for them to say, 'No, don't buy it,'" he told the *New York Times*.[23] After no one objected, Nemont decided to go ahead.

To its credit, Huawei delivered. For several weeks, Chinese technicians slept in the Nemont offices, working around the clock to install 3G networks and train local technicians. "There were pizza boxes everywhere," one of the Nemont employees recalled. "Everyone was exhausted. But we worked together, and we got it done." There was pride in having accomplished something big on a shoestring budget. The partner that made it possible, however, was striking. A Chinese company helped Nemont do what the U.S. government could not, and what large U.S. corporations would not.

## "FOR OUR VERY SURVIVAL"

By the time its engineers arrived in Glasgow, Huawei had been connecting some of the world's most remote and dangerous places for over a decade. In the mid-1990's, Ren Zhengfei realized that his company needed to start competing internationally. If Huawei failed, Ren believed, it would struggle for a shrinking piece of China's domestic market.[24] "We were forced to go into the international market for our very survival," he later explained.[25]

After staying close to home for its first overseas project in Hong Kong, Huawei targeted riskier, more overlooked markets. At first glance, its timing could not have been worse. It often arrived as crises were bubbling up or boiling over. But that also meant Huawei faced less competition, as Western companies were often departing or waiting until the business environment became safer. To establish itself in emerging markets, Huawei concentrated on regional anchors. Success in Russia, for example, could make it easier to enter other former Soviet states.

In these riskier environments, Huawei honed its sales pitch, and its staff became more experienced working with foreigners. It developed a potent recipe combining low costs, fast delivery, and attention to customers. "Huawei's products may not be the best, but so what? What is core competitiveness?" Ren asked his team. "It's choosing me and not choosing you!"[26]

Huawei courted international markets with urgency, but also persistence and patience. In 1997, it entered Russia by forming a joint venture, Beto-Huawei, with a local telecommunications company to make switches. The following year, the Russian government defaulted on its sovereign debt, devalued its currency, and suspended payments from commercial banks to foreign creditors.

But Huawei was patient. "The ensuing financial crisis was more like a heavy snowfall that froze the entire land," one of Huawei's first employees in Russia recounts. "Therefore, I had no choice but to wait, to transform from a wolf into a hibernating polar bear."[27] When the employee saw Ren two years later, the only victory he could point to was a thirty-eight-dollar contract for batteries. But Ren believed it was still too early to leave Russia. "If one day the Russian market recovers but Huawei is blocked at the door, then you can jump off this building," he joked darkly.[28]

The Chinese government opened doors for Huawei's early ventures abroad. In Russia, for example, China's ambassador intervened to have Huawei's joint venture approved. "Political considerations were the only thing that broke the stalemate," admitted a former Huawei employee and author of a book praising Huawei's accomplishments.[29] A major breakthrough came in 2001, when a Russian government delegation visited Huawei's headquarters and signed a $10 million contract.[30] By 2003, Russia was one of Huawei's largest markets with more than $100 million in annual sales.[31] Ren's persistence paid off, as did his ability to leverage the Chinese government.

Huawei struggled to establish its brand. Overseas customers could not pronounce its name and associated China with low-tech, low-quality goods. After learning that Beto-Huawei was Chinese, one Russian executive asked, "A Chinese high-tech company? You're not selling electric kettles, are you?"[32]

Huawei's employees were still learning, but they were willing to go where Western companies would not. After spending thirteen months in Russia, one intrepid employee agreed to help set up Yemen's national network. "Yemen is poor, with rather harsh conditions all-around: high temperatures, high altitudes. Sanitation, transportation and safety were all very inadequate," he recalled. "The scorching sun was directly overhead and the power was out. The sweltering heat was unbearable. We slept in the cellar."[33] Reflecting on his work, he later explained, "Actually, compared to my childhood growing up in a poor Hunan village, to my days spent running barefoot over the ridges in the fields, I don't think it was tough. I found my place at Huawei."[34]

Huawei's flexibility allowed it to thrive in dramatically different markets. In 1999, its first project in Africa was a cellular network in Kenya. When an employee arrived in Naivasha, a large town sixty miles northwest of Nairobi, he found that "the hotel room had no phone, no television, and no bathing facilities." He spent the next nine months setting up and troubleshooting the system, working one evening until 3:00 a.m. to replace failed parts. The next year, he was in Ethiopia setting up the same cellular equipment. Ethiopia's mountainous terrain was even more challenging, and the system's antenna required special modifications to withstand high winds.[35] In a publication for Huawei employees, he nostalgically recounts working through nosebleeds, stomaching unfamiliar food, and doing it all alone.

Even more telling was Huawei's success in dealing with different customers. Kenya and Ethiopia share a border, but their telecom sectors are worlds apart. Competing in Kenya required bidding on open contracts and working with other private companies such as Vodafone. Ethiopia's government, in contrast, held a monopoly of the telecom sector that blocked most Western firms. Huawei succeeded in both environments by courting government officials, offering rock-bottom prices, and delivering projects quickly. A trail of corruption allegations and convictions failed to slow its advance.[36] As of 2019, Huawei had built an estimated 70 percent of Africa's 4G networks.[37]

Huawei's culture idolizes self-sacrifice, and Ren has made enduring hardship the expectation rather than the exception for employees. "Many countries are impoverished. Some even have malaria," he told employees in 2000. "Overseas employees don't receive much compensation. Their wages aren't very different from domestic ones. The main thing is the fighting spirit of Huawei employees."[38] In 2006, during another internal talk, Ren, who has a penchant for exaggeration, estimated that more than 70 percent of Huawei's employees in Africa had contracted malaria.[39]

Employees' accounts of their experiences abroad read like a mixture of New World settlers from the past and science fiction explorers of the future, the Pilgrims meet *Prometheus*. "We lived in a neighborhood called 'Dreamland,'" one employee wrote five years into his time in Sudan. "In a dark, low-ceilinged hut, bunks for seven or eight people were packed into a room . . . The dilapidated building in front of our room was the client's business hall."[40] Glasgow, Montana, is remote but luxurious by comparison.

The company is quicker to forget personal tragedies. When Ren jokingly demanded that his employee jump off a building should Huawei's Russian ventures be unsuccessful, that employee could laugh. But an investigative report counted six unnatural deaths from 2006 to 2008, including three suicides.[41]

Ren's paramount concern, critics suggest, is not employee safety but corporate earnings. In 2007, Huawei paid 7,000 employees with longer tenures to quit and sign new short-term contracts. The move was widely criticized for evading a new Chinese labor law that allowed employees with ten or more years of service to sign open-ended contracts.[42] Huawei directors also take a "self-discipline" pledge that declares, among other promises, "We love Huawei as much as we love our lives."[43]

Even when talking about employee safety, Ren cannot help but talk about expenses and profit. "We must do everything we can to keep them safe and avoid doing anything too risky," he explained to employees in 2015.[44] Huawei's office in Yemen, he suggested, "can install steel plates on the interiors, replace window glass with laminated glass, and introduce mechanical ventilation systems." "The Yemen office only needs to pay installation costs," he qualified. He continued, "When we risk our lives to provide products or services in the face of war or violence, then the price of our products should go up . . . We're not trying to extort anyone, but we need to let carriers understand our situation. That way, we can break even in small countries."

Huawei's comfort with discomfort has sometimes backfired. By 2000, the company had offices in Cuba, Burma, and Iraq—all countries under U.S. sanctions.[45] In 2002, it was accused of breaking U.N. sanctions on Iraq by supplying high-tech fiberglass parts that could be used for air defense systems.[46] Huawei has also helped the North Korean government build and maintain a wireless network, according to documents leaked to the *Washington Post*.[47] In 2018, the United States accused Huawei of violating sanctions on Iran, and Canadian authorities arrested Huawei's CFO, Meng Wanzhou, who is also Ren's daughter.

As Huawei broke into foreign markets, the United States mostly ignored it, and in some cases assisted it. As the U.S. invasion of Iraq looked increasingly likely in early 2003, Huawei began scouting opportunities. In February, a month before the invasion, a Huawei employee traveled to Iraq's semiautonomous Kurdish region and began negotiations for expanding a mobile network. "Day by day, the situation in Iraq became increasingly tense. U.S. soldiers gradually completed the deployment of their offensive forces. The flames of war were truly about to ignite at any second," the employee recalled. But the start of the war seems to have only been a temporary obstacle. "The decision to re-expand into the Iraqi market was a topic being discussed by the company's senior leadership," the employee explained. By May, he was back in northern Iraq to continue the project.[48]

The U.S. invasion of Iraq was a gift to Huawei. To disrupt their adversary's communications, U.S. forces crippled Iraq's telecommunications infrastructure during the attack. Afterward, Huawei was happy to help rebuild. In 2007, as the security environment kept most Western firms away, Huawei won a $275 million contract to help build a wireless network for Iraq.[49] In 2013, a Huawei employee reflected on five years in Iraq, recalling "the rising smoke on the banks of the Tigris River while mortars whistled in the air," "the gloomy Hummers and tanks of the U.S. military patrolling the roads and streets," and "the party celebrating the successful launch of new networks and the awarding of new contracts."[50]

Huawei found opportunities in Afghanistan as well. In 2003, Afghanistan's government signed a contract with Huawei and ZTE for a cellular network.[51] The following year, the Asian Development Bank (ADB), in which the United States and Japan are the largest shareholders, provided a loan to Roshan, Afghanistan's largest mobile provider. Roshan initially bought equipment from Alcatel and Siemens, but after further review, ADB approved replacing it with Huawei equipment, which it noted had "lower lifecycle costs and more configuration flexibility."[52] U.S. and coalition forces provided security for these projects, just as they did for ZTE when it built Afghanistan's broadband network.

Huawei's staff endured harsh conditions in Afghanistan and expanded operations after the United States announced in 2009 that it was sending additional troops. An employee recalled the challenges: "Our local staff was held hostage once . . . We always kept some bulletproof vests in the office. Two colleagues in the office contracted typhoid."[53] With foreign money pouring in and the security environment improving, Huawei's office expanded from a single employee in 2009 to twenty employees the following year, and soon it was working with all four of Afghanistan's leading telecom providers. Afghan Wireless, which is the nation's second-largest mobile provider and is owned by a U.S. company and the Afghan government, rolled out Afghanistan's first 4G LTE network in May 2017 using Huawei equipment.[54]

Huawei's expanding role in Afghanistan and Iraq raises uncomfortable questions about U.S. strategy, or lack thereof. As an Asian foreign minister told Jon B. Alterman, a leading U.S. scholar of the Middle East, "The United States has been fighting but not winning in the Middle East for 20 years, while China has been winning but not fighting for 20 years."[55] The United States provided security at great financial and human cost, and Chinese firms took advantage of new commercial opportunities. Before the United States came to see Huawei as a national security threat, U.S. forces were effectively relying on Huawei equipment in military operations overseas.[56]

By the time Nemont was looking at vendors for its 3G network in Glasgow and other rural areas, Huawei had established a long track record of connecting difficult places. Even as it grew and won contracts in European cities, Huawei still viewed rural and developing markets as critical to its success. Its networks were connecting U.S. government personnel in Iraq, climbers on Mount Everest, and an expanding share of humanity. "We are committed to providing networks for society . . . whether in the low-oxygen highlands, the scorching deserts, the freezing Arctic Ocean, hazardous areas filled with mines, forests, rivers, oceans . . . Wherever there are people on the earth, there will be coverage,"[57] Ren promised his employees in 2011.

## "THIS GIGANTIC TASK"

"Look, the spillway!" Hunter said excitedly, as we were driving back to town. He pointed at the Fort Peck Dam, a massive public works project that President Franklin Delano Roosevelt (FDR) started in the 1930s. It was releasing water, an event that is rare enough that local media report on it. We pulled over for a closer look.

Standing on a bridge above the spillway's sixteen gates, it is easy to get nostalgic about the days when the U.S. government did big projects. On one side, there is a lake with a shoreline that is longer than California's coast. On the other, a spillway that looks like a giant concrete bowling lane carries water back to the Missouri River. The dam's sheer size and scope are breathtaking. Stretching two miles wide, it became the world's largest earth-filled dam when it was only one-fifth complete. After eight decades, it is still churning out electricity for Montana and neighboring states.

I was slightly embarrassed to admit to Hunter and Handran that I had never heard of the project before. Quite literally, it is the biggest piece of American history in which Glasgow has played a leading role. But I was also intrigued. After seeing rural America's connectivity challenges, the dam surprised me. Hundreds of feet below us, the water roaring through it whispered that big things were possible. Could they be once more?

That evening, the dam loomed as large in my mind as it did in the surrounding landscape. Since stepping off the train in Glasgow, most of what I had seen hinted at a gap between private and public interests. Large U.S. companies did not see the value in the area's small market. The U.S. government provided limited support. A foreign company had filled the void. The dam was a monument to a different approach but, as I learned, also a fundamentally different era.

Life around the construction of the Fort Peck Dam was harsh and chaotic. The undertaking was so big that thousands of men and women were assigned to it, under the supervision of the U.S. Army Corps of Engineers. Three shifts were organized to keep the work progressing twenty-four hours a day, seven days a week, for nearly seven years. The Army noted in a 1936 report that the deaths, when adjusted for working hours, were below the U.S. average.[58] Two years later, a landslide killed eight men. Altogether, sixty people were killed while working on the project.

During the project's early years, ten to fifteen families were arriving in Glasgow every day, stretching the town beyond its limits.[59] Temporary towns sprung up with names such as Square Deal, New Deal, and Delano Heights. One housing advertisement in the local newspaper promised: "River front, three miles from the dam, residence lots and garden spot to lease, plenty of good water and shade. No floods. Far enough apart so if one house burns it won't burn them all: $2.50 a month."[60] Unable to afford such luxuries, many workers lived in dilapidated dwellings without electricity or running water.

The frontier spirit that created Glasgow half a century earlier had returned. When the journalist Margaret Bourke-White visited the Fort Peck construction site in 1936, she found "a pinpoint in the long, lonely stretches of northern Montana so primitive and so wild that the whole ramshackle town seemed to carry the flavor of the boisterous Gold Rush days. It was stuffed to the seams with construction men, engineers, welders, quack doctors, barmaids, [and] fancy ladies." Her photos became the cover for *Life* magazine's first issue. Looking at these photos and reading workers' accounts make the Fort Peck Dam feel even more foreign.

The closest modern parallel for the rawness of these scenes is not American. Like Huawei's early employees, dam workers left their homes and set out for an unknown landscape. They arrived and endured unforgiving conditions. With government support, companies were eager to push the boundaries of what was technically possible. Instead of pausing for years of risk assessments, the project started quickly and the builders troubleshot as they went. The grind continued all day, every day, for years. They got it done.

During the Great Depression, job creation was among the project's short-term objectives. Supplies and services were sourced from around the country: power distribution systems from Dallas, tunnel drilling from New York, tunnel gates from Baltimore, electric transmission lines from Los Angeles, sewage systems from Sioux City, substation buildings from Pittsburgh, and so on.[61] Taking this broader supply chain into account, the project's total employment was likely closer to 40,000 or 50,000 workers.[62]

The project's scale is difficult to square with its cost. In total, it cost $100 million, roughly $2 billion in today's money. That's a major investment, but one that pales in comparison to today's megaprojects. The first phase of New York City's Second Avenue subway line cost $2.7 billion—per mile—and an extension is expected to cost even more.[63]

Venturing inside the dam provides some clues to this scale-cost mystery. Building the dam was not easy, but its design is elegant. The structure has two power plants, one installed in 1951 and the other in 1961. A staff of twenty people operates the facility. The system through which water runs, turbines spin, and electricity is generated is simple enough that it can be explained to the groups of elementary school students that come for tours each year. The complexity of modern infrastructure comes with a higher cost.

Construction of the Fort Peck Dam was far from perfect, of course. In addition to worker fatalities, the project had other social and environmental costs. Residents were relocated and disputes arose over whether the government paid fair prices for their land. Several more dams were constructed along the Missouri River, and in the process, Native Americans were forced off their land with little or no compensation. Sediment from Fort Peck and other dams on the Missouri have decimated certain fish species.[64]

But the project was also part of a longer-term vision. As FDR explained during a visit to Fort Peck in 1934, months after the project was approved: "It is because we have undertaken this gigantic task that will take us more than a generation to complete; because we have undertaken it now and the people of the United States understand the objective of the idea, that I feel very certain we are going to carry it through to a successful completion."[65]

Electrification was among those objectives. In 1935, FDR created the Rural Electrification Administration (REA) to close the gap between the 90 percent of urban Americans that had electricity and the 90 percent of rural Americans that did not.[66] Of the 37,000 farms near Fort Peck Dam, only 12 had electricity in 1937.[67] Private companies concentrated on urban areas, where demand was higher and markets were larger. Like today's largest internet providers, they didn't see the value of venturing into sparsely populated areas, where customers were often poorer.

The REA encouraged rural communities to establish cooperatives, self-owned utility companies, that purchased electricity from public and private sources or generated it themselves. To make these ventures feasible, the REA offered low-interest, long-term loans for large projects as well as individual households. Nearly all these loans were fully repaid, making the cost to U.S. taxpayers relatively low.[68] The cooperatives doubled the number of farms receiving electricity and constructed more distribution lines than private companies had in the previous half century.[69]

Rural life was transformed. "When we hooked a power line up to rural people, it wasn't just a matter of electricity in the house. It brought them up out of the mud, out of the dark. They came into the 20th century," recalled a Montana resident and former cooperative manager.[70] The economic benefits were significant as well. Electrification increased agricultural employment, rural farm population, and rural property values.[71] Bridging the electrical divide produced long-lasting benefits, and those areas that gained early access experienced higher economic growth for decades. By the time of FDR's death in 1945, the ratio was reversed, with 90 percent of rural American homes having electricity.

It is hard to imagine the Fort Peck Dam being built today. The government's leading role would be anathema to many politicians, including perhaps Montana's own elected officials. A jungle of red tape, from federal and state regulations, would stand in the way. Would enough American workers sign up for such an undertaking? The sheer scale and speed of this megaproject seems like a thing of the past. Most critically, so does the vision that guided it.

## "ELECTRICITY OF THE TWENTY-FIRST CENTURY"

It is practically gospel among American leaders that broadband is as critical today as electricity was last century. As FCC chairman, Pai underscored the need to "make sure the next generation of Americans has access to the 21st-century version of electricity, which is broadband."[72] "Broadband has become the electricity of the twenty-first century," declares Brad Smith, Microsoft's president and chief legal officer.[73] Senator Michael Bennet, a Democrat, writes, "In the 21st century, not having access to high-quality broadband is like not having access to electricity."[74]

But using electricity as a touchstone also reveals a gap between grand rhetoric and action. Broadband access has improved across the United States, but the digital divide persists and widens at higher speeds. In rural areas, roughly one in four Americans still do not have access to basic fixed broadband services, according to the FCC's 2019 report.[75] The real number is likely closer to one in three.[76] At 100 Mbps/10 Mbps, only half of rural households have access, compared to 92 percent of nonrural households.[77]

For all the talk about the importance of broadband, investment has been decidedly less sweeping. In 2020, the FCC unveiled the Rural Digital Opportunity Fund, which plans to spend $20.4 billion over a decade to improve broadband access. But the FCC's own highly conservative estimate suggests it would cost $80 billion to connect the entire country with broadband. Factoring in the increased demand that 5G will put on networks, a study by the consulting firm Deloitte estimated that between $130 billion and $150 billion is needed over a five-to-seven-year period.[78]

A digital infrastructure package that is truly transformational could have several parts. As Susan Crawford outlines in her book *Fiber*, a national infrastructure bank could be established to provide equity, loans, loan guarantees, and insurance. Build America Bonds, which were used after the 2008 financial crisis, could be revived. Alongside the physical infrastructure, Elsa B. Kania, an expert on emerging technologies and Chinese military innovation, has suggested that a "digital works program" could also include "training of workers in critical digital skillsets, such as cyber security and data science."[79]

The American Jobs Plan, a $2 trillion package proposed by the Biden-Harris administration, could provide the breakthrough for broadband access that has so far proved elusive. Agreeing with members of both parties, the administration notes, "Broadband internet is the new electricity." The proposal backs that claim with real resources, including $100 billion for achieving full access to broadband, as well as investments in other infrastructure, R&D, worker training, and additional areas important for competing globally.[80] Encouragingly, Congress is also investing in emerging technologies through the U.S. Innovation and Competition Act, a bipartisan effort that puts $250 billion toward R&D and advanced manufacturing over five years.

Strategic domestic investments could also give momentum to technologies that make the United States and its partners more competitive in supplying wireless networks globally. A major shift is underway from traditional wireless networks, which tightly combine hardware and software, to an open approach that separates hardware and software. In the traditional approach, the network hardware and software are proprietary, forcing operators like Nemont to choose one vendor to supply everything. Huawei has excelled in this game by providing a low-cost radio access network (RAN), which makes up a considerable portion of network costs.

Open RAN networks could tilt the playing field in favor of the United States.[81] By virtualizing parts of the network that are currently served by proprietary hardware, Open RAN allows operators to mix and match different network components from different vendors. For operators, the potential upside is greater vendor choice up front, lower deployment costs, and less risk of being locked into a single vendor. The United States stands to benefit because its companies are leading providers of the specialized software and semiconductors that Open RAN relies upon.

There are already promising examples of Open RAN being deployed around the world. Parallel Wireless, a company based in New Hampshire, has experience building Open RAN networks at all speeds, from 2G to 5G, across six continents.[82] They have worked with operators in Africa, Latin America, and Southeast Asia—beating Chinese competitors in the process—as well as Wisconsin, Idaho, and other rural areas in the United States. "Our commercial market in communications infrastructure equipment is being distorted by a state actor," CEO Steve Papa says, pointing to China's heavily subsidized approach. "We can let that happen or we can counter it in a similar way."[83]

But the technology is still maturing. The flipside of greater vendor choice is greater complexity. Despite extensive testing, there are still kinks to work out as networks combine components from different suppliers. Smaller operators may not have the technical expertise to sort out these new dynamics, while larger operators may not have the patience. Some may still prefer the ease of going with a single vendor, even if it is more expensive. The largest U.S. carriers, including

T-Mobile, AT&T, and Verizon, have expressed interest in Open RAN but have not yet fully embraced it in their 5G rollout plans.

It could take anywhere from several years to a decade for Open RAN to replace the old way of building networks. The issue has bipartisan support in the U.S. Congress, which included $750 million for developing 5G networks and accelerating Open RAN in the 2021 defense bill. A larger digital infrastructure package could build on those efforts by incentivizing Open RAN adoption and investing in wireless chip innovation. Doing so would shorten the timeline for wider adoption within the United States, help U.S. companies scale, and position them to succeed in foreign markets. It could disrupt the status quo, putting China on the defensive not merely with security warnings but with commercially superior alternatives.

A domestic digital infrastructure push would require broad public support, and thankfully, Americans seem to understand the "objective of the idea," as FDR would put it. Nine in ten Americans support using public funds to expand internet access, according to a 2020 poll, and over 60 percent believe it should be an "immediate concern" for Congress.[84] There will be challenges, of course. As Crawford writes, "The incumbents will fight to the death to ensure that the federal government does none of this."[85] Industry groups have rushed into action to influence the American Jobs Plan's broadband investments.[86]

When I was visiting Glasgow in 2019, the U.S. government's more immediate focus was tearing something down. In May 2019, Trump's executive order banning Huawei forced Nemont to freeze a planned expansion of its networks. Later that year, the FCC voted to mandate the removal of existing Huawei equipment. But it was not until Congress passed a second COVID-19 relief package in late December 2020 that funding was authorized for replacing the equipment.

Even with $1.9 billion in funding made available, the replacement process might continue to creep along. Carriers need to solicit bids from vendors, a process that will take months. It will take even more time for the winning vendors to replace the equipment. Meanwhile, some carriers are starting to struggle to repair their existing equipment, leaving areas without service in extreme cases.[87]

It is unclear whether the government's measures will adequately cover costs associated with replacing the equipment. Nemont, for example, will have to replace several hundred antenna radios across its eighty-plus cell towers. Above and beyond the equipment's cost, there are labor costs for removal and installation. Like other rural carriers, Nemont outsources tower-climbing activities because the insurance is too expensive to maintain. Altogether, Nemont estimates the costs could hit $50 million.[88] This herculean effort is designed to make networks more secure, but it will not necessarily make them any faster.

Unlike electricity, broadband is a moving target, and the arrival of 5G is likely to widen the divide. U.S. carriers are offering different services under the "5G" label, which has created confusion over their availability and utility for different environments. The fastest version uses high-frequency millimeter waves and promises download speeds of up to 1 to 2 Gbps (forty to eighty times the speed of the current 25 Mbps standard). But these waves only travel fifty to three hundred yards, they do not penetrate obstacles, and the infrastructure needed to utilize them is expensive. Short distances and high costs are not a winning recipe for rural areas. "It could drastically affect our network in rural areas," Hunter worries.[89]

Rural America will be slower to get 5G, and the version it gets will be slower as well. It is easy to imagine precision farming benefiting from faster broadband in rural America. But it is difficult to imagine a critical mass of rural customers being willing to pay enough for providers to deploy ultra-expensive 5G hotspots. "The multiple-gigabit, ultralow-latency promise of [millimeter wave] 5G won't arrive any time soon—and it may not arrive at all, until those communities have already grown enough to not be so rural anymore," cautions Jim Salter, a reporter for *Ars Technica*.[90]

The 5G that reaches rural America will be less transformational than advertised. As part of their merger agreement, T-Mobile and

Sprint have promised to provide 5G coverage to 97 percent of the country within three years and 99 percent within six years. Their approach uses a lower frequency, 600 MHz, which travels further and is better at penetrating obstacles. But this approach will produce only modest gains: 20 percent faster on average than 4G networks, according to T-Mobile statements. The result would be speeds closer to 30 Mbps, faster than rural America's status quo, but only a small fraction of what their urban counterparts would have access to.[91]

If 5G ushers in the ultra-connected environments that many observers predict, it could exacerbate the digital divide in dramatic ways. Cities are incorporating wireless sensors to make everything from traffic flows to garbage disposal more efficient. All large cities already have at least one smart project, according to a 2018 poll of U.S. mayors, as compared to only 7.5 percent of small towns.[92] Much faster wireless networks could greatly expand the scope of these activities. Rural areas, in contrast, stand to gain only a slightly faster version of what they currently have. In the longer term, the divide between connected and superconnected could look as stark as the divide between unconnected and connected does today.

To be sure, there is more than a little hype around today's 5G claims. It is sobering to recall that boosters once dubbed 3G "the dawn of a great revolution in cellular telephony" and then spent several years struggling to roll out the technology, while several major companies ultimately failed to recoup their investments.[93] But just as faster wireless networks enabled ride-sharing services such as Uber and Lyft, 5G could enable activities that are not immediately apparent. Not all those changes will be unabashedly "good." There will also be disruptions, jobs created and lost, in the process. The increased connectivity of devices, the Internet of Things, also creates security challenges, as the next chapter explains.

But areas with 5G stand to gain much more than a head start on downloading movies. Their schools could use augmented virtual reality in lessons, allowing students to virtually visit and interact with the places and things they are studying. Their cars could communicate with the road, other vehicles, and their surroundings, improvements that could speed commutes and reduce accidents. Their hospitals could provide superior medical care with better patient monitoring, staff management, and supply-tracking systems. Factory floors could become more productive. The sum of these changes—smarter schools, safer roads, better hospitals, stronger businesses—begins to feel like two different worlds. It's the Flintstones versus the Jetsons.

No one wants to be left behind, especially developing and emerging markets. At home, the U.S. government can mandate that Nemont replace its equipment, but it will need a more compelling argument for persuading communities beyond U.S. borders. China's offer is financially attractive, and most developing countries view information security as a secondary concern rather than a vital need. Their choices, like Nemont's, ultimately come down to price. That's why competing with China's state capitalism will require the U.S. government to think as much about economics as security.

The security argument has limits even among U.S. allies, as former secretary of defense Mark T. Esper discovered when addressing the Munich Security Conference in February 2020. "Reliance on Chinese 5G vendors . . . could render our partners' critical systems vulnerable to disruption, manipulation, and espionage," he warned. "It could also jeopardize our communication and intelligence sharing capabilities, and by extension, our alliances."[94] Esper had the room's attention. Sitting in the audience were officials from NATO countries.

Toomas Hendrik Ilves, the former president of Estonia, stood up and asked a pointed question to which he already knew the answer: "Many of us in Europe agree that there are significant dangers with Huawei, and the U.S. for at least a year has been telling us, do not use Huawei. Are you offering an alternative?"[95] The room applauded. Over the next year, governments and major network operators in nearly all NATO member states raised barriers to Huawei's participation in their 5G rollouts—with Hungary, Iceland, Montenegro, and

Turkey being the exceptions—but Ilves had put his finger on a critical weakness in the U.S. strategy.

Even as European countries restrict Huawei's access to their 5G networks, they are far from ready to fully disconnect from Chinese technology. The E.U.'s largest economies, Germany and France, are wary of China retaliating in other sectors. "The idea of getting into a situation in which German companies are torn between two emerging tech ecosystems—being forced to decide between different digital spheres—haunts businesses," says Maximilian Mayer, a scholar at University of Bonn.[96]

Chinese diplomats have not been subtle. "If Germany were to take a decision that leads to Huawei's exclusion from the German market, there will be consequences," China's ambassador to Germany, Wu Ken, warned in December 2019. "The Chinese government will not stand idly by."[97] One in three German cars are sold in China, and Wu suggested that China could declare German cars unsafe.

No German leader wants to risk losing the jobs those sales support, but allowing the auto industry to steer Germany's foreign policy is even more dangerous. After all, if Chinese diplomats are willing to threaten auto sales, effectively weaponizing the flow of physical goods, how will they behave in the future when dealing with countries whose networks depend on Chinese technology? For German leaders, giving in to the demands of last century's industry may mean giving up the future.

But when they look to the future, German and French leaders also worry about depending on U.S. tech companies. "We Europeans have a decision to make. And I say in all candour that I consider neither the Chinese nor the US digital model to be an option," German foreign minister Heiko Maas said in October 2020.[98] "It's time to have our own technological sovereignty and not depend only on American or Chinese solutions!" French president Emmanuel Macron said in December 2020.[99] These are not the rallying cries of transatlantic allies eager to embrace the United States.

Of course, Europe is more than Germany and France. But the

power of business interests can be felt elsewhere, especially in the United Kingdom, which is looking to strengthen trade and investment ties after leaving the European Union. The pull of Chinese money is even stronger toward Europe's eastern edge, where Hungary, Greece, and others are jockeying to attract investment. It is hard to expect Europe's smaller economies to stand up to Chinese threats until the continent's largest economies are willing to do so.

Beyond Europe, developing countries are much more reluctant to limit their options. When U.S. officials visited Brazil in October 2020, they offered to finance purchases by Brazilian telecom providers of non-Chinese telecom equipment.[100] While this was a step in the right direction, U.S. officials may have been asking for too much, or not offering enough. The following month, Brazil's four largest telecom companies declined to meet with them. "We should be able to freely make our best financial decisions," an industry source explained.[101] For many countries, that means remaining in the middle and pitting competing offers against each other rather than choosing sides.

At the end of his remarks, Esper urged the audience: "In short: let's be smart; let's learn from the past; and let's get 5G right so we don't regret our decisions later. The reality of the 21st century is that many economic decisions are also national security decisions." But the reality is that for most people, economic concerns are paramount, whether in rural America or Afghanistan. Being smart requires offering affordable alternatives that speak to their needs and aspirations. And the past suggests that in the absence of an attractive U.S. vision, backed by resources that match its rhetoric, China's networks will thrive.

# CHAPTER FOUR

# FIVE HUNDRED BILLION EYES

It was a bright cold day, and the cameras automatically adjusted, their lenses squinting in the late afternoon sun.[1] They watched Guo Bing, a law professor, leave his office at Zhejiang Sci-Tech University in Hangzhou. They watched him on the street. They watched him all the way home.

Guo is lucky. He enjoys a degree of privacy not shared among all Hangzhou's residents. In some rental units, cameras watch residents from *inside* their homes. Having failed to stem the flow of China's internal migrants, the largest movement of people anywhere in the last century, the police have taken a page from George Orwell's *1984*. They call this program "Building Intelligent Communities."[2]

The CCP has always watched citizens, but technology now extends its gaze further and deeper into their lives than ever before.[3] Its explicit goal is nothing less than total surveillance of every inch of public space, and every face, fed back into a central database. It aims to achieve this by building an "omnipresent, fully networked, always working and fully controllable" system. It is "a top-level push for video surveillance that's globally unprecedented," explains Charles Rollet, a leading industry analyst.[4] By the end of 2020, China planned to install 626 million cameras, nearly one for every two people.[5]

Hangzhou is the unofficial capital of China's surveillance-industrial complex. It is home to China's three largest surveillance camera manufacturers: Dahua, Hikvision, and Uniview. With generous government support, they have graduated from selling basic equipment to producing increasingly advanced systems. Between 2010 and 2020, Hikvision and Dahua's combined market capitalization soared from $8 billion to $76 billion.[6]

Having grown rapidly at home, China's surveillance giants aim to dominate global markets. Together, Hikvision and Dahua supply nearly 40 percent of the world's surveillance cameras.[7] Chinese surveillance technology is being used in more than eighty countries, on every continent except Australia and Antarctica, according to Sheena Chestnut Greitens, a leading expert on authoritarian politics and foreign policy.[8] "If the plans of Xi and the Party are successful, it will mean the return of totalitarianism dressed in digital garb," writes Kai Strittmatter, a veteran journalist, in *We Have Been Harmonized*. "And for autocrats all over the world, that will provide a short-cut to the future: a new operating system that they can order in from China, probably even with a maintenance agreement."[9]

Indeed, these twin trends—China's draconian surveillance at home and its bulk export of these systems abroad—have led many observers to conclude that China is "exporting authoritarianism."[10] Only China has companies that are competitive at every step of the process, from manufacturing cameras to training AI to deploying the analytics, Rollet points out. Chinese companies never question the government's use of these capabilities, and government subsidies fuel their global expansion.[11]

Yet the "exporting authoritarianism" narrative also oversimplifies the challenge.[12] It overlooks more complicated questions about why countries are importing these technologies, factors influencing how they are used, and limitations to the technologies themselves. It is a mirror version of the same mistake that U.S. policymakers made at the end of the Cold War, when they believed the United States was exporting democracy by selling technology. Throughout, technology has remained a tool.

"Surveillance is used in democracies and autocracies," observes Steven Feldstein, author of *The Rise of Digital Repression*.[13] "The bigger question is whether a regime will choose to use these tools in violation of existing norms and principles." Indeed, Western companies have long sold surveillance equipment around the world. After the Tiananmen Square protests in 1989, Chinese authorities took footage from traffic cameras and broadcast it over Chinese state television to identify protesters. Those cameras were manufactured in the United Kingdom and paid for by the World Bank.[14]

Chinese-manufactured cameras now watch Tiananmen Square as well as public spaces in the United Kingdom, the United States, and other democracies. The ubiquity of Chinese equipment suggests that the motives for purchasing it are not purely political and have strong commercial drivers, which have received less attention from U.S. officials. Depending on local conditions, the same technology can be used in dramatically different ways, from counting customers and improving traffic safety to preventing public assembly and contributing to the worst human rights violation in recent history.

## SHARP EYES

The scope and increasing sophistication of China's surveillance model is stunning, yet it is far from perfect. In its quest for godlike vision, the CCP has also created confusion, waste, and resentment. The Party requires local officials to roll out surveillance networks, even if their communities lack the supporting infrastructure, and requires even poor communities to replace older cameras with high-definition models.[15] In 2019 alone, one third of all counties in China purchased surveillance equipment.[16]

Fed by massive state spending, cameras have flocked like birds into public spaces, landing on traffic lights at intersections, on street corners, on building tops, and above doorways. In 2005, China announced

Skynet, an urban surveillance program "to fight crime and prevent possible disasters."[17] Its name comes from a Chinese saying: "Heaven's net is vast—scattered wide yet misses nothing." A decade later, China expanded these efforts into the countryside with a program called "Sharp Eyes." The project's Chinese name literally translates to "snow-bright," referencing an old Maoist slogan: "The eyes of the masses are as bright as snow."

Sharp Eyes goes beyond even Orwell's dystopia. In Oceania, the authoritarian state in *1984*, the Thought Police watch citizens. Sharp Eyes makes that possible with unprecedented scale, and in some communities, it also allows citizens to watch each other. From their couches, residents can flip from state news to video feeds of their neighborhood. Or they can access video from an app on their phones, alerting authorities with the push of a button if they see something unusual. The system is cruelly clever, offering up a voyeur's buffet and tapping into social pressures that date back more than a thousand years, when collective neighborhood organizations were first created.[18]

Local governments are eager to take credit for their efforts, and state media highlight Sharp Eyes successes almost daily. In these stories, surveillance systems are the superheroes. They fight crime, find lost children, and help elderly citizens at home. Unmentioned is how these systems are used to monitor suspected protestors and dissidents, surveillance targets whom Chinese officials refer to as "key persons."[19] Few dare to ask whether the money spent on surveillance equipment, which can run into the millions of dollars for a single county, would have been better spent on other priorities.[20] After all, the government is watching.

More recently, a smarter breed of camera has landed in China's public spaces. High-definition cameras automatically adapt to glare, low lighting, and fog, providing sharper images in all conditions around the clock. They automatically pan, tilt, and zoom to track moving objects. Their video feeds into AI-powered software that catalogs license plates, counts people, and analyzes faces. This data can be paired with devices that capture unique codes from mobile phones, increasing authorities' confidence in identifying individuals.[21]

In China's surveillance state, everyone is famous. But the cameras' gaze cuts much deeper than that of the paparazzi trailing movie stars. They do more than simply record your likeness. They judge your gender, age, and ethnicity. They check your body temperature for signs of illness. They measure and evaluate the way you walk. After enough takes, some companies claim their cameras can recognize you from behind. They don't just watch you. They quantify you.

Even though expectations of privacy are lower in China than in many Western countries, Chinese citizens are wary of constant scrutiny and haphazard applications of facial recognition. In the first major public survey in China of data protection views, conducted in 2019, a third of respondents said they had not signed agreements before having their faces scanned.[22] More than half expressed concern about being tracked. Overwhelming majorities preferred traditional identification methods and worried about data security. These concerns are not a rejection of facial recognition, but they suggest a desire to set limits and establish stronger protections.

In November 2019, Guo became the public face of Chinese privacy concerns after filing a lawsuit against Hangzhou Safari Park. Located southwest of the city, the park's lions, tigers, and monkeys have made it one of Hangzhou's most popular tourist attractions. Despite the name, which suggests a natural environment, it is essentially a conventional zoo that segregates animals into exhibits. The most open element is a trolley that shuttles visitors through several larger exhibits, where park staff stand watching, sometimes just feet away from the animals.

The park had sent Guo a strange text message in October: "Dear annual pass holder, the park's annual pass system has been upgraded to a facial recognition system for park entry. The previous fingerprint recognition system has been eliminated. Starting from today, users who have not registered using facial recognition will be unable to properly enter the park. If you have not yet registered, please bring your fingerprint-verified annual pass to the annual pass center to do so as soon as possible. Enjoy your visit!"[23]

"I don't think of myself as a technological 'conservative,'" Guo explained, "but when I encounter facial recognition and similar technological innovations, I'll often ask a few more 'why's.'"[24] After talking with colleagues, he filed a lawsuit with the local district court. Guo also submitted a proposal to local authorities to ban property managers from collecting biometric data.[25] Launching these efforts in Hangzhou, home to China's largest surveillance companies, is like campaigning against chocolate in Hershey, Pennsylvania.

But Guo was not looking to play David and slay the surveillance state's Goliath. His legal moves have been focused on businesses using facial recognition technology, not the government. "I can still accept that public security and related government departments will collect facial information out of certain public interest considerations, but for an animal amusement park to also collect facial information, I have some doubts about its safety and privacy," Guo explained. "If a breach occurs, who will bear the responsibility?"[26]

The Chinese government is not deaf to these concerns, but it is reluctant to give up any power. A draft law on personal information, expected to be finalized in mid-2021, proposes steep penalties for companies that mishandle personal information and requires that data from surveillance systems in public areas only be used for public security purposes.[27] Guo called the first draft "an improvement," but also noted that it was vaguely worded.[28]

In November 2020, the court partially sided with Guo and ordered the park to delete his facial recognition data and pay him the equivalent of $158. It did not, however, agree with Guo's claim that the park's notice regarding the collection of facial recognition data was inherently invalid and infringed on visitors' privacy rights.[29] Both Guo and the park appealed the decision.

Regardless of the final outcome, Guo's stand is already rich with symbolism. The most serious official challenge to China's surveillance laws comes from a place of amusement. More fundamentally, the business in question is the ultimate expression of surveillance taken to the extreme. It allows people to watch creatures who do not fully understand how and why they are being watched—and certainly never consented. In the name of safety, it deprives those being watched of their natural lives. The world's biggest safari park is China's surveillance state.

## "HISTORY HAS STOPPED"

In China's northwestern province of Xinjiang, the government has forced more than one million Uyghur, Kazakh, and other predominantly Muslim minorities into camps. While the Uyghurs have been persecuted for decades, the Chinese government began taking more extreme steps in 2009 after protests in Urumqi, Xinjiang's capital, left nearly two hundred dead and hundreds more injured.[30] When reports surfaced of the camps, Chinese officials denied them, and then claimed that attendance was voluntary.

But leaked Communist Party planning documents detail a system for managing what U.S. officials have called "the largest mass incarceration of a minority population in the world today."[31] Bethany Allen-Ebrahimian, who led the reporting on these documents for the International Consortium of Investigative Journalists, noted how their "style combines standard Chinese bureaucratese with Orwellian doublespeak."[32] Like Oceania's "Ministry of Love," which dispenses torture, China calls its detention centers "reeducation camps" and its prisoners "students."

Life inside the camps is brutal, according to survivor accounts. Every day is strictly managed to strip prisoners of their individuality and convert them into supplicants of the state. Prisoners are forced to repent and confess. They are bombarded with state propaganda videos and drilled with lessons in Mandarin and Communist Party ideology.

The only choice they have at meals is inhumane, former detainees told *The Telegraph*. They can yell "Long live Xi Jinping!" and receive a steamed bun or helping of rice. Or they can remain silent and taste the sharp pain of an electric cattle prod.[33] "Power is in tearing human minds to pieces and putting them together again in new shapes of your own choosing," observes O'Brien, the antagonist in Orwell's *1984*.[34]

The camps rely on constant surveillance and heavy punishment. State documents call for prisons to ensure "full video surveillance coverage of dormitories and classrooms free of blind spots." The smallest of infractions can extend a prisoner's captivity. "You enter the camp with 1,000 points. You can't gain points. You can only lose them if you yawn or smile," a survivor explained.[35] "If you ever went under 500 points, you'd have to stay for another year." This is the calculus of a system designed to harm, one that only points downward. Release is won not by rising, but by minimizing how far you fall.

There is no freedom from China's labor camps. Prisoners return to communities that have been blanketed with cameras and security forces. After using malware to monitor Uyghurs' phones for years, the Chinese government's methods have become even more overt.[36] It requires them to install applications that monitor their location, calls, and messages. They must submit to "health checks" that take blood and DNA samples and contribute to the state's growing biometric database.[37]

China's digital repression goes hand in hand with low-tech techniques for control. Growing beards and wearing hijabs is strictly prohibited, and in addition to "minority detection," Chinese surveillance companies offer "beard detection" among their facial analytics.[38] The government does not stop after separating Uyghurs from their identities. In daily "antiterrorism" security exercises, it drills them for battle with an invisible and fictional enemy that resembles a dark and deeply warped caricature of their former selves.

As Chinese authorities try to erase identities, they have razed and repurposed the physical spaces that anchor Uyghur culture. In Kashgar, a historic trading post and home to Uyghur holy sites, the city's oldest buildings were destroyed in 2009, a historic loss that authorities claim was for earthquake safety.[39] The state's paranoia has turned Kashgar's Id Kah Mosque, a centuries-old building and peaceful place of worship, into a machine for cataloging Muslims. Checkpoints around the city monitor individuals' movements, feeding them into a database with details about their families, education, and past activities.[40]

Hotan, an oasis town in southwestern Xinjiang, was for centuries a thriving hub for trade and gathering point for Uyghur pilgrims. Entering its bazaar requires submitting to a facial scan and showing an ID card.[41] In the town square is a statue of Kurban Tulum, a Uyghur farmer and politician, shaking hands with Mao. Less than a mile away, a thousand-year-old Uyghur cemetery and sacred shrine was bulldozed in 2019.[42] Officials claimed the move was for development and to "promote a spacious, beautiful environment for all of the city's people."[43] Part of the space was replaced with a parking lot.

"Do you realize that the past, starting from yesterday, has been actually abolished?" asks Winston, the protagonist in *1984*. "Every record has been destroyed or falsified, every book has been rewritten, every picture has been repainted, every statue and street and building has been renamed, every date has been altered. And that process is continuing day by day and minute by minute. History has stopped. Nothing exists except an endless present in which the Party is always right."[44]

The CCP wants to control the future by rewriting the past. Satellite imagery suggests that two-thirds of Xinjiang's mosques have been destroyed or damaged as a result of government policies since 2017, according to the Australian Strategic Policy Institute.[45] Those that have not been torn down have been outfitted with cameras. One Hikvision project required installing cameras at the entrances of nearly one thousand mosques in a single county in Xinjiang.[46] Between 2016 and 2017 alone, Hikvision and Dahua won over $1 billion in contracts for surveillance projects in Xinjiang, according to Rollet's research.[47]

Far from being appalled by China's repressive tactics, plenty of foreign leaders are intrigued. They see an opportunity to acquire tools that could reduce crime and spur growth in their cities.[48] Of course, the authoritarian-leaning among them also see an opportunity to monitor their domestic challengers and cement their control. But mayors in developing countries are just as focused on creating jobs and improving city services as their counterparts are in wealthier countries. They have fewer resources, which can make Chinese technology even more appealing.

Hikvision, the largest of the Hangzhou trio, has become the world's surveillance heavyweight thanks to generous state support at home and low-cost sales abroad. Its facilities can churn out 260,000 cameras daily—two for every three people born each day.[49] In 2019, it produced nearly a quarter of the world's surveillance cameras, with sales in more than 150 countries.[50]

The company began as a state entity and maintains close ties. The China Electronics Technology Group Corporation (CETC), a fully state-owned defense-industrial conglomerate, is Hikvision's largest shareholder and straddles the military and civilian sectors, producing everything from lasers to washing machines.[51] CETC supplied Kashgar's military-style command and surveillance system, the facial recognition system at Hotan's bazaar, and a vast police program that aggregates data and flags people deemed potentially threatening, among other projects in Xinjiang.[52] "Our goal is to lead the development of China's electronics industry and build the cornerstone of national security," CETC's chairman said in 2017.[53]

Since its public listing on the Shenzhen Stock Exchange in 2010, Hikvision has strengthened its ties with the Chinese government. In 2015, during its first Party meeting, Hikvision's chairman emphasized the importance of integrating Party policies with business development goals.[54] Weeks later, Chinese leader Xi Jinping visited Hikvision's headquarters to review the company's products and R&D center. "The great rejuvenation of the Chinese nation is just around the corner," he told the workers.[55] Later that year, the government provided Hikvision with a $3 billion line of credit.[56]

China's surveillance giants have also benefited from U.S. technology and investment. Hikvision has purchased programmable chips from Nvidia to train its AI algorithms. The company also claims to have partnered with Intel, Sony, and Western Digital, which was still advertising its partnership with Hikvision at trade shows in early 2019.[57] In 2005, Seagate partnered with Hikvision to release what it called the first hard drive developed specifically for surveillance equipment. When Seagate announced the first hard drive developed for AI surveillance in 2017, it quoted representatives of Hikvision, Dahua, and Uniview. "As a strategic partner, Seagate's advanced technology will help Dahua to reach a new top in the AI field," said the director of Dahua's domestic sales operations center.[58]

## "BUILD YOUR SMART LIFE"

Even if you have never set foot in China, Hikvision's cameras have likely seen you. By 2017, Hikvision had already captured 12 percent of the North American market.[59] Its cameras watched over apartment buildings in New York City, public recreation centers in Philadelphia, and hotels in Los Angeles.[60] Police departments used them to monitor streets in Memphis, Tennessee, and Lawrence, Massachusetts, and to watch over a crime lab in Colorado.[61] London and more than half of the U.K.'s twenty next largest cities have purchased and deployed Hikvision cameras.[62]

Hikvision's reach requires a map to fully appreciate it. The search tool Shodan allows users to locate internet-connected devices. In April 2020, I searched for Hikvision cameras and found over 105,000 devices in the United States. The results map, which displays devices with red dots, looked like a pandemic tracker, with clusters of activity in major cities. Houston led the way with over 2,500 devices. Los

Angeles, Chicago, and Miami all had more than 1,000 devices. Even in rural Montana, red dots popped up here and there. As I zoomed in, I discovered a device connected to a Nemont customer in Westby, Montana (population: 168).

Hikvision's competitive pricing won over suppliers to some of the U.S. government's most sensitive sites. Offering huge discounts to American redistributors, the company's cameras eventually made their way to Peterson Air Force Base in Colorado, home to the North American Aerospace Defense Command and military units that were later integrated into the U.S. Space Force.[63] The U.S. embassies in Kiev, Ukraine, and Kabul, Afghanistan, also installed Hikvision cameras.

Hikvision cameras became so ubiquitous that the U.S. government struggled to find them all. When Congress banned U.S. government agencies from using Hikvision and Dahua cameras in 2018, amid concerns the devices could covertly send information back to China, it gave them a year to rip out the equipment.[64] But more than ninety different companies had relabeled the cameras with their own brands, according to IPVM, the surveillance industry research group. In some cases, agencies had no option but to disassemble suspected equipment and inspect their parts.

Hikvision's U.S. subsidiary, EZVIZ, has tried to put a friendlier face on its products. Downplaying its real origins, EZVIZ emphasizes that it is based in City of Industry, California. At one point, its ads even suggested the company was started by three millennials from the Midwest who were "video-obsessed."[65] Since arriving in the United States in 2015, the EZVIZ brand has expanded from cameras to doorbells, locks, and even automated curtains. Its products are sold by Home Depot, Walmart, and other major retailers. "Build Your Smart Life with EZVIZ," its Amazon page beckoned in 2020.[66]

Smart homes are at the center of a rise in internet-connected devices. As the cost of processors and sensors has plummeted, and broadband speeds have risen, more devices are being connected to the internet. Washing machines, televisions, even toasters now come with automated features that require internet connectivity. In 2020, Cisco estimated the number of all internet-connected devices, inside and outside homes, at fifty billion. By 2030, it projects there will be five hundred billion internet-connected devices.[67] Put differently, that is five hundred billion eyes and ears.

Surveillance cameras may seem like an extreme example, but the constant collection of data by other devices carries serious risks as well. Fitness watches and bands are increasingly popular and often track movements, heart rate, and sleep patterns. Xiaomi, a leading Chinese manufacturer of phones and other gadgets, sells a fitness band with a military-grade sensor and thirty-day battery life for thirty-five dollars. Its motto is "Understand your every move."[68] These types of products offer new forms of convenience, but they often lack proper privacy and security safeguards.

Consumers do not seem too worried, even if some governments are taking a closer look. Through mid-2020, Xiaomi had shipped more than thirteen million fitness bands, more than any other supplier in the world.[69] The company's latest model had received more than sixteen thousand five-star Amazon reviews by the end of the year. Then in January 2021, the U.S. Defense Department added Xiaomi to a blacklist of companies with alleged ties to the Chinese military.[70] The order, which was blocked by a federal judge and later retracted, forced U.S. investors to divest from the company but did not stop Americans from buying Xiaomi products.

Connected homes are a convenience dream and a security nightmare. There are microphones not only on smartphones but also in speakers, alarm clocks, TVs, cars, refrigerators, and most places where people spend their time. An internet-connected refrigerator seems benign, but as Laura DeNardis explains in *The Internet in Everything*, it could reveal private details about an individual's health as well as when that person is home.[71] It could also provide an avenue to access other devices on the same network.

U.S. officials' public warnings have largely gone unheeded. As

U.S. Director of National Intelligence James Clapper told Congress in 2016, "Intelligence services might use the [Internet of Things] for identification, surveillance, monitoring, location tracking, and targeting for recruitment, or to gain access to networks or user credentials."[72] Devices can also be used to launch attacks. Seven months after Clapper's warning, a botnet named "Mirai" infected more than half a million devices, many of them Dahua webcams, and used them to knock major websites offline.[73]

As the internet expands ever further into the physical world, security remains too often an afterthought rather than a primary selling point for consumer devices. "Being first to market is paramount," explains DeNardis. Designing devices that are more secure and can be patched in the future when vulnerabilities are discovered requires more time and money. These incentives suggest that companies will keep security to the bare minimum until consumers or regulators demand otherwise. Nor are these risks limited to Chinese companies. As cybersecurity expert James A. Lewis observes, "Chinese actors appear to have little trouble accessing U.S. data and devices even if they do not use Chinese services or were not made in China."[74]

Hikvision is fighting for a lucrative opportunity to watch your front door, and it is even hoping you will welcome it inside. In 2018, the Consumer Electronics Show, which is for electronics what the Detroit Auto Show is for cars, gave EZVIZ an innovation award for its "Smart Door Viewer." The device watches through a peephole, examines faces, and compares them against a user-defined database.[75] In a press release about the award, EZVIZ claimed the company had humble origins, "starting off as a small team with the ambition to bring innovative technologies to more people."[76]

Press pause for a moment, and let this sink in. The same technology that contributes to the greatest human tragedy of this century may also watch over streets in your city, buildings in your neighborhood, and even the living room next door.

The presence of common technology is chilling, but the differences in how it is used are glaring. In the United States, for example, surveillance laws are still being developed, with some cities outlawing facial recognition and others allowing it, and momentum is growing for instituting limits. But in the meantime, longer-standing U.S. civil liberty and privacy laws limit the government's ability to use these tools. In China, and other authoritarian countries, there are no real limits to security services, and no signs of any serious challenge to them.

## BIG BROTHER'S BLIND SPOT

While trying to learn more about how these tools work, I discovered that Hikvision's training and certification courses were still open. Topics ran the gamut from license-plate recognition to thermal cameras. Curious to see how the company was pitching its products, especially in the face of mounting human rights concerns, I enrolled in two professional certification courses.

The first course, Hikvision's sales training for North America, promised to cover "the key topics crucial to effectively positioning and selling Hikvision products." Trainees would "learn the fundamentals of video surveillance," "master the essential configuration of Hikvision devices," and "overcome general installation challenges using Hikvision devices." What it provided was a peek into an alternative reality.

The course began by proudly recounting Hikvision's rise from minor player to market leader in just a decade. A timeline illustrated this rapid growth and major milestones, such as opening its first U.S. office in 2006, followed by operations in India, Amsterdam, Russia, and Dubai. It touted Hikvision's 14,500-employee salesforce, its 8 percent of annual revenue invested in R&D, and its presence in over 150 countries. These stats would be helpful for sales reps introducing the Chinese company to potential customers. "The name of the company is *what*?" I could hear English speakers asking.

Some customers would have already heard about the company, of course. And their first impressions may not have been positive. Because of the company's growing challenges in the United States, I expected the course would include some suggested answers to frequently asked questions: What is the relationship between Hikvision and the Chinese government? Does Hikvision sell equipment to Chinese security forces in Xinjiang?

But these topics were ignored entirely. There was no mention of human rights issues, let alone allegations of violations. There was no explanation for how a large customer, the U.S. government, became Hikvision's most vocal critic. There was not even a hint of the company encountering trouble in the U.S. market. Hikvision described itself as a thriving company with no obstacles and only upside ahead.

Yet the course made a direct appeal to help Hikvision's image. "Social media exposure, speaking engagements, and promotion of cybersecurity initiatives help the installer and integrator with their customers. If the home or business owner does research on Hikvision they will see a great company. Don't get us wrong, we are a great company, but the Internet is where people go to get their facts these days. If we look good, you will look good with your customer." The reality, of course, is much less flattering. In early 2021, Google's top suggested question for a search of the company's name was "Why is Hikvision banned?"

The second course was more revealing of the equipment's capabilities and limits. Designed for surveillance industry professionals, it covered how to design, install, and operate Hikvision systems. While the sales course described what the "smart" features can do, this technical course explained how they work and how to properly set up cameras to use them. Smart functions such as "object removal detection," which notices when items go missing, depend on the camera making a model of the scene's background and using that model to detect changes.

Most of the case studies focused on protecting private property.

"Intrusion detection," which triggers an alarm when a person or vehicle enters a defined zone, was shown guarding an oil pump. "Line-crossing detection" was protecting a fence alongside a road. "People counting" and "heat-mapping" were used in a department store to monitor foot traffic. The course argued that surveillance is often viewed as an expense, but the data it provides, such as showing a store owner where customers spend the most time, is valuable intelligence that can be used to increase revenue.

Not mentioned was how these capabilities can be used in dramatically different ways. People-counting can boost grocery store revenues, and it can alert repressive governments when large groups are gathering. Line detection can alert local police when a car is heading the wrong way down a street, and it can alert them when people come and go from a dissident's house. Automated alarms can keep people out of danger, and they can keep people from being free. Every night, hours apart but under the same moon, Hikvision cameras watch over Minnesota's public schools and Xinjiang's camps.[77]

One feature stood out among the rest. "Privacy shields" allow the user to block areas within a camera's view from being monitored. Imagine drawing a virtual shade on the outside of a house to prevent yourself from looking in it. In twenty-plus hours of course materials, this was the only function that was designed to limit surveillance. It could be a strong selling point for markets with privacy concerns, particularly in North America, but it was only mentioned in passing. The course quickly returned to discussing how to enhance a camera's field of vision.

Hikvision's facial recognition arsenal offers a single system to dole out punishments and rewards. "Recognise people from your blacklist and notify security to take action to reduce risks," a brochure says. "Recognise whitelist customers so they can experience exclusive VIP service from the moment they arrive."[78] Looking beyond the racist terms, which industry professionals have advocated replacing, it does not require much imagination to see the potential for abuse. With facial recognition, a club owner can spot valued patrons and lavish them with free drinks. A despot can use the same technology to identify, track, and silence opponents. Whether you're being welcomed to heaven or hell, thanks to AI surveillance, the wait is getting shorter.

Both courses were naturally focused on showcasing the products' capabilities, but they did occasionally hint at limitations. The people-counting feature, Hikvision explained, is only 90 percent accurate when traffic is heavy. Softening customer expectations, one slide noted, "Entertainment TV is fiction. What they do on *CSI* and *NCIS* and other programs is not reality. A CCTV system is NOT going to have unlimited zoom with crisp images."

These systems are increasingly sophisticated, but I came away thinking it is still a stretch to call them "smart." Light reflecting off glass and tile, for example, can confuse the camera. Leaves swaying in the wind can be falsely identified as new objects. Animals and even small bugs, especially those with wings, can trigger alarms. Users can adjust alarm sensitivity and are encouraged to place cameras at optimal vantage points. But errors remain relatively common, making authoritarian uses of these tools even more dangerous.

These risks are not readily advertised to prospective customers. Hikvision sometimes advertises its facial recognition accuracy rate as "above 90 percent," allowing customers to imagine that it could be higher, perhaps even close to perfect. One reseller of Hikvision products claims its cameras provide facial recognition with an accuracy greater than 99 percent.[79] Facial recognition products have biases that arise from the data used to train them. Hikvision's algorithms are most accurate on people from East Asia, and least accurate on people from Africa, according to third-party tests.[80]

Hikvision markets its DeepinMind series as "a smart-thinking Network Video Recorder (NVR) with a 'mind' of its own, one that can analyze the content and make informed decisions for you."[81] But in 2018, an independent evaluation by IPVM, a leading surveillance industry research group, found the system was riddled with errors.[82] It mistakenly identified rabbits and vehicles as people and missed people in other cases. The test conceded that the system was partially correct, after falsely identifying an SUV as a person, in that the SUV was in fact not wearing a backpack. Another test the following year, after the system was updated, indicated that DeepinMind made fewer errors but still consistently misidentified people and experienced false alarms.[83]

With more training and data, these systems are improving, but I would not trust them to make decisions. It is one thing to have a system miscount the number of people who spent time in the produce section of a grocery store and quite another to have a system misidentify an individual as the suspect of a crime. Tests show that facial recognition technology in particular has pervasive gender and racial biases, leading to increased false positives for women and minorities.[84] These are not theoretical risks, nor are they limited to Chinese suppliers. By the end of 2020, three Americans had been wrongly arrested because of false positives in facial recognition.[85] All of them were Black men.

As the course continued, it delved deeper into surveillance capabilities while ignoring all constraints. The objective of every training scenario was to expand the ability to surveil and detect. In every case, the person behind the camera accumulates power, while for good or bad, the person on camera becomes a target. The authoritarian approach does not question this imbalance. It makes little or no effort to minimize harm.

There were no principles offered for responsible use. "THINK before you look," I imagined. Absent from the course was any reminder to check local guidelines. Some U.S. cities, for example, have banned local authorities from using facial recognition. In the examples of businesses using surveillance equipment to gather information, there was no suggestion that customers should be asked for their consent. I thought of Guo's lawsuit against Hangzhou Safari Park.

The use of military language, common in the surveillance industry, heightens the sense that these tools can easily become weapons.

Cameras can be set to "patrol," meaning they pan and tilt at predefined intervals, scanning areas on a loop. "Intrusion detection" sounds like a method for defending a bank or a military base, a system that only catches bad guys. Hikvision's cameras do not check identities. They "capture" faces.

When I finished both courses, I was relieved to be done but also unsatisfied. After passing two exams, I was technically qualified to sell and install systems that use AI to identify faces and analyze behavior. I was taught the difference between RAID 0 and RAID 5 data storage systems. I learned how to set up an intrusion-detection zone and configure where the alerts would be sent. But I remained utterly unequipped to deal with the privacy and human rights concerns these systems raise.

This ethical blind spot is hardly limited to Chinese surveillance companies, or even the surveillance industry writ large. Oracle has marketed police applications of its software in countries with poor human rights records, including China, Brazil, Mexico, Pakistan, Turkey, and the United Arab Emirates, as Mara Hvistendahl has reported.[86] More fundamentally, private companies' bulk collection of personal data, what Harvard professor Shoshana Zuboff has dubbed "surveillance capitalism," has wide-ranging implications not only for privacy but also for social control.[87]

Many technology companies have sought to cast themselves as high-tech hardware stores, simply selling tools to customers who are ultimately responsible for how they are used. When asked whether Huawei could be held accountable for the Chinese government's use of its products in Xinjiang, Ren Zhengfei replied, "The situation is similar to say a carmaker in Spain. Can a carmaker determine who it will sell the cars to? What the carmaker sells is just the car itself. What will be put into the car is determined by the driver. The carmaker does not sell drivers, just cars."[88]

But Huawei, Hikvision, and others are not merely exporters of consumer goods. They sell capabilities as well as methods. To borrow Ren's metaphor, they provide driver training and sometimes even chauffeurs. They do not check to see if you have a bad driving record or even necessarily a license to drive. They have been willing to sell any product they have to anyone who will buy, with very few exceptions.

That laissez-faire approach appears increasingly unsustainable. As more communities debate the merits of AI-powered surveillance, companies will be forced to play a more active role in preventing harm. Companies that engage constructively in this conversation can earn trust and stand to profit from helping to address social concerns. Like the environmental movement, a market for socially responsible AI could emerge.

The United States could work with its partners and allies to lead this movement. "As the economies of Africa, Latin America, and Southeast Asia move forward with their development and urbanization processes, why not support a global initiative around smart cities that includes support for technological innovation, environmental sustainability, and good governance," argues Liz Economy, a leading China expert and senior fellow at the Council on Foreign Relations.[89] Such an effort would challenge China's current activities by drawing a stark contrast and offering a superior alternative. Companies that press forward without safeguards may find their clientele shrinking to a list of names they would not care to advertise.

For a company whose motto is "See far, go further," Hikvision has appeared shortsighted, if not willfully blind, to the backlash building against its brand. Evidence of the company's role in Xinjiang's camps surfaced as early as 2018.[90] But it was not until 2019, after Western investors began divesting, that the company issued its first environmental, social, and governance report.[91] "Over the past year, there have been numerous reports about ways that video surveillance products have been involved in human rights violations," it noted. The report was heavy on passive voice and light on specifics.

Hikvision's concern for human rights appears superficial. It promised to incorporate the U.N.'s Universal Declaration of Human Rights, among other provisions, into its practices and hired a U.S. law firm, Arent Fox LLP, to conduct an internal review, which it has not made public. After waiting for a copy of the review, a Danish pension fund finally divested from Hikvision in November 2020, noting that it had "lost patience with the company."[92] Hikvision also appointed a chief compliance officer, who is vaguely responsible "for promoting the compliance construction covering areas of human rights protection, data security and privacy protection as well as social responsibility, etc." Apparently, Hikvision could not be bothered to finish the sentence and fully articulate the position, which could have been titled chief complaint officer. Perhaps it assumed that investors and customers just needed a bit of assurance and did not care to dig too deeply.

Social risks are an even greater blind spot for Hikvision's clientele, including the Chinese government. Fear about social unrest is what motivates the construction of a surveillance state that attempts to reach deeper into citizens' lives. By clumsily imposing more invasive measures, however, it could strengthen the very forces of resentment that it fears the most. When China's systems do not deliver the precision they promise, it is not just privacy advocates and dissident groups who are disappointed. After enough errors, even supporters of surveillance measures begin asking questions.

## "SAFE CITIES"

The gap between what Chinese surveillance companies promise and what they deliver may be even greater overseas. With Beijing's financial and diplomatic support, they are moving into more of the world's cities. Their sales pitch is incredibly attractive: next-generation technology delivered affordably today. But in their haste for quantitative dominance of foreign markets, the quality of their projects can fall short.

Imagine yourself as the mayor of major city in an emerging economy. You face a cascade of reinforcing crises. The COVID-19 pandemic broke your health system and threatens to reemerge. Even worse is the financial fallout. Debt is dangerously high, limiting your ability to borrow and finance development projects. Meanwhile, a demographic time bomb is ticking: your population is overwhelmingly young, and already there are not enough jobs to go around. Crime is increasing and threatens to scare off foreign investors. Your political prospects are as uncertain as the city's future. You are up for reelection in two years.

Like a genie, a company arrives and promises to grant you three wishes. You ask for help with the health crisis, higher economic growth, and lower crime. All these wishes, the company says, can be delivered by making your city smarter. Temperature-sensing cameras can help identify people with fevers. Measuring traffic flows and enforcing driving laws can help improve congestion. Facial recognition and behavior analysis can identify wanted criminals and alert the police to unusual behavior, such as running or wandering near restricted areas. These capabilities will be fed into a central database and command center.

The command center they show you looks like NASA's mission control, something available only to the world's richest countries. Rows of workstations are arranged in concentric arcs. All face a towering wall with giant screens. Maps appear to show the locations of vehicles, the identities of people, and a variety of alerts. With everything spiraling out of control, the command center is a government administrator's Eden. The local media would beg for a tour. They would write stories about leapfrogging to the forefront of innovation and the prosperous future that a smarter city offers. The outside world would have to take notice. Foreign investors would see greater opportunity and less risk.

All this comes in a single package that can be customized to your needs and your budget. "The Hikvision Safe City Solution provides sound, stable, and reliable municipal security," the company explains. "All componentry, software, and services in the Safe City Solution reinforce public administration, improve people's lives, and boost substantial, long-term development."[93] To sweeten the deal, China's state banks will provide a subsidized loan that is repayable over twenty years. By that point, the city should be transformed. The project will pay for itself. Even if it does not, you will have moved on, so it will be someone else's problem.

The allure of China's offer is easy to understand. Governments around the world want the efficiency and safety that new remote sensing and surveillance technology promises. As the cost of computing power has plummeted and broadband speeds have risen, cities are deploying automated cameras and sensors to improve everything from garbage collection to emergency responses.

The expansion of Chinese technology into foreign cities worries U.S. policymakers, who view these projects as not merely made by China but made for China. During a trip to Kenya's capital, Nairobi, Senator Marco Rubio was alarmed to see the delegation's movements monitored by one of Huawei's flagship projects. "Literally at every intersection, some picture snapped," Rubio said in 2019.[94] "They know what hotel you're staying in, they know what WiFi network you're on. It provides them more and more opportunity for that company and [Beijing] to access your corporate information and steal it."

China's wiring of the world's cities has outpaced policymakers' ability to respond. In August 2019, Rubio and Senator Ron Wyden asked the State Department to warn Americans about the risk of traveling to foreign cities using Chinese technology. "Supplying technology to countries with poor rights records might not only benefit local authoritarians; it might also benefit China," they cautioned.[95] They cited a *New York Times* report, which estimated that there were more than eighteen countries using Chinese systems. The reality is even more jaw-dropping: Chinese firms have exported "smart city" products and services to more than one hundred countries, according to research by Katherine Atha, James Mulvenon, and colleagues at the research firm SOS International.[96]

Even local leaders in the United Kingdom have turned to Chinese vendors. The city of Bournemouth negotiated a smart city contract with Alibaba that would have involved the Chinese company controlling large amounts of data, according to the *Financial Times*.[97] The deal was aborted after the central government intervened. But the threat remains significant enough that the British intelligence agency GCHQ published guidelines in May 2021 warning local authorities about using foreign suppliers for smart city systems.[98]

China's most active companies sell their products under the banner of "Safe Cities," a bumper sticker that puts security first. There is no universal definition for what constitutes a smart city, and even applications of the same equipment can vary depending on local conditions. Hikvision and Huawei are China's leading providers globally, followed by Dahua and ZTE, according to SOS International.[99] Their sales to nondemocratic countries have fueled criticism that China is "exporting authoritarianism."

The real story is more complicated, of course. Many countries were not exactly thriving democracies before importing Chinese gear. Chinese surveillance companies do not sell superior capabilities, but they are more willing to provide them to anyone who can pay. Some U.S. companies are even withholding their facial recognition products from U.S. law enforcement until there is a federal law regulating it.[100] Several have also called for the U.S. government to institute export restrictions on facial recognition technology.

If the market for surveillance equipment were a gun show, Chinese firms would be the dealers that do not ask for background checks. They do not particularly care who you are, or how you might use their products. And if you would prefer to do the sale in the parking lot, rather than inside the venue where people are watching, they are happy to oblige. Fewer conditions, more options, and less scrutiny is the essence of the Chinese surveillance sales pitch—all this at a cost you can afford or are made to believe you can afford because of all the benefits these tools will bring.

Surprisingly few people have asked if the genie actually makes these wishes come true. Advocates trumpet massive gains in efficiency and safety. Critics warn that these systems make the government omnipresent. While they disagree on the ultimate objective of China's digital infrastructure projects, both sides of this debate tend to assume the technology works. A closer look suggests that China's "Safe City" exports have a more mixed track record. Eager to win business, companies have been willing to stretch the truth.

Some sales pitches promise nothing short of a miracle.[101] In its marketing materials, ZTE promises its systems will improve government efficiency by reducing transportation costs by 20 percent to 30 percent, administrative approval times by 40 percent to 50 percent, and telecom costs by 50 percent to 70 percent. If that were not enough, the same slide promises to reduce poverty and illiteracy, create new employment opportunities, and attract foreign investment.[102]

After adopting Huawei's Safe City solution, the company claims, an anonymous city called "XX" experienced a 15 percent reduction in violent crime, a 45 percent increase in case clearance rate, and a reduction in emergency response time from 10 minutes to 4.5 minutes. But wait, there's more: "citizen satisfaction" in the city increased from 60.2 percent to 98.3 percent. Apparently, those 1.7 percent of citizens who were not satisfied are either very demanding or very brave to admit their dissatisfaction.

China's Safe City builders have left a trail of suspicious and potentially dangerous claims. Hikvision, Dahua, and Uniview have all falsified tests required to export their products to South Korea.[103] Selling into the global response to the COVID-19 pandemic, Hikvision and Dahua have exaggerated the capabilities of their heat-sensing cameras, falsely claiming they could take the temperatures of up to thirty people per second.[104] These promises persuaded an Alabama school district to spend $1 million on Hikvision fever cameras, wasting public resources and putting the community at risk.[105]

Many governments sign on the dotted line because they may benefit politically regardless of whether the project actually works. Prestige is a major factor. Announcing a "smart city" project signals a move into the vanguard of advanced development. It taps into what sociologists call the "technological sublime"—a powerful attraction that incentivizes decisionmakers to add bells and whistles beyond what they actually need.[106] Every camera installed in the city is a visible reminder that the government is watching. Command centers, direct in name and sophisticated in appearance, are the perfect projects for governments wanting to appear technologically advanced and in control. The security aesthetic—the appearance of control—attracts governments to Safe City systems like Lamborghinis attract people who want to appear rich.

Pakistan spent $100 million to outfit its capital of Islamabad with a Huawei Safe City system. Huawei installed nearly 2,000 cameras, more than 500 kilometers of fiber-optic cable, and an LTE wireless network. By far the most visibly impressive addition was a cavernous, 3,000-square-foot command center with seventy-two screens. It is designed to withstand level nine earthquakes and massive explosions. Huawei delivered presentations to government officials to build support for the project. "Those who have been to our Safe City CCC Command Center, they were definitely very impressed with our huge screens," a Huawei representative recalled.[107]

The system's actual performance has been less impressive, as Sheridan Prasso reported for Bloomberg.[108] In 2018, murders, kidnappings, and burglaries in Islamabad all rose from the previous year, and total crime was up 33 percent, according to data from Pakistan's National Police Bureau.[109] Half of the cameras were not functioning. That same year, the speaker of Pakistan's national assembly raised these issues in a meeting with Huawei and Chinese government representatives, pointing out in a press release that "there were some error[s] and defects in the Islamabad Safe City project, and we want to remove these defects after consultation with the concerned authorities for [a] safe and secure Capital city."[110]

Some errors were human. In early 2019, images showing people in their cars, taken from what appeared to be Islamabad's Safe City cameras, were leaked online. Officials insisted that the images were not from their cameras and that operating procedures were in place at the command center to prevent unauthorized access. But they also admitted that three external government agencies also had control over Safe City cameras in the capital.[111] The command center was acknowledging that it was not always in control.

In Lahore, five hours south of Islamabad, city officials got more from Huawei than they thought they had paid for. The city installed 1,800 cameras, which technicians later discovered were equipped with Wi-Fi transmitting cards that they could not access.[112] Huawei explained that the cards were included in the surveillance system's bidding documents and were designed to provide technicians with remote access. But skeptics pointed out that the system already had remote access enabled through the cameras' primary wired network. A second entry point increased the risk of unauthorized access.

Was China spying on Pakistan? The Lahore evidence is far from conclusive. Given the challenge of getting China's smart city exports to work in foreign capitals, it is hard to believe that Lahore's cameras currently provide a centralized and crisp view to officials in Beijing. But China's stakes in Pakistan are higher than in most places. Chinese officials have touted the China-Pakistan Economic Corridor, a $25 billion-and-growing collection of infrastructure projects, as the flagship of Xi's signature foreign policy vision, the Belt and Road Initiative.[113] China also has an estimated 10,000 to 15,000 Chinese nationals working abroad on these projects to protect.[114] A desire for real-time surveillance would not be surprising.

The method, however, is questionable. Wi-Fi access could allow a third party to download selected footage, or larger amounts of footage if the proper equipment was installed within close proximity. This could work if one or two cameras were known to surveil high-value targets. But bulk transmission would need to occur through fiber-optic cables. As it happens, Huawei installed a fiber-optic line between Pakistan and China in 2018.[115]

Regardless, the greater and more immediate risk to Pakistan is not that the cameras have a dual function but that they do not work. Having borrowed significant sums for Safe City equipment in Islamabad, Lahore, and other major cities, Pakistan needs these projects to succeed. Having borrowed much more for other projects, and given longer-standing challenges, Pakistan's finances leave little room for an economic slowdown or unexpected events.

As Senator Rubio learned, Kenya is another proud host of Huawei's Safe City solutions. A Huawei promotional video on the project, which includes 1,800 cameras in Nairobi and Mombasa, is designed to feel like a spy thriller.[116] It opens with a military-style satellite view from above, complete with crosshairs, and zooms into Nairobi. "For some time now, Kenyans have been thinking that these CCTV cameras installed both in Nairobi and Mombasa counties are inactive," the narrator says. "However, this is far from the truth. Unbeknown to Kenyans, security agencies have already activated the new Safaricom security system." Rather than downplay the system's capabilities and provide assurances about privacy, Kenya's security forces brag about it. "Those cameras are very accurate and very clear," a senior police administrator says in the video. "Anybody who does anything is being watched."

When I visited Nairobi in 2019, I expected the gaze of these cameras would be uncomfortable. My movements would be tracked and watched. I would fall under the crosshairs. But as I walked the streets, I realized just how ridiculous that expectation was, even bordering on paranoid. I was just another tourist. The Chinese state, if they were watching, must have a lot of free time on its hands. Wandering from block to block for hours, getting a feel for the surveillance system's physical footprint, I would have wasted some low-level bureaucrat's workday.

As the sun went down, I understood, in a small way, how the threat of physical danger can outweigh privacy concerns. The eyes following me most closely were on the same streets, and not watching for either government. I was obviously a foreigner, an easy target in a city with high crime rates. On unfamiliar terrain, privacy was the last thing I wanted. I stayed under the streetlights. Instead of avoiding the cameras, I tried to remain within their fields of vision. I felt safer knowing that they were watching, a feeling that was the opposite of the paranoia I had expected. It may have been just as false.

Later, I learned that these cameras have been less impressive than advertised. Huawei claims its Safe City solutions dramatically reduced crime in Nairobi and Mombasa.[117] However, the year after the system's installation, Kenya's National Police Service reported a smaller decrease in Nairobi's crime rates than what Huawei had publicized, while crimes rates in Mombasa increased significantly.[118] In 2017, crime in Nairobi skyrocketed 50 percent, rising above pre-installation levels. Crime ebbs and flows because of a myriad of factors, of course. But companies attempting to take credit for reducing crime should expect questions when crime moves in the opposite direction.

Few care to ask questions. Many governments have consumer protection agencies that guard against fraud. But when the government is the customer, as it typically is with smart city projects, public scrutiny is limited. After the sale is made, both sides are incentivized to portray the product as a success. Pointing out that the systems do not work as promised will expose the government to criticism that it squandered public money and did not do its job effectively. Many countries are also reluctant to risk jeopardizing their relationship with the Chinese government, a major lender and trading partner. Consequently, governments may spend less time rigorously evaluating whether these projects work than publicly portraying them as successful.

In Machakos County, a two-hour drive from Nairobi, China is helping Kenya build a digital city from scratch.[119] In 2008, the government announced the Konza Technopolis, which it hopes will become a world-class technology hub.[120] "By leveraging the smart city framework, Konza will be able to optimize its city services, creating a sustainable city that responds directly to the needs of its residents, workers, and visitors," the government says.[121] But the project has fallen behind schedule, and the government hopes to complete the city's roads, water, and other basic infrastructure by the end of 2021.[122]

Founding a tech hub is exactly the type of sweeping, legacy-building project that gets leaders excited. Everyone wants to be the mayor of their own Silicon Valley. The problem is that many of the world's best-known innovation hubs grew through a mixture of state support and organic growth. Creating a tech hub from scratch is mind-bendingly difficult. Even with tax exemptions and other financial incentives to offer, Konza is still struggling to convince Kenyan and Western companies to relocate from Nairobi and other major cities, where the real commercial action remains.

The Kenyan government seems undeterred by these challenges, even a dozen years after the project was announced. Officials are now studying the feasibility of creating a "Digital Media City" within Konza.[123] It is an intriguing prospect, given Kenya's vibrant entertainment and media sector, which has seen double-digit growth in recent years. Yet creating a city within a city that itself is not complete also has the hint of promotional spin gone too far. The more missions Konza is given, the less likely it is to do any of them well.

But Chinese companies are rushing for a piece of the action. With the project's financial future uncertain, China's Export-Import Bank stepped in and offered a $172.7 million concessional loan.[124] Huawei was contracted to develop the project, including a surveillance system and a data center, which is intended to provide services to the government as well as the private sector. John Tanui, former deputy head of Huawei's Kenya branch, was named as Konza's CEO in 2015.[125]

To supply the city's electricity, the Kenyan government commissioned the China Aerospace Construction Group to build a forty-kilometer power line to link the development to the national grid, an effort also funded by China's Export-Import Bank.[126] Even if the Technopolis bubble bursts, Chinese firms will still get paid for building it.

## SMARTER EYES

On March 31, 2020, Chinese leader Xi Jinping donned a blue surgical mask and set out to visit Hangzhou. COVID-19 was tearing across the world, but new infections and deaths reported in China were falling. Every day, the public was more restless for life to return to normal, while the world was angrier with China. Xi wanted to encourage Chinese citizens to remain disciplined. He wanted to show the world that China's response to the outbreak was sophisticated. He wanted everyone to know that he was in control.

His destination of choice was the Hangzhou City Brain Operation Command Center. In 2016, Alibaba and Hikvision partnered to build a system that uses AI algorithms and inputs from over 4,500 traffic cameras to manage traffic lights, alert authorities to accidents, ease traffic congestion, and provide users with real-time traffic and travel route recommendations.[127] Since becoming operational, the system has helped reduce traffic by 15 percent and cut emergency response times in half, according to company statements.[128] "We are able to locate people with only one photo, even a photo of a person's back," Alibaba researchers claim about a similar system in Quzhou.[129]

While "City Brain" gets the credit for these improvements, old-fashioned methods surely helped. Hangzhou capped the number of new vehicle registrations per year and maintains the world's largest bike-sharing program.[130] Nor is there anything particularly revolutionary about automating traffic lights. In 2018, Alibaba exported a second version of the system to Malaysia's capital of Kuala Lumpur.[131]

Congestion there continued to increase, according to data from the geolocation company TomTom, but the "City Brain" brand remains untarnished.[132]

At the command center, Xi looked over Alibaba's cutting-edge displays. One large screen showed a 3D map of Hangzhou, indicating the changing populations within different city districts and buildings. Another tracked the city's traffic congestion, with a banner at the top displaying the number of vehicles in transit and average speeds on major roads and highways. A third monitored the health of Hangzhou residents, categorizing their COVID-19 infection statuses using a color-coding system and calculating the daily change in infection rates.[133]

Xi called for making cities "smarter," peppering his remarks with references to big data, cloud computing, blockchain, and AI. He called for using these technologies, which he dubbed "new infrastructure," to modernize China's governance system from the ground up.[134] The technologies were new, but the twin goals, development and control, remained unchanged.

Xi did not mention the dangers that come with collecting so much personal data. In January, an independent researcher discovered that City Brain's data was available to unauthorized users.[135] The previous year, an Alibaba-hosted database that monitored citizens in parts of Beijing was left unprotected for weeks, allowing anyone to access the system's facial recognition data.[136] The database made references to City Brain and included functions to identify Uyghurs, but Alibaba denied that its signature AI platform was being used.

Xi did not have time for these nuances. He was trying to pull off one of the greatest public relations magic tricks in recent history. Despite being the source of the COVID-19 outbreak, and having wasted precious time while attempting to cover it up, China was positioning its response as a model for the world. It was doing this by sending masks and medical experts to other countries and by championing technological solutions for virus detection and contact tracing.[137]

Chinese companies were already answering Xi's call. More than five hundred Chinese companies were claiming to use AI in response to the pandemic, according to Jeffrey Ding, an AI expert and author of the "ChinAI" newsletter.[138] Some of these applications more than stretched the truth. Dahua, for example, was aggressively marketing its temperature-sensing cameras as helping to identify people with fevers. It misleadingly suggested that its equipment could accurately read people wearing hats and check crowds getting off trains, for example, claims that IPVM debunked.[139]

China's response to the coronavirus pandemic also revealed the difficulties of integrating and centralizing different datasets. As different levels of government launched their own health-monitoring systems, and Chinese companies did their part to help, the result was duplication and confusion.[140] Residents were told to use different health applications on their phones that made use of different data points. The government was forced to resort to low-tech, Mao-style techniques of surveillance and control, manually knocking on doors to keep tabs on residents.[141] China's cities were apparently not yet "smart" enough.

This challenge has fragmented the central vision that Chinese authorities hoped to achieve through Sharp Eyes. The poorest communities still lack the basic infrastructure to make these systems function. There is no standard plan for setting up these systems, so they have been rolled out unevenly. In reality, Chinese authorities are far from achieving their goal of fully centralized and actionable surveillance.

The Communist Party's ability to see has outpaced its ability to think. There are simply too many video feeds, scattered across too many different systems, to watch and process in bulk. Government officials and academics are discussing how to avoid these "data islands." Even the brain behind the "City Brain" has expressed concerns. "Cities are burdening themselves with too many smart systems," Wang Jian, the founder of Alibaba Cloud said in 2018. "Installing ten cameras on one utility pole is not a smart plan."[142] But it is good business for

Hikvision, Dahua, and other Chinese surveillance companies. "Smart city constructions are turning cities into monsters," Wang warned.

Something similar might be said about the Hangzhou Safari Park. Despite the park's eagerness to embrace AI surveillance systems to track its customers, it appears to have failed at providing much more essential forms of security. In May 2021, after local residents shared their sightings on social media, the park belatedly admitted that three leopards had escaped.[143] They had been at large for more than two weeks. Search parties fanned out with dogs, drones, and live chickens as bait. Apparently, "big cat detection" was not yet included in the park and surrounding area's surveillance systems.

China's state surveillance model is inefficient by design and application. It purposefully enlists the masses to police each other, and it fuels an industry that thrives on duplication. These incentives are so powerful that they may actually prevent the government from achieving the fully centralized view it desires. If the sheer technological challenge can be solved, which is a colossal one, the government would still likely keep the "mass" in its surveillance model, as Mulvenon and his colleagues explain.[144]

A more efficient surveillance state would mean fewer cameras and fewer security forces. But the CCP's goal is maximum control rather than efficiency. The prospect of downsizing security forces, even if the technology allowed it, carries its own risks to stability. If there were an authoritarian guide to governance, mass layoffs of security forces would be near the top of the "Do Not Do" list. Instead, the government hires security forces in droves.

The atrocities in Xinjiang are revealing of the model's limits as well. The shocking and inhumane way technology is being used can make China's methods, and the technology itself, appear more advanced than they are in reality. "In associating China's repression in Xinjiang with sophisticated, AI-driven policing models, we may be assuming too much," cautions Yuan Yang, deputy Beijing bureau chief for the *Financial Times*.[145] Indeed, China's approach is "driven by political objectives that are blunt and indiscriminate." Rather than harnessing technology to identify only a few individuals, authorities are targeting an entire ethnic group.

This approach can be seen in actual lines of code for a Xinjiang policing mobile app, reverse-engineered as part of an investigation by Human Rights Watch. The app, which feeds into a system that aggregates data and designates people as potentially threatening, flags behaviors such as "not socializing with neighbors, often avoiding using the front door," and a myriad of other actions and characteristics. "Gathering information to counter genuine terrorism or extremist violence is not a central goal of the system," explains Maya Wang, the investigation's lead researcher.[146] By scoring users on their ability to carry out tasks, the app also serves as a tool for government supervisors to monitor lower-level officials. Those on the frontlines doing the controlling, after all, must be controlled.

All surveillance systems face a fundamental trade-off between precision and recall, explains political scientist Jennifer Pan in *Welfare for Autocrats*. Systems that favor "precision" minimize false positives (people who are falsely flagged as posing a threat). Systems that favor "recall" minimize false negatives (people who do pose a threat who go unflagged). Chinese officials, wanting to avoid social unrest and justify large security budgets, have clearly prioritized the latter. Their goal is not to minimize harm from false identifications but to ensure that no potential threats go unnoticed.[147]

Taking its cue from Xi, Hikvision has set its eyes on becoming smarter. In 2019, it was added to the list of China's national champions for AI, a designation that provides prime access to government contracts.[148] Hikvision's focus on AI makes sense, given its expertise in processing images and vast amounts of data, but it faces competition from SenseTime, Megvii, and other Chinese companies. Hikvision's annual reports do not instill much confidence, reading more like techno-babble word clouds than windows into the company's operations. In its 2019 report, the company claims in a single sentence that it "put forward the 'big data-AI fusion' concept, which integrates AI and perceptive big data to achieve perceptive intelligence, and integrates AI and multidimensional big data to achieve cognitive intelligence; it expands from focus on products to focus on systems, from focus on technologies to focus on businesses expansion, from focus on single business to focus on businesses across multiple industries; in the cooperation ecosystem built through the open platform, it provides users with complete intelligent industry and smart city solutions."[149]

It is impossible to know exactly how much is real and how much is rhetorical—or whether the confusing sentence was merely written by AI. Globally, there is no widely agreed upon definition for what constitutes AI, leaving room for companies to hype their products. When MMC Ventures, an investment firm, examined 2,830 European start-ups classified as AI companies, it found that 40 percent of them did not use AI at all.[150] Hikvision has been pushing the limits of video applications of AI, but given that its products still sometimes identify cars as people, claiming to offer "cognitive intelligence" for entire cities seems like a stretch.

But Hikvision knows what its biggest customer wants. And even if the technology is not yet mature, the sales opportunity has already arrived. In 2020, Chinese cities and counties began implementing the next phase of Sharp Eyes, which focuses on AI, cloud, big data, and other "core technologies," according to state media. It is tempting to dismiss these buzzwords as fluff, but some projects are already underway. Sharp Eyes is starting to look even more menacing.

In Zhucheng City, in the southeastern province of Shandong, local authorities are rolling out "smart mediation" and "smart corrections."[151] Citizens can file complaints electronically, and government mediators collect information and make recommendations by streaming video. Not only has the satisfaction rate reached 100 percent, state media claim, but the system's big data analysis generates early warnings that prevent disputes. This false certainty makes the system feel less like *Judge Judy* than *Judge Dredd*.

Local authorities are also taking a page from *Minority Report*. Citizens who have committed offenses ranging from prostitution to political dissent are tracked at literally every step. Electronic wristbands monitor their heart rate, blood pressure, and other diagnostics, and transmit data to local authorities in real time. By analyzing large amounts of location data, the authorities build "space-time" profiles of corrections subjects that predict behavior. This provides godlike powers, according to state media, "to shatter traditional models of supervision that know only of the present but not the past, and to achieve precise characterizations of the activity trajectories of community corrections subjects."

Big data analysis is not required to see the terrifying trajectory of the CCP's own space-time profile. The Party's past demonstrates a willingness to crush even peaceful opposition by force. Its present includes genocide and crimes against humanity.[152] The CCP is building a society in which any challenge to its rule, including protests of any scale, can be cut down before it grows. Every tool—next-generation networks, connected devices, cloud computing—is being aimed at that goal.

The CCP is still sharpening its digital surveillance arsenal, as new systems spring forth in a disjointed manner, but it does not need a perfect system. It combines high-tech surveillance with old-fashioned intimidation. "The all-seeing eye doesn't have to be looking at you for the panopticon to function," writes Strittmatter. "All that matters is that you feel it might be—even if in reality, it isn't there yet."[153] Official accounts inflating China's surveillance capabilities serve this end and may even attract interest from foreign buyers.

What works for the CCP at home, however, will face greater challenges abroad. China spends far more than any other country does on these systems, making its own model expensive, if not impossible, for many countries to replicate, even if some of the same tools and techniques can be transplanted. Perhaps overly accustomed to receiving praise from the state, Chinese surveillance companies sometimes exaggerate their capabilities and are vulnerable to questions about the performance of their systems.

"If we believe everything we read in the news, we might believe that our world is on the verge of a dramatic and possibly terrible change because of artificial intelligence and new computational technologies," writes Pan. "If we read political science research, aside from research on social media, computational technologies might as well not matter. The reality is likely somewhere in between, and likely hidden in the nuances of how politics work."[154]

Given its politics, there is little question that the CCP will continue harnessing technology to further strengthen its control at home. China's surveillance giants, meanwhile, will continue selling to anyone willing to buy.

# CHAPTER FIVE

# A CREASE IN THE INTERNET

It takes 230 milliseconds for data to travel from Los Angeles to Hangzhou, China's surveillance camera–industry capital. That's roughly the blink of an eye, easy to miss if you're not looking closely. But in December 2015, Doug Madory *was* looking closely, and he did not like what he saw. Data should have been traveling from Los Angeles to Washington, D.C. Instead, it was racing through a submarine cable on the bottom of the Pacific Ocean, hopping into China, and then boomeranging back to Los Angeles and onward to Washington.

Madory begins most mornings by poring over tables of data that measure the internet. At a small start-up called Renesys, he helped build a vast monitoring system that sends out hundreds of millions of probes each day. Each of these "traceroutes" is fired off from a known origin to a target destination. On the way, it records information about the nodes it passes through and the time between the origin and each of those nodes. In bulk, these measurements provide a granular, albeit imperfect, map of the internet.

Madory's specialty is Border Gateway Protocol (BGP) routing, which is like the internet's postal system.[1] BGP routing decides how to send data between autonomous systems, or ASes, which are like local post office branches. Internet service providers such as Verizon and Comcast have ASes, as do universities and large businesses, and each AS has a block of internet protocol (IP) addresses assigned to it. When you access a website, your computer connects to your local AS, which uses BGP to find the best path to the AS hosting the website. The best route depends on speed, cost, and other factors.

Unlike the Postal Service, however, ASes are not all part of the same organization. They are "autonomous," as the name suggests, and they have different relationships with each other. The larger entities sell access to smaller entities. Some are peers, meaning they agree to exchange traffic for free. Each has its own table of routes learned from adjacent ASes, which may have learned them from yet more ASes and so on, a process called "route by rumor." It is like asking for driving directions from a stranger, who only knows them because she heard them from a friend.

Navigating networks has become more dangerous in recent years. Before BGP was invented over lunch in 1989, scrawled on two napkins, the internet was small enough that researchers often knew the people on the other end of these connections by name.[2] By the end of 1989, there were about 500 ASes, a number that climbed to nearly 100,000 in 2020.[3] What began as a quaint neighborhood has exploded into a bustling metropolis, humming with valuable activity as well as accidents and crime.

As Madory dug into the data, he found the source of the problem.[4] SK Broadband, a South Korean company, had announced more than 300 Verizon routes for just over a minute, but that was enough to begin a cascade that convinced other ASes around the internet that SK Broadband was Verizon. The announcement was made through a China Telecom AS that was peering with SK Broadband. As a result, networks around the world began sending data intended for Verizon through China Telecom. It was a crease in the map of the internet.

Pointing to this incident and others, U.S. national security experts warn that China is intentionally redirecting data flows. By changing routing conditions, these "network shaping" tactics increase the likelihood that traffic moves across connections where China has the ability to monitor it. "Vast rewards can be reaped from the hijacking, diverting, and then copying of information-rich traffic going into or crossing the United States and Canada," researchers Chris C. Demchak and Yuval Shavitt wrote in a study of China Telecom's routing behavior that suggested "malicious intent."[5]

Routing experts agree that China Telecom failed to take preventative actions, but they caution that it is usually impossible to tell the difference between honest mistakes and malicious BGP hacks.[6] A detailed study of China Telecom's most infamous incident, in 2010, concluded that it was likely an accident but could not rule out malicious intent.[7] The leak impacted about 8 percent of U.S. routes, including data traveling to the U.S. Senate and U.S. military branches, as well as IBM, Microsoft, and other commercial sites.[8] Because sensitive data is encrypted, some experts speculate that China is copying re-routed data to decode in the future, following breakthroughs in quantum computing. However, Madory cautions that the 2010 leak was "so minimal and short-lived, it would be impossible to intercept traffic effectively—whether encrypted or not."[9]

Whether Chinese authorities are redirecting traffic, or Chinese carriers are driving recklessly, there is no question that Beijing wants even greater control of global data flows. In 2014, while calling for China to become a "cyber great power," Chinese leader Xi Jinping explained that "network information flows across national borders." "The flow of information guides the flow of technology, capital and talent," he stressed. "The amount of information controlled has become an important indicator of a nation's soft power and competitiveness."[10]

The challenge for Beijing is that greater connectivity requires giving up some control. The world's largest internet hubs are neutral and open, making it easy for companies to connect with each other. Neutrality, however, is anathema to Chinese authorities, who view the global internet as a threat to their rule. Their unyielding obsession with control makes it harder to achieve scale in global networks.

This tension is playing out in three areas. At home, China's Great Firewall requires all incoming traffic to pass through its state-owned carriers, enabling Chinese officials to monitor, censor, and disrupt data flows. Under the sea, China is growing its share of cables that carry the vast majority of international data. In foreign markets around the world, Chinese cloud providers are setting up new data centers. Piece by piece, China is redrawing the map of the internet.

## THE BIG THREE

Like a medieval castle, China's domestic network has only a handful of entry points. By forcing international connections into these choke-points and requiring foreign carriers to use one of China's three state-owned telecom firms, Beijing has an unrivaled ability to monitor, censor, and cut off traffic. But this fortress-style approach also creates economic costs at home and vulnerabilities abroad.

The Big Three—China Telecom, China Unicom, and China Mobile—are China's network gatekeepers. Collectively, these state-owned companies control 98.5 percent of China's international bandwidth.[11] Anyone looking to connect with China's network must reach an agreement with them. The Big Three, in turn, ultimately answer to China's State Council, giving the government final say over their operations.

Foreign cloud providers are not floating easily over the Great Firewall, either. China prohibits foreign companies from directly providing cloud computing services and requires them to partner with Chinese firms, hand over their technology and intellectual property, and submit to government assessments.[12] Amazon and Microsoft have gone ahead, albeit with arrangements that offer a more limited selection of their services. Microsoft's user guide for cloud services in China notes diplomatically, "The network latency between China and the rest of the world is inevitable, because of the intermediary technologies that regulate cross-border internet traffic."[13]

China has strengthened its fortress-style approach in recent years, even as its internet population has exploded. As of early 2021, it had only 564 registered ASes, according to Kirtus G. Leyba, a computer science expert at Arizona State University.[14] The United States, in contrast, had 17,715 of these. In 2009, Chinese authorities could intercept 90 percent of international traffic by monitoring the country's ten largest ASes. A decade later, they could accomplish the same goal using only two ASes.[15]

China's Great Firewall operates at these chokepoints and in the provincial-level access points just beyond them. It reads traffic between China and the outside world and uses several methods to terminate requests for banned content. The moniker is actually somewhat misleading, as China's Great Firewall is less disruptive than a traditional firewall, which can drop data packets in flight and would produce greater delays to international traffic.[16]

Yet China's incoming traffic still faces what a group of researchers call "the Great Bottleneck."[17] China's international data flows are asymmetric. Data entering China experiences significant slowdowns and instability, while data exiting China is relatively fast and stable. The Big Three are responsible for managing the points at which data is slowed. Over 70 percent of these bottlenecks are located within China, a fact that suggests they are a feature in China's network strategy rather than a bug or a result of inadequate international connections.

Friction is one of the most powerful tools in China's censorship strategy. Making information slightly more difficult or costly to obtain can be a powerful deterrent for many individuals, as political scientist Margaret E. Roberts explains in *Censored: Distraction and Diversion Inside China's Great Firewall*.[18] Do you want to wait longer for that foreign movie to download, or stream an approved title right now?

Wealthier and more technically savvy individuals can still find ways to access the information. In the past, one popular method was using a virtual private network (VPN) to access blocked content. In recent years, however, even these tools have been heavily curtailed. Friction is strategic because it reveals those who are willing to pay a higher cost, allowing the government to target them further if it wishes.

In October 2020, a phantom app for Android appeared to offer a new way to circumvent the Great Firewall. The app, Tuber, allowed Chinese internet users to browse content on Google, Twitter, YouTube, and other sites normally blocked by Beijing. It was an instant hit, downloaded more than five million times in less than a day. But this was no rogue operation. China's largest cybersecurity firm was behind the app, which appeared to have received state approval. Then, just a day after its official launch, the app was gone.

"Tuber's brief existence suggests the Great Firewall could be replaced by the Great Filter," explains David Bandurski, codirector of the China Media Project at the University of Hong Kong.[19] Instead of banning sites, such a system would allow for more localized tracking of user behavior. The app, according to those who had a chance to test it, still filtered video content and search results. It also required users to provide their mobile phone numbers, which are linked to unique national IDs, and asked for permission to access contacts.[20]

Lowering the drawbridge in such a controlled fashion may also allow China's nationalist commentators to march onto foreign platforms in greater numbers, where they could spar with China's critics and defend official positions. It could also give them ammunition to claim, however implausibly, that China is relaxing restrictions and opening up.

But the Great Bottleneck also has its champions, including some powerful interest groups.[21] Because international traffic is unstable, more foreign companies must locate their servers within China. That's more opportunities for Chinese security services to monitor foreign activities and extra business for Chinese data centers. Chinese companies in search, social media, e-commerce, and other online services also benefit when their foreign competitors are more difficult to access. The Great Bottleneck further protects Chinese internet companies from foreign competition.

The Big Three have turned their slow incoming traffic into a marketing opportunity. Like other carriers, they sell different tiers of international transit. China Telecom, for example, sells four tiers of bandwidth to AS operators, the fastest of which costs $38,000 a month to maintain, plus a $10,000 service charge.[22] Naturally, these services are too expensive for everyone except large companies. In this way, the friction supporting China's censorship is preserved and state-owned firms have another source of revenue. The state wins twice.

The Big Three do not play well with others—or even always with each other. In most of the world, large operators agree to peer and exchange similar amounts of traffic for free. But in China, these exchanges come with a price. China Mobile has been forced to pay its two siblings upward of $280 million a year.[23] While Chinese authorities eliminated these fees for the Big Three in 2020, payments by smaller domestic network operators continue. After all, by limiting connectivity among China's networks, the fees preserve a hierarchical network structure that serves China's security interests.[24]

Behind its fortress, China is perfectly positioned to cut itself off from the global internet.[25] In 2009, the Chinese government demonstrated this capability on a regional scale as part of its crackdown in Xinjiang. For half a year, internet access was cut off along with most mobile text messaging and international phone services. Even when services were initially restored, people found their text messages were capped and international websites were blocked.[26]

Internet shutdowns powerfully demonstrate the state's reach, but their bluntness can also backfire. Rather than penalize specific individuals and behaviors, shutdowns touch everyone in a geographic area. When Xinjiang lost internet access, business managers had to travel to Gansu, a neighboring province, to communicate with customers.[27] These measures are often justified in the name of stability, but they can also stoke resentment.

China is developing more sophisticated methods of control. Access Now, a nonprofit that tracks internet shutdowns, counted only a single shutdown in China during 2019, out of 213 worldwide, which occurred during the lead-up to the thirtieth anniversary of the Tiananmen

Square protests. The actual count is surely higher, given that China's censorship makes it hard to detect and verify shutdowns, but it may also reflect the government's stronger hold on information flows.

Just as China keeps the "mass" in its surveillance model, as chapter 4 explained, it does the same with its censorship model. The government employs some two million internet censors, giving it an online content army that is roughly the size of the PLA's active-duty forces, and draws on a network of more than twenty million part-time volunteer internet trolls.[28] This combined force has powers that extend beyond blocking and deleting content. Roberts and her colleagues estimate that the government fakes 448 million social media comments each year, often to support government positions or change the subject from undesirable topics.[29]

China's censors sprang into action in early January 2020, a ProPublica investigation revealed.[30] As rumors began circulating about a novel virus, they removed videos of bodies on the street and arguments in hospitals. They purged memorial messages for Li Wenliang, a Chinese doctor who warned about the outbreak only to be threatened by the police before dying of the virus. They promoted articles that downplayed the severity of the crisis, avoiding the words "fatal," "lockdown," and other terms that might cause alarm. They highlighted the heroic deeds of CCP members.

But the CCP's cowardice comes through the timeline of events. Even before the virus had been identified definitively, authorities were racing to downplay it. China's censors moved ahead of its medical experts. Social control was prioritized over public safety. Instead of sharing vital information with Chinese citizens, and the global community, the government suppressed it. And while Chinese censors worked frantically to assure everyone that the CCP was firmly in control, the outbreak was spiraling into a global pandemic. Truth was the pandemic's first casualty.

There's a double-sided nature to this power. The CCP avoided mass unrest. But at what cost? During the next crisis, citizens may recall how the government got the virus under control, but they will surely also recall being deceived. Remembering Li Wenliang's fate, anyone with important knowledge is more likely to remain silent. The more successful China's censors are at convincing others to adopt their positive narratives, the less likely that negative information, vital truths such as the emergence of a new virus, will make its way to authorities.

But in an era of increasing rivalry, China's fortress may offer other strategic advantages. Domestic traffic does not leave the country, which makes foreign surveillance more difficult. Fewer access points limit the "attack surface," the sum of available routes that foreign attackers could take. This approach is not without its drawbacks, however. Attackers could concentrate their efforts on a handful of routes, and upon gaining access to one of China's major carriers, could impact a greater share of China's users than if China's network was more complex.

Forcing international data flows into tightly controlled entry points can also facilitate offensive measures, such as China's Great Cannon, a tool that compromises foreign visitors to Chinese sites. In 2015, the Great Cannon intercepted traffic to Baidu servers and, for a portion of those requests, replaced the response with a malicious script, according to an investigation by Bill Marczak and his colleagues at Citizen Lab.[31] The script enlisted foreign computers in a distributed denial-of-service attack against GreatFire, a nonprofit that provides tools for Chinese users to circumvent censorship.

But China's fortress also carries colossal costs. "The extremely hierarchical topology . . . and the tight control of a tiny number of centrally controlled international gateways, mean the country does not experience or interact with the global Internet, but only a subset of it," the Internet Society explains.[32] This benefits the Big Three but harms millions of Chinese firms, particularly small and medium-sized businesses, which face higher fees, longer wait times, and limited access to international networks.

Enforcing censorship rules requires companies to walk a tightrope between competing legal and commercial interests.[33] On the one side, companies must follow government orders to remain in business. On the other side, they need to attract users with content. Striking the right balance—weighing the cost between noncompliance and losing users—requires time and staff. Managers navigate competing directives from government agencies. Social media companies hire tens to hundreds of staff as censors.[34] Censorship gives birth to bureaucracy.

Restricting access to information also harms innovation. After China banned Google in 2014, the value of Chinese patents dropped 8 percent, according to one estimate.[35] These restrictions could harm China's national champions if applied more stringently. Huawei, for example, used a paper from a Turkish mathematician to help develop its 5G processes. It has the resources to maintain access to the outside world, but many start-ups do not. It is impossible to tally the full toll these measures take: companies that were never founded, patents that were never filed, and ideas that were never formed.

China's fortress also constrains its influence in global networks. Mainland Chinese cities are conspicuously absent from the rankings of the world's most connected hubs. In 2020, eight of the world's top ten hubs, as measured by international bandwidth capacity, were in Europe and the United States. The other two were Hong Kong and Singapore.[36]

Hong Kong acts as a buffer between China's domestic network and the world, but China's passage of a draconian national security law in 2020 threatens its hub status. In January 2021, one of Hong Kong's largest internet providers blocked a pro-democracy website, the first instance of full website censorship under the new law and a warning that China's fortress may be expanding.[37]

Hong Kong and the world's other leading hubs all have internet exchange points that are "carrier-neutral," meaning they are owned and operated independently. Neutrality leads to growth by removing barriers to access and promoting competition. When carriers own exchanges, they can block competitors from operating within them or charge egregiously high fees. Fewer operators make the location less attractive to other networks.

China's first attempt at a carrier-neutral exchange shows how the state's insistence on control limits greater connectivity. In December 2015, Song Wang, the CEO and cofounder of ChinaCache, thought he saw an opening. Speaking at the Wuzhen World Internet Conference, Chinese leader Xi Jinping called on countries to "speed up the building of global Internet infrastructure and promote inter-connectivity."[38] Of course, that proposal was prefaced by an even lengthier call for protecting digital sovereignty. But Wang was preparing to launch mainland China's first neutral internet exchange, and he embraced Xi's emphasis on connectivity as support for his venture.[39]

Wang and his colleagues pieced together a compelling offering. They chose the Tianzhu Free Trade Zone, near Beijing's main international airport, hoping to enjoy looser government oversight. They also enlisted the help of the Amsterdam Internet Exchange, a nonprofit-run hub that is one of the world's largest exchanges, hosting more than 800 networks. "By working with AMS-IX, we are hoping to bring the advance[d] international IXP standards into Mainland China as soon as possible," Wang wrote in a blog on ChinaCache's website.[40] The company built two more exchanges, in Shanghai and Guangzhou, and signed up major Chinese tech companies, including Alibaba, Tencent, Baidu, and JD.[41]

But ChinaCache struggled to scale up, stumbling operationally and leaving a long trail of litigation in its wake. In 2016, one of its facilities was disconnected for several hours, an exchange operator's worst nightmare. Leading service providers promise 99.999% uptime, or "five nines," which translates into just under five and a half minutes of unplanned downtime annually. The following year, the company lost more than a third of its customers.[42] The company's partners, vendors, and investors have accused it of construction delays, late equipment payments, and misleading statements. In May 2019, Chinese authorities arrested Wang for bribery. Four months later, NASDAQ halted trading of ChinaCache's shares and delisted the company.

Even if ChinaCache avoided these missteps, its mission—to provide an open, neutral internet exchange—was fundamentally incompatible with China's fortress. As of early 2021, China had 14 internet exchanges, and its largest commercial exchange, based in Beijing, hosted 18 companies, all of them Chinese.[43] The United States had 140 internet exchanges.[44] China's embrace of the Big Three, and its ban on foreign operators, crushes the demand for interconnections that would exist in a more diverse and open environment.

The Big Three look much smaller on the global stage. A study of traffic to the world's one hundred most popular websites found that eight of the ten ASes that carried the most traffic were headquartered in the United States, including the top three.[45] China only had two of the top thirty ASes, which ranked eleventh and thirteenth and were run by China Telecom and China Unicom, respectively. This underperformance is all the more striking given China's large internet population and that fourteen of the top thirty most popular sites are Chinese.[46] The Big Three benefit from a massive protected market but, unlike their U.S. competitors, cannot easily welcome international connections at home. Instead, they must physically go abroad.

When they do go abroad, the Big Three depend heavily on U.S., European, and Japanese networks. China Telecom's most active international AS provides transit for 326 ASes globally.[47] Level 3 runs the United States' most active AS, which provides transit for more than seventeen times as many ASes, including thirty-two times as many customers.[48] Indeed, Level 3 is a provider to China Telecom, as are the top ASes in Japan (operated by NTT), the European Union (operated by Telia), and Australia (operated by Telstra). The dominance of these carriers is a function of first-mover advantages in setting up the internet's early connections, as well as the openness of the countries in which they have heavily invested.

With its connections concentrated on foreign soil, China's international traffic is more vulnerable to surveillance. Madory's internet-monitoring tools, used to detect and examine routing incidents, send traceroutes from servers around the world. Nearly two-thirds (63 percent) of traceroutes destined for China entered Chinese networks through the United States, while another 17 percent entered through Western Europe. The math is simple but striking: 80 percent of China's international traffic is passing through U.S. and European hands.[49]

## ALL-RED ROUTES

To reduce this reliance on foreign carriers, China is building more subsea cables, which carry the vast majority of international data. The technology is new, but China's global activities echo those of imperial Britain in the late nineteenth century. Just like Britain's telegraph cable strategy from the past, China is investing in commercially viable routes as well as those that could serve strategic functions. Cable by cable, it is building a high-capacity, high-speed network spanning Asia, Africa, Europe, and South America.

At first, Britain's motives were mainly commercial. Its companies laid the first submarine cables in the 1850s, and their innovative materials and cable-laying techniques dominated the market. Britain's largest telegraph company manufactured two-thirds of the world's cables during the nineteenth century and almost half thereafter.[50] China aims to achieve similar dominance through Made in China 2025, including capturing 60 percent of the global market for fiber optics.[51]

Toward the end of the nineteenth century, with the strategic importance of telegraph cables clear, the British government began developing a smaller system of cables, called the "All-Red Routes," touching only the British Empire and its possessions. Without this system, its communications were vulnerable to being monitored as they passed through foreign territory and could easily be disrupted during a conflict. By the eve of World War I, a British military journal boasted that Britain had a system of cables "spread like a net all over the world."[52]

China has moved faster than its predecessors along the ocean floor. In 2009, Huawei Marine was created through a joint venture between Huawei and Global Marine, a U.K.-headquartered company that traces it heritage back to the British Eastern Telegraph Company. While venturing into this new territory, Huawei followed a familiar playbook. It partnered with a foreign company that had the technical expertise it lacked, benefited from Chinese state financing to pursue projects that allowed it to learn, and gradually took over more of the technical functions. In its first decade of operation, the company was involved in 104 projects and deployed more than enough submarine cable to encircle the world.[53]

Three flagship projects reveal China's ambitions to connect continents and suggest that its motives are not purely commercial. The first project, designed to carry finance and trading information across the Atlantic, previewed the difficulties that Huawei would later face in Western markets. In 2010, Hibernia Networks, a U.S. telecom services provider, announced it was building a new system, the Hibernia Express, to connect trading centers in New York, New Jersey, and London. For Huawei Marine, a young company eager to prove itself, the project offered a shortcut to joining the elite ranks of leading cable producers, long dominated by Western and Japanese companies.

Huawei Marine's short track record already signaled big ambitions. Strategically, the company sought out progressively more challenging projects to learn and demonstrate its capabilities. Its first cable, connecting Tunisia and Italy, was short and did not need to use repeaters, which are critical for longer projects.[54] But even short international cables are complex undertakings. "Aside from dealing with the sea and the weather, during the construction process, we also had to engage in arduous negotiations with customs, the navy, fishermen, ports, shipping and other related departments," a Huawei employee recalled. The Hannibal cable, named after the Carthaginian general, was completed in late 2009.[55]

Huawei's first cable with repeaters and branches was a humbling experience.[56] The project was designed to connect Trinidad and Tobago to Guyana with a branch into Suriname, totaling only one-sixth the Hibernia Express's length. Nexans, a Norwegian company, manufactured the cable. Although Huawei provided the repeaters and hardware, it leaned heavily on its U.K. partner, Global Marine, to pull everything together and lay the cable. Huawei engineers spent long hours in Chelmsford, United Kingdom, testing the hardware before traveling to Rognan, Norway, where they combined the hardware and the cable. "The submarine cable integration work was a completely unfamiliar concept to us," a Huawei employee recalled.[57]

In this trial, there was plenty of error.[58] The cable planning team did not realize the three countries had festivals at different times and struggled to find hotels. After the cable was installed, engineers in Guyana tried to call Trinidad using a telephone line that is deployed with the cable and allows the landing stations to communicate. When the Suriname landing station answered the phone instead, they realized the signal carrier had been installed backward. But the team pressed on, learned from its mistakes, and completed the cable in May 2010.[59]

The Hibernia Express was in another league. The project aimed to shave five milliseconds off the roundtrip time between New York and London. While such an improvement might seem miniscule, financial institutions were hungry for the first new transatlantic cable in over a decade. Algorithmic trading was pushing trading volumes higher, and traders wanted the edge that faster systems could offer.

Security and reliability are paramount for financial trading. Submarine cables carry over $10 trillion in transactions every day, including activity that flows through the world's stock exchanges.[60] If these cable networks are disrupted, a chief of staff to the U.S. Federal Reserve chairman once explained, "the financial services sector does not grind to a halt, rather it snaps to a halt."[61]

Huawei knew it needed to make Hibernia an offer it could not refuse. In 2007, Hibernia had selected Huawei to upgrade its existing terrestrial systems in Europe, as well as subsea systems connecting Canada, the U.S. East Coast, and England.[62] But Huawei's submarine track record was still thin. Eager to demonstrate that it could build a transatlantic cable, it offered $250 million in financing for the project. The leading cable producers had longer track records, but none matched Huawei's financial package.

In 2012, Huawei Marine won the contract to produce and install the cable.[63] "Project Express is an exciting one for Huawei," said Nigel Bayliff, the company's CEO, who called it a "significant and technically challenging system."[64] For the young company, this was like moving from being an extra on daytime TV to a starring role in a blockbuster film. Proving it could deliver and meet the standards of U.S. and European regulators, especially in an area as critical as financial information flows, promised to open up even deeper access to their markets. The Chinese government, meanwhile, would have a national champion embedded in the West's financial information infrastructure.

Huawei's celebration, however, was premature. After Congress issued its report on Huawei and ZTE, U.S. authorities took a more skeptical look at the proposal. Hibernia tried to assure U.S. officials that it ultimately would control the systems, regardless of who produced and deployed them, but U.S. officials were unpersuaded. Facing the prospect of an indefinite delay, Hibernia dropped Huawei for SubCom, a U.S. cable producer.

Since being kicked off the Hibernia Express in 2013, Huawei Marine has not built a cable touching the United States.[65] The company has been forced to make its mark in the Global South, where its financial incentives are even more enticing and the geopolitical environment is more welcoming. Shunned by the West, Huawei would connect the rest.

Huawei Marine's first transatlantic cable proved even more historic than the Hibernia Express. In 2017, it announced the South Atlantic Inter Link (SAIL), a system connecting Brazil and Cameroon that aimed to become the first connection across the South Atlantic. Its approach to building the cable brought together all China's trademark ingredients for megaprojects abroad: government-to-government dealmaking, Chinese state financing, and a preference for speed over safeguards. Despite gaping holes in its commercial logic, SAIL raced ahead, lifted by political winds.

Speed was essential because the project faced competition. Three years earlier, the Japanese firm NEC, one of the world's three largest suppliers of submarine cables, announced a cable between Brazil and Angola called the South Atlantic Cable Systems (SACS). Huawei Marine needed to adhere to a tight timeline, or its Japanese competitor would win the headlines. That overriding desire to be first may have come at the cost of the project's commercial viability.

Huawei Marine's SAIL project was a government-to-government affair. China Unicom took an ownership stake alongside Camtel, which is owned by Cameroon's government and has struggled financially. To make the project's $136 million price tag palatable, the Export-Import Bank of China provided an $85 million loan and China Unicom provided $34 million in financing.[66] With the two governments aligned, the deal closed, and the project started promptly.

On September 4, 2018, Huawei wrote the press release its executives had been dreaming about since getting kicked out of the Hibernia project: "This marks a significant milestone: for the first time, two continents, Africa and Americas, in the Southern Hemisphere are fully connected."[67] It was also South America's first international cable in eighteen years that did not go directly to the United States. Huawei hinted at broader geopolitical consequences: "This cable will allow immediate links of BRICS with connections to Brazil, South Africa in Southern Hemisphere, and connections to China, Russia and India in Eurasia."

Two years later, evidence had yet to emerge that the SAIL cable was handling significant traffic, according to Madory's data. "We could confirm and analyze the activation of the SACS cable from day one," he said, contrasting it with the Japanese project. "A similar low-latency route between Brazil and Cameroon has simply never appeared."[68] Cameroon backed the SAIL project to help modernize its economy, which is dominated by agriculture. But demand for the project was not there to begin with and has not materialized. Huawei Marine got its demonstration project, and Cameroon got a pile of debt.

China could convert that debt into strategic advantage. With its financial position weakened in the aftermath of the COVID-19 pandemic, Cameroon could look to offload the cable. China Unicom is the obvious candidate to purchase Camtel's share. Commercially and politically, it would be a risky play. The cable's traffic is likely to remain low. By taking full ownership of the cable, China would play right into the hands of its biggest critics, who warn that Beijing is using "debt-trap diplomacy" to seize strategic assets. On the other hand, China would gain sole ownership of a cable that connects two continents where it is increasingly active. It would control a line into the Western hemisphere that does not touch U.S. territory.

By laying its own cables, China is following in the footsteps of Western imperial powers.[69] The competition over modern networks is fierce, and the stakes are even higher given the importance of data flows, but it is different in a critical way. As anthropologist Nicole Starosielski explains in *The Undersea Network*, "With the breakup of colonial empires, the focus of securing the cable network shifted from routing via one's territory or colonial holdings to having national control over the processes of building, operating, and maintaining the cable network."[70] Viewed in this light, the creation of Huawei Marine was China's shortcut to greater network security.

China does not need to take territory to control cable systems.

Meeting the connectivity needs of developing countries requires significant investment, and China's financial packages can appear alluring. China can also exploit the desire among some countries to diversify away from U.S.-dominated networks. "Our communication routes with the world are mainly through the United States," Brazil's secretary of telecommunications, Maximiliano Martinhão, acknowledged in 2013, following the Edward Snowden leaks. "This creates a vulnerability in Brazilian communications."[71] With the construction of the SACS and SAIL cables, Brazil gained two independent links to Africa.

China is not alone in capitalizing on the demand for alternatives. A European-funded cable, EllaLink, connects Brazil to Portugal and is slated to begin service in mid-2021. "Data Security was previously touted as a key reason for the cable, with communications between Brazil and the EU currently routed through North America," says the project's CEO, Philippe Dumont.[72] The project will include an extension from Sines, Portugal, to Marseilles, France, a rising hub for Asian carriers and critical node in Huawei Marine's most ambitious project yet.

China's third flagship project, the cleverly named PEACE cable, has the strongest echoes of Britain's telegraph cable strategy. The project was originally named the Pakistan East Africa Cable Express. Billed as the shortest connection between Asia and Africa, it also draws a line between China's current and future military ambitions.

The Asian end of the cable lands in Pakistan's Gwadar Port, the southern terminus of the China-Pakistan Economic Corridor, or CPEC, the $25 billion-and-growing portfolio of infrastructure projects that Chinese officials have called the flagship of the Belt and Road Initiative. Despite being called a "corridor," the effort is light on cross-border infrastructure projects.

An important exception is a fiber-optic cable that Huawei installed across the China-Pakistan border in 2018. Before this connection was completed, Pakistan had to rely on submarine cables landing in

Karachi, leaving it dependent on companies from rival India. "The network which brings internet traffic into Pakistan through submarine cables has been developed by a consortium that has Indian companies either as partners or shareholders, which is a serious security concern," a senior Pakistani military official said in 2017, while advocating for the approval of the Huawei cable.[73]

China stands to gain as well. "All the cables connecting China with countries in Europe are routing via Hong Kong and Singapore in which routes are relatively simple and lack of [sic] an effective protection mechanism. In the event of geological disasters or man-made destruction, the stability of the submarine cable will be affected," explains a press release for the PEACE cable.[74] A leaked Chinese planning document goes further, noting that "China's telecom services to Africa need to be transferred in Europe, so there is certain hidden danger of the overall security."[75]

So far, however, the terrestrial cable has carried relatively little, according to industry analysts. Pakistan only announced that the cable was operational in July 2020, two years after it was inaugurated. It is possible that the route is running and operating in a manner that is difficult to detect. The connection could also become more active after the PEACE cable connects Gwadar to Djibouti. Or it could join Gwadar Port on the list of white-elephant projects.

Gwadar Port's lackluster commercial performance has fueled speculation about its purpose. China has helped finance and expand the port well beyond any immediate commercial demand. Pakistani leaders had been angling for a port in the underdeveloped area for decades and may have offered naval access. "We have asked our Chinese brothers to please build a naval base at Gwadar," Pakistan's defense minister told the *Financial Times* in 2011.[76]

From Pakistan, the PEACE cable's next stop is Djibouti, where China opened its first overseas military base in 2017. Djibouti has enticed some of the world's major powers to pay for access to its shores by offering a comparatively safe harbor in a stormy neighborhood. It also hosts military facilities for the United States, France, Italy, and Japan. "God has not given us oil," says a senior advisor to Djibouti's president, "but he has given us a strategic point."[77]

China was late to the party, but it has been expanding its footprint in Djibouti in recent years. Beyond its military base, China has invested in a free-trade zone with logistics, business, and manufacturing facilities. The zone's initial phase covers just a square mile, but it is intended to ultimately span eighteen square miles of prime coastal real estate.[78] During a boat ride along Djibouti's coastline in 2019, I watched as the Chinese military base blended almost seamlessly into the port and logistics infrastructure that rises up nearby. Local fishermen said they were harassed by Chinese troops if they strayed too close to the base. China rents this territory, but its presence does not feel temporary.

Evicting China would be difficult for Djibouti, which has allowed its most raucous tenant to become its largest lender. The country's construction spree has pushed its debt dangerously high, and China holds an estimated 57 percent of its foreign debt.[79] U.S. officials have warned that China could take over another port, which Djibouti repossessed from the Dubai-based company DP World in 2018.

The action beneath Djibouti's waters has received less attention but may be even more important. Djibouti is a critical chokepoint in global communications, with at least eleven cables completed or planned to land on its shores.[80] The Big Three are investors in five of these cables. Huawei and ZTE have been working with Djibouti Telecom, the country's state-owned monopoly, since the mid-2000s.

China's expanding presence complicates U.S. operations in the region. The U.S. military has dedicated underseas connections, often called "black fiber." But it relies on privately owned infrastructure for the vast majority of its communications, up to 95 percent, according to a 2009 estimate.[81] The deployment of drones outfitted with increasingly sophisticated sensors drives the demand even higher for reliable bandwidth. When three submarine cables between Egypt and Italy were cut in December 2008, U.S. drone flights in Iraq decreased from hundreds to tens a day.[82]

The U.S. military is also keeping an eye on the PEACE cable's planned expansion to Seychelles, almost 1,000 miles off the coast of Africa. Seychelles stands to benefit from gaining a second submarine connection, increasing its resiliency to disruptions. But the island nation also hosts U.S. forces, including drone operations that fly into Somalia. Ensuring that U.S. government communications do not pass through Chinese-built or -operated systems could become more difficult after the PEACE cable lands.

The PEACE cable connects China's present and future military capabilities in other ways. The cable's main investor, Hengtong Group, has won praise from the Chinese state for "military-civil fusion," the term of art for companies whose work benefits China's military. The company has captured a quarter of China's market for fiber-optic cables and has formal research partnerships with the Chinese PLA. The chief operating officer of the PEACE cable is a former Hengtong employee.

The PEACE cable has grown since being announced. In 2018, Orange, France's largest carrier, agreed to land the cable in Marseilles via the Suez Canal. The cable was renamed the Pakistan and East Africa Connecting Europe cable system, preserving the precious acronym. Orange is state-owned, but its participation does not imply naivete. The landing could provide France with monitoring opportunities. "The French are really saying, 'Sure, you can park that cable right here. We'll watch that for you,'" an industry expert told me.[83]

Taken together, these projects hint at a new map that is emerging. With the SAIL cable, China gained a route between South America and Africa. With the PEACE cable, it gains routes between Asia, Africa, and Europe. China has also explored opportunities to connect South America and Asia. Collectively, these routes outline a China-centric global network that did not exist a decade ago.

There are limitations to these new routes. Like all international cables, they will remain vulnerable to foreign interference as they pass through international waters. They are not contiguous, and unlike the British "All-Red Routes," China will not own the foreign territory on which these systems land. But many of these new connections land in countries in which China's growing commercial activities, and hefty loan portfolio, could insulate it from scrutiny.

In this underseas contest, China is not yet at par with foreign companies. In 2019, Hengtong acquired Huawei Marine, bringing the company further under Chinese control. The rebranded company, HMN Technologies, has less than 10 percent of the submarine cable market, a rising but still distant fourth place to its American, European, and Japanese competitors.[84] Hengtong still relies on Global Marine to test, install, and repair some systems. Its dependency is less a matter of acquiring ships than mastering the skills required to successfully deliver these complex projects on its own.

Despite these limitations, China's rapid rise is striking. In just over a decade, it has graduated from depending upon foreign firms to controlling the fourth major submarine cable company in the world. It has graduated from purchasing cables to producing them domestically. Hengtong's next objective is easy to guess: becoming self-sufficient in installing and repairing cables would provide the Chinese champion end-to-end control over the submarine cable process. From a strategic perspective, the ability to install and repair cables is just as important as producing and owning them.

Hengtong barely hides its nationalist mission. A press release available only on the Chinese-language version of its website declares: "Hengtong Marine had the courage to break the industrial monopoly held by international submarine cable giants, to develop its own submarine fiber optic cables, to promote the development of global informatization, to provide powerful support for the modernization of our country's national defense, to march onto the international market, to construct a high-end international submarine cable, and to achieve 'global quality from China.'"[85]

The key to Britain's dominance of global telegraph networks was not only ownership of cables but unrivalled technical expertise. In the late 1890s, Britain owned twenty-four of the world's thirty cable-repair ships.[86] When World War I erupted, the British were better prepared than anyone to maintain communications among their forces while monitoring and disrupting enemy communications. British ships moved quickly to cut enemy lines at the war's outset. For some German officials, the guns of August were followed by a deadly silence.[87]

## THE NEW PERIPHERY

China's existing network periphery, the places where it connects with the global internet, is overwhelmingly beyond its borders and concentrated in countries where its political relations are fraying.[88] Out of commercial and strategic necessity, Chinese companies are looking to emerging markets in Asia, Africa, and Latin America for growth. They are building a new network periphery, one that uses Chinese technology in countries where China has greater influence.

As they venture into new markets abroad, Chinese cloud providers face fierce competition. Amazon pioneered the first cloud offerings in 2006 and has invested heavily in its cloud business. Every day during 2016, it was adding enough server capacity to support the storage and computing needs of a Fortune 500 company.[89] In 2020, Amazon controlled nearly a third of the global market for cloud services, according to Canalys, a research firm, and was followed by Microsoft and Google, respectively. Collectively, these top three cloud providers, all U.S. companies, control more than half the global market.[90]

Alibaba is a cloud giant within China but an infant outside it. It launched Alibaba Cloud, also known as Aliyun or AliCloud, in 2009 and won nearly half of China's market by 2020. Its international service, launched five years later, offers fewer capabilities and has been much slower to win customers. In 2019, Alibaba Cloud earned only 10

percent of its revenue outside China and, unlike the largest U.S. providers, only became profitable at the end of 2020.[91] China's domestic
market is so big, however, that Alibaba is the world's fourth-largest
cloud provider, winning almost 6 percent of the global market.[92]

Cleverly, Alibaba is positioning itself as a bridge into China, turning the barriers that foreign firms face to its advantage. Even in its
most magnanimous interactions, China's Great Firewall slows traffic
down. Data packets are often lost en route, which can wreak havoc on
otherwise efficient systems. Alibaba offers itself up as an experienced
navigator of these barriers, a guide for everyone stuck on the outside.
Its services are best for those connecting near China's borders, outper-
forming the competition when linking mainland China and Singapore or mainland China and Hong Kong, according to the U.S. firm
ThousandEyes.[93]

AliCloud is even more attractive to Chinese firms going global
than Western firms trying to get into China. Alibaba has partnership agreements with the Big Three that include cooperation on cloud
computing. It has positioned itself as the preferred provider for the
Chinese state, winning 105 government contracts between 2016 and
2019.[94] Chinese state-owned enterprises provide a natural path for
expansion. Many already have overseas operations, and they would
naturally prefer to have access to the same data and services. In 2020,
Alibaba announced it would invest $28 billion into its cloud division
over three years.[95]

But Alibaba is not China's only rising cloud provider. Weeks later,
Tencent one-upped Alibaba's announcement with a pledge to invest
$70 billion in cloud computing, AI, and other priorities over five
years.[96] As the world's largest gaming company and developer of the
popular app WeChat, Tencent has positioned itself as a provider of AI
cloud applications such as image recognition, natural language recognition, and machine learning. As of early 2021, Tencent was operating
twenty data centers outside of China and planning to open another six
to ten foreign locations by the end of the year.[97]

Plenty of others are competing for a piece of the action. In November 2020, China Telecom announced that it would make cloud computing its "main business in the future."[98] Baidu aims to deploy five million "intelligent cloud servers" by 2030.[99] Kingsoft controlled 5.4 percent of the Chinese market in 2019 and company documents note, "We will focus on 'Belt and Road' countries, where the cloud markets are less saturated and present more attractive opportunities."[100] While each company has its own value proposition, all face common challenges in scaling globally.

Huawei claims to have provided cloud services in more than 140 countries, including more than 330 projects for governments.[101] Public announcements, however, suggest that closer to forty countries were using these services as of early 2021.[102] While some cases may not have been publicly announced, it is also possible that many of those "governments" are subnational entities within China. But it is still a significant amount of foreign activity, and an area that Huawei aims to grow. After U.S. sanctions limited its access to semiconductors, Huawei made the strategic decision to double down on cloud computing.[103] "It is our goal to make it as convenient for customers to use Huawei's cloud services as it is to use electricity," Ren Zhengfei told his employees in 2020.[104] The pandemic provided a boost, accelerating global adoption of cloud services by one to the three years and growing Huawei's cloud revenue by 168 percent during 2020, according to Ken Hu, the company's rotating chairman.[105]

The success of Huawei's government cloud services in developing markets is striking when compared to the scrutiny its 5G hardware has received in developed markets. In the latter, many governments debated whether Huawei could be safely limited to the periphery of national networks and ultimately decided to restrict its equipment altogether. In the former, Huawei is providing some of the most sensitive government functions. Its cloud services touch everything from government communications to social security and health records, budgets, and even electronic elections.[106] As Huawei gets squeezed out of advanced economies, it is burrowing deep not merely into developing markets but literally into their governments.

The global data center boom is just beginning, as James Hamilton, vice president and distinguished engineer on the Amazon Web Services team, explains.[107] Netflix has one of the world's largest content delivery networks, which includes about 1,000 locations globally, providing a rough barometer for the number of "regions" that each global cloud provider will ultimately need to cover. Each of those "regions," however, will need anywhere from three to tens of data centers in order to be sufficiently protected against power outages, natural disasters, and other risks. Depending on the number of global providers, the result could be anywhere from 10,000 to 100,000 data centers worldwide.

That map would look very different than it does today. Globally, in mid-2020, there were approximately 540 hyperscale data centers, each of which houses at least 5,000 servers across 10,000 square feet, according to Synergy Research Group. The United States was home to 38 percent of these centers. The United Kingdom, Germany, Japan, and Australia were home to a combined 21 percent. China was home to 9 percent.[108] Several factors are pulling data centers into new locations, including rising demand in emerging markets, calls for storing data locally, and technology that benefits from processing data closer to the user. Hyperscale facilities are already being augmented with smaller, more diffuse data centers that are likely to multiply in the coming years.

China's cloud ambitions in advanced markets face fierce competition and security concerns. Alibaba Cloud has made small steps into the United States and Europe using co-location providers but struggles to compete against U.S. cloud giants. After choosing a cloud provider, most customers stick with that provider to avoid the hassle of transitioning into a new system. Even if Chinese companies offer lower pricing, it is hard to see why foreign customers would incur those transition costs to choose a foreign provider that offers less functionality.

Rising concerns over Chinese technology and data security add another hurdle. China's far-reaching cybersecurity laws put foreign data at risk. "No information contained on any server located within China will be exempted . . . No communication from or to China will be exempted. There will be no secrets. No VPNs. No private or encrypted messages. No anonymous online accounts. No trade secrets. No confidential data. Any and all data will be available and open to the Chinese government," explains Steve Dickinson, an expert on Chinese law.[109]

Addressing these concerns will require companies to provide customers with more control over their data and much greater transparency. Alibaba chose Singapore as the headquarters for its international cloud services unit, and the company's executives claim it follows Singapore's data laws.[110] But Alibaba also notes that its customers cannot choose the path their data follows, including what jurisdictions it passes through, and cannot obtain documentation showing the path their data takes.[111]

Chinese cloud providers also face regulatory hurdles at home that have limited their ability to serve the financial sector, an important source of revenue and opportunities to hone their capabilities. As Kevin Xu, author of *Interconnected*, a newsletter on Chinese technology, explains, "With banking and securities customers being off limit, Chinese cloud vendors won't have the chance to build cloud-native products for two of the most demanding use cases in the industry."[112]

Given these challenges, Chinese providers have set their sights on emerging markets in Asia, Africa, and Latin America. As of 2020, they had barely made a dent in these markets, according to International Data Corporation, a market research and advisory firm.[113] Alibaba had captured a mere 0.3 percent of the Asia-Pacific market for public cloud services, excluding Japan and China. Huawei led the way among Chinese firms in Latin America as well as the Middle East and Africa, winning 0.9 and 0.7 percent of those markets, respectively. But

Huawei's year-on-year growth in those markets was 155 percent and 125 percent, respectively, hinting at bigger things to come.

For China, the global cloud competition is fiercest closest to home, in Southeast Asia, which has an internet economy that is expected to triple in value by 2025, hitting $300 billion.[114] Positioning itself for that prize, in 2021 Alibaba Cloud announced a $1 billion commitment to train 100,000 developers and support 100,000 start-ups in the region over three years. Singapore is the region's incumbent hub, offering a business-friendly environment and opportunities to connect with twenty-seven cables landing on its shores.[115] All China's major cloud providers have operations in Singapore, viewing the city-state as a regional launching pad. But space in Singapore is already at a premium, making it one of the most expensive hubs in the world.[116]

There is more room for growth across the Singapore Strait, where Jakarta, Indonesia's capital, is emerging as an alternative hub. In 2018, Alibaba was the first global cloud provider to open a local data center in Indonesia, and it opened a second center the following year. Google followed suit in 2020. Both providers have used co-location, tapping into existing data centers rather than building stand-alone facilities. Tencent plans to open two data centers in Indonesia by the end of 2021, Microsoft is standing up new operations, and Amazon has announced plans to launch services by 2022, as well.[117]

India, once a promising market, is becoming a major question mark for Chinese companies. In June 2020, Chinese and Indian troops clashed over contested territory in the Himalayas, bringing relations between the two nations to their lowest point in decades. New Delhi subsequently banned more than 100 Chinese apps, including TikTok, which had an estimated 125 million users in India. But India's market is far from closed to China, as chapter 7 explains in greater detail, and it remains highly dependent on Chinese hardware. In 2019, India imported nearly two-thirds of its equipment for data centers from China and Hong Kong.[118]

In Africa, China's global cloud footprint could follow its state-owned enterprises. The continent is home to about 17 percent of the world's population but less than 1 percent of worldwide data center capacity. In early 2020, the city of London had about four times as much data center capacity as did all of sub-Saharan Africa.[119] "Africa is the last frontier for sustainable double-digit growth," says John Melick, former chairman of the Djibouti Data Center.[120]

For Alibaba Cloud, however, Africa remains largely uncharted territory. As of mid-2021, China's largest cloud provider did not yet have a dedicated data center in Africa, which is striking given the heavy involvement of Chinese companies across the continent. Whale Cloud, an Alibaba subsidiary, is providing cloud services in South Africa.[121] The company was previously part of ZTE, and known as ZTEsoft, before Alibaba acquired and rebranded it.

Africa's biggest customers in recent years have been governments. Huawei is providing cloud services for at least fifteen African governments and the African Union, according to CSIS research, and has ambitions to provide public cloud services across the continent. It is leasing capacity at a data center in Johannesburg, South Africa, the continent's incumbent hub, and plans to set up additional centers in Kenya and Nigeria, which have the next greatest concentrations of international firms.[122]

As Africa develops, U.S. cloud companies are in a comparatively strong position to expand. Microsoft and Amazon's investments in South Africa overshadow Huawei's.[123] New submarine cables are improving the continent's access to international bandwidth.[124] Google is building Equiano, a cable that stretches from Portugal to South Africa, with a branch connecting Nigeria.[125] Facebook is supporting 2Africa, a cable that will connect sixteen countries on the continent and includes China Mobile among its partners.[126] In contrast to China's government-to-government approach, the private sector has largely driven these efforts.

The third frontier is Latin America. The region, which stretches from Mexico through Chile, has a combined population of 650 million, with two-thirds having internet access. The United States is Latin America's incumbent hub, even though it is not technically part of the region. In the shadow of the United States, however, Chinese companies have political angles of attack.

In Brazil, the region's next most central node, and elsewhere, Chinese companies are positioning themselves as alternatives to the United States. An overwhelming amount of Brazil's traffic, including 84 percent of paths from its networks to the world's top 100 websites, traverses the United States.[127] Amazon, Google, and Microsoft have all established data centers in Brazil. At the same time, Brazilian officials have tried to diversify the country's connections, as their interest in the SACS, SAIL, and EllaLink cables indicates.

Huawei is trying to capitalize on that interest and longer-standing regional grievances, racing ahead of Alibaba to build its own data centers in Mexico, Chile, and Brazil. The strategy, Huawei's regional president explained, is "to form a giant triangle of improved coverage and better connectivity in Latin America."[128] Alibaba has taken a more cautious approach by forming local partnerships that resell its cloud services in Mexico and Brazil. As of mid-2021, Alibaba had not opened a data center in the region.[129]

Huawei is spinning U.S. criticism as part of its sales pitch. "Latin America has been caught in many traps, like the middle income trap, the widening gap between the rich and the poor, and the financial crisis," Ren Zhengfei told journalists from the region in December 2019. "All of these were actually caused by the U.S.'s Monroe Doctrine. The U.S. wanted to control Latin America and treated the region like its backyard, which caused all this. China is investing in Latin America now, but the region still maintains its sovereignty, and by investing in Latin America, China is actually building a ladder to help them out of these traps."[130]

Chile, which calls itself the country of poets, may seem an unlikely hub for storing zeros and ones, but it has won the attention of the world's largest cloud providers. The country's population is less than a tenth of Brazil's, but it offers a 4,000-mile coastline with a growing number of submarine cables landing on its shores, a comfortable climate for operating energy-intensive data centers, and favorable tax incentives.

In 2015, Google became the first major player to launch a data center in Chile, which it expanded three years later. The facility uses a solar array in the Atacama Desert to provide 100 percent renewable energy. In 2019, Google completed a new submarine cable that stretches 10,500 kilometers from Valparaíso, Chile, to Los Angeles, California, and announced a second data center. According to the Chilean government, fifteen data centers were being expanded or newly built in 2019.[131] Alibaba is reportedly considering joining that list.[132]

Chile could become a more critical node in China's expanding network. In 2019, Huawei Marine completed a 1,780-mile submarine cable along Chile's southern coast, which it proudly advertises as the "southernmost submarine cable in the world."[133] Several months later, Huawei opened a data center in Paine, near the capital of Santiago, and announced plans to invest $100 million in the country. While the data center is co-located instead of being independent like Google's facilities, these steps indicate bigger ambitions.

Both projects were intended to position Huawei for its largest international connection yet: South America's first direct connection to Asia. The Chilean government wanted a submarine cable to Asia, and naturally, Huawei Marine wanted to build it. But in July 2020, the Chilean government selected Japan's proposal for the cable, which is intended to run from Chile to Australia and New Zealand, stopping short of China.[134] Chile has not ruled out having a second cable, although it would be hard to justify from a purely commercial perspective. Like Brazil and other emerging hubs, however, Chile could benefit from stoking competition in related areas. Undeterred, Huawei announced in September 2020 that it was opening a second data center.[135]

As China charts a new network periphery, the southern tip of South America may remain enticing. As Ren explained to a journalist from neighboring Argentina, "Your country is at the end of the world and is geographically secure. Even if there is a great war in the rest of the world, Argentina will be safe and sound."[136] A student of history, Ren is surely familiar with the race to lay the world's first undersea cables, which began as a commercial competition, intensified as national security concerns grew, and ultimately became part of the battlefield.

## DEFENDING THE MAP

The telegraph race holds lessons for the United States as well. As new routes fanned out across the globe during the decades before World War I, it was not uncommon for countries to impose fees on foreign operators for access to their territory. Britain adopted a different strategy and lowered fees and other barriers to attract more foreign connections. Openness was critical in turning London into the central hub for international communications and finance that it remains today.

Having embraced a similar strategy for decades, the United States is adopting a more defensive posture, applying greater scrutiny to its domestic networks, internet exchanges, and submarine cables. The desire for greater protection is only natural given China's expanding activities and track record of cyberattacks, espionage, and cooperation between Chinese companies and the PLA. But the United States must consider how each decision could impact its position within global networks. The consequences are not as straightforward as they might initially appear.

Nearly two decades after granting them licenses, the FCC began showing China Telecom and China Unicom the door. In 2019, the agency rejected China Mobile's application for a license to carry calls between the United States and foreign countries, which it had filed in 2011. "The underlying foundation of trust that is needed for a mitigation agreement to adequately address national security and law enforcement concerns is not present,"[137] the commissioners concluded in a unanimous decision, which was the FCC's first denial of an application on national security and law enforcement grounds.[138]

It was the end of an eight-year ordeal for China Mobile, but for China Telecom and China Unicom, a new battle was just beginning. In April 2020, the FCC asked four Chinese carriers, including China Telecom and China Unicom, "to demonstrate that they are not subject to the influence and control of the Chinese government."[139] As Kate O'Keeffe of the *Wall Street Journal* pointed out, the FCC was essentially asking the state-owned companies to prove that they were not state-owned.[140] In November, Trump issued an executive order banning U.S. investment in companies linked to China's PLA, including China Telecom and China Unicom.[141] In the following months, the FCC began the process of revoking China Telecom and China Unicom's licenses.[142]

The United States is also reassessing its subsea connections. In June 2020, the U.S. government partially blocked the activation of the Pacific Light Cable Network, the first direct link between Los Angeles and Hong Kong. The cable's sections between Los Angeles, the Philippines, and Taiwan were activated, but the section extending to Hong Kong was ordered to remain dark. U.S. officials concluded that the cable's landing in Hong Kong and its majority ownership by Dr. Peng Telecom, a Chinese company, presented a risk that could not be overcome. Weeks later, China's national security law effectively took Hong Kong off the map, and companies planning subsea routes are already looking elsewhere in the region.[143]

But if the United States severs or blocks too many connections, global networks may adapt in ways that do not favor American interests. U.S. companies could build cables with alternative landing points and move more of their computing power overseas. Canada and Mexico could position themselves as alternative gateways. Tijuana, for example, could become a hub on the West Coast. Several U.S. carriers already have connections running through the area and could provide transit into the United States. The United States could lose business as well as access for monitoring projects.

Kicking Chinese companies out of U.S. internet exchange points presents similar trade-offs. As of 2021, China's Big Three had set up a total of sixty-two points of presence in the United States, including in Los Angeles, Seattle, New York, and other major cities.[144] Companies face low marginal costs for making new connections where they are already present, and so U.S. carriers have been happy to exchange traffic with Chinese carriers in their own backyard. The downside is that more connections between U.S. and Chinese carriers mean more opportunities for routing errors to propagate. If forced to connect with Chinese carriers overseas, fewer U.S. carriers would make the effort.

Demchak and Shavitt, the researchers who believe China Telecom's suspicious routing behavior is no accident, have called for "Access Reciprocity."[145] They point to a striking imbalance: China bars foreign companies from having points of presence within its network, while Chinese companies have access to U.S. networks. They propose establishing a fairer balance. If points of presence were proportionate to customer populations, for example, U.S. companies should have more points of presence in China to serve its larger population base. If China refuses the demand for reciprocal access, they call for the United States, and potentially allied countries, to block traffic to and from Chinese points of presence.

Other experts caution that gaining access for U.S. companies in China would be commercially beneficial but would not address the underlying risks that U.S. networks face. Creating more traffic handoff points on Chinese territory could raise the risk of Chinese authorities spying on U.S. firms. More fundamentally, as long as U.S. networks remain open to operators that do not take proper precautions—whether foreign or American—they remain vulnerable to routing errors and hijacks. In June 2019, for example, a Swiss company's routing mistake sent traffic intended for some of Europe's largest mobile networks, including traffic from the United States, through China Telecom's network.[146]

Focusing on reciprocity also overlooks the disproportionate advantages that flow to the United States through its open networks. Chinese points of presence on U.S. territory increase the global share of internet traffic that flows through the United States. That wave of data brings commercial benefits, and it is also a gift to U.S. intelligence agencies that monitor foreign communications. Exactly how big this gift is, and what is done to "unwrap" it, is classified, of course. But public statements and declassified documents suggest that U.S. centrality in global data flows provides vital information.[147]

Inadvertently, an allied approach to enforcing reciprocity might make some traffic less secure when it leaves the United States. Unless a complete decoupling of data flows were to occur, traffic would still need to travel between allied and Chinese networks. Instead of those exchanges happening on allied territory, they would occur in foreign countries with lower security standards, making allied data more vulnerable.[148] Perversely, those foreign countries, non-allies by definition, would gain commercially and strategically by attracting redirected data flows.

Redrawing the map of the internet would produce other unintended consequences. Less efficiency would mean higher costs for U.S. companies and consumers, and basic assumptions about routing would become invalid. That could make abnormal routing behavior even more difficult to detect. Inspecting anomalies would become even more burdensome, as Madory and other analysts would have to figure out whether a suboptimal route was the best option given these restrictions.

Rather than limit data flows to trusted partners, the United States could develop technologies that do not rely on trust and encourage wider adoption of best practices. Quantum-encryption techniques, for example, promise to increase security in even the riskiest environments. Best practices such as the Internet Society's Mutually Agreed

Norms for Routing Security, or MANRS, can help prevent routing incidents and respond to them faster.[149] "A real solution," advises the Internet Society, "lies not in controlling the interconnections, but ensuring that the Internet routing protocol, BGP, operates in a secure manner."[150]

Like wearing a mask to prevent the spread of a virus, MANRS benefits people around the user rather than the user itself. Universal participation would make everyone better off. By walking around without a mask, however, China Telecom risks getting kicked out of others' networks. Belatedly, China Telecom officially joined MANRS in December 2020, the same day that the FCC announced its license would be terminated. Somewhat ironically, the communications director of China Telecom's Americas subsidiary publicly thanked Madory on Twitter for "championing this issue over the years."[151]

The December 2015 incident and the delay in addressing it, as Madory points out, were not China Telecom's responsibilities alone. He had spent several months trying to convince Verizon to take action. While Verizon was slow to act, Madory managed to convince other major providers to deploy filters that blocked Verizon routes being carried by China Telecom. Eventually, the routing error was fixed around April 2018. The original incident lasted less than a minute, but its consequences persisted for two and a half years.[152] As of mid-2021, Verizon had not yet joined MANRS. Nor had China Unicom or China Mobile.[153]

Since its invention, the global internet's openness has carried great rewards but also significant risks. China's activities have sparked a necessary recalibration and greater scrutiny of these risks, particularly within U.S. networks. But battening the hatches and hunkering down with friends is not a viable long-term strategy. It would be a mistake for the United States to take significant steps toward emulating Beijing's fortress-style approach.

After all, China is drawing a new map of the global internet because the current version overwhelmingly favors the United States and its allies. The dominance of U.S. cloud providers stems from first-mover advantages but also domestic investments in physical infrastructure and openness to foreign connections. Chinese cloud providers are giants at home, but they remain infants beyond their borders. As China strives to turn its national champions into true global champions, the stage is set for an intensifying competition in third markets.

Winning will require the United States to balance domestic security measures with a greater emphasis on commercial offense abroad. It must speak to the needs and aspirations of the half of the world that has yet to come online. Working with partners and allies, it must think creatively about how to adjust the risk-reward calculus that has kept their companies out of these markets. A more intrepid approach will include building data centers and laying subsea cables to connect emerging economies. It may also include harnessing new technologies and, quite literally, reaching for the stars.

# CHAPTER SIX

# THE COMMANDING HEIGHTS

"Ten!" thundered Commander Yin Xiangyuan, beginning the final countdown at Xichang Satellite Launch Center at 9:43 a.m. on June 23, 2020. If he and his colleagues in mission control were nervous, only their eyes showed it. To prevent the spread of COVID-19, their faces were covered with surgical masks. Everyone watched the launch vehicle, a white rocket towering twenty stories above the launch pad. As pressure built inside it, white smoke drifted out its trunk and into the morning air.[1]

From top to bottom, the launch vehicle was a monument to Chinese nationalism. Near the top, a red Chinese flag was painted on the side of its nose cone. Its base was a Long March 3B rocket, named after the strategic retreat by Chinese Communist forces that began in 1934 and carried Mao Zedong to power. Most important was the payload: the final piece of China's third-generation Beidou global navigation satellite system, an alternative to the U.S. GPS system.

Beidou is the child of a marriage between China's scientific and military communities, and plenty of family members were there to watch. The Chinese government usually releases footage of its satellite launches only after they are successful, but in a rare change of policy, this launch was broadcasting live, so the world could see China join the elite ranks of the leading space powers. Only the United States, the European Union, and Russia had built truly global navigation satellite systems.

Developed during the Cold War to position nuclear weapons, global navigation satellites are critical for military operations, helping forces coordinate their movements and guiding munitions to targets. They are used even more heavily beyond the battlefield, with 6.4 billion receivers installed in cell phones, cars, and other consumer applications worldwide.[2] Using ultraprecise atomic clocks, these systems provide timing for everything from consumer ATMs to stock exchanges to mobile networks. They keep the world running.[3]

Having launched the first Beidou satellite in 2000, China's long march toward global positioning independence was now nearing the finish line.[4] But success was not guaranteed, and China's high-altitude ambitions had come crashing down before. In 1996, the Long March 3B rocket's maiden flight ended in tragedy after a control system error sent the rocket and the U.S. satellite it was carrying into a nearby town. Officially, six people died and fifty-seven people were injured. But, according to later testimonials, the deaths of local villagers could have run into the hundreds, making it possibly the worst launch disaster in history.[5]

The rocket was improved in subsequent years, but its recent track record is far from flawless. In April 2020, a Long March 3B rocket failed from the Xichang launch site, raining debris on Guam.[6] The launch to complete the Beidou system, originally scheduled for early June, was postponed because of issues with the rocket's engine.[7]

"Ignition. Lift off!" mission control said, and the rocket began its ascent. The China Central Television broadcast followed the rocket and cut to a split screen. On the left, a computer-generated animation displayed the rocket's coordinates, height, and speed. On the right, a camera on the rocket's midsection provided a live feed of the engines and the shrinking ground below. Every satellite launch is carefully choreographed, but this one was made for TV.

The launch vehicle's final act came twenty-six minutes into the flight, when the satellite detached. As the rocket's upper stage drifted into space, it kept the camera trained on the satellite, a boxy structure floating 140 miles above blue oceans. Two arms unfolded like accordions on either side of the satellite. They sparkled when fully extended, the sunlight bouncing off their solar panels.

An orderly wave of applause briefly filled mission control. No one yelled. No one whistled. No one clapped much louder or longer than anyone else. "[The] satellite has successfully entered its predetermined orbit," Zhang Xueyu, the launch center's director, announced matter-of-factly from a podium. Above him was a large screen with a short message in gold calligraphy on a red background: "Congratulations . . . the 55th satellite of the Beidou satellite navigation system was a complete success."

The sober tone was telling. China had joined one of the world's most elite clubs, yet Chinese officials were already looking to the next milestone. Even before the third-generation Beidou system was fully in place, they had already announced plans to upgrade it by 2035. Chinese officials view the system as constantly evolving and never complete.

If China wants to catch up with the United States in space, it cannot slow down. While China's state-owned enterprises labored on the Beidou system—technology that the United States basically achieved in the 1990s—U.S. companies have been pioneering more innovative technologies. Just a week after China completed its Beidou system, Elon Musk's SpaceX launched a third-generation GPS satellite from Cape Canaveral, Florida, for the U.S. Air Force.

Once dismissed as a fantasy, SpaceX now handles about two-thirds of NASA launches, having dramatically cut costs with reusable rocket components.[8] NASA spends about $152 million for each launch, which SpaceX has cut to $62 million. Musk is confident the company can realize even more savings in the future, even speculating that launch costs could plummet to $2 million.[9] Musk, who has a talent for making headlines, also knows how to appeal to U.S. bureaucrats. He offered that projection at the first-ever U.S. Air Force Space Pitch Day.

SpaceX is also working to deliver a new satellite constellation that sounds like science fiction and could upend global communications. It is one of several companies planning to launch massive constellations of low earth orbit, or LEO, satellites that will provide global broadband. If these efforts succeed, some of the world's most remote places could come online.

Hanging in the balance are massive amounts of data, a prize that could pit Western companies against Chinese incumbents in developing markets. Almost all the biggest tech companies, from Amazon to Facebook to Google, are looking to the sky. "Whoever gets the most data wins," Masayoshi Son, CEO of Softbank and a major investor in OneWeb, another satellite broadband provider, said in 2017.[10]

In the coming years, the competition to provide satellite internet will unfold on three levels. In space, companies are jockeying for finite real estate in Earth's orbit. The battle over spectrum, the frequency bands that carry communications, is even fiercer. Ultimately, the competition returns to the ground, where states retain the power to grant "landing rights" to satellite service providers.

China is vulnerable across all three levels, but it will not back down. Space is central to its military strategy and, increasingly, its commercial ambitions. As China's top military general, Xu Qiliang, explained in 2009, "The 21st century is the century of informatization, as well as the century of aerospace. The aerospace and information ages have already simultaneously arrived, and the information and aerospace fields have become the new commanding heights of international strategic competition."[11]

The term "commanding heights" is apt for both political and military reasons. It harkens back to Marxist thought and was used by Vladimir Lenin to argue that the state must control steel and coal production, the railways, banking, and other critical sectors. In other words, these are activities that are too important for the state to leave to the invisible hand of the market. As the CCP steers China's economy further into the twenty-first century, it plans to keep a tight grip on the aerospace sector.

But the term also rings true as a military metaphor. The evolution of warfare can be summarized as a quest for progressively higher ground. In ancient times, generals learned to position their forces on hills for strategic advantage. The advent of air power elevated the battlefield again. As Xu explained, "If you control the sky, you control the ground, the oceans, and the electromagnetic domain, thus seizing the strategic initiative."[12] Both the U.S. military and China's PLA agree: space is the ultimate high ground.[13]

## "AN UNFORGETTABLE HUMILIATION"

China is a latecomer to space, but with its Beidou Navigation Satellite System, it has proven that it can move quickly when its military and commercial stars align. Beidou, named after the Chinese term for the Big Dipper, was formally started in 1994. Over the next quarter-century, Chinese engineers approached the challenge of building a global satellite navigation constellation in three phases. At each step, foreign threats pushed them forward.

Cleverly, China has cast the Beidou program as a purely benign public good and an example of its return to the forefront of innovation. In 2019, China even sponsored an exhibit at the Vienna International Center in Austria. "From the Compass to BeiDou," on display in the months leading up to an annual U.N. conference on satellites, highlighted the country's contributions to navigation and timing systems. "We'd like to show the importance of navigation in the development of the society to enhance people's understanding," the deputy director of China's satellite navigation office said at the exhibit's opening.[14]

But China's Beidou system, like its American counterpart, has military roots. In 1970, China launched its first satellite, the Dong

Fang Hong-1, or "The East is Red-1," named for the iconic Maoist revolutionary anthem. The satellite weighed more than the first satellites launched by the Soviet Union, the United States, France, and Japan—combined. It had only basic functionality and was designed to collect telemetry data and transmit it back to Earth.[15] But the satellite lifted China's national ambitions and, during its brief twenty-eight-day life, broadcast its namesake song on loop.[16]

China's investment in space and in other strategic technologies gained momentum in March 1986, when four of its top strategic weapons scientists wrote to Deng Xiaoping.[17] The letter stressed that technological development was inherently tied to the international struggle for power, warning that if China remained aloof, it would fall behind.[18] Deng took only two days to decide. "Action must be taken on this matter immediately; it cannot be put off," he wrote on a copy of the report.

Two events during the 1990s starkly highlighted U.S. power in space and China's vulnerability. The first Gulf War provided a spectacular demonstration of GPS on the battlefield.[19] Chinese military officials watched the United States use its space capabilities for targeting, intelligence gathering, and communications on the battlefield.[20] "The events of this war show that electronic warfare has already become the primary means of combat in modern joint campaigns," a Chinese military journal later observed. "The official debut of space [as a] battlefield is simply a matter of time."[21]

China's vulnerability became even clearer during the Taiwan Strait crisis in 1996. The crisis began the year before, when Taiwan's president, Lee Teng-hui, aided by the U.S. Congress, defied Chinese pressure and delivered a speech at Cornell University. As Lee's reelection was approaching, China announced large-scale military exercises and fired three missiles into the East China Sea, just over ten miles from a Taiwanese military base.

The first missile hit its intended location, but China's military lost the second and third. Years later, a retired Chinese colonel attributed the failure to the United States' cutting off GPS coverage. "It was a great shame for the PLA . . . an unforgettable humiliation. That's how we made up our mind to develop our own global [satellite] navigation and positioning system, no matter how huge the cost," he told the *South China Morning Post* in 2009. "Beidou is a must for us. We learned it the hard way."[22]

To improve its satellite capabilities, China was already looking to the United States. Beijing enlisted the help of U.S. companies, including Loral Space and Communications and Hughes Electronics Corporation, to troubleshoot a series of recent launch failures. Their recommendations improved the reliability of China's Long March rockets, according to a Congressional report issued in 1999.[23] The U.S. government fined the companies, and Congress tightened restrictions on satellite exports to China. But China had already acquired key pieces of the satellite puzzle, including design and guidance system improvements.

China launched its first Beidou satellite in 2000, just as Chinese military officials began describing space as vital for waging war in all other domains.[24] Of course, China continued to insist that the Beidou program, and its other activities in space, was peaceful. Upon joining the European Union's project to build Galileo, a global navigation satellite system announced in 2003, the Chinese Foreign Ministry declared, "China is willing to actively participate in the development and future applications of the Galileo system in accordance with the principles of equality and mutual benefit."[25]

Galileo provided a shortcut for China to improve its Beidou system.[26] In its arrangement with the European Union, spelled out in twelve contracts that have not yet been made public, China was tasked with manufacturing and testing technologies related to signals interference, satellite positioning, and ground-based receivers, among other functions. Participation gave Chinese scientists better access to their European counterparts, and China was able to purchase and reverse-engineer atomic clocks, a vital component for navigation systems.

Meanwhile, China's $228 million contribution to the program was spent on Chinese companies, which retained ownership of the hardware and intellectual property.

China completed Beidou's first phase in 2007, successfully delivering its fourth satellite, the minimum number required for a functioning system. The system mainly covered Chinese territory, and its performance was largely experimental. But China had made a major leap. It now had the essential ingredients, and it was demonstrating that it could combine them correctly and deliver the final product into space.

From there, China raced toward global coverage. By the end of 2012, the Beidou system had sixteen satellites in orbit and opened for commercial use, serving China and neighboring countries in the Asia-Pacific.[27] In 2018, China added another eighteen satellites to achieve global coverage, launching more successful missions that year than any other country, a historic first for the Chinese space program.[28] "From now on, no matter where you go, BDS will always be with you," proclaimed a spokesman for the program.[29]

As it pushed toward completing the Beidou system, China was combining its space and cyber capabilities with an eye toward winning future wars. In late 2015, the PLA established the Strategic Support Force, a new organization charged with integrating space, cyber, and electronic warfare capabilities into military operations.[30] A single organization was now responsible for what Chinese military planners call "information support" and "information dominance," positioning the PLA to operate during a conflict while paralyzing enemy systems.[31] The following year, China released a white paper that announced its intention to complete a "stable and reliable space infrastructure" by 2021.[32]

China's Beidou system even outperforms GPS in some respects. It is more accurate than GPS in the Asia-Pacific region, although slightly less accurate globally.[33] Its satellites occupy fewer orbital planes, making maintenance easier, a benefit of having learned from the systems that came before it.[34] The system also allows users to send short text messages, and its larger footprint increases its availability. In 165 capital cities, Beidou satellites provide more extensive coverage than GPS does, according to an investigation by *Nikkei Asia*.[35]

The PLA has access to even more powerful Beidou services, which provide a location accuracy of ten centimeters, and has wasted no time in using them. In August 2020, it deployed rocket systems equipped with Beidou functionality to ground forces at its Eastern Theater Command, which oversees activities in the Taiwan Strait.[36] Chinese joint naval–air exercises in the Taiwan Strait the following month may have also tested the capabilities of Beidou-enabled military assets.[37] The humiliation of events a quarter century ago has not been forgotten.

## FOSTERING DEPENDENCY

As it has in other digital dimensions—wireless networks, connected devices, and undersea cables—China has gone from latecomer to leading provider of satellite services, especially for developing markets. It stands to benefit commercially, politically, and strategically. Its partners, meanwhile, risk becoming dependent on Beijing.

China's partners are eager to gain access to advanced navigation capabilities, making Beidou a lucrative bargaining tool. "The difference in accuracy can be critical in warfighting environments, making the 10-centimeter claim a very big deal for potential [Belt and Road Initiative] partners with military aspirations," explains Rob Miltersen, an analyst at the U.S. Air Force's China Aerospace Studies Institute.[38] Pakistan was the first to gain access to Beidou's military capabilities, while Saudi Arabia and Iran have both signed cooperation agreements.[39] In the future, Beijing could also offer Beidou access as a sweetener when selling arms.

China's satellite diplomacy is all the more intriguing because it does not have any military allies in the traditional sense of the word. Unlike Washington, which has a network of relationships that are formalized in treaties, Beijing has preferred to cultivate partnerships. China offers up impressive-sounding labels during state visits, ranging from the humdrum "partnership" to the grander "comprehensive strategic partner," with many other variations in between. By the end of 2016, China had twenty-four varieties of partnerships with seventy-eight countries, or almost half of the countries with which it had official diplomatic ties.[40] But these arrangements remain less formal. A willingness to share Beidou's restricted military services could signal deeper ties.

Ironically, the U.S. military occasionally benefits from the Beidou system as well. "My U-2 guys fly with a watch now that ties into GPS, but also Beidou and the Russian [GLONASS] system and the European [Galileo] system so that if somebody jams GPS, they still get the others," General James Holmes, then head of U.S. Air Combat Command, said in 2020, referring to the U-2 high-altitude reconnaissance aircraft.[41] Of course, the United States only has access to the civilian versions of the Chinese and Russian positioning systems. Garmin, a U.S. company, makes the watches, which are available to the public.

China wants more of the world to have Beidou on their wrists, in their pockets, and in their cars. Hundreds of millions of devices include Beidou functionality, from phones to farm equipment. Naturally, Beidou's usage is greatest in China, where more than 70 percent of cell phones are Beidou-compatible. There are 6.5 million vehicles using Beidou, which the state media proudly advertise as "the world's largest dynamic monitoring system for operating vehicles." Altogether, China's satellite navigation sector pulled in $64 billion in 2019.[42]

When China exports electronics, increasingly it is exporting the Beidou system. Leading Chinese mobile phone brands, including Huawei, Xiaomi, Oppo, and Vivo, include Beidou service by default. In 2020, the four brands sold 42 percent of all smartphones worldwide, with a reach extending into at least ninety countries and territories.[43]

DJI, which produces upwards of 80 percent of the world's commercial drones, equips its products with Beidou functionality.[44] Watches, fitness trackers, and other "wearables" are increasingly outfitted with satellite positioning, and Chinese manufacturers are strong in these areas as well. The market for satellite navigation devices is projected to grow to about $360 billion by 2029, when there will be nearly ten billion receivers installed worldwide.[45]

As they compete for a slice of that market, foreign suppliers are incorporating Beidou into their devices as well. Samsung has offered products supporting Beidou functionality since 2013, while Apple's iPhone began to do so in 2020.[46] The world's two largest auto manufacturers, Volkswagen and Toyota, are planning to include Beidou functionality in their vehicles. The cost of adding Beidou alongside other systems is marginal, and it is increasingly necessary for companies to compete within China and the region more broadly. The Asia-Pacific region, where Beidou's coverage is best, accounts for more than half of the global navigation satellite system market.[47]

Chinese automaker Geely is going a step further and plans to launch its own satellite constellation to provide data for autonomous vehicles. Given Geely's investments in several foreign car brands, including Volvo, Daimler, and Proton—a Malaysian manufacturer—its satellite efforts, if successful, could reach well beyond China. The company has produced two experimental satellites and is building a $326 million factory that aims to churn out five hundred smaller, LEO satellites a year by 2025. "With our feet on the ground, we should always keep an eye on the wider universe," says the company's founder and chairman, Li Shufu.[48]

Many people are unaware their devices can use Chinese navigation services. Beidou works alongside existing systems because China coordinated its deployment with the European Union, Russia, and the United States.[49] Having access to multiple navigation services can improve performance, while not coordinating could interfere with other systems. One thorn in the side of China's Beidou program is that many devices refer to all these services as GPS, the name of the U.S. system, by default. Chinese officials have proposed replacing the "GPS signal" label on devices with a more generic label: "Satellite navigation signal."[50] Having finally joined the global navigation club, China wants recognition.

The recognition that Beidou receives may not be what China had in mind. Some commentators have warned that China could use its network to track Beidou-enabled devices. Most devices, however, only have the ability to receive signals and cannot send them to the Beidou system. Some devices, particularly those with a search-and-rescue function, do include the ability to transmit signals to Beidou. That ability is openly advertised and used to justify a higher cost for the product.

China is unlikely to conceal functions in Beidou devices en masse. Most satellite navigation receivers cost less than six dollars.[51] Adding the ability to transmit signals is considerably more expensive, and someone would have to foot the bill. Using the send function also consumes energy, which would degrade the device's performance. It would cost even more to disguise this capability, which typically requires additional physical hardware. Doing all this in bulk would also virtually guarantee that someone would discover the hidden functionality.

There are much easier ways to obtain location data. The simplest method is to purchase it. Many users do not realize their location data is being recorded, packaged, and sold.[52] Others share it knowingly without fully understanding the risks. The rise of wearables creates more opportunities for collection and unintended consequences. In 2018, the U.S. military revised its technology policies after Strava, a fitness app, released a global heat map of user activity.[53] Nathan Ruser, a twenty-year-old college student at the time, was the first to point out that the map revealed the locations of undisclosed U.S. military bases.[54]

China also uses the Beidou network to strengthen scientific partnerships, deepen political ties, and market products. In 2018, China and the Arab League established a center in Tunisia to promote Beidou usage. "The center could serve as both a window to showcase the BDS, and a platform for promoting international exchanges and cooperation," said the director of China's Satellite Navigation Office. The center arranges joint research, testing activities, and workshops that highlight the benefits of Beidou and the Chinese products using it.[55] China provides scholarships to Arab students studying navigation systems, lifting their prospects as well as Beidou's.

The China-Arab States Beidou Cooperation Forum provides another stage for Chinese companies to sell their products. In addition to speeches and product exhibitions, these gatherings include "trainers" who demonstrate Beidou's newest applications for security, transportation, and agriculture.[56] In 2019, the forum released the results of a technical test conducted on the Beidou system, which used ground stations built by Chinese companies.[57] Unsurprisingly, it declared the system a resounding success.

The Beidou system's ground infrastructure receives less attention than its satellites do, but it has quietly expanded to every continent as well as the Arctic. China has built thirty global reference stations, which improve the system's precision. It is technically possible this ground infrastructure could be used for malicious activities as well, such as jamming enemy signals.[58] The United States has not allowed Beidou stations on its territory, nor has it allowed Russia's GLONASS stations.[59] But not all U.S. allies have been as cautious. Australia hosts two stations, while Canada and the United Kingdom each host one station.[60]

Beidou's terrestrial footprint overlaps even more strongly with China's Belt and Road Initiative. Brazil, Pakistan, Nigeria, Russia, and Sri Lanka all participate in the Belt and Road and host global reference stations. China has suggested that it wants to build a much larger network of smaller ground stations abroad, including potentially 1,000 in Southeast Asia, and has conducted extensive outreach to Thailand.[61] Officials have even called for building a "Belt and

Road Space Information Corridor" that integrates remote sensing, navigation, and communications satellites, an ambitious and amorphous goal they predict will take a decade to achieve.[62]

There is a strong logic to combining these capabilities along the Belt and Road. Chinese companies are busy building communications networks, pipelines, and power grids in foreign countries, and all these systems rely on precise timing. "This means that Beidou will play a role, not only for surveying and planning of key construction sites, but also for the basic operation of much of the infrastructure once it is completed," explains Dean Cheng, an expert on China's military and space capabilities.[63] Likewise, once countries look to China for these turnkey systems, they may find it tempting to return to Chinese vendors for related technology. Buy a 5G network from Huawei, for example, and there might be benefits to having a Chinese satellite system that integrates more easily with it.

The United States' experience with GPS suggests that China could gain immensely from wide adoption of Beidou. Since GPS was made available for commercial use in the 1980s, it has contributed $1.4 trillion to the U.S. private sector, according to a government-sponsored study.[64] The technology is so widely incorporated into daily life that losing access to GPS, the same study estimated, would cost the U.S. economy $1 billion a day. That toll could rise even higher, to $1.5 billion a day, if access were lost during the planting season for U.S. farmers. All this underscores just how much modern economies depend on satellite navigation systems.

The stakes are rising as China's Beidou system is being deployed. New technologies are emerging that rely heavily on precision timing and positioning. Beidou could eventually serve smart cities, autonomous vehicles, and advanced communications networks around the world. China stands to gain commercially, just as U.S. companies have benefitted from GPS. But as more critical infrastructure relies on Beidou, China could also gain coercive leverage over its partners. It could threaten to cut off access, or it could do so without warning at the outset of a conflict, reversing the roles from its experience during the 1996 Taiwan Strait crisis. Becoming independent from GPS was just the first step. Beijing wants the world to depend on Beidou.

## "THIS BOLD AND STRATEGIC STEP"

China is also carving out a niche as the go-to provider for developing countries that want their own communications satellites.[65] For about $250 million, only a fraction of which is required up front, countries can acquire their own communications satellite. China provides generous financing, often covering up to 85 percent of the cost through its Export-Import Bank and the China Development Bank. Satellite financing typically takes half a year or longer after the initial contract is signed, but China pays upon signing. Along with the satellite, China also provides ground stations, testing, training, launch, and operations support.

China's starter kit for countries with space ambitions has wide appeal—and widely ignored risks. Every leader gets to play the role of President John F. Kennedy, igniting citizens' imaginations as they reach for the stars, even if China is doing the heavy lifting. National pride is evident in even the satellites' names. Venezuela named its Chinese-made satellite "Simón Bolívar." Bolivia went with "Tupac Katari," named after an eighteenth-century indigenous leader. As of early 2021, at least nine countries have bought or are in the process of buying communications satellites from China, which is following in the footsteps of U.S. and European companies that have sold satellites for decades.[66]

China's most popular model is the DFH-4, a behemoth that weighs as much as an elephant and has solar panels spanning over a hundred feet.[67] It is geostationary, meaning the speed of its orbit matches the earth's rotation, so it appears to hover over one spot. To avoid export restrictions, it is manufactured without U.S. components.

All China's foreign satellite sales run through the China Great Wall Industry Corporation, which U.S. officials have labeled a "serial proliferator" for sharing military technology.[68] Founded in 1980, the company is a subsidiary of the state-owned, defense-industrial conglomerate China Aerospace Science and Technology Corporation (CASC) and was sanctioned for exports to Pakistan in the 1990s and Iran in the 2000s.[69] In addition to selling satellites and satellite capacity, China Great Wall provides launch services, attracting customers that already have their hardware and are looking to hitch a ride. As it has grown, the company has spun its own web of subsidiaries, including hotel and real estate operations. Great Wall does not actually build anything and acts as a trading company of sorts, extracting rents from CASC and increasing the inefficiency of China's state-run approach.

Many of China's customers have struggled. The cost of the satellite, after all, is only one part of running a satellite company, which spans engineering, marketing, and customer service, plus building out terrestrial infrastructure in remote places. After joining the elite club of satellite operators, these new members have to compete against better-resourced incumbents with more experience. Nor is bandwidth demand unlimited. In Asia—and increasingly around the world—the glut of new entrants into the satellite market is outpacing demand for bandwidth access, especially as high-throughput satellites are poised to further boost capacity.[70]

The results are often disappointing. As Blaine Curcio, a leading expert on Chinese aerospace companies and founder of Orbital Gateway Consulting, explains, "While a country may feel national pride in seeing a rocket with its flag launch into space, the pride has been short-lived, as many a legacy satellite have ended up costing the country more money than it delivers in benefit."[71]

Nigeria became China's first foreign satellite customer in 2004. The satellite, Africa's first, carried prestige for both parties. "This bold and strategic step in the development of a key ICT infrastructure will forever change the destiny not only of Nigeria but the entire

Africa,"[72] predicted Robert Boroffice, the director of Nigeria's space agency.

Boroffice's mission was ambitious. As he explained, "The main aim of the NigComSat-1 project is to provide a critical and innovative collaboration for capacity-building and the development of satellite technology for a quantum transformation in the telecommunication, broadcasting and broadband industry in Africa, while at the same time providing new opportunities and challenging platforms for business in rural and remote regions through access to strategic information in the new world economic order."[73]

All those objectives were noble, but there was a tension among them. If the project's main aim was to develop Nigeria's indigenous technical capabilities, its commercial performance should have been a secondary concern. If the project's main aim was to transform industry, commercial performance and profitability should have been paramount. If the main aim was to expand rural and remote access, technical training and commercial performance should have taken a back seat to affordability. By tying all these goals to a single satellite, Nigeria was setting itself up for disappointment.

Problems became apparent well before launch. When Nigeria announced a call for bids in 2004, twenty-one companies expressed interest, but the competition was quickly whittled down. Israeli and Russian firms were reportedly unable to meet the project's requirements, while U.S. and European companies angered Nigerian officials by questioning their specifications. "A senior representative of this company came to visit us and was arrogantly telling us what we needed, and why we didn't want what our [request for proposals] said," Boroffice told *SpaceNews*. "I told him I was expecting him to ask two questions he didn't ask, and I posed these questions to him myself: Do you see people living in trees here? Do you see lions or hyenas running in the streets? This company was not taking us seriously."[74]

China Great Wall was the only company to submit a bid by the deadline. Having invested heavily in developing the DFH-4, which had not yet been launched, it was eager to demonstrate the satellite and break into foreign markets.

With one untested option in hand, Nigeria went ahead. In late 2004, it signed a $311 million deal that included the satellite and its launch, along with training, insurance, and options on a future satellite.[75] Nigeria only needed to cover about a third of that cost, however. In 2006, days before becoming the first African country to enter into a "strategic partnership" with China, Nigeria received a $200 million credit from the Export-Import Bank of China for the project.[76]

While Nigeria was waiting for delivery, China launched its first DFH-4 satellite. Sinosat, another subsidiary of CASC, bought the satellite to provide digital and live broadcast TV services. This maiden mission was intended to demonstrate the DFH-4 for an international audience. The satellite made it into orbit, but its solar arrays and antenna did not deploy. It was dead on arrival.

Nigeria's satellite fared only slightly better. In May 2007, it launched from Xichang, and both sides declared the operation a success. Nigerian president Olusegun Obasanjo lauded the launch as "the best gift" that he and the Nigerian people could have received.[77] "This satellite embodies my country's consistent mission towards the peaceful use of outer space for the benefit of mankind," a Chinese official said.[78] A year later, however, the satellite's solar arrays malfunctioned, and it began losing power. Designed for fifteen years, it lasted just one and a half years.

Instead of walking away from the project, Nigeria doubled down. A Chinese insurer covered the loss, and Nigeria entered into a new contract with China Great Wall for a replacement satellite that launched in 2011. The replacement satellite was successfully delivered, but the Nigerian company managing it, NIGCOMSAT, remains unprofitable and bloated with midlevel staff.[79] China Great Wall has stepped in, according to industry experts, trying to assist NIGCOMSAT in selling satellite capacity so it can get paid for the first satellite and potentially justify selling a second one.[80]

Political support is building for a new course. In June 2020, the Nigerian Federal House of Representatives ordered an audit of the company. "There is little or nothing to show for these huge investments," Ndudi Elumelu, the minority leader, pointed out. He pointed to procurement irregularities, unauthorized spending, and alleged bribery. Two months later, a House committee opened an investigation into the deals that financed the launch of the replacement satellite, including $500 million in Chinese loans.[81]

Nigeria's uncertain path toward privatization could lead even closer to China. In 2018, China Great Wall and Nigeria announced a $550 million deal for two satellites.[82] Under its original contract, Nigeria was required to assume 15 percent of the total costs, with China providing the rest of the financing. When that arrangement became untenable, however, China Great Wall offered to provide the satellites for an equity position in NIGCOMSAT, according to Adebayo Shittu, Nigeria's communications minister at the time.

The deal remains a mystery. It has yet to be finalized, and since Shittu left office in 2019, there has been little mention of the equity offer. It is possible the offer was never real, and it was only announced for domestic political purposes. Even that possibility is intriguing, however. It implies that Nigeria's governing elite believes that the country's citizens would be more excited about the announcement of a second satellite than worried about Chinese ownership of a company so clearly linked to the nation's security. That political calculus would suggest yet again that fear alone will not stop China's Digital Silk Road in emerging markets.

Positioning itself as the hub of an emerging satellite network, China stands to gain commercially and politically by playing matchmaker among its partners. After buying a DFH-4 satellite from China, Belarus was looking for a partner to provide the satellite's monitoring services.[83] China Great Wall oversaw the bidding process, which Nigeria won, and hosted Nigerian officials for the launch of the Belarusian satellite in 2016. China also retained a stake in the satellite, with China

Satcom owning several of the satellite's transponders that provide coverage over Africa, the Middle East, and southern Europe.[84] The following year, Nigeria and Belarus expanded their cooperation with an agreement to provide satellite backup services for each other. Representatives from China Great Wall attended the signing ceremony.[85]

China's equity investments in foreign satellite operators, while limited to date, also have a strategic dimension. Laos, a country of 7.5 million people and an average annual income of $2,570, would appear to have more pressing needs than acquiring its own satellite. But in 2015, China delivered the nation's first and only communications satellite. "The launch of the satellite by China is a special gift to Laos to mark [our country's] 40th anniversary," Hiem Phommachanh, the Laotian minister of posts and telecommunications, said.[86] Chinese leader Xi Jinping called it "a significant manifestation of [the] China-Laos comprehensive strategic cooperative partnership under new circumstances."

But those circumstances are less a partnership than a game of monopoly that Laos is losing. Having borrowed heavily for other infrastructure projects, Laos's debt is dangerously high, and China is by far its largest creditor. The $259 million communications satellite added to those obligations. Essentially, China was both the seller and the buyer, setting itself up as the satellite's majority stakeholder. Doing so dramatically reduced the upfront costs for Laos, but at the expense of its control over its own satellite.

By coopting Laos, China gained access to a rare resource: a parking spot for another geostationary satellite. The International Telecommunication Union (ITU), a U.N. agency, assigns these spots, called orbital slots, on a first-come, first-serve basis, so competition is fierce. Countries game this system by filing for more orbital resources than they need. As a result, not all slots are occupied by a satellite in orbit, but all have been claimed via so-called paper satellites.[87] By working with and through Laos, China gained access to an additional slot.[88]

Nigeria and Laos are not the only countries that might be having buyer's remorse after doing business with China Great Wall. Venezuela's first and only communications satellite failed in March 2020, four years earlier than planned.[89] The following month, Indonesia's satellite did not reach orbit after the Long March 3B rocket carrying it exploded. The satellite was insured, but its failure was embarrassing. Despite these public disappointments, China has largely escaped public criticism from its partners, who may want to avoid jeopardizing other economic opportunities.

China's preference for opaque dealmaking raises the social costs of its satellites. In 2012, China launched Sri Lanka's first satellite amid questions about its true ownership. A Sri Lankan company, SupremeSAT, leased part of the Chinese-made satellite, claimed the lease was an equity investment, and attempted to name the entire satellite "SupremeSAT-1," giving the impression that it owned it. After failing to receive state approval for funds, the company may have diverted funding intended for the country's power sector with help from Rohitha Rajapaksa, son of then president Mahinda Rajapaksa.[90] With Chinese financing and technical assistance from China Great Wall, Sri Lanka also built a satellite control center and established a space academy—showpiece projects that cost at least $20 million.

Yet the political appeal of China's satellite offerings remains strong, all the more so because China is willing to sell to anyone while keeping the details secret. Cambodia, DR Congo, and Nicaragua have all signed deals, and Afghanistan has expressed interest.[91] With all these countries facing serious financial challenges, their satellite project timelines have been repeatedly delayed, and some may not reach the stars anytime soon. Meanwhile, China's existing customers, including Nigeria, Pakistan, and Brazil, are planning to acquire additional satellites.[92] Even for loss-making programs, expansion is more politically convenient than cutting losses.

As geostationary communications satellites become more sophisticated and less expensive, China's starter kit could find more buyers.[93] High-throughput satellites, which use multiple beams and reuse spectrum, promise to dramatically decrease data transfer costs.[94] In late 2017, China successfully deployed its first international commercial satellite using this technology for Algeria.[95] In the future, these advances could provide countries with significantly more bandwidth than older geostationary satellites provide for roughly the same cost. But they may also face competition from new technology at lower altitudes.

## "REBUILDING THE INTERNET IN SPACE"

The next generation of communications satellites will fly even closer to home and could upend the global connectivity contest. At the start of 2021, about 1,800 communications satellites were in operation, collectively carrying only about 1 percent of international data. But space is about to get a lot more crowded, as some of the biggest names in technology jockey to bring satellite internet to the masses.

Over the next decade, tens of thousands of communications satellites could be launched, the vast majority of them into low earth orbit, or LEO, between 500 and 2,000 kilometers high. The companies behind these efforts are competing to provide low-latency, high-speed internet globally. The winners stand to make fortunes from connecting users and carrying untold amounts of data.

Elon Musk's SpaceX is building the biggest constellation of all. Called Starlink, the constellation is composed of 500-pound satellites, each the size of an office desk. Starlink launched its first wave of satellites in 2019, plans to have nearly 12,000 satellites operating by mid-2027, and has applied to launch another 30,000 afterward. "In the long term, it would be like rebuilding the internet in space," Musk explains.[96]

These mega-constellations could usher in the next chapter for global connectivity.[97] Their impact is likely to be felt first in rural markets within developed economies, but they could eventually expand broadband access in developing and emerging markets as well. The companies at the vanguard of these efforts are almost exclusively U.S. and European. They face daunting technical and commercial obstacles, but if they succeed, they could capture some of China's most promising growth markets.

Lower means faster. With less distance to travel and less interference, the signals from LEO satellites deliver communications faster than their geostationary siblings at higher altitudes. But LEO satellites also move faster than the earth rotates. As a result, they must be launched in bulk to provide coverage over a single area. A LEO constellation is like a relay team. Each satellite provides coverage for about five minutes and then hands off to a satellite that is entering the coverage area.[98]

Using intersatellite links, lasers that beam information between satellites, LEO satellites can even outperform terrestrial networks.[99] In the vacuum of outer space, data can travel faster than it does through fiber-optic cables on the ground. Intersatellite links effectively turn satellite constellations into mesh networks, which are potentially more resilient, less reliant on terrestrial systems, and capable of delivering internet to some of the most remote locations on Earth.[100]

Nations that control LEO constellations could enjoy several strategic advantages. LEO satellites are cheaper to replace, and the failure of one or even a handful of LEO satellites will not stop the rest of its network from operating. Signals are more difficult to jam at lower altitudes, so LEO satellites could also serve as a backup to geostationary global navigation satellites. Future LEO systems could provide more accurate positioning services as well as early warning capabilities, even detecting hypersonic weapons that older geostationary systems might miss.

The U.S. military is already experimenting with LEO satellites.[101] Among other efforts, the Pentagon has turned to Starlink as the government develops a secure and resilient global communications and control system that connects land, sea, air, and space assets.[102] The

U.S. Air Force has already tested Starlink connections using attack and refueling aircraft. "What I've seen from Starlink has been impressive and positive," Air Force acquisition chief William Roper told reporters after a live-fire exercise using the satellites in 2020.[103]

For consumers, the main selling points are availability and speed. Over long distances, LEO satellites reduce the number of "hops" between systems. Musk likes to give the example of data traveling from Seattle, where SpaceX established its second office, to South Africa, where he grew up. Without satellites, that data would travel through a submarine cable, trace the outline of several continents, and may pass through twenty routers and repeaters along the way. Using Starlink could reduce that chain to three or four hops, Musk says.[104]

Musk's example is convenient because the distance between Seattle and South Africa isn't—they're located more than 16,000 kilometers apart. For shorter journeys, such as Los Angeles to Rio de Janeiro, Brazil, which is closer to 6,000 kilometers, Starlink will have less of an advantage. There will be a "tipping point" for distances— approximately 3,000 kilometers—below which Starlink and other LEO constellations will be slower than their terrestrial counterparts.[105]

LEO constellations could help close the digital divide, and many operators claim to be serving a wider social good. "Shouldn't everyone have access to the world's information?" asks OneWeb, which is developing its own LEO constellation. "As a global citizen, we are on a mission to close the connectivity gap, and that includes not overlooking those who live in the most remote and rural regions of the world," says a senior representative at Intelsat, another provider.[106]

Amazon and Facebook have released few details about their LEO satellite plans but have hinted at broad social benefits. Amazon founder Jeff Bezos announced a $10 billion investment in Project Kuiper, which could include 3,200 satellites, according to the company's filings with the FCC. Amazon says the project "has made significant progress towards our goal to serve tens of millions of people who lack basic access to broadband internet" and is being led by "a diverse, world-class team of experts who are passionate about bridging the digital divide."[107]

Facebook has been even more secretive. Its satellite project, code-named Athena, is managed by a subsidiary called PointView LLC, according to a *Wired* investigation. The company's FCC filing notes that it aims to "efficiently provide broadband access to unserved and underserved areas throughout the world."[108] Athena is experimenting with E-band and aims to provide even faster speeds, up to 10 Gbps for downloads and 30 Gbps for uploads.[109] Facebook also experimented with giant solar-powered drones but found aircraft manufacturing too costly.[110]

For a decade, Google took to the sky with Project Loon. "We had a hunch that balloons flying freely on the winds could be controlled just enough to act like floating cell phone towers in the sky," recalls Astro Teller, the head of Google X, often called the company's "moonshot factory."[111] Google's balloons flew in the stratosphere, between 50,000 and 70,000 feet, using solar-powered pumps that automatically inflated and deflated. Each balloon cost tens of thousands of dollars and provided bandwidth speeds similar to those of 4G/LTE networks.[112]

The technology was refined over the years, as Google's balloons logged more than a million flying hours and traveled enough distance to make one hundred trips to the moon.[113] The atmospheric data that Google collected allowed the balloons to optimize their travel routes, enabling fewer balloons to cover more territory for longer periods of time and to reach their intended destinations faster. In 2017, Project Loon provided communications to Puerto Rico after Hurricane Maria, demonstrating its value for humanitarian relief efforts.

Loon's biggest challenges were less technical than political and commercial. Some countries feared the balloons could become a floating surveillance network for the U.S. government, while others wanted to shield local companies from foreign competition. Indian officials blocked Project Loon after claiming it would interfere with cellular services. In 2020, Kenya became the first country to use Project

Loon equipment during non-emergency situations.[114] Details about the contract remain secret, although Google executives hinted at one point that they could eventually charge as little as five dollars a month for the service.[115]

But in January 2021, Loon's CEO, Alastair Westgarth, announced that the venture was winding down. "We talk a lot about connecting the *next* billion users, but the reality is Loon has been chasing the hardest problem of all in connectivity—the *last* billion users: The communities in areas too difficult or remote to reach, or the areas where delivering service with existing technologies is just too expensive for everyday people," he explained.[116] Loon had discovered that many of the people it aspired to connect could not afford 4G phones or did not see enough value in connecting to the internet. "While we've found a number of willing partners along the way, we haven't found a way to get the costs low enough to build a long-term, sustainable business," Westgarth acknowledged.[117]

Musk makes no secret that Starlink's overriding goal is profit, and providing satellite communications is merely a means to that end. Starlink's target market is the "three or four percent hardest to reach customers for telcos, or people who simply have no connectivity right now, or the connectivity is really bad," he says. While many details are still being worked out, early signs suggest Starlink will not be cheap. In early 2021, beta users were paying $499 for a user terminal and $99 per month for services. The actual cost of a user terminal might be closer to $2,400, meaning that Starlink is heavily subsidizing them.[118] While costs could drop as production quantities increase and manufacturing processes improve, without considerable financial support, these terminals are likely to remain out of reach for many of the world's would-be internet users.

Musk has a greater social aim, but it is extraterrestrial. His long-term goal is not to connect Earth but to settle Mars. "The whole purpose of SpaceX is really to help make life multiplanetary," he says.[119]

"What's needed to create a city on Mars? Well, one thing is for sure: a lot of money. So, we need things that will generate a lot of money."[120] SpaceX's launch business stands to max out at around $3 billion a year, Musk estimates, while Starlink could rake in $30 billion a year by serving only about 3 to 4 percent of the market.[121]

Even Starlink's terms of service were written with interplanetary ambitions. "For Services provided on Mars, or in transit to Mars via Starship or other colonization spacecraft, the parties recognize Mars as a free planet and that no Earth-based government has authority or sovereignty over Martian activities," the user agreement notes. "Accordingly, Disputes will be settled through self-governing principles, established in good faith, at the time of Martian settlement."[122] Services provided to those of us on Earth, in the meantime, will follow the laws of California.

Musk is aware that others before him have failed. During the 1990s, several companies tried to deliver large LEO constellations. "Guess how many LEO constellations didn't go bankrupt? Zero," Musk explained in 2020. "Iridium is doing okay now, but the Iridium One went bankrupt. Orbcomm went bankrupt. Globalstar? Bankrupt. Teledesic? Bankrupt . . . There's a bunch of others that didn't get very far and also went bankrupt." Being "not bankrupt," Musk declared, would be a "big step."[123]

Companies have failed more recently as well. In late 2019, LeoSat, a company that had planned to launch up to 108 LEO satellites, folded after its investors backed out.[124] In 2020, OneWeb and Intelsat both filed for bankruptcy and have reemerged with new ownership structures. OneWeb was auctioned off to the U.K. government and Bharti, an Indian firm. As a consequence of leaving the E.U., the United Kingdom lost access to Galileo's advanced services, including for its military, at the end of 2020. It may have an interest in using the OneWeb constellation to provide global positioning services in the future.

To avoid Icarus's fate, LEO satellite companies will have to cut costs dramatically.[125] One reason for optimism is that satellite construction and launch costs are declining. A single SpaceX Falcon 9 missile can carry sixty Starlink satellites into orbit. After launch, SpaceX can retrieve and reuse the first stage of the missile, and it is experimenting with ways to retrieve the nose cone as well.

Excitement about satellites tends to emphasize launches rather than equally critical developments on the ground.[126] To operate at full power, Starlink could require upwards of 120 ground stations, more than Telesat and OneWeb combined, according to an MIT study.[127] These ground stations would be outfitted with an estimated 3,500 gateway antennas, and each would cost anywhere from $1 million to $4 million.[128] Operators also need to offer user terminals, which will receive the signals, at affordable prices. Starlink's $499 terminal, as noted earlier, is heavily subsidized.

It all adds up. The cost of deploying a large LEO constellation could range from $5 billion to $10 billion with operating costs upwards of $1 billion to $2 billion a year. Starlink could spend up to $33 billion before it begins turning a profit in 2031, according to a projection by Morgan Stanley.[129] But the same study estimates that Starlink will have over 360 million subscribers by 2040, when it will be pulling in $90 billion in annual revenue. Such a long horizon is inherently risky, holding out the tantalizing prospect of massive rewards in later years. If Musk stays the course, his Mars mission could gain a powerful funding stream, or it could burn up in low earth orbit.

The LEO race may well become a marathon. For now, SpaceX is raising money with ease, including a $1.9 billion funding round that closed in August 2020 and another $850 million round in February 2021. Amazon and Facebook have record piles of cash on hand. For companies with tighter budgets, such as OneWeb, the path ahead may be more challenging. China, however, has the resources to begin another long march.

## "THE BEST FRENEMIES"

China is charting a different course into low earth orbit. Its companies are behind in the race to launch LEO constellations, but they have generous state support, making profitability less of an immediate concern. This second-mover, state-backed strategy allows China to see what works and emulate foreign successes, avoiding the costs that pioneers incur. But as China waits, foreign companies are claiming orbital slots and critical spectrum for operating the satellites. Missing the LEO moment could come back to haunt Beijing.

China's space industry remains firmly in the hands of the state, despite recent steps toward commercialization.[130] As of mid-2019, private Chinese aerospace firms had raised less than $1 billion, according to Curcio.[131] In comparison, China's two largest state-owned aerospace companies, China Aerospace Science and Technology Corporation (CASC) and China Aerospace Science and Industry Corporation (CASIC), pulled in $75 billion in revenue that year alone.[132]

What China's LEO efforts do share in common with those of U.S. companies is that few details have been made public. Some confusion among foreign observers stems from the fact that similarly named companies, CASC and CASIC, have pursued similarly named LEO constellations, Hongyan and Hongyun, respectively. Although specifics are sparse, the overall trend is clear. China is stepping up its LEO activities in response to those abroad and it is doing so by fueling competition between its own state champions. Both CASC and CASIC launched their first LEO broadband satellites in December 2018.

China's seriousness can be seen in its ability to push these plans forward even during the COVID-19 pandemic. In December 2020, CASIC, which is headquartered in Wuhan, completed China's first "smart manufacturing" facility for satellites. The plant, which began operating in May 2021, automates component installation, assembly, and testing, and is designed to produce as many as 240 small satellites a year.[133]

CASC and CASIC are "the best frenemies ever," as Curcio puts it. Having two similarly sized companies working on similar projects might seem inefficient, but the Chinese government could stand to benefit from the resulting competition. Larry Press, a professor of information systems at California State University, notes that China used a similar approach of pitting state-owned companies against each other during the 1990s to deliver domestic internet and more recently to develop AI.[134]

China's champions also work together. CASIC often serves as a subcontractor on CASC-led projects, and CASIC's first Hongyun satellite was launched on a CASC rocket. Cooperation on launch services is not unusual among private sector competitors, either. Bezos's aerospace firm, Blue Origin, has contracts to provide services to Telesat and OneWeb, both LEO competitors.[135] Likewise, Musk has said that SpaceX is open to providing launch services to its competitors. But CASC and CASIC have much deeper ties and ultimately answer to the same owner.

CASC is the primary contractor for China's space program, managing the Long March rockets, among other initiatives. Its main LEO broadband project is called Hongyan, or "wild goose," a reference to the ancient practice of using geese to deliver messages, which, according to legend, dates back to the Han Dynasty. The constellation is designed to have 320 satellites, with 60 operating by 2023, and the full constellation in place by 2025.[136]

CASIC has deeper ties with the Chinese defense industry and less experience in developing satellites. Its main LEO project is called Hongyun, or "rainbow cloud." When it was announced, the constellation was originally described as including 156 satellites. But after foreign competitors announced larger plans, the system was expanded to 864 satellites. Hongyun's original 156 satellites should be operational by around 2023, according to Chinese officials, and the constellation is designed to focus on countries participating in China's Belt and Road Initiative. Actually providing those services, however, still requires Beijing to negotiate landing rights and receive approval from each country, a potentially massive diplomatic effort.[137]

Like Google and Facebook, CASIC is experimenting with other flying platforms. Pulling from the state's deep pockets, it has budgeted roughly $15.4 billion on Hongyun and four other "cloud" (-yun) projects.[138] Project Xingyun is a smaller, 80-satellite LEO constellation that is designed to use narrowband frequencies and intersatellite links to produce an Internet of Things network.[139] Project Feiyun aims to build a solar-powered drone-based network to facilitate long-distance emergency communications, internet, and ground observation.[140] Project Kuaiyun intends to use stratospheric, lighter-than-air aircraft to rapidly provide emergency services. Lastly, Project Tengyun seeks to develop a two-stage, horizontal take-off and landing, reusable space-plane by 2030.[141] These projects also carry advertising value, positioning CASIC at the cutting-edge as it jockeys for a greater share of CASC's business.

The big question is whether Beijing can successfully integrate these efforts. China's Fourteenth Five-Year Plan, which spans from 2021 to 2026, calls for an integrated network of communications, Earth observation, and navigation satellites. In an important step toward consolidation, in April 2021, China created a state-owned company, China Satellite Network Group, that will be responsible for all satellite internet operations.[142] The new company is expected to combine the Hongyun and Hongyan projects into a single constellation, tentatively named Guowang, or "national net(work)," and make use of China's ITU applications for two LEO constellations that include nearly 13,000 satellites in total.[143] "The interesting thing will be whether Xingyun also gets integrated into this project," says Curcio.[144]

Novel as these efforts may seem, they lag behind those of foreign commercial space companies. In the past, this second-mover approach has worked for China's other industries, particularly its railway and telecommunications companies. "We can see what works and then can improve upon it and mass market," an employee of a Chinese aerospace company told researchers at the Institute for Defense Analyses.[145] If history repeats itself, and LEO satellite constellations fail as they did during the 1990s, China will have avoided a potentially costly quagmire. If one or two succeed, it can try to mimic those successes, adapting them to its own target markets.

But arriving second in space is risky. With gold-rush urgency, companies are already laying claim to the most promising bands of spectrum, which the ITU regulates. "The harsh reality for anyone trying to make a real impact on global connectivity is that no matter how good your network is, success is not possible without the right spectrum," says Ruth Pritchard-Kelly, vice president of regulatory affairs for OneWeb.[146] Companies that make it through the ITU process first can enjoy "priority" status, which means they are not required to make as many adjustments to deconflict frequencies as companies that show up later.

The three most sought-after bands for the new generation of LEO satellites are Ku, Ka, and V. The trade-off is that higher frequencies offer higher speeds but smaller range. Ku, the band containing the lowest frequencies of the three, covers the widest geographic scope with a single beam and is the most resistant to weather interference. The Ka band's higher frequencies offer more bandwidth, which translates into greater speeds. The V band, the option with the highest frequencies, is the least commercially developed. Its frequencies often cannot penetrate buildings and fade when they encounter rain or moisture in the air.

While the satellite race favors early action, it is much more complicated than just showing up first. Companies must navigate past incumbents using similar frequencies, competitors that want the same chunk of spectrum, and national governments with their own political and national security priorities. Battles are fought in legal filings and counter-filings, nationally and internationally. Adding urgency, in 2019, the ITU began pushing companies to use or lose their spectrum.

Under new rules, companies have to deploy 10 percent of their constellations within nine years and half within twelve years, and complete their constellations within fourteen years of their initial filings.[147]

Clearing these milestones is only the beginning of the race, which continues as companies seek access to individual markets. Winning priority status from the ITU makes it easier for companies to access markets that follow ITU guidance, and to raise money from investors, but it does not guarantee market access. Markets that are relatively open often accept requests from companies to use ITU-approved frequencies or require minor modifications. But others can impose unworkable conditions or deny the requests to protect their own companies or to guard against perceived security risks.

Given all these obstacles, the path ahead for LEO constellations to provide global coverage is likely to prove longer and more winding than expected. Securing priority rights does not guarantee financial success. In March 2020, OneWeb launched thirty-four satellites and met the ITU's 10 percent milestone. Just days later, it filed for bankruptcy. The last-minute launch was strategic, enhancing the company's value for potential buyers. The company's spectrum rights were arguably its most valuable asset. Its failure, however, highlighted the risks that come with moving first. The eventual winner will have the resources to stay the course through this complex approval and coordination process.

The playing field could shift over time because the second movers are also among the best resourced. Amazon and Facebook are sitting on record amounts of cash, and China's state-backed approach has even more staying power. Laggards can become leaders through acquisitions. Amazon was rumored to be among the potential bidders for OneWeb, as were two unnamed Chinese organizations.[148] China's state champions could also acquire companies from the country's fledgling commercial space sector. "Like Amazon, China has funds for the long run," observes Press.[149]

## TOO FAR FOR COMFORT

But if China waits too long, the coming wave of LEO mega-constellations could undercut its advantage in overlooked markets. As chapter 3 recounted, China's network providers have thrived in rural and less-wealthy markets, from Naivasha, Kenya, to Glasgow, Montana, that Western companies overlooked. With LEO constellations, however, Western companies could serve those markets without building all the ground infrastructure that has deterred them in the past.

In July 2020, I visited one of SpaceX's Starlink gateways, tucked away in a clearing on a small hill, down a dirt path, off a rural road without signs. Hidden behind a tall green fence, a cluster of white domes, each roughly four feet in diameter, looked skyward. A small brick building, likely housing a power supply and fiber-optic connections, was positioned across from the fence. The entire footprint was small and inconspicuous, an understatement to the constellations of hundreds of satellites traveling overhead at 17,000 miles per hour.

SpaceX is quietly rolling out dozens of these gateways across the United States, including one in Conrad, Montana, just a few hours' drive from Glasgow. In 2020, the company preliminarily won $886 million in funding, over ten years, from the FCC's Rural Digital Opportunity Fund auction to provide service to hundreds of thousands of customers in thirty-five states. It is a significant bet on SpaceX and its technology, given the companies that have come before it and failed.

But after using Starlink for a week, I came away more convinced of its potential. The system arrived in a large gray box, which included a white satellite dish roughly two feet in diameter, a tripod stand, a wireless router, and ethernet and power cables. All I had to do was find a spot outside with an unobstructed view of the sky, and a Starlink mobile app even helped make sure no trees were in the way. When activated, the satellite pivoted automatically to assume the most effective angle. The entire process, from opening the box to connecting to the internet, took less than thirty minutes. It was impressively simple.

The connection held up well against everything that a New England spring could throw at it: dense clouds, hard rain, and strong winds. It usually clocked above 100 Mbps and occasionally approached 200 Mbps for downloads. It wasn't flawless. My video and audio briefly cut out during a meeting, and the meeting application warned that the connection was unstable. Coverage will improve as more satellites come online. But even in this early phase, as I worked, so did Starlink. A day into using the system, I forgot that my data was going into space.

The appeal was easy to understand. I was accustomed to using a fiber-optic connection, so the lack of noticeable change was a success. For customers without a fast connection, or perhaps any connection, the system could offer a major improvement. In the part of rural New England where I was using the system, the cost of accessing a hard-wired internet connection can be prohibitive for residents. For a single home, the ditch-digging and cable-laying work can cost thousands of dollars. Avoiding that construction process and paying less for a Starlink system could seem like a bargain.

But SpaceX and other LEO broadband providers may need a bigger push to go into lower-income countries. Most are starting by focusing on gaining access to the U.S. and European markets, where potential revenue per customer is highest. Despite their mission-driven rhetoric about connecting the unconnected, these companies still need the commercial math to work. "This is not a democracy movement. This is a business," says Peter B. de Selding, cofounder of Space Intel Report.[150]

Affordability will be key. Demand is strong in developing and emerging economies, but prospective customers will not be able to shell out a hundred dollars a month, let alone a few hundred dollars for a user terminal. Bringing the internet to 90 percent of Africa, according to the U.N. Broadband Commission, may involve providing satellite or other wireless solutions to 10 percent to 20 percent of the continent's rural population. The average village, however, has fewer than five hundred people, each of whom might only be able to afford paying two or three dollars per month.[151]

Cost cutting will only go so far, and someone will have to foot the bill. Realistically, profit-driven satellite providers will have to find ways of subsidizing services to low-income markets. Partnering with the World Bank and other multilateral development banks is one option. While the development banks have supported geostationary satellite broadband in the past, they have been reluctant to back LEO satellites, given their use of still-nascent technology and longer history of financial struggles.

A coalition of internet companies could share costs, but they face major barriers. To antitrust advocates, this scenario sounds like a nightmare, extending the reach of the biggest tech companies deep into the markets of the future. Of course, these companies stand to profit from connecting more users. Facebook, for example, is seeing its fastest user growth in Africa and the Asia-Pacific. As income levels rise in these emerging markets, average revenue per user will likely increase. But shareholders are unlikely to support spending resources on a long-term, socially driven venture, even if commercial rewards loom over the horizon.

Then there is the philanthropic scenario, in which a superrich individual or group of wealthy donors foots the bill. With the world's first internet pioneers now growing old, improving global connectivity would seem an attractive legacy to leave. Bill Gates, the founder of Microsoft, invested heavily in Teledesic, an ambitious LEO effort that folded in 2002.[152] He has since focused on global health. "Which is more important, connectivity or malaria vaccine?" he asked the *Financial Times* in 2013. "If you think connectivity is the key thing, that's great. I don't."[153]

Mark Zuckerberg, the founder of Facebook, begs to differ. "Connecting everyone in the world is one of the great challenges of our generation," he said in 2015.[154] "In the long term, I do think it could be good for our company, as well, if you look at it in a 10-, 20-, 30-year time horizon because a lot of these countries and economies will develop, and over time will be important."[155]

Jeff Bezos announced in early 2021 that he would be stepping down as Amazon's chief executive to focus on his other "passions," including Blue Origin.[156] The company is geared toward making space travel cheaper, safer, and more accessible with reusable launch vehicles. Its mission has appeared unhurried. "We are not in a race . . . We will go about this step by step because it is an illusion that skipping steps gets us there faster. Slow is smooth, and smooth is fast."[157]

But the clock is ticking. Beyond aligning incentives, Western satellite companies still have to secure rights in developing markets. They have the lead in developing and deploying technology and in securing priority rights in developed markets and at the ITU. But the longer they wait to secure rights in developing markets, the better China's chances become. Once China closes the gap in LEO satellite technology, its existing commercial and political ties, backed by state financing, could give it an edge in developing markets.

Eventually, the same characteristics that helped Chinese firms forge connections on the ground could carry Chinese LEO satellite services into foreign markets. State subsidies and financing could allow Chinese constellations to provide services at low cost. China's state-driven approach will continue to resonate with leaders wanting to expand internet access while still maintaining control over communications. Although few details are available about its constellations, they are likely to carry China's vision for cyber sovereignty into orbit.

Starting with China itself, Western satellite providers will need to decide whether, and how, to accommodate governments that do not want their citizens to access the open global internet. Intersatellite laser links, which allow satellites to exchange data without passing through a ground-based intermediary, could reduce costs and improve performance. But the same technology also presents a major challenge to authoritarian governments, threatening to cut them out of the loop and provide their citizens with unrestricted, unmonitored access to the global internet.

So far, Western satellite companies have mostly deferred to the governments they are courting for landing rights. OneWeb's experience in Russia is disappointingly familiar to how Western companies made concessions during their rush into the Chinese market. After Russian officials expressed their concerns, the company agreed to drop intersatellite laser links and pass all Russian traffic through ground stations in Russia.[158] OneWeb gave up additional control by agreeing to become a minority partner in the company providing these services in Russia.

Mark Rigolle, the former CEO of LeoSat, explained how this puts companies using intersatellite links at a disadvantage. "In a country like China—they are not the only country but they are a big country that will require us to route everything through the gateway before it goes out of the country or comes in from abroad, so one of [our unique selling points] is kind of lessened," he told *SpaceNews* in 2018.[159] These changes are expensive to make as well, increasing the required amount of ground infrastructure. Companies not making these changes, however, face the prospect of being locked out of markets.

In November 2019, before OneWeb had declared bankruptcy, company executives made a trip to China, where they announced plans to build three ground stations. They signed an agreement with the city of Sanya, in China's Hainan province, but both sides may have gotten ahead of themselves. The central government had not yet provided its blessing. After the meeting, Hainan officials received a stern call from their counterparts at China's Ministry of Industry and Information Technology.[160]

Musk acknowledges that not all countries will want Starlink's services. In 2015, he half-jokingly remarked, "We could conceivably continue to broadcast and [countries would] have a choice of trying to shoot our satellites down or not. China can do that. So probably we shouldn't broadcast there. If they get upset with us, they can blow our satellites up."[161] China has other coercive tools it could employ before taking aim at Starlink satellites, however. Authorities could threaten to close Tesla's factory in Shanghai, for example, and block it from the Chinese market, where it has been a best-selling electric car brand.

Overcoming the twin challenges of affordability in developing markets and accessibility in authoritarian countries may require support from wealthy democracies. The United States and its partners could pool their resources and make satellite broadband part of an allied approach to improving global connectivity. The effort could be framed not in opposition to any country but in support of the billions of people that remain unconnected.

While hardly a panacea, expanding access to satellite internet would be a bold move that helps the world and challenges China's push into emerging markets. As those markets mature, companies from the United States and allied countries would be better positioned to provide other services as well. Doing so would help move the United States from complaining about Chinese networks to competing with them. It would put China on the defensive.

# CHAPTER SEVEN

# WINNING THE NETWORK WARS

China's rise has completely reversed a causal arrow that guided U.S. foreign policy. For two decades, leading thinkers proclaimed that technology would promote democracy around the world. But that consensus has crumbled, giving way to a much darker outlook. Freedom is not flourishing. Digital authoritarianism is on the march.

Now the hope is that democracies will promote technology. Democrats and Republicans alike are calling for the United States to band together with fellow democracies to compete with China. Proposals range from a small club of five countries that reduces supply chain vulnerabilities to a much larger "Alliance of Free Nations" that would tackle technology among other issues. What they all have in common is the belief that democracy is the central trait around which a coalition should be built.

These calls are as alluring as the original idea that technology was on the side of democracy. Then, as now, a material issue—the provision of hardware and know-how—is being elevated into a moral imperative. The solution seems self-evident, and all too easy. It does not appear to demand much, if any, sacrifice. We only need to be ourselves, lock arms with friends, and the rest will follow.

Like the original hope that technology could help democracy, there is real promise in democracies working together on technology. But realizing that promise will not be cheap, easy, or inevitable.

Success will require a heavy dose of realism that was missing the first time around.

Any strategy for competing with China must, of course, begin at home. The United States still has its own communities to connect and a digital divide that will widen if left to market forces. It must push forward the frontiers of technology by educating and attracting the next generation of innovators, ensuring they have the resources to succeed and the competitive space for new businesses to flourish. It must fashion data policies that protect citizens' privacy and their security. These domestic efforts are urgent and necessary, but not sufficient.

China presents a challenge of scale. Its population of 1.4 billion provides Chinese companies with preferred access to the world's largest market of middle-class consumers and the government with access to an ocean of data. The Chinese government's ability to direct resources, even if inefficient and wasteful, is giving a boost to emerging technologies and subsidizing the cost of Chinese equipment globally. Even as they answer Xi's call to build "new infrastructure" at home, Chinese companies are doubling down in emerging markets.

The competition is already too close for comfort. In 2018, the United States and China were neck and neck in their shares of global R&D spending, at 28 percent and 26 percent, respectively.[1] But China's spending is growing faster and may have surpassed the United States in 2019, according to the National Science Board.[2] Chinese companies have graduated from pirating to pioneering in emerging areas such as facial recognition, digital payments, and quantum communications.

Yet China's dominance of global networks is far from assured. The United States remains ahead in critical areas, including cloud computing and satellite technology as well as advanced semiconductors. Maintaining this edge requires a strategy that promotes further innovation while defending against China's illegal acquisition of technologies. Nor is innovation at home sufficient by itself. To have the resources for supporting continued innovation, U.S. companies must commercialize their research and sell it widely. Lacking China's scale, the United States must compete in foreign markets.

But as U.S. policymakers have attempted to course-correct in recent years, their focus on defensive measures has overlooked the importance of going on the offensive in foreign markets. Export controls, equipment bans, license revocations, restrictions on foreign investment, and prosecuting IP theft are all important tools. They can defend the U.S. market and disrupt Chinese supply chains, but they will not win this global competition. China's tech companies rose not only through stealing technology and receiving generous state subsidies but also by providing services to overlooked markets. Competing globally will require offering better alternatives.

A winning strategy, which combines defense and offense, will require a coalition to carry out. In the absence of a coalition, China can pit companies against each other to access their technology, just as it did during the 1990s when Nortel, AT&T, and other global telecom companies undercut each other. Without the commercial incentives that a coalition could offer, U.S. and allied companies are likely to remain focused on the largest, wealthiest markets, overlooking the developing world. In both cases, only a coalition can offset China's scale.

A coalition for this twenty-first-century challenge will be fundamentally different from those that confronted last century's threats. It should be framed to attract rather than exclude, emphasizing the positive alternatives it offers. It should recognize that perfect security is impossible and that resilience is a better framework for planning.[3] It should reflect that global networks are first and foremost a technological and economic issue with intelligence and military implications rather than the other way around. Call it the Coalition of Open and Resilient Economies, or CORE.

Flexibility will be key. Different groups of countries will more naturally align on some issues but not all. Unanimous consensus should not be required for action. While governments will drive the action, companies must be integrated more deeply into the policy-planning process. The private sector is not only at the forefront of innovation but literally on the frontlines of the Network Wars. Governments must do a better job of understanding the risk-reward calculus that companies face as they consider how to invest and what markets to pursue.

It helps to think about this coalition in network terms. There will be a group of wealthy democracies with strong common interests that give the coalition a critical mass. Collectively, a group of seven U.S. allies—Australia, Canada, France, Germany, Japan, South Korea, and the United Kingdom—could offset China. These seven countries collectively outspend China on R&D, and although the pandemic has clouded their economic prospects, they are still projected to account for roughly a fifth of global GDP in 2030.[4] All these countries are U.S. treaty allies and democracies.

But the coalition's mission must extend beyond simply protecting wealthy democracies. It must also engage and support rising hubs on the periphery, large economies in the developing world with a mixture of overlapping and distinct interests. These divisions will be fluid. As the coalition succeeds over time, parts of the periphery will join the core, and countries at the outer edge of the periphery may move closer as well.

Two bridges are especially critical to building this coalition. The first bridge stretches across the Atlantic. Despite common values, the United States and Europe look at global networks differently. Lacking a technology champion of similar size, some European leaders view U.S. technology companies as even more threatening than Chinese companies. The European Union is trying to position itself as a middle option between the open U.S. model and the state-centric Chinese model. Disagreements over data flows, content regulation, and digital taxes all threaten to derail transatlantic cooperation.

The second bridge connects the core and the periphery. It begins with India, which is expected to become the world's most populous country in the coming years, making it the critical swing state in the global network competition. The CORE must give India a clear path to full participation in the coalition, and it must also reach out to emerging economies, which are expected to account for 70 percent of global growth and half of global GDP by 2030.[5] Many countries in the periphery will hedge and extract as much as possible from all sides. Failing to compete, however, will hand China the markets of tomorrow.

Neither of these bridges can be built overnight. The skepticism that the United States faces in Europe and India stems from asymmetries in power, reflecting America's strengths in the tech sector. Competing in developing markets will require incentives to shift the risk-reward calculus of companies that have grown comfortable operating in rich economies. At each step, China will try to sow division and undercut the competition. But the alternative is unacceptable: a Sino-centric future that is already being woven into existence, one connection at a time.

## THE ARSENAL OF DEMOCRACIES

The United States has overcome greater challenges before. During World War II, FDR famously called upon American businesses to ramp up production. Speaking to Americans in a radio broadcast on December 29, 1940, he issued an industrial call to arms: "We must be the great arsenal of democracy."[6]

Can the United States now lead an arsenal of democracies? The list of areas for cooperation runs long. To spur innovation, the group could share data, coordinate investments, and conduct joint R&D. It could lead global standard setting at the ITU and other bodies. It could work to make supply chains more resilient. It could impose common export controls on sensitive technology, refuse to transfer technology to China as a condition of doing business, take action against IP theft, and help deter economic coercion. With a common front, all these actions would be more likely to succeed.[7] Without it, China will have room to extract, coerce, divide, and dominate.

But all this is much easier said than done, as past pushes for democratic unity remind us.[8] In 2000, the Clinton administration helped create the "Community of Democracies," which grew to include 106 countries.[9] After several years of meetings, its sole accomplishment was a statement criticizing Burma in 2003.[10] But the core concept remained attractive, and in the following years, U.S. foreign policy experts proposed a "Concert of Democracies."[11] With President Biden calling for a global democracy summit, some version of the idea appears poised for action.

Republicans have long embraced the idea as well. On the presidential campaign trail in 2007, Senator John McCain called for a "League of Democracies" and promised to convene a summit of democracies during his first year in office.[12] Toward the end of the George W. Bush administration, the State Department convened policy-planning officials from several democracies, an effort that the Atlantic Council, a U.S. think tank, continued in subsequent years.[13]

But the sharp reality of international politics could again deflate lofty proposals for democratic coalitions. When push comes to shove, the United States has pragmatically worked with other countries regardless of their governance style, allying with the Soviet Union during World War II; supporting dictators in Argentina, the Philippines, Iran, and elsewhere during the Cold War; and working with Kuwait and Saudi Arabia during the first Gulf War. As Democratic and Republican foreign policy leaders were calling for democracies to unite in 2008, the United States continued to work with an authoritarian regime in Pakistan, out of necessity.[14]

Critics of using democracy as the flag around which to rally and compete with China point out that many key partners are only partially democratic at best. "The United States will find it hard, if not impossible, to work with less liberal or nondemocratic states if it sees things primarily through an ideological prism," cautions Elbridge Colby, a former senior official in the U.S. Department of Defense, and Robert D. Kaplan, a journalist and geopolitical analyst, in *Foreign*

*Affairs.* "It's no use for the United States to have Denmark or the Netherlands onboard but not Indonesia, Malaysia, Singapore, Thailand, or Vietnam."[15]

National interests, not ideology, should be the guiding compass for U.S. policy, but there is also a realist case for convening democracies, particularly on technology issues. America's most essential partners, in economic and technological terms, are democracies. Democracies have common interests in networks that expand access to information, encourage free speech, and protect users' privacy and security. Even as democracies struggle to uphold their own ideals, they put a greater emphasis on individual rights than the authoritarian alternatives do.

Yet there are also differences among democracies that will prevent collective action unless they are addressed. There is not a universal democratic position on technology issues but a range of positions. Organizing around what is common is a logical first step, as long as it does not distract from the need to address real differences and the need to work with non-democracies and the developing world. The CORE could begin naturally as a group of democracies, but it would have the flexibility to include other partners as interests and issues require.

In the past, calls for democratic coalitions have struggled because there was no common threat menacing enough to catalyze action. "McCain pines for the 'vital democratic solidarity' of the Cold War and sees a league of democracies as a way to revive it," Charles A. Kupchan, a scholar and senior official in the Obama and Clinton administrations, wrote in 2008. "But yesterday's solidarity was the product of an alliance against an external threat, not of an alignment based exclusively on regime type."[16] Threats from terrorist groups did not appear universal enough, and climate change did not appear urgent enough.

China's rise, however, is beginning to push its competitors together. Thought leaders in the United States, Europe, and Asia agree that the best way to deal with China is through increased collaboration among like-minded states, according to a 2020 survey by CSIS.[17] More than two-thirds of those thought leaders support banning

Chinese firms from their 5G networks. A growing majority of Americans support building up relations with allies, even if that harms relations with China.[18] And while the calls for democratic coalitions have come mostly from Americans in the past, more European leaders are pounding the drum.[19]

Some elected leaders are already taking action. The Inter-Parliamentary Alliance on China, or IPAC, announced in June 2020 on the anniversary of the Tiananmen Square protests, has grown to include legislators from eighteen countries and the European Union.[20] "Some countries—we hadn't even asked—had heard about it and then jumped in," one of the founding cochairs, Sir Iain Duncan Smith, recalled.[21] The cochairs for each country are from rival political parties, allowing the group to represent both the political Left and Right. The group has issued statements addressing China's persecution of predominantly Muslim minorities in Xinjiang, forced labor in Tibet, Taiwanese participation in the World Health Organization, clashes along the India-China border, and the national security measures imposed on Hong Kong. It accomplished more during its first six months than the Community of Democracies did in several years.

IPAC's growing ranks reveal a desire for cooperation among democracies, but it also runs the risk of becoming unwieldy like the Community of Democracies before it. The combined strength of democracies looks even more formidable as the list of partners grows, so there is a natural temptation to expand the group, but coordination challenges quickly mount. The closest thing the field of international relations has to a scientific law is that mature constitutional democracies do not go to war with each other.[22] Perhaps equally valid is that if you get enough democracies together, they will not go anywhere with each other.

Given these challenges, some proposals may be overly ambitious in their initial membership. Richard Fontaine and Jared Cohen have called for a "new grouping of leading 'techno-democracies,'" which they dub the "T-12." Their list includes six of the G-7 (the United

States, France, Germany, Japan, Canada, and the United Kingdom) and adds Australia, South Korea, Finland, Sweden, India, and Israel. They propose expanding this group to a T-20 within five years. It is an admirable goal, and one that recognizes the importance of scaling beyond a core group of rich democracies. But India may not be ready yet, as explained later in this chapter, and admitting it prematurely could sink the effort at the outset.

Other proposals are too narrow. One such idea is repurposing the Five Eyes intelligence alliance for technology issues.[23] Born from Allied efforts to monitor enemy communications during World War II, the group includes the United States, the United Kingdom, Canada, Australia, and New Zealand. As Anthony R. Wells, who worked for both the British and U.S. intelligence services, writes in his history of the alliance, it is "a powerful international diplomatic force, and undoubtedly the most successful intelligence organization ever in the world."[24]

But for practical and political reasons, the Five Eyes alliance is not the best organizing framework. Its secrecy is a barrier to cooperation with the private sector, where many solutions will reside. As Wells writes, "Five Eyes governments have tended to be behind the curve in responding to technological change, . . . woefully slow and ponderous, with the result that the commercial, non-defense intelligence world is far more ahead of the technical game because of the ability to innovate quickly and effectively."[25]

The Five Eyes alliance will remain important for aspects of the U.S.-China technology competition that are closely related to signals intelligence. It is well-positioned to collaborate on quantum computing, for example, and develop the next generation of encryption techniques. But for commercial applications, the intelligence group has less to offer. "GCHQ might be just the people to eavesdrop on Russian undercover agents operating in the UK, but they're not really your go-to guys to put up cell towers," observes Alan Beattie of the *Financial Times*, referring to the U.K.'s equivalent of the NSA.[26]

The second challenge is political. One of the main themes that U.S. officials have emphasized when criticizing Chinese telecommunications equipment is the risk of espionage. Those warnings will ring hollow if the alternatives are being led by an intelligence alliance. This would be particularly damaging in Europe, where the Snowden leaks still sting. For German and French officials in particular, that incident was a reminder that they remain outside the most trusted inner circle.

The right size for the initial coalition, therefore, is likely somewhere between the T-12 and Five Eyes. The United Kingdom has proposed a D-10 group, which includes G-7 members plus South Korea, Australia, and India.[27] Others have proposed a D-10 grouping that is similar but includes India as an observer and the European Union as a member. In practical terms, it is better to start smaller, accomplish a few concrete objectives, and then expand. What all these groupings have in common is that European countries make up the largest bloc. Convening is only the beginning. Collective action will require bridging the transatlantic divide.

## EUROPE'S DANGEROUS SIGNALS

Calls for cooperation now echo in Op-Ed pages, think tank reports, and speeches by officials from both sides of the Atlantic. The door is open, especially following Trump's departure from office, to more closely coordinate defensive actions such as export controls and investment screening.[28] Going on the offensive, the United States and Europe can increase cooperation in developing 5G alternatives and setting technology standards at international bodies. Making progress in these areas, however, will require tolerating disagreements in other areas, particularly cloud computing.

The United States, China, and Europe are playing different games in global networks.[29] To put it crudely, the United States is playing Monopoly. It has the world's largest technology companies and, like a tycoon, is trying to clear a path for further expansion. China is playing Risk. The state oversees China's defensive posture at home and its companies' march into markets abroad. The European Union is playing Red Light, Green Light. Lacking its own tech giants, it is acting like a traffic cop, exercising regulatory power and requiring others to obey its rules.

As the European Union does this, it is sending conflicting signals that hint at deeper divisions. In early December 2020, the European Commission released a paper that called for a "new transatlantic agenda for global cooperation" and declared, "As open democratic societies and market economies, the EU and the US agree on the strategic challenge presented by China's growing international assertiveness."[30] It was a love letter intended to make the most of Biden's victory.

By the end of the month, however, the European Union was sending a very different signal. It announced a major investment agreement with China, putting it on a course for deeper ties, instead of stepping back and conducting a joint reassessment with the United States. Regardless of whether the deal is finalized, its announcement was revealing. It "shows that the EU, with Germany leading the way, still believes that economic and broader strategic interests can be neatly separated—an idea that is no longer accepted in Washington," explains Noah Barkin, a veteran journalist and senior visiting fellow at the German Marshall Fund.[31]

Fundamental differences in threat perceptions cannot be wished away. Despite sharing common values with their American counterparts, E.U. officials remain much more ambivalent about taking a stronger stand that might impact economic ties with China. There is also lasting damage from the Trump administration, which levied tariffs on European exports, withdrew from the Paris Agreement and the Iran nuclear deal, and shunned multilateral institutions. These actions, which European leaders viewed as reckless unilateralism, eroded trust and exacerbated longer-standing concerns.

Transatlantic perceptions plummeted during Trump's time in

office. By the spring of 2018, more people in Germany and France, the European Union's two largest economies, viewed U.S. power and influence as threatening than viewed China or Russia that way.[32] In September 2020, only 41 percent of U.K. citizens expressed a favorable opinion of the United States, the lowest rating on record. In France and Germany, U.S. favorability ratings fell to levels similar to those at the start of the Iraq War, and only one in ten people in those countries expressed confidence in Trump.[33]

This damage will not be easy to repair, according to a survey by the European Council on Foreign Relations conducted after Biden's victory in 2020. Majorities in key European countries—including Germany, France, and the United Kingdom—believe the U.S. political system is broken, believe that China will be more powerful than the United States within a decade, and would want their governments to remain neutral in a conflict between the United States and China. "Europeans appear keen to forge their own path rather than fall into line behind America's China policy," write Ivan Krastev and Mark Leonard, who oversaw the survey.[34]

At the same time, European perceptions of China have been hardening, even if they do not align neatly with views in Washington. In 2019, the European Commission branded China a "strategic competitor," "an economic competitor in pursuit of technological leadership," and "a systemic rival promoting alternative models of governance."[35] The European Union has announced enhanced investment screening mechanisms and unveiled its own initiative for connecting Europe and Asia, which includes a focus on digital connectivity.[36] China's response to COVID-19, human rights abuses, repression in Hong Kong, and diplomats' aggressive rhetoric has further harmed its image.

Beijing's missteps, combined with aggressive U.S. diplomacy and export controls, helped align the United States and Europe's major economies on 5G. In January 2020, the European Union announced a "5G Toolbox" that includes recommendations to mitigate security risks while leaving decisions and implementation to individual countries.[37]

The United Kingdom initially decided to allow Huawei equipment in the non-core parts of its 5G network, but in July 2020, it announced a ban, citing concerns over Huawei's ability to source reliable and secure components following U.S. sanctions.[38] The same month, France announced a de facto phaseout of Huawei equipment from its 5G networks by 2028.[39] In April 2021, the German government adopted a new process for evaluating 5G equipment, including an evaluation of the manufacturer's "trustworthiness" and a requirement to meet the "security policy goals" of Germany, the E.U., and NATO. But the German government has not singled out Huawei by name, and it is unclear whether, and how, it will exercise these powers.[40]

As of mid-2021, governments and major network operators in twenty-four of the E.U.'s twenty-seven member countries had adopted measures to restrict Huawei from their 5G networks. The holdouts are not exactly embracing Huawei, either. Austria and Malta are heavily dependent on Chinese vendors for their 4G networks, which would make a full "rip-and-replace" extremely costly.[41] Instead, they are likely to increase their supplier diversity as they add new equipment, meaning less market share for Huawei. Hungary remains the singular, but unsurprising, exception to the rule, given how aggressively it has courted Chinese investment and taken steps to weaken collective E.U. statements against China in the past.

The experiences of Austria, Malta, and others that became dependent on Huawei as their primary vendor highlights a basic challenge that transatlantic cooperation could help address. Huawei and its major competitors all sell proprietary equipment that is not designed to operate with other products. Consequently, network operators shopping for 4G and 5G solutions typically go with one company to provide all their equipment. Going with a single vendor simplifies the process, but it can create dependency. The more equipment that is added, the more expensive it becomes to switch vendors later on.

Coordinated investments in Open RAN networks, described in chapter 3, could allow operators to combine components from different vendors, reduce costs, and avoid lock-in. Companies in the United States, Japan, and Korea are leaders in producing the software and key components for Open RAN, and some are already working together. Dish Network, which aims to provide 5G coverage to 70 percent of the U.S. population by 2023, has partnered with Fujitsu. Rakuten, which rolled out the first 5G network using Open RAN in 2020, has a majority stake in Altiostar, a Massachusetts-based Open RAN provider. With support from CORE governments, these activities could be extended further and scaled faster in emerging markets.

Another area where greater transatlantic cooperation is both urgent and possible is international standard setting. The E.U.'s large market and stringent regulations mean that its rules often become the global standard, a phenomenon that Anu Bradford, a law professor at Columbia University, has dubbed the "Brussels Effect." Rather than forgo market access, or develop an E.U.-specific product line, many multinational corporations adopt E.U. standards as their default. The European Union is also strong at international standard-setting bodies, where China has been stepping up its efforts.

Three international standard-setting bodies are especially important. Technologies that adhere to standards set by the International Organization for Standardization (ISO), the International Electrotechnical Commission (IEC), and the ITU cannot be banned in international trade, according to WTO rules.[42] Other countries, especially developing economies, often look to these bodies for guidance as they set their own domestic standards. As of 2019, the European Union held more leadership positions in the ISO and IEC than did the United States or China.[43]

Transatlantic cooperation is urgently needed at these organizations, beginning with choosing the right leadership. For example, the United States and its European partners could work together to elect the ITU's next director-general and replace the Chinese incumbent, Houlin Zhao, when he steps down in 2022.[44] Coordination in working groups is needed to push forward socially responsible standards in emerging areas such as AI surveillance, while blocking Chinese proposals to hand governments more control over the internet.[45]

But the United States' 5G campaign in Europe also hints at challenges to come. Convincing European countries to avoid Chinese 5G equipment should have been comparatively easy. They are wealthy democracies, after all, with strong views on protecting privacy and the resources to afford more expensive alternatives. There are also two European providers of 5G equipment, Nokia of Finland and Ericsson of Sweden, giving them a commercial incentive to promote alternatives to Chinese equipment.

Falling trust in the United States has opened opportunities for China in Europe. In a 2019 advertising campaign, Huawei was even brazenly suggesting that it was the partner with common values. "It is crucial to roll out 5G the European way, in line with European values," the company claimed.[46] Some countries recoiled when pushed publicly by U.S. diplomats. Few countries wanted to explicitly exclude Huawei, hoping to avoid retaliation from Beijing, and instead adopted objective screening criteria for their network equipment that Huawei will nevertheless struggle to meet.

The Biden administration can seize the opportunity to improve perceptions, but deeper differences have not disappeared after Trump's defeat. European thought leaders, like their American counterparts, are calling for a democratic coalition, but they have different goals in mind. In their eyes, the threat is not merely China's authoritarian approach but also the power that U.S. companies possess. "Without deliberate and immediate efforts by democratic governments to win back agency, corporate and authoritarian governance models will erode democracy everywhere," warns Marietje Schaake, president of the Cyber Peace Institute and a former member of the European Parliament.[47]

The United States could remove obstacles to cooperation by adopting national data privacy regulations aligned with the E.U.'s own General Data Protection Regulation (GDPR), encouraging greater competition in the digital economy, and working on a digital tax treaty.[48] All these steps could be worthwhile in their own right, and there is growing bipartisan support for them in Congress, even if there are still disagreements about specifics.

But Europe is not cozying up with the United States to offer a unified alternative to China's vision for global networks. It is positioning itself as an alternative to China and the United States. "The European Union is well-placed to play a global leadership role in strengthening the governance of cyberspace, as an effective 'third way' buffer between the dominant American and Chinese paradigms," says a working paper from the European Commission.[49] "Unless we find new ways to democratise access to data and break through this vicious circle, today's winners will also be the winners of tomorrow."[50]

The underlying problem is that Europe does not consider itself among today's winners. The United States is home to 68 percent of the market capitalization of the world's seventy largest digital platforms, according to a U.N. study, and China is home to another 22 percent. Europe is home to only 3.6 percent.[51] The same study found that seven companies—Microsoft, Apple, Amazon, Google, Facebook, Tencent, and Alibaba—account for two-thirds of the digital market's total value. Without a champion of its own in that league, Europe is reluctant to defend a system it views as benefitting others.

Germany comes closest but is still far away. Europe's largest tech company is the German firm SAP, a business software provider that has more than two hundred million customers and advertises that 77 percent of the world's transaction revenue touches one of its systems. As of early 2021, Alphabet, the parent company of Google and the fourth largest U.S. tech firm, was worth more than the thirty leading companies on Germany's DAX index put together.[52] Only one E.U. company, Deutsche Telekom, is ranked by Forbes within the top twenty digital firms. In contrast, twelve of the top twenty were U.S. companies.[53]

The European Commission's data strategy envisions a dramatically different landscape by 2030. "Competitors such as China and the US are already innovating quickly and projecting their concepts of data access and use across the globe," it writes.[54] The Commission has called for the European Union to capture a share of the global data economy that is at least equal to its economic weight, double its global market share of semiconductors, and double the number of E.U. tech companies worth at least $1 billion.[55] These ambitions are admirable, but such grand targets also feel like they could have been pulled from Chinese policy documents.

European officials are also calling for "digital sovereignty," a phrase that sounds a bit like China's vision of cyber sovereignty.[56] "The aim is to create a single European data space—a genuine single market for data, open to data from across the world," says the European Commission's data strategy. "This favourable context, promoting incentives and choice, will lead to more data being stored and processed in the EU." The document advises this should all come about "not by fiat, but by choice." But realistically, most companies currently storing data outside the European Union will not choose to move, which comes with higher costs, unless they are forced to.

The E.U.'s late and somewhat convoluted entry into the global cloud competition illustrates the limits of this approach. European officials have expressed concerns about the U.S. CLOUD Act, passed by Congress in 2018, which helps the U.S. government obtain cross-border data from companies for law enforcement investigations.[57] Their arguments may sound similar to warnings that U.S. officials make about Chinese companies, which are legally required to provide any assistance necessary, including supplying access to restricted facilities, data, and equipment in state intelligence activities.[58]

The major difference, of course, is that the U.S. approach is based on rule of law and mutual consent. The CLOUD Act is not imposed on other countries by fiat and simply authorizes the U.S. government to negotiate bilateral agreements over data access with foreign governments. Having already reached a deal with the United Kingdom, the U.S. government is negotiating with the European Union over a bilateral agreement that would uphold laws on both sides and provide reciprocal access. But as perceptions of the United States plummeted in Europe during Trump's tenure, and U.S. cloud providers continued to grow, more European lawmakers began calling for the European Union to invest in its own cloud alternatives as a matter of sovereignty.

In June 2020, Germany and France launched GAIA-X, named after the Greek goddess of the Earth.[59] "We are not China. We are not the United States. We are European countries with our own values," declared Bruno Le Maire, France's finance minister, when speaking about the project.[60] "In order to achieve digital sovereignty, we need to start approaching data processing the way major American and Chinese companies—the hyper-scalers—approach it," says German economy minister Peter Altmaier.[61]

A more apt name for the project is Proteus, a Greek god known for shape-shifting. In official documents, the project's true form can be difficult to decipher. The German government explains that the effort is "a Europe-wide platform for storing data in external data centres," which sounds like a European cloud. Another official document declares, "The road map for GAIA-X foresees the creation of an international, non-profit society governed by Belgian law . . . that will shape the framework for the GAIA-X ecosystem and provide key functionalities."[62] Translation: GAIA-X is creating a nonprofit that will help define what GAIA-X becomes.

Adding to the hype, and reflecting the confusion surrounding the effort, international media have dubbed it "Europe's bid to get cloud independence" and "Europe's answer to the power of U.S. and Chinese cloud giants."[63] But the German government explains, "No competitive product to existing offers should be created."[64] Indeed, non-European companies are barred from sitting on the board of directors, but they are otherwise welcome to take part in the initiative, as long as they commit to GAIA-X principles—an offer that has been extended even to Huawei.[65]

One reason for skepticism is that the rhetoric around GAIA-X is not being backed up with serious resources. The European Commission plans to provide only 2 billion euros over seven years for cloud computing and aims to attract additional funding from member states and companies, bringing the total to 10 billion euros.[66] That is less than Amazon's cloud computing services pull in during a single quarter.[67]

Harnessing the E.U.'s regulatory power, GAIA-X is essentially a gatekeeper of existing cloud services. Although the specifics are still under development, it could become a sort of one-stop shop that brings together Europe's smaller cloud providers. Doing so could increase their visibility and encourage the creation of shared pools of data for innovation. In theory, this could give users of GAIA-X more choices and allow them to move more easily between cloud providers. The aim is to reduce the barriers to entry for new providers, but it is hard to imagine competing with the superior services, scale, resources, and global reach of today's cloud giants.

While GAIA-X is not likely to give birth to European tech titans, it could handicap U.S. companies and unintentionally boost Chinese cloud providers in the developing world. Its underlying goal, to promote European providers, means that the "price of admission" is likely to be higher for U.S. companies. Placing additional costs on U.S. providers means they will have fewer resources for expanding into developing markets.

The E.U.'s focus on digital sovereignty, captured in GAIA-X, has its own dangers. It evokes aspirations that are common in smaller markets around the world, but the path it offers will be challenging for the European Union itself and even more difficult, if not impossible, for smaller economies. The concept is also easily misused. The E.U.'s vision of digital sovereignty has individual rights at its core. Governments in China, Russia, Iran, and elsewhere wave the same banner but toward less altruistic ends. One country's digital sovereignty can look like digital nationalism to everyone else, and in extreme cases, it masks digital authoritarianism.

Realistically, the United States and its European partners will not be able to neatly merge their different visions for global networks. Asymmetries in global market share, as well as long-standing differences on security and privacy, stand in the way of complete alignment. As the scholars Henry Farrell and Abraham L. Newman write, "EU-US interactions over privacy and security have never reached a stable equilibrium, where all parties are better off with the particular institutional setup than a feasible alternative given everyone else's actions, and surely never will." What they see, instead, is "ongoing and heated contestation."[68]

But transatlantic cooperation will endure and can even benefit from that ongoing struggle, if differences are honestly acknowledged and effectively managed. One new and encouraging avenue for cooperation is the EU-U.S. Trade and Technology Council, created in June 2021 to work through issues ranging from investment screening and export controls to artificial intelligence. As Germany's defense minister, Annegret Kramp-Karrenbauer, said in October 2020, "This constant friction with America is a good thing, a productive thing. This friction entails confrontation, discourse, and dispute—and perpetually questioning oneself. This is the essence of an open society."[69] Friction will be a natural part of the CORE. Policymakers should temper their expectations accordingly, and while strengthening the CORE, they must not lose sight of the developing world, where China is forging ahead.

## THE SWING STATE

The United States and its partners must prepare for a world that could look dramatically different by century's end. Europe and Asia will recede, demographic trends suggest, while Africa and the Arab world rise. Nigeria, the world's twenty-eighth-largest economy in 2017, is projected to become the world's ninth largest economy, according to researchers at the University of Washington's Institute for Health Metrics and Evaluation.[70] During the same period, India will move from seventh to third place. Turkey will move from seventeenth place to ninth place by mid-century, before settling at eleventh place by 2100. These are projections, of course, and plenty could change in the coming decades. But they provide a glimpse of a world in which emerging economies have arrived.

In the face of these trends, rich democracies cannot become a digital island. Countries rated "free" in Freedom House's Freedom on the Net rankings are expected to decline in their collective share of global GDP from 48 percent to 38 percent by 2050. Meanwhile, countries rated "not free" are expected to grow their share from 22 percent to 30 percent.[71] These are very rough, back-of-the-envelope measures of economic power. But economic power ultimately underwrites technological and military power. The CORE will need to offset demographic decline by reaching out to the developing world.

They will be pushing on an open door, as developing countries are already embracing digital solutions. Among the top thirty countries with the greatest digital revenue as a share of GDP, sixteen are in the emerging world, according to Ruchir Sharma, chief global strategist for Morgan Stanley Investment.[72] Since 2017, digital revenue has been growing more than twice as fast in developing countries as in developed countries. And the potential for additional growth is vast.

The developing world is still coming online. More than half the world have limited or no access to the internet.[73] More than a third of countries still lack internet exchange points.[74] A third of the world's population live in countries where 1GB mobile broadband plans are unaffordable for average earners.[75] Among those with mobile connections, only 15 percent of users are expected to use 5G by 2025, while nearly 60 percent of mobile users will rely on 4G.[76] The "race" for 5G, and global networks more broadly, is just getting started.

The world's rising middle class will help decide the winner. A historic tipping point was reached in 2018, when for the first time in human history, the world's poor and vulnerable citizens were no longer the global majority, according to calculations by Homi Kharas of the Brookings Institution.[77] The middle class, defined as households spending $11 to $110 per day per person, is the largest and fastest-growing consumer segment in the global economy. The challenge is that by 2030, a quarter of global middle-class consumption will happen in China, according to Kharas and Brookings scholar Meagan Dooley.[78]

As the CORE looks to expand, India should be at the top of its list, if not in a category all its own. India is projected to have the second-largest share of middle-class consumption, 13 percent of the world's total, by 2030.[79] India's middle class is already driving demand for devices and services. In 2018, Indian users downloaded more apps than users everywhere besides China and spent more hours on social media than users in China and the United States.[80] A quarter of the world's mobile subscription growth by 2025 will occur in India, by which point Indians will have nearly a billion smartphones.[81] After China, no one else comes close.

India is the critical swing state. With India on board, the CORE would have eight of the world's ten largest economies in 2030.[82] The combined economic weight of the United States and India will continue to exceed China's share of global GDP in 2050, after which point China's share is expected to decrease.[83] India has a deep pool of technical talent, especially in software and services. It could become the CORE's ambassador to the developing world, and a primary commercial beneficiary of that outreach.

The same attributes make the prospect of losing India's cooperation just as troubling. If India tips toward Beijing, the CORE loses its most natural counterweight to China. It would face two countries that collectively constitute more than a third of the world's population. Of course, it is entirely possible that India will remain nonaligned, which would be a major lost opportunity and could make it less likely that other emerging economies gravitate toward the CORE.

The momentum is strongly in Washington's favor. Common perceptions of China are driving greater cooperation between the United

States and India in military exercises, cybersecurity talks, and intelligence sharing.[84] The United States and India have long appeared to be a natural match, the world's oldest democracy and the world's largest democracy. That promise now appears to be materializing.

India is also cooperating more closely with key U.S. allies. The Quad, a strategic forum composed of the United States, Japan, India, and Australia, was inspired by coordinated disaster-relief efforts that followed the Indian Ocean earthquake and tsunami in 2004. After several attempts faltered, the group is now benefitting from top-level political participation and working-level cooperation on technical issues. The four countries held their first leaders-level summit in March 2021 and, among other actions, created a working group focused on critical and emerging technologies.[85] This is exactly the type of bridge-building work that the United States must lead, helping to steer the Quad "from its novel *form* of dialogue toward joint *functional* action by the group," as Evan A. Feigenbaum and James Schwemlein write for the Carnegie Endowment.[86]

Despite this progress, India's alignment with the CORE must be continuously cultivated rather than assumed. Even when U.S. and Indian threat perceptions of China converged during the Cold War, disagreements persisted about the correct course of action. The lesson for New Delhi and Washington, as the scholar Tanvi Madan explains, is that both ends and means must be aligned, expectations must be carefully managed, and the relationship should be institutionalized. "Nature might bring the two countries together as they deal with China, but without nurture, any such alignment will be unsustainable," she writes.[87]

Washington has at times gotten ahead of itself, acting as if alignment was inevitable, or already achieved. "America and India will bring light to the darkest corners of our Earth," President George W. Bush proclaimed after signing a civil nuclear agreement in 2006.[88] During his final trip to India as U.S. secretary of state, Mike Pompeo declared, "What's become very clear now is there is a battle, and the battle in the world is between freedom and authoritarianism, and India, like the United States, has chosen democracy and freedom."[89] The problem with these black-and-white framings is that they miss the vast gray area where many developing countries reside.

India has not formally picked a side, even as it now leans toward the United States. Although Indian prime minister Narendra Modi has distanced himself from the nonaligned movement that guided decades of Indian foreign policy, he is still hedging. Recent improvements in U.S.-India ties have come in the security domain. In the economic realm, however, India's preference for indigenization has thrown up barriers to cooperation, including the highest applied tariffs among major economies.[90] In Washington, it can seem as if there is not one India but two, depending on whether security or economic issues are being discussed.

Beijing knows that divisions remain, and it will try to exploit them. "There is an upper limit to the closeness of U.S.-India [relations]," says Ye Hailin, one of China's top South Asia experts. Even within characteristics the United States and India share, Ye is eager to point out differences: "We must remember one thing: these two countries may both speak English, but the English of one country is hamburger-flavored, and the English of the other country is curry-flavored. They are two different things."[91]

In a sense, India's challenge is Europe's dilemma magnified. India wants its own tech champions and greater control of its data, but it has fewer resources and manufacturing capabilities and is more dependent on Chinese technology. In 2014, Modi launched "Make in India," an attempt to boost domestic manufacturing by removing barriers to foreign investment and raising tariffs on imports of electronics and other manufactured goods that has fallen short of expectations.[92]

Much of India's networks are Made in China. India imports about 90 percent of its telecommunications equipment, 40 percent of which was sourced from China in 2019.[93] That same year, India also imported nearly two-thirds of its data center equipment from China and Hong Kong.[94] Three of India's four largest carriers—Airtel, Vodafone

Idea, and BSNL—rely on Huawei and ZTE equipment for 30 percent to 40 percent of their networks.[95] Affordability is, and will remain, a major driver for India's decisions.

Indian consumers may not be ready to give up on Chinese equipment. In 2020, following a standoff between Indian and Chinese troops along their disputed border, India banned more than one hundred Chinese apps. But several months after the initial clash, Chinese tech giant Xiaomi remained India's most popular smartphone supplier, winning nearly 30 percent of the country's smartphone market in the second quarter of 2020. The Chinese companies Vivo, Realme, and Oppo took third, fourth, and fifth places, respectively. Altogether, these four Chinese firms captured two-thirds of the Indian smartphone market.[96]

Affordability may still trump security concerns. Indian security experts assume that any foreign equipment will come with espionage risks. "Concerns over foreign surveillance would always loom large, whether it is Huawei (China), Nokia (Finland), Cisco (USA), or Ericsson (Sweden)," explains Munish Sharma, a scholar at the Institute for Defence Studies and Analyses (IDSA) in New Delhi.[97] Some believe that New Delhi can still have the best of both worlds: equipment from the cheapest provider and security from effective supervision. "This dependency [on China] does not prohibit states from having enough oversight on these developments to ensure that the tools are not misused," write Ajey Lele and Kritika Roy for IDSA.[98]

Yet the Indian government is beginning to take a harder position on Chinese suppliers of 5G equipment. In late 2019, the government said it would allow all suppliers to participate in its 5G trials. But when it officially announced the suppliers for those trials, which are scheduled to last for six months during 2021, Chinese vendors did not make the cut.[99] New procurement rules will allow only "trusted sources," echoing the spirit of screening measures adopted by wealthier democracies.[100] The tide may be turning, owing to China's mistakes and India's longer-standing desire to favor domestic suppliers.

Like Europe and others, India wants to harvest the value of its own data. Thought leaders in India find both Washington and Beijing's approaches to data flows lacking.[101] But instead of participating in international discussions on these issues, India has been conspicuously absent. It declined to join e-commerce talks at the WTO and data flow initiatives at the G-20.[102] In the meantime, India is moving toward adopting the Personal Data Protection Bill, national legislation that experts have called "a crude amalgamation of provisions in the [European Union's] GDPR with authoritarian leanings."[103]

Another area where India's recent actions fall short of its potential is the government's use of internet controls. India is the world's leader in internet shutdowns, which have increased in recent years.[104] In August 2019, the government cut off all communications to Jammu and Kashmir, depriving the region's thirteen million people of mobile internet, broadband, landline services, and cable TV. It became the longest shutdown in the democratic world, running until January of the following year.[105] Reports also suggest that the government has used spyware to target activists, journalists, and lawyers representing marginalized groups.

Ultimately, India's participation in the CORE should be based on actions, not aspirations. In 2020, India scored 51 out of 100 in Freedom House's Freedom on the Net index. The average score for the other countries in the proposed D-10 grouping was 77.[106] In 2021, Freedom House's annual democracy ranking downgraded India to "partly-free." The last time India received that rating was 1997, the same year that G-7 nations prematurely invited Russia to join their club. They hoped that Moscow was moving toward deeper economic and democratic reforms.[107] Instead, Russia's authoritarian turn weakened the group until it was kicked out in 2014.

To avoid repeating that mistake, the CORE should work with India to agree upon a roadmap for its full participation in the coalition. India is hosting the G-20 in 2023, which provides one natural milestone. In the lead-up to that summit, it could take steps to reduce its internet controls, adopt strong criteria for screening 5G vendors, and lower barriers to trade with other CORE members. The summit itself could include a focus on data flows, building on efforts started during Japan's host year in 2019.

India's reforms could be incentivized with policies that help its manufacturing ambitions, as Robert K. Knake, a senior fellow at the Council on Foreign Relations, has proposed.[108] Companies in CORE countries, for example, could receive tax incentives for moving telecommunications production from China to India. The United States, for example, sources over 90 percent of its laptops and nearly three quarters of its cell phones from China.[109] Shifting some of this manufacturing to India would help CORE countries become more resilient by diversifying their supply chains. Strengthening India's manufacturing capabilities would also have the benefit of decreasing its reliance on China.

A more open India could become the CORE's ambassador to the developing world. Indian officials understand firsthand the trade-offs around cost and security that drive decisions. Rather than avoiding international talks on data flows, India could act as a bridge between the wealthier economies and other emerging markets such as Brazil, Indonesia, and South Africa.[110] With a stronger manufacturing sector, India could offer solutions that are designed with lower-income markets in mind. India's first priority, of course, will be getting more of its own citizens connected, and it will build valuable capabilities while doing so. That experience and expertise, supported by financing and investment from other CORE members, could be a powerful combination for connecting more of the developing world.

## UPGRADING AMERICAN STATECRAFT

When FDR called Americans into action during the early days of World War II, he recognized that only a major change could meet the challenge. "This can be accomplished only if we discard the notion of 'business as usual,'" he said.[111] As the United States looks to rally a coalition to compete with China in global networks, it will also require three major shifts in strategy to break away from old habits.

The first shift is how the United States and its allies think about and pay for security. There is no question that national security leaders are increasingly grappling with digital threats. "Today, disruptive technologies are changing warfare as much as did the Industrial Revolution," NATO secretary general Jens Stoltenberg said in October 2020. "Conflicts are increasingly defined by bytes and big data. As much as by bullets and battleships."[112] But bullets and battleships still dominate military budgets. "More spending on cyber is a no-brainer," says Admiral James Stavridis, a former Supreme Allied Commander of NATO.[113]

Digital issues must be elevated in government budgets. NATO members, for example, pledge to spend 2 percent of their GDP on defense annually. Safa Shahwan Edwards, deputy director of the Atlantic Council's Cyber Statecraft Initiative, proposes that alliance members commit to spending 0.2 percent of their GDP on cybersecurity and digital defense modernization. Some members already meet this goal, but most would need to double or triple their spending.[114]

Many European countries have been failing to meet their original defense spending pledge for years, but investing in cyber and digital defense could be more politically feasible. For example, NATO members could be allowed to count some spending on critical digital infrastructure with a direct application to NATO communications, such as select 5G systems, toward their overall spending obligations.[115] As Stoltenberg explained, "A ship from one NATO country can always sail next to a ship from another. But if they can't share information, if their radar and tracking systems cannot communicate, they may as well be in different oceans."[116]

The United States should reflect this shift in its own budgets as well. Although some trends are heading in a positive direction, the U.S. federal budget is painfully resistant to change. The Department of Defense requested $9.8 billion for cyber activities in its fiscal year

2021 budget, which includes $789 million for cloud computing and $1.5 billion for 5G connectivity. That sounds like a massive amount of funding, but it amounts to just 1.4 percent of the total budget. Simply trimming bloated administrative spending would save the Defense Department $125 billion over five years, according to an internal study.[117]

Better aligning resources also requires updating how the U.S. government is staffed. The Defense Department has almost thirty times as many musicians as the Commerce Department has foreign commercial service officers.[118] In recent years, roughly two dozen U.S. foreign commercial service officers have been spread across the entire Middle East and Africa. They are present in only eight of sub-Saharan Africa's forty-six countries. Meanwhile, China is expanding its diplomatic footprint and has ten to forty government representatives in Africa for every U.S. foreign commercial service officer there.[119] In 2019, China overtook the United States as the country with the most diplomatic posts worldwide.[120]

The United States should put more resources toward financing digital infrastructure. Congress has taken promising steps in recent years, including creating the U.S. International Development Finance Corporation (DFC) and reauthorizing the U.S. Export-Import Bank. But collectively, these two institutions are capped at $195 billion in exposure, and budget rules constrain the DFC's ability to take equity positions. To put this into perspective, global needs for ICT investment are estimated at $8.9 trillion through 2040.[121] Both agencies aim to catalyze financing from the private sector, such as from pension funds and institutional investors, where the real firepower resides. But there is no escaping the fact that more public resources are needed.

The second major shift is how these resources are applied. The U.S. government must become more entrepreneurial in how it approaches foreign markets and emerging technologies. Imagine, for example, if the U.S. government had a foreign technology venture fund and portfolio managers. Working with U.S. embassies, the portfolio managers could identify promising start-ups and nurture technological development locally. They could target larger transitioning economies, such as Brazil, Indonesia, and Nigeria, which will shape regional trends and are important markets in their own right.

This would require adopting a mindset that is more comfortable with failure. Like venture capital investors in the private sector, these portfolio managers would place bets knowing that many will fail. In the U.S. government's case, however, even those bets that do not succeed commercially could provide valuable insights into local dynamics. With those insights and a real stake in local ventures, the United States would be more effective in encouraging countries to adopt policies that favor openness and resilience.

The United States could share the risks, and rewards, with partners and allies. Nirav Patel, a former senior official at the U.S. State Department and cofounder of the Asia Group, a consultancy, proposes creating an Asia-Pacific Technology Fund with a multilateral bank, such as the Asian Development Bank. The fund would have a general partner structure and allow companies to participate in individual projects as co-investors and become limited partners over time.[122] Involving more partners in this way, and bringing together the public and private sectors, will naturally require some trial and error. But in the absence of these types of creative alternatives, China will continue filling the void.

A greater tolerance for risk would also enable the U.S. government to invest in technologies that challenge authoritarian networks. The Open Technology Fund (OTF), an independent nonprofit and grantee of the U.S. Agency for Global Media, supports tools such as Tor and Signal that help dissidents communicate securely and reconstitute their websites after an attack. The fund receives only $21 million a year from Congress, while helping more than two billion people in more than sixty countries access the internet. The organization should be asked what it could do with two, four, or even ten times that budget.

While technology is often viewed as the problem these days, efforts such as OTF harness technology to provide creative solutions.

Tim Hwang, a leading AI expert, recommends sharing knowledge about how to defeat authoritarian applications of AI, for example, by feeding these systems "adversarial examples" that disrupt their abilities to accurately identify people and objects.[123] A group cochaired by Eric Schmidt and Jared Cohen recommends investing in advanced encryption and novel packet routing technology, among other areas.[124] Expanding the availability of satellite broadband, as chapter 6 proposed, is another promising avenue.

Skeptics will warn that these actions blur the line between the U.S. government and the private sector. But the U.S. government already places bets. The Defense Advanced Research Projects Agency, or DARPA, famously invested in projects that helped develop the internet and GPS. The United States also places bets on people through exchange programs and scholarships. Thankfully, even Republicans in the U.S. House of Representatives, among them critics of big government, are calling for some of these steps to compete with China, suggesting there is bipartisan ground for action.[125]

The third major shift is how the United States makes its sales pitch to the world. Even as the Trump administration worked to expand alternatives for other countries, it remained narrowly focused on the dangers of Chinese equipment. For example, when announcing that the U.S. government would offer financial assistance to developing countries for purchasing secure telecom equipment, a senior official previewed the two themes the U.S. government planned to hit. The first was that Chinese equipment was vulnerable to espionage. The second was that Chinese financing would trap them.[126] These arguments might win applause from some U.S. audiences, but they do not resonate in most developing countries.

Getting the message right will require more empathy. Warnings against espionage mean little, as developing countries assume that risks come with any foreign technology. Warnings against debt traps, meanwhile, can sound paternalistic and empty, turning developing countries into unwitting victims and overlooking the fact that few asset seizures have occurred from Chinese lending.[127] The overall effect is like a prospective customer going to a Ford dealership to test drive a car, only to have the sales rep launch into a tirade against the Honda dealership across the street. A savvy sales rep sells the benefits of their product, not the shortcomings of their competitors.

In developing countries, affordability will continue to drive decisions. Beyond providing financial assistance, the United States can improve how countries assess costs and reach those decisions. The initial price tag on Chinese projects often only includes the upfront costs associated with construction. After getting something up and running, there are operations and maintenance costs as well. Ignoring those expenses is a recipe for disaster. It's like buying a car and assuming you won't need to fill it up with gas (or recharge it), or ever take it to the mechanic. That is a safe scenario only if you plan to never drive the car.

Consider the experience of Papua New Guinea, which borrowed $53 billion from the Export-Import Bank of China to have Huawei build a data center in its capital. An assessment commissioned by the Australian government suggested that Huawei deliberately used poor cybersecurity standards for the project. Espionage risks naturally won the headlines, but the report also noted that the data center fell into disrepair because not enough money was set aside for operations and maintenance.[128] Instead of simply warning about espionage and debt traps, U.S. officials should point out that the data center also failed because it was a dud. Huawei looks like the car dealer who knowingly sold a lemon.

The United States and its partners will be more competitive when project estimates reflect actual costs. This requires helping developing countries factor in not only standard maintenance and operations costs but also added expenses associated with cybersecurity. Whether accidental or intentional, Huawei's equipment, for example, has more bugs than some of its competitors have, making it more vulnerable to hacks.[129] Risk mitigation can be expensive. Not mitigating risks can be even more expensive. The United States and its partners in the

CORE should help developing countries objectively analyze these trade-offs.[130]

When the United States does talk about the shortcomings of Chinese equipment, it should highlight experiences such as Papua New Guinea's and focus on the gap between promises and benefits. Some Chinese tech companies, overly eager to sell, have promised capabilities they cannot deliver, as chapter 4 showed in the case of China's surveillance and Safe City technology. These advertised benefits are a major driver for foreign governments and companies purchasing the equipment. Drawing attention to false claims, and instances when equipment fails, would be a better defensive strategy in developing markets.

Waging an overtly geopolitical struggle is likely to backfire in the developing world. Developing countries are not ready to give up doing business with the world's largest trading nation. They are not ready to turn away the world's largest bilateral creditor. Few view the United States and China in such Manichean, good-versus-evil terms. For most, development and growth are higher priorities than democratic governance. Their leaders are looking to keep their options open, generate competing offers, and avoid dependence on a single outside partner. Few view China as a partner of first choice. But the United States must compete, or, for many, China will be the only choice.

## "THE WORST POSSIBLE DAY"

It does not take a crystal ball or Hollywood screenwriters to imagine a world wired by China. The warning signs are already here, many of them featured in the tour this book has provided. Some of them might look innocuous: blinking green lights in the basement of a local telecom provider in Glasgow, Montana; cameras mounted on lampposts in London; thousands of miles of fiber-optic cable, running underground and across the ocean floor. Even as China's digital footprint grows, it remains mostly out of sight and out of mind.

The future is taking shape most clearly in the developing world, where this competition will unfold. The same hardware is already wreaking havoc. Servers at the African Union headquarters send data to Beijing covertly in the dead of night. Cameras watching over Pakistani streets come equipped with hidden hardware, while others malfunction. A subsea cable stretches across the South Atlantic and adds little but debt to Cameroon's economy. Laos's first satellite is actually owned by Beijing. These are the early signs of digital dependency.

Picking up today's warnings and looking much further ahead, Amy Webb, a leading American futurist, previews a chilling scenario in *The Big Nine: How the Tech Titans and Their Thinking Machines Could Warp Humanity*. The year is 2069, and China sits at the center of a network of more than 150 countries, all of them dependent upon Beijing for communications, trade, and finance. They have pledged to uphold the "Global One China Policy." The United States and what remains of its allies are considering their options when China preempts them with a final AI-guided attack that is "brutal, irreversible, and absolute," wiping out the populations of the United States and its allies.[131] Farewell, democracy.

China's own strategists understand the stakes. "The control of an information society [is] the doorway to the opportunity to dominate the world," declares Shen Weiguang, the information-warfare guru introduced in chapter 1.[132] Shen penned those words in 1999 as part of his unnervingly titled book, *The Third World War: Total Information War*. They have only become truer as communications technology pushes deeper into society. Very little of daily life, whether in smart cities, such as Nairobi, Kenya, or rural towns, such as Glasgow, Montana, exists apart from digital infrastructure. As society's digital dependence increases, so does the power that comes with controlling these systems.

China stands to gain intelligence and coercive powers it can exercise every day as well as weapons for what Thomas Donahue, a cybersecurity expert and former U.S. intelligence official, calls "the worst possible day."[133] Every day, Beijing would have its finger on the pulse of the global economy. It would know the movement of energy grids, cargo ships, and farming equipment. It could reach deeper and detect the energy usage of a building, the contents of a cargo container, and the yield of a tractor. By amassing this data, Beijing could construct a potent early-warning system.

Knowledge of even these seemingly arcane details is power. Knowing farm yields, for example, Beijing could spot and exploit market inefficiencies, profiting from price fluctuations. It could help client states prepare for and prevent social unrest that accompanies rising food prices. By tracking the precise contents of the world's cargo ships, Beijing could decide to stockpile critical supplies before the rest of the world is aware that a shortage is coming. Spikes in energy usage at military installations could reveal that foreign troops are mobilizing. For China's leaders, surprise could become a thing of the past.

China would know more of the world's secrets, while concealing its own information. Beijing would have eyes and ears not merely walking around foreign capitals but woven into foreign government buildings, public security command posts, and data centers. It would learn about scientific breakthroughs as they are made, corporate mergers and acquisitions as they are contemplated, and patents before they are filed. It would be a fly on the wall for sensitive deliberations. It would enter most negotiations from a position of overwhelming strength.

China's information advantage would amount to an epic twist in the competition between state-controlled and more open economies. State planners have long struggled to make economic decisions with the efficiency of markets, as the Soviet Union's collapse highlighted. China's position at the center of global networks could cure that fatal flaw. If China's digital infrastructure efforts are uncontested and perfected, a scenario that must be considered, however unlikely, Beijing could ultimately possess better information than its rivals relying on open markets.

Armed with these advantages, Chinese leaders could be tempted to intervene more frequently in foreign countries. Foreign interventions are fraught with risk. The world simply has too many variables, many of them unknown, and the likelihood of unintended consequences looms large. But when leaders believe they have overwhelming advantages and superior information, success appears more likely and risks appear more manageable. Chinese leaders could become more confident in their ability to prevail in international disputes, whether over trading terms or physical territory. The likelihood of conflict could rise.

China's advantages would extend to the battlefield as well. The U.S. National Intelligence Council's *Global Trends 2040*, the latest forecast in a series that is published every four years, warns, "Dominance in major power competition and more specifically on the battlefield may increasingly depend on harnessing and protecting information and connecting military forces. Belligerents are increasingly likely to target their adversaries' computer networks, critical infrastructure, electromagnetic spectrum, financial systems, and assets in space, threatening communications and undermining warning functions."[134]

On the worst possible day, Beijing would have its hand on the throat of its adversaries. In a conflict, China could wreak havoc on countries' critical infrastructure. "Strategically the objective of information-war is to destroy the enemy's political, economic, and military information infrastructures, and, perhaps, even the information infrastructure for all of society," Shen explains. "This includes destroying and paralyzing the enemy's military, financial, telecommunications, electronic, and power systems, and computer networks."[135] The full and unimpeded realization of China's DSR points to a world in which China wins conflicts without firing a shot.[136]

To be clear, China is far from possessing this power. The CCP's view is becoming sharper and reaching further, but it remains fragmented and overwhelmed by data. Collecting such a massive amount of information is only the first step. The much harder technical challenge is making sense of it. From a purely technical standpoint, it is unclear that China can achieve this far-reaching yet perfectly centralized view even within its own borders. Doing so globally is exponentially more difficult.

Nor is network power without limits. China would be more likely to temporarily disrupt systems, especially in ways that allow some form of deniability, than to outright destroy them. Hitting the kill switch on another country's critical infrastructure, or set of countries, is not a card that can be played without significant risks and fast diminishing returns. The target could retaliate, including with conventional military force. The world would be watching, and even bystanders to the conflict may well decide that they should reduce their dependence on Chinese systems before it is too late.

Thankfully, it is not too late.

## ADVANCING FREEDOM

The belief that technology would promote democracy arose during a moment of American triumphalism.[137] The belief that democracies should promote technology is arising during a moment of despair. As the public mood shifts from hope to fear, there is a risk that paranoia will take hold and lead the United States to squander its still-superior power. In the coming years, American leaders and their counterparts in CORE countries will struggle to get the balance right between action and overreaction.

Anxiety about China's technological ambitions is hitting hard because it is overdue. China has risen rapidly, closing gaps in wireless networks, internet-connected devices, subsea cables, and global navigation satellite systems. Its ambitions have only grown, and it has set its eyes on taking the commanding heights. It aims to dominate the physical connections that carry data from the ocean floor to outer space and everything in between. Most shocking of all are its dystopian applications of technology at home. China's digital dream looks increasingly like a nightmare, and the United States and its partners are waking up to that reality.

Awareness of these risks is necessary to spur action. If the American public does not view China as a long-term competitor, the United States will struggle to formulate and sustain a strategy that will need to span administrations, parties, and even decades. Without common threat perceptions, the transatlantic bridge will remain disjointed, inefficient, and weak in its collective action. If India views China more as an irritant than an existential threat, it will chart a path outside the CORE. If threat perceptions continue to converge, the CORE stands a better chance of achieving the critical mass it needs and coordinating that collective strength.

But there is a line between anxiety and paranoia, and crossing it carries dangers all its own. During World War II, FDR made the horrific decision to force 120,000 people of Japanese ancestry into internment camps. Because today's challenge is primarily economic and technological, the signs are more subtle, but the risks are real. The United States must guard against xenophobia and racism as well as protectionism. These ills do not simply spring forth on their own. Historically, they have been pushed forward by groups using a foreign threat to advance their own agendas.

There is no quick fix for avoiding these pitfalls, no permanent guardrails that can prevent the plunge. It will require sustained vigilance and a willingness to ask often and honestly whether the United States, as it competes with China, is becoming a better version of itself. Anxiety can be harnessed toward productive ends, just as President Truman invoked the threat of the Soviet Union to build support for the U.S. interstate system. Similarly, responding to China today could involve making the domestic investments—in infrastructure, but also education, research, and better immigration policies—that will help the United States maintain its competitive edge.

Some will caution that the bigger risk is underreacting to the threat that China presents. Given the stakes of losing, this line of thinking goes, it is better to err on the side of overreaction. The problem is that this misses what should be the real objective: to depict China as it actually is, and to respond to that reality.[138] An effective strategy requires not only recognizing China's strengths but also identifying and exploiting its weaknesses. Depicting China as a juggernaut striding effortlessly toward global dominance is doing the CCP's work for it.

"Confidence is *the* essential ingredient," advises Ryan Hass, a former U.S. diplomat and leading China expert.[139] Projecting confidence at home will help keep alarmist and dishonest voices in check. Projecting confidence abroad is more likely to attract partners. And the United States has plenty of reasons to be confident.[140] It is the world's leading hub for international data, home to the world's most innovative companies, and the linchpin in a global network of partners and allies that China lacks. Beijing's domestic barriers constrain its companies' ability to innovate and expand. As long as Chinese officials continue giving in to their own paranoia, China will face an uphill battle to overtaking the United States as world's chief network operator.

The United States and its allies should brace themselves for a long competition. The Network Wars are not likely to be decided in a single winner-take-all confrontation. Victory will not look like the end of World War II in Europe, when streets filled with music and parades. It is harder to celebrate things that do not happen, and winning will require preventing disasters and weathering disruptions. Success is less about securing an enemy's surrender than building resilient systems. Much of the work will be technical, repetitive, and unglamorous.

During the network battles and crises to come, it is worth keeping in mind that China has fewer reasons for confidence but has an easier time faking it. Democracies' flaws and mistakes are often on display for the world to see. Amid the outrage that comes with each failure, it is easy to forget that awareness of these shortcomings often stems from strengths: transparency, independent media, and rule of law. Openness, in turn, drives adaptation. In contrast, the true extent of China's flaws is more likely to remain unknown, perhaps until Beijing can no longer manage them. Behind the CCP's obsession with control is deep insecurity.

Embracing a realistic view of technology does not mean giving up on the aspirations that motivated and indeed blinded so many leaders from the internet's earliest days. There is a vast amount of good that communications technology does every day, and incredible potential over the horizon to expand access and improve lives. But it is now painfully apparent that expanding access does not guarantee positive outcomes. Connectivity is not an unalloyed good. Believing otherwise unburdened governments, companies, and citizens of responsibility.

Recall Reagan's words to a London audience in 1989: "More than armies, more than diplomacy, more than the best intentions of democratic nations, the communications revolution will be the greatest force for the advancement of human freedom the world has ever seen."[141] That "revolution" sounded like it would run on autopilot. Already unleashed, it simply needed time to gather momentum. But far from being a utopia, the digital world now reflects and amplifies real world problems. Inequality, tribalism, and crime all thrive online.

Once the myth that connectivity is purely "good" falls away, the breadth of the challenge becomes clearer. There is nothing inevitable about the advancement of human freedom. Realizing the positive potential of communications technology will require even more diplomacy. It will require wealthy democracies to live up to their own principles while reaching out to developing countries. It will require overhauling traditional concepts of security.

None of this will be fast, easy, or cheap. So much needs to be done that it is all too alluring to imagine that ever-smarter technology will provide a shortcut, a magic fix, an upgrade to the human condition. But rather than pin our hopes on tools or grand forces, we must shift our focus to humanity itself. In different degrees, each of us bears responsibility for deciding how networks are used. Governments must plan wisely. Companies must act with care. Citizens must demand accountability. Humans must be the greatest force for freedom.

# ACKNOWLEDGMENTS

This book would not have been possible without the kindness, care, and wisdom of many people.

The Center for Strategic and International Studies has provided a professional home for the past five years. Thank you, Dr. John Hamre, Craig Cohen, Josie Gable, and Matthew Goodman for your leadership and support. The team behind the Reconnecting Asia Project has my gratitude as well. Andrew Huang chased down a long list of research requests and dove deep into technical details with speed and precision. Emily Cipriani provided early assistance with translations. Laura Rivas and Joseph Yinusa provided targeted research support. Maesea McCalpin kept us all on track.

Thank you to colleagues who have advised the Reconnecting Asia Project and myself: Bushra Bataineh, Michael Bennon, Jude Blanchette, Victor Cha, Heather Conley, Alexander Cooley, Judd Devermont, Bonnie Glaser, Michael Green, Grace Hearty, Scott Kennedy, Agatha Kratz, Sarah Ladislaw, James Lewis, Greg Poling, Peter Raymond, Richard Rossow, Daniel Runde, and Stephanie Segal.

While navigating new terrain, I benefited from the guidance of more experienced travelers, especially Blaine Curcio, Steven Feldstein, Allie Funk, Sheena Chestnut Greitens, Caleb Henry, John Melick, John McHugh, James Mulvenon, Charles Rollet, Victoria Samson, Adrian Shahbaz, Patrick Shannon, David Stanton, Brian Weeden, and several others who will remain anonymous.

I'm especially grateful to Andrew Hill at the *Financial Times* for overseeing the Bracken Bower Prize, an exceptional opportunity for aspiring writers. Thank you to Allan Song and the Smith Richardson Foundation for their generous support, and to Doron Weber at the Sloan Foundation for encouraging my initial exploration of technology issues.

A literary all-star team made this book possible. Hollis Heimbouch and Wendy Wong at HarperCollins made every page smarter, every chapter smoother, and somehow made it all fun. Plaegian Alexander's careful eye sharpened the final text. At Profile, Ed Lake's feel for international audiences helped make this a truly global story. Toby Mundy has a gift for defying the laws of ideas, making concepts bigger and sharper at the same time, and I'm lucky to have him as an agent.

Thank you to friends and family for tolerating slow responses, missed calls, and unpolished versions of some of the stories told in these pages. My parents and in-laws were generous hosts and helpers at key moments during a year of isolation, providing the company, change of scenery, and peace of mind to continue writing. After a year of co-confinement, I'm more mystified than ever about the source of my partner's endless energy. It's inspiring to see the passion she brings to her work, the loyalty she brings to friends and family, and the love she brings to our daughter, Harper. Most of all, thank you, Liz.

# NOTES

## CHAPTER ONE   THE NETWORK WARS

1.  Ronald Reagan, "The Triumph of Freedom" (speech, 1989 Churchill lecture, London, June 13, 1989), London Broadcasting Company (LBC) / Independent Radio News (IRN) Digitisation Archive, Global Radio UK Ltd., http://bufvc .ac.uk/tvandradio/lbc/index.php/segment/0007100432001.

2.  Nicholas D. Kristof, "The Tiananmen Victory," *New York Times*, June 2, 2004, www.nytimes.com/2004/06/02/opinion/the-tiananmen-victory.html.

3.  Andrew Higgins, "A Correspondent Shares 25 Years of Perspective," *Sinosphere* (blog), *New York Times*, June 3, 2014, https://sinosphere.blogs.nytimes.com /2014/06/03/live-blogging-the-25-tiananmen-square-anniversary/.

4.  Nicholas D. Kristof, "Satellites Bring Information Revolution to China," *New York Times*, April 11, 1993, www.nytimes.com/1993/04/11/world/satellites-bring -information-revolution-to-china.html.

5.  Nicholas D. Kristof, "Death by a Thousand Blogs," *New York Times*, May 24, 2005, www.nytimes.com/2005/05/24/opinion/death-by-a-thousand-blogs.html.

6.  Toru Tsunashima, "In 165 Countries, China's Beidou Eclipses American GPS," *Nikkei Asia*, November 25, 2020, https://asia.nikkei.com/Politics/International -relations/In-165-countries-China-s-Beidou-eclipses-American-GPS.

7.  "Yi tong zhongguo qianding gong jian 'yidai yilu' hezuo wenjian de guojia yi lan" 已同中国签订共建'一带一路'合作文件的国家一览 [List of Countries That Have Signed Cooperation Documents with China to Jointly Build the "One Belt One Road"], Belt and Road Portal, last modified January 30, 2021, www .yidaiyilu.gov.cn/gbjg/gbgk/77073.htm.

8.  Jason Miller, "Ban on Chinese Products Starts Today despite Confusion over Acquisition Rule," Federal News Network, August 13, 2020, https://federal newsnetwork.com/acquisition-policy/2020/08/ban-on-chinese-products-starts -today-despite-confusion-over-acquisition-rule/.

9.  David Shepardson, "FCC Begins Process of Halting China Telecom U.S. Operations," Reuters, December 10, 2020, www.reuters.com/article/usa-china-tech /fcc-begins-process-of-halting-china-telecom-u-s-operations-idUSKBN28K2 ER; John McCrank and Anirban Sen, "NYSE to Delist Three Chinese Telecoms in Dizzying About-Face," Reuters, January 6, 2021, www.reuters.com/article /us-china-usa-telecom/nyse-to-delist-three-chinese-telecoms-in-dizzying-about -face-idUSKBN29B1TR.

10. Ellen Nakashima and Jeanne Whalen, "U.S. Bans Technology Exports to Chinese Semiconductor and Drone Companies, Calling Them Security Threats," *Washington Post*, December 19, 2020, www.washingtonpost.com/technology/2020 /12/18/china-smic-entity-list-ban/.

11. "The Clean Network," U.S. Department of State (archive), accessed February 22, 2021, https://2017-2021.state.gov/the-clean-network/index.html.

12. "China's Got a New Plan to Overtake the U.S. in Tech," Bloomberg, May 20, 2020, www.bloomberg.com/news/articles/2020-05-20/china-has-a-new-1-4-trillion -plan-to-overtake-the-u-s-in-tech.

13. Arjun Kharpal, "In Battle with U.S., China to Focus on 7 'Frontier' Technologies from Chips to Brain-Computer Fusion," CNBC, March 5, 2021, www.cnbc .com/2021/03/05/china-to-focus-on-frontier-tech-from-chips-to-quantum -computing.html.

14. James Crabtree, "China's Radical New Vision of Globalization," *Noema Magazine*, December 10, 2020, www.noemamag.com/chinas-radical-new-vision-of -globalization/.

15. Daniel W. Drezner, Henry Farrell, and Abraham L. Newman, eds., *The Uses and Abuses of Weaponized Interdependence* (Washington, D.C.: Brookings Institution Press, 2021).

16. Rebecca MacKinnon, *Consent of the Networked: The Worldwide Struggle for Internet Freedom* (New York: Basic Books, 2012); Evgeny Morozov, *The Net Delusion: The Dark Side of Internet Freedom* (New York: PublicAffairs, 2011).

17. John Perry Barlow, "A Declaration of the Independence of Cyberspace," Electric Frontier Foundation, February 8, 1996, www.eff.org/cyberspace-independence.

18. Translation as paraphrased in Timothy L. Thomas, *Dragon Bytes: Chinese Information-War Theory and Practice* (Leavenworth, KS: Foreign Military Studies Office, Fort Leavenworth, 2004), 46.

19. Thomas, *Dragon Bytes*, 51.

20. "Freedom of Expression and the Internet in China: A Human Rights Watch

Backgrounder," Human Rights Watch, accessed February 28, 2021, www.hrw
.org/legacy/backgrounder/asia/china-bck-0701.htm; "Zhonghua renmin gong
heguo jisuanji xinxi xitong anquan baohu tiaoli" 中华人民共和国计算机信息系
统安全保护条例 [Regulations of the People's Republic of China on the Security
and Protection of Computer Information Systems], The Central People's Government of the People's Republic of China, last modified August 6, 2005, www
.gov.cn/flfg/2005-08/06/content_20928.htm.

21. "The 11 Commandments of the Internet in China," Reporters Without Borders,
last modified January 20, 2016, https://rsf.org/en/news/11-commandments
-internet-china; for the full set of regulations, see "Provisions on the Administration of Internet News Information Services (Chinese Text and CECC Full
Translation)," Congressional-Executive Commission on China, accessed February 26, 2021, www.cecc.gov/resources/legal-provisions/provisions-on-the-admini
stration-of-internet-news-information-services#body-chinese.

22. William J. Clinton, "Full Text of Clinton's Speech on China Trade Bill" (speech,
Paul H. Nitze School of Advanced International Studies, Johns Hopkins Univer-
sity, Baltimore, MD, March 9, 2000), https://www.iatp.org/sites/default/files
/Full_Text_of_Clintons_Speech_on_China_Trade_Bi.htm.

23. Greg Walton, *China's Golden Shield: Corporations and the Development of Surveillance
Technology in the People's Republic of China* (Montreal: International Centre for Human Rights and Democratic Development, 2001), https://ia803005.us.archive
.org/35/items/230159-china-golden-shield/230159-china-golden-shield.pdf.

24. Jonathan Ansfield, "Biganzi Q&A: Li Xinde Shares Tips of His Trade," China
Digital Times, September 21, 2006, https://chinadigitaltimes.net/2006/09
/biganzi-qa-li-xinde-shares-tips-of-his-trade/.

25. Nicholas D. Kristof, "Slipping over the Wall," *New York Times*, August 24, 2008,
www.nytimes.com/2008/08/24/opinion/24iht-edkristof.1.15583418.html?
searchResultPosition=15.

26. Sheena Chestnut Greitens, "China's Surveillance State at Home and Abroad:
Challenges for U.S. Policy" (working paper, Penn Project on the Future of U.S.-
China Relations, 2020), https://cpb-us-w2.wpmucdn.com/web.sas.upenn.edu
/dist/b/732/files/2020/10/Sheena-Greitens_Chinas-Surveillance-State-at
-Home-Abroad_Final.pdf.

27. American Telephone and Telegraph Company, "Annual Report for the Year
Ending December 31, 1908," March 16, 1909, in *The Commercial & Financial
Chronicle* 88 (New York: William B. Dana Company, 1909), 829, https://books
.google.com/books?id=v3dIAQAAMAAJ.

28.  Tom Wheeler, *From Gutenberg to Google: The History of Our Future* (Washington, D.C.: Brookings Institution Press, 2019), 184.

29.  James Currier, "The Network Effects Manual: 13 Different Network Effects (and Counting)," *NFX* (blog), January 9, 2018, https://medium.com/@nfx /the-network-effects-manual-13-different-network-effects-and-counting-a3e0 7b23017d.

30.  Sophia Chen, "Why This Intercontinental Quantum-Encrypted Video Hangout Is a Big Deal," *Wired*, January 20, 2010, www.wired.com/story/why-this -intercontinental-quantum-encrypted-video-hangout-is-a-big-deal/.

31.  Momoko Kidera, "Huawei's Deep Roots Put Africa beyond Reach of US Crackdown," *Nikkei Asia*, August 15, 2020, https://asia.nikkei.com/Spotlight/Huawei -crackdown/Huawei-s-deep-roots-put-Africa-beyond-reach-of-US-crackdown.

32.  Paul Brodsky et al., *The State of the Network: 2020 Edition* (San Diego, CA: Pri-Metrica, Inc., 2020), 8, www2.telegeography.com/hubfs/assets/Ebooks/state-of -the-network-2020.pdf.

33.  Tim Rühlig, *China, Europe, and the New Power Competition over Technical Standards,* (Stockholm: The Swedish Institute of International Affairs, 2021), 3, www.ui.se /globalassets/ui.se-eng/publications/ui-publications/2021/ui-brief-no.-1-2021 .pdf.

34.  Daniel Fuchs and Sarah Eaton, "How China and Germany Became Partners on Technical Standardization," *Washington Post*, November 16, 2020, www.washing tonpost.com/politics/2020/11/16/how-china-germany-became-partners -technical-standardization/.

35.  Ghalia Kadiri and Joan Tilouine, "A Addis-Abeba, le Siège de l'Union Africaine Espionné par Pékin" [In Addis Ababa, the Headquarters of the African Union Were Spied on by Beijing], *Le Monde,* January 26, 2018, www.lemonde .fr/afrique/article/2018/01/26/a-addis-abeba-le-siege-de-l-union-africaine -espionne-par-les-chinois_5247521_3212.html.

36.  Huawei, "Huawei and the African Union Sign a MoU to Strengthen Their Technical Partnership on ICT," press release, May 31, 2019, www.huawei.com/za /news/za/2019/huawei-the-african-union-sign-a-mou.

37.  Raphael Satter, "Exclusive-Suspected Chinese Hackers Stole Camera Footage from African Union—Memo," Reuters, December 16, 2020, www.reuters.com /article/us-ethiopia-african-union-cyber-exclusiv/exclusive-suspected-chinese -hackers-stole-camera-footage-from-african-union-memo-idUSKBN28Q1DB.

38.  Peter Suciu, "Is China Using Hacked OPM Data?," ClearanceJobs, April 19,

2019, https://news.clearancejobs.com/2019/04/19/is-china-using-hacked-opm
-data/; Erik Larson, "Chinese Citizen Indicted in Anthem Hack of 80 Million People," Bloomberg, May 9, 2019, www.bloomberg.com/news/articles/2019-05-09
/chinese-national-indicted-by-u-s-grand-jury-over-anthem-hack; Eric Geller,
"U.S. Charges Chinese Military Hackers with Massive Equifax Breach," *Politico*,
February 10, 2020, www.politico.com/news/2020/02/10/us-charges-chinese
-spies-with-massive-equifax-hack-113129.

39. Zach Dorfman, "Beijing Ransacked Data as U.S. Sources Went Dark in China,"
*Foreign Policy*, December 22, 2020, https://foreignpolicy.com/2020/12/22/china
-us-data-intelligence-cybersecurity-xi-jinping/; Zach Dorfman, "China Used
Stolen Data to Expose CIA Operatives in Africa and Europe," *Foreign Policy*, December 21, 2020, https://foreignpolicy.com/2020/12/21/china-stolen-us-data
-exposed-cia-operatives-spy-networks/.

40. "China-Linked Group RedEcho Targets the Indian Power Sector amid Heightened Border Tensions," Insikt Group, Recorded Future, February 28, 2021, www
.recordedfuture.com/redecho-targeting-indian-power-sector/.

41. Shreya Jai, "From Thermal to Solar Units, China Dominates India's Power Sector," *Business Standard*, June 18, 2020, https://www.business-standard.com/article
/economy-policy/from-thermal-to-solar-units-china-dominates-india-s-power
-sector-120061701894_1.html.

42. Evelyn Cheng, "China's Xi: 'No Force Can Stop the Chinese People and the
Chinese Nation,'" CNBC, last modified October 1, 2019, www.cnbc.com/2019
/10/01/china-70th-anniversary-xi-says-no-force-can-stop-the-chinese-people
.html.

43. China Unicom, "Shengshi huacai keji fu neng: Guoqing shengdian beihou de
liantong qi da liangdian—beijing liantong yuanman wancheng qingzhu xin
zhongguo chengli 70 zhounian huodong tongxin fuwu baozhang" 盛世华彩 科
技赋能: 国庆盛典背后的联通七大亮点—北京联通圆满完成庆祝新中国成立
70周年活动通信服务保障 [Golden Age Splendor and Technological Empowerment: Seven China Unicom Highlights behind the National Day Ceremony—
Beijing Unicom Successfully Provides Security for Communications Services at
the 70th Anniversary Celebrations of the Founding of New China], press release,
October 1, 2019, www.chinaunicom.cn/news/201910/1569940668782066081
.html.

44. Jessie Yeung, James Griffiths, and Steve George, "Hong Kong Protesters Hit
the Streets as China Marks 70 Years of Communist Rule," CNN, last modified
October 1, 2019, www.cnn.com/asia/live-news/china-hong-kong-oct-1-live-intl
-hnk/h_6551c3607349db6d0d8babac4dda0a32.

45. Eva Dou, Natasha Khan, and Wenxin Fan, "China Claims U.S. 'Black Hand' Is behind Hong Kong Protests," *Wall Street Journal*, August 9, 2019, www.wsj.com /articles/china-claims-u-s-black-hand-is-behind-hong-kong-protests-115653 56245.

46. Melanie Hart and Jordan Link, "Chinese President Xi Jinping's Philosophy on Risk Management," Center for American Progress, February 20, 2020, www .americanprogress.org/issues/security/news/2020/02/20/480680/chinese -president-xi-jinpings-philosophy-risk-management/.

47. Qiao Long 乔龙, "Liusi tian wang, zhongguo yulun jiandu wang zai zao gongji" 六 四天网, 中国舆论监督网再遭攻击 [The June 4th Network and the China Pub- lic Opinion Supervision Network Were Attacked Again], Radio Free Asia, Au- gust 18, 2015, www.rfa.org/mandarin/yataibaodao/meiti/ql2-08182015102821 .html.

48. Li Xinde 李新德, "Tianjin dong li: Zhejiang yi gongsi pi zhi 'ju zhi zui' rang qian fading daibiao ren dan ze" 天津东丽: 浙江一公司被指 '拒执罪' 让前法定代表 人担责 [Tianjin's Dongli District: A Zhejiang Company Charged with "Refus- ing to Comply with Criminal Penalties" Lets Its Former Legal Representative Shoulder the Blame], *Yulun Wang* 舆论网 [Opinion Network] (blog), October 14, 2019, https://wemp.app/posts/2691d0e9-d092-4948-9fbe-d77041c21958; Li Xinde 李新德, "Tianjin dong li: Qian fading daibiao ren pi zhi 'ju zhi zui' jingfang huiying: Zeren yongjiu zhi" 天津东丽: 前法定代表人被指 '拒执罪' 警方回应: 责任永久制 [Tianjin's Dongli District: Former Legal Representa- tive Is Charged with "Refusing to Comply with Criminal Penalties," Police De- partment's Response: [He] Bears Ultimate Responsibility], *Yulun Wang* 舆论网 [Opinion Network] (blog), October 18, 2019, https://wemp.app/posts/8c42ff1e -525b-4aab-b4e8-f67f38986c9f.

49. "Zhongguo yulun jiandu wang chuangban ren lixinde bei pan wu nian" 中国 舆论监督网创办人李新德被判五年 [Li Xinde, Founder of the China Public Opinion Supervision Network, Receives a Five Year Sentence], Radio Free Asia, January 13, 2021, www.rfa.org/mandarin/yataibaodao/renquanfazhi/pl -01132021153542.html.

50. Ansfield, "Biganzi Q&A."

51. Katherine Atha et al., *China's Smart Cities Development: Research Report Prepared on be- half of the U.S.-China Economic and Security Review Commission* (Vienna, VA: SOS Inter- national LLC, 2020), 56–57, www.uscc.gov/sites/default/files/2020-04/China _Smart_Cities_Development.pdf.

52. Sheridan Prasso, "Huawei's Claims That It Makes Cities Safer Mostly Look

Like Hype," Bloomberg, November 12, 2019, www.bloomberg.com/news/articles /2019-11-12/huawei-s-surveillance-network-claims-face-scrutiny?sref=VZP f2pAM.

53. Reuters, "Kenya Secures $666 Million from China for Tech City, Highway," April 26, 2019, www.reuters.com/article/us-kenya-china/kenya-secures-666 -million-from-china-for-tech-city-highway-idUSKCN1S21KG.

54. Tim Stronge, "Does 70% of the World's Internet Traffic Flow through Virginia?," *TeleGeography Blog*, TeleGeography, May 30, 2019, https://blog.telegeography .com/does-70-of-the-worlds-internet-traffic-flow-through-virginia.

55. John Markoff, "Internet Traffic Begins to Bypass the U.S.," *New York Times*, August 29, 2008, www.nytimes.com/2008/08/30/business/30pipes.html.

56. "AWS, Microsoft, Google, Alibaba Share in Cloud Market," InfotechLead, April 2, 2020, https://infotechlead.com/cloud/aws-microsoft-google-alibaba-share-in -cloud-market-60638.

57. Jared Cohen and Richard Fontaine, "Uniting the Techno-Democracies," *Foreign Affairs*, November/December 2020, www.foreignaffairs.com/articles/united -states/2020-10-13/uniting-techno-democracies.

## CHAPTER TWO    CTRL + C

1. Northern Telecom Ltd., *Annual Report 1994*, February 23, 1995.

2. Northern Telecom Ltd., *Annual Report 1992*, February 25, 1993.

3. As quoted in Northern Telecom Ltd., *Annual Report 1992*.

4. Nick Waddell, "The Nortel Orbitor: The iPhone Killer That Was a Decade Ahead of Its Time," Cantech Letter, November 9, 2011, www.cantechletter.com /2011/11/nortels-orbitor-the-iphone-killer-that-was-a-decade-early/.

5. *The Future of Warfare: Hearing before the Committee on Armed Services, United States Senate*, 114th Cong. (2015) (statement of General Keith B. Alexander, Ret., former director of the National Security Agency), https://www.govinfo.gov/content /pkg/CHRG-114shrg99570/html/CHRG-114shrg99570.htm.

6. Northern Telecom Ltd., *Annual Report 1994*.

7. Milton Mueller and Zixiang Tan, *China in the Information Age: Telecommunications and the Dilemmas of Reform* (Westport, CT: Praeger, 1997), 26–29.

8. "Nortel Underlines Ties with China's Market," *People's Daily*, July 27, 2001, http://en.people.cn/english/200107/27/eng20010727_75951.html.

9. Sun Ying Shea, "Major Barriers in Telecommunications Technology Transfer: Northern Telecom's Perspective" (master's thesis, Department of Communication, Simon Fraser University, 1992), 41, https://summit.sfu.ca/item/3834.

10. Robert D. Atkinson, "Who Lost Lucent?: The Decline of America's Telecom Equipment Industry," *American Affairs* 4, no. 3 (2020): 99–135, https://american affairsjournal.org/2020/08/who-lost-lucent-the-decline-of-americas-telecom -equipment-industry/.

11. Ann Walmsley, "The Deal That Almost Got Away: Nortel's Bid to Be a Global Player Was Pinned to a Crucial Chinese Contract," *Report on Business Magazine, Globe and Mail*, August 1995, https://search.proquest.com/docview/194517 403.

12. Swapan Kumar Patra, "Innovation Network in IT Sector: A Study of Collaboration Patterns among Selected Foreign IT Firms in India and China," in *Collaboration in International and Comparative Librarianship*, ed. Susmita Chakraborty and Anup Kumar Das (Hershey, PA: IGI Global, 2014), 154, https://books.google .com/books?id=quNGAwAAQBAJ.

13. Brenda Dalglish, "China Comes to Call," *Maclean's*, May 2, 1994, https:// archive.macleans.ca/article/1994/5/2/china-comes-to-call.

14. Xing Fan, *China Telecommunications: Constituencies and Challenges* (Cambridge, MA: Program on Information Resources Policy, Harvard University, Center for Information Policy Research, 1996), 146–47, www.pirp.harvard.edu/pubs_pdf/fan /fan-p96-4.pdf.

15. U.S. General Accounting Office, *Export Controls: Sale of Telecommunications Equipment to China*, GAO/NSIAD-97-5 (Washington, D.C.: U.S. General Accounting Office, 1996), www.gao.gov/assets/230/223441.pdf.

16. Marlin Fitzwater, "Statement by Press Secretary Fitzwater on Multilateral Export Controls" (speech, White House press statement, n.p., May 24, 1991), in George H. W. Bush, *Public Papers of the Presidents of the United States: George H. W. Bush (1991, Book I)* (Washington, D.C.: U.S. Government Publishing Office, 1992), 558–59, https://www.govinfo.gov/content/pkg/PPP-1991-book1/html /PPP-1991-book1-doc-pg558.htm.

17. U.S. Department of Commerce, *Background Paper for Assistant Secretary Sue Eckert Meeting* (Washington, D.C.: U.S. Department of Commerce, 1994), China and the US, National Security Archive, George Washington University, Washington, D.C., https://search.proquest.com/docview/1679077299.

18. William J. Clinton, "Remarks to the Seattle APEC Host Committee" (speech,

Asian-Pacific Economic Cooperation conference, Seattle, WA, November 19, 1993), The American Presidency Project, University of California, Santa Barbara, https://www.presidency.ucsb.edu/documents/remarks-the-seattle-apec-host -committee.

19. See chapter 13 in Michael J. Green, *By More than Providence: Grand Strategy and American Power in the Asia Pacific Since 1783* (New York: Columbia University Press, 2017) and chapter 5 in Bob Davis and Lingling Wei, *Superpower Showdown: How the Battle between Trump and Xi Threatens a New Cold War* (New York: Harper Business, 2020).

20. Norman Kempster and Rone Tempest, "U.S. Imposes Sanctions on China, Pakistan over Missile Deal: Arms Technology: Export of Satellite Gear to Beijing Is Banned. Both Asian Nations Deny Violating Controls," *Los Angeles Times*, August 26, 1993, www.latimes.com/archives/la-xpm-1993-08-26-mn-28209-story .html.

21. U.S. Department of Commerce, *Assistant Secretary Sue Eckert Meeting.*

22. White House, *A National Security Strategy of Engagement and Enlargement*, White House Report 19960807 039 (Washington, D.C.: White House, 1996), 2–3, https:// history.defense.gov/Portals/70/Documents/nss/nss1996.pdf?ver=2014-06-25-.

23. Hugo Meijer, *Trading with the Enemy: The Making of US Export Control Policy toward the People's Republic of China* (New York: Oxford University Press, 2016), 156–57.

24. William J. Clinton, "Remarks and a Question-and-Answer Session with Silicon Graphics Employees in Mountain View, California" (speech, Mountain View, CA, February 22, 1993), The American Presidency Project, University of California, Santa Barbara, www.presidency.ucsb.edu/documents/remarks-and-question -and-answer-session-with-silicon-graphics-employees-mountain-view. See also William J. Clinton, interview by John Culea (reporter, KFMB-TV), San Diego, CA, October 22, 1993, The American Presidency Project, University of California, Santa Barbara, www.presidency.ucsb.edu/documents/interview-with-john -culea-kfmb-tv-san-diego.

25. White House, *National Security Strategy*, 1.

26. William J. Clinton, "Remarks in a Town Meeting with Russian Citizens in Moscow" (speech, Moscow, January 14, 1994), The American Presidency Project, University of California, Santa Barbara, www.presidency.ucsb.edu/documents /remarks-town-meeting-with-russian-citizens-moscow.

27. U.S. General Accounting Office, *Export Controls*, 9.

28. "Joining Forces: SCM/Brooks Telecommunications L.P. of Chicago . . . ,"

*Chicago Tribune*, May 5, 1993, www.chicagotribune.com/news/ct-xpm-1993-05 -05-9305060330-story.html.

29. Jeff Gerth and Eric Schmitt, "The Technology Trade: A Special Report; Chinese Said to Reap Gains in U.S. Export Policy Shift," *New York Times*, October 19, 1998, www.nytimes.com/1998/10/19/us/technology-trade-special-report -chinese-said-reap-gains-us-export-policy-shift.html.

30. James C. Mulvenon, *Soldiers of Fortune: The Rise and Fall of the Chinese Military-Business Complex, 1978–1998* (New York: Routledge, 2015).

31. John Polanyi, "Education in the Information Age," in Northern Telecom Ltd., *Annual Report 1994*, http://sites.utoronto.ca/jpolanyi/public_affairs/public_af fairs4g.html.

32. John Polanyi, email correspondence with author, December 4, 2020.

33. Northern Telecom Ltd., *Annual Report 1994*, 34.

34. Ray Le Maistre, "Huawei Reports 2008 Revenues of $18.3B," Light Reading, April 22, 2009, www.lightreading.com/huawei-reports-2008-revenues-of-$183b /d/d-id/667148; "Nortel Reconfirms 2008 Outlook, to Offer Notes," Reuters, May 21, 2008, www.reuters.com/article/idUKN2138018820080521.

35. As quoted in Xiao Wei 肖卫, *Yingxiang zhongguo jingji fazhan de ershi wei qiye lingxiu* 影响中国经济发展的二十位企业领袖 [Twenty Enterprise Leaders That Influence China's Economy] (Shenyang, China: Shenyang chubanshe 沈阳出版社 [Shenyang Publishing House], 2000), 12; this was the source cited in Peilei Fan, "Promoting Indigenous Capability: The Chinese Government and the Catching-Up of Domestic Telecom-Equipment Firms," *China Review* 6, no. 1 (2006): 9–35, www.jstor.org/stable/23462007?seq=1.

36. "Opening Speech at the 12th National Congress of the Communist Party of China," *China Daily*, September 1, 1982, https://cpcchina.chinadaily.com.cn /2010-10/20/content_13918249.htm.

37. Cheng Dongsheng 程东升 and Liu Lili 刘丽丽, *Huawei Zhenxiang* 华为真相 [The Truth of Huawei] (Beijing: Dangdai zhongguo chubanshe 当代中国出版社 [Contemporary China Publishing House], 2003), 30.

38. "'Du shang xingming' gao yanfa huawei weisheme zheme pin" '赌上性命' 搞 研发 华为为什么这么拼 ["Betting Your Life" on R&D: Why Huawei Works So Hard], *People's Daily*, November 23, 2018, http://ip.people.com.cn/n1/2018 /1123/c179663-30417549.html.

39. Cheng and Liu, *Truth of Huawei*, 216–17.

40. Deng Yingying, "China's National Innovation System (NIS) in the Making: Case Studies of Three Indigenous Chinese Companies" (master's thesis, University of Massachusetts Lowell, 2003), 44–45; Evan S. Medeiros et al., *A New Direction for China's Defense Industry*, MG-334-AF (Santa Monica, CA: RAND, 2005), 218, www.rand.org/pubs/monographs/MG334.html; Bruce Gilley, "Huawei's Fixed Line to Beijing," *Far Eastern Economic Review*, December 28, 2000, www.web.pdx .edu/~gilleyb/Huawei_FEER28Dec2000.pdf.

41. Deng, "China's National Innovation System (NIS)," 45; Gilley, "Huawei's Fixed Line to Beijing."

42. Qing Mu and Keun Lee, "Knowledge Diffusion, Market Segmentation and Technological Catch-Up: The Case of the Telecommunication Industry in China," *Research Policy* 34, no. 6 (August 2005): 759–83, https://doi.org/10.1016/j.respol .2005.02.007.

43. Deng, "China's National Innovation System (NIS)," 45–46.

44. Cheng and Liu, *Truth of Huawei*, 103.

45. Cheng and Liu, *Truth of Huawei*, 284–86.

46. Mu and Lee, "Knowledge Diffusion," 759–83.

47. Deng, "China's National Innovation System (NIS)," 47–48; Mu and Lee, "Knowledge Diffusion."

48. Chuin-Wei Yap, "State Support Helped Fuel Huawei's Global Rise," *Wall Street Journal*, December 25, 2019, www.wsj.com/articles/state-support-helped-fuel -huaweis-global-rise-11577280736.

49. Yuan Yang and Nian Liu, "Huawei Founder Ren Zhengfei in His Own Words," *Financial Times*, January 15, 2019, www.ft.com/content/aba92826-18db-11e9-9e 64-d150b3105d21.

50. Deng, "China's National Innovation System (NIS)," 47–48.

51. "Huawei gongsi jibenfa (dinggao)" 华为公司基本法(定稿) [The Huawei Company Basic Law (Finalized)], Geren tushu guan 个人图书馆 [Personal Library], accessed February 23, 2021, www.360doc.com/content/20/0925/16/20390846 _937558376.shtml.

52. Li-Chung Chang et al., "Dynamic Organizational Learning: A Narrative Inquiry into the Story of Huawei in China," *Asia Pacific Business Review* 23, no. 4 (2017): 541–58, https://doi.org/10.1080/13602381.2017.1346910. On Deng's use of the concept, see Gao Yi 高屹, "Lishi xuanzele dengxiaoping (72)" 历史选择了

邓小平 (72) [History Chose Deng Xiaoping (72)], *People's Daily*, August 1, 2018, http://cpc.people.com.cn/n1/2018/0801/c69113-30182455.html.

53.  Cheng and Liu, *Truth of Huawei*, 41.

54.  Cheng Dongsheng and Liu Lili, *The Huawei Miracle: English Edition* (Beijing: China Intercontinental Press, 2019), 52.

55.  This source notes that Chen gave the book: Tian Tao, David De Cremer, and Wu Chunbo, *Huawei: Leadership, Culture, and Connectivity* (Los Angeles: SAGE, 2017), loc. 2015 of 6460, Kindle; this source notes the title of the book: Johann P. Murmann, Can Huang, and Xiaobo Wu, "Constructing Large Multinational Corporations from China: East Meets West at Huawei, 1987–2017," in *Academy of Management Annual Meeting Proceedings 2018* (Chicago: Academy of Management, 2018), https://doi.org/10.5465/AMBPP.2018.10189abstract.

56.  Michael E. McGrath, *Setting the PACE in Product Development: A Guide to Product and Cycle-Time Excellence* (Boston: Butterworth-Heinemann, Elsevier, 1996), 172, https://books.google.com/books?id=W2TZvWAaMLoC.

57.  Tian, De Cremer, and Wu, *Huawei*, loc. 4944, Kindle; "Huawei Technologies: A Trail Blazer in Africa," *Knowledge@Wharton*, April 20, 2009, https://knowledge.wharton.upenn.edu/article/huawei-technologies-a-chinese-trail-blazer-in-africa/.

58.  Xiaobo Wu et al., "The Management Transformation of Huawei," in *The Management Transformation of Huawei: An Overview*, ed. Johann Peter Murmann (Cambridge, UK: Cambridge University Press, 2020), 40, www.alexandria.unisg.ch/259512/1/Murmann_Huawei_Overview.pdf.

59.  Tian, De Cremer, and Wu, *Huawei*, loc. 5012-5016.

60.  Tian, De Cremer, and Wu, *Huawei*, loc. 4884.

61.  Tian, De Cremer, and Wu, *Huawei*, loc. 4914-4939.

62.  Tian, De Cremer, and Wu, *Huawei*, loc. 5685.

63.  Tian, De Cremer, and Wu, *Huawei*, loc. 5660.

64.  Tian, De Cremer, and Wu, *Huawei*, loc. 5656.

65.  Murmann, Huang, and Wu, "Constructing Large Multinational Corporations," 34.

66.  Tian, De Cremer, and Wu, *Huawei*, loc. 4941.

67.  Tian, De Cremer, and Wu, *Huawei*, loc. 5676.

68.  Spencer E. Ante, "Huawei's Ally: IBM," *Wall Street Journal*, last modified October

10, 2012, www.wsj.com/articles/SB100008723963904432949045780468720362 96296.

69. Tian, De Cremer, and Wu, *Huawei*, loc. 4941.

70. Clinton, "Speech on China Trade Bill."

71. *China in the WTO: What Will It Mean for the U.S. High Technology Sector?: Joint Hearing before the Subcommittee on International Economic Policy, Export and Trade Promotion and the Subcommittee on East Asian and Pacific Affairs of the Committee on Foreign Relations, United States Senate*, 106th Cong. (2000), www.govinfo.gov/app/details /CHRG-106shrg66498/context.

72. Richard Younts (executive vice president, Motorola Inc.), testimony on *China in the WTO*.

73. Frank Carlucci (chairman of the board of directors, Nortel Networks), testimony on *China in the WTO*.

74. Jiang Zemin, "Accelerate the Development of Our Country's Information and Network Technologies" (speech excerpt, Third Session of the Ninth National People's Congress and the Third Session of the Ninth National Committee of the Chinese People's Political Consultative Conference, Beijing, March 3, 2000), in *On the Development of China's Information Technology Industry* (Amsterdam: Academic Press/Elsevier, 2010), 255–56.

75. Jiang Zemin, "Report on an Inspection Tour of the US and Canadian Electronics Industries," in *On the Development of China's Information Technology Industry*, 59–72, www.oreilly.com/library/view/on-the-development/9780123813695/B978012 3813695000027.xhtml#fn0010.

76. Jiang Zemin, "Revitalize Our Country's Electronics Industry," *People's Daily*, September 11, 1983, in *On the Development of China's Information Technology Industry*, 73–77, www.oreilly.com/library/view/on-the-development/9780123813695/B9780 123813695000039.xhtml#fn0010.

77. Jiang Zemin, "Gradually Explore a Chinese Style Development Path for the Electronics Industry," in *On the Development of China's Information Technology Industry*, 85–112, www.oreilly.com/library/view/on-the-development/9780123813695/B97 80123813695000052.xhtml#fn0010.

78. Jiang Zemin, "Initiate a New Phase in the Electronics Industry's Services for the Four Modernizations," in *On the Development of China's Information Technology Industry*, 155–77, www.oreilly.com/library/view/on-the-development/9780123813695 /B9780123813695000118.xhtml#fn0010.

79. Jiang Zemin, "Strive to Accomplish the Two Historic Tasks of Mechanizing and

Informationizing Our Army" (speech excerpt, enlarged meeting of the Central Military Commission, Beijing, December 11, 2000), in *On the Development of China's Information Technology Industry*, 261–62, https://learning.oreilly.com/library /view/on-the-development/9780123813695/B9780123813695000210.xhtml# B978-0-12-381369-5.00021-0.

80. Jiang Zemin, "Speech at the Opening Ceremony of the 16th World Computer Congress" (speech, opening ceremony, 16th World Computer Congress, Beijing, August 21, 2000), in *On the Development of China's Information Technology Industry*, 257–59, https://learning.oreilly.com/library/view/on-the-development/9780123 813695/B9780123813695000209.xhtml#B978-0-12-381369-5.00020-9.

81. "Jiang Zemin Says E-Commerce Will Transform China," *New York Times*, August 22, 2000, www.nytimes.com/2000/08/22/technology/jiang-zemin-says-ecommerce -will-transform-china.html.

82. Walton, *China's Golden Shield*.

83. Zixue Tai, "Casting the Ubiquitous Net of Information Control: Internet Surveillance in China from Golden Shield to Green Dam," in *International Journal of Advanced Pervasive and Ubiquitous Computing* 2, no. 1 (2010): 53–70, http://doi.org /10.4018/japuc.2010010104.

84. Tai, "Casting the Ubiquitous Net," 55.

85. Mueller and Tan, *China in the Information Age*, 52; "Golden Projects," CNET, June 27, 1997, www.cnet.com/news/golden-projects/.

86. As quoted in Zixue Tai, *The Internet in China: Cyberspace and Civil Society* (New York: Routledge, 2006), 241.

87. Tai, *Internet in China*, 240–42.

88. Walton, *China's Golden Shield*, 15.

89. Walton, *China's Golden Shield*, 6.

90. GE Industrial Systems, "GE Industrial Systems Acquires Nortel Networks Lentronics Product Line," press release, August 25, 2001, www.gegridsolutions.com /multilin/pr/nnlentronics.pdf.

91. M. Perez, "SONET-Based System Enhances Reliability," *Transmission & Distribution World* 52, no. 12 (2000): 60–63; Walton, *China's Golden Shield*, 6.

92. Walton, *China's Golden Shield*, 6.

93. Walton, *China's Golden Shield*, 18.

94. Nortel Networks, *OPTera Metro 3500 Multiservice Platform: Release 12.1 Planning and*

*Ordering Guide—Part 1 of 2*, NTRN10AN (Canada: Nortel Networks, 2004), www .manualslib.com/manual/113141/Nortel-Ntrn10an.html?page=2#manual.

95. Walton, *China's Golden Shield*, 21.

96. Thomas C. Greene, "Nortel Helps Stalk You on Line," *The Register*, February 1, 2001, www.theregister.co.uk/2001/02/01/nortel_helps_stalk_you/.

97. "Nortel Breaks China Record," Light Reading, February 13, 2001, www.light reading.com/ethernet-ip/nortel-breaks-china-record/d/d-id/572665.

98. "China Telecom Awards Nortel Networks China's Largest Ever Optical Contract," *Fiber Optics Weekly Update*, February 16, 2001.

99. Walton, *China's Golden Shield*, 21.

100. "Nortel Wins China Metro Deal," Light Reading, June 27, 2002, www.lightread ing.com/cable-video/nortel-wins-china-metro-deal/d/d-id/581602.

101. Tom Blackwell, "Exclusive: Did Huawei Bring Down Nortel? Corporate Espionage, Theft, and the Parallel Rise and Fall of Two Telecom Giants," *National Post*, February 24, 2020, https://nationalpost.com/news/exclusive-did-huawei -bring-down-nortel-corporate-espionage-theft-and-the-parallel-rise-and-fall-of -two-telecom-giants.

102. *United States of America v. Huawei Technologies Co., Ltd. et al.*, 18 CR 457 (S-3) (AMD), 7 (E.D.N.Y., 2020), www.justice.gov/opa/press-release/file/1248961/download.

103. Mark Chandler, "Huawei and Cisco's Source Code: Correcting the Record," *Cisco Blogs*, Cisco, October 11, 2012, https://blogs.cisco.com/news/huawei-and -ciscos-source-code-correcting-the-record.

104. Corinne Ramey and Kate O'Keeffe, "China's Huawei Charged with Racketeering, Stealing Trade Secrets," *Wall Street Journal*, February 13, 2020, www.wsj.com /articles/chinas-huawei-charged-with-racketeering-11581618336.

105. G. V. Muralidhara and Hadiya Faheem, "Huawei's Quest for Global Markets," in *China-Focused Cases: Selected Winners of the CEIBS Global Case Contest*, ed. CEIBS Case Center (Shanghai: Shanghai Jiao Tong University Press, 2019), 72, https:// books.google.com/books?id=efGKDwAAQBAJ.

106. Eric Harwit, *China's Telecommunications Revolution* (Oxford: Oxford University Press, 2008), 131.

107. Chandler, "Huawei and Cisco's Source Code."

108. Plano Economic Development Board, "Progress Report 2002," n.d., 5, https:// planotexas.org/ArchiveCenter/ViewFile/Item/55.

109. Bill Hethcock, "Huawei Makes Plano Expansion Official," *Dallas Business Journal*, November 11, 2009, www.bizjournals.com/dallas/stories/2009/11/09/daily
27.html.

110. Carol D. Leonnig and Karen Tumulty, "Perry Welcomed Chinese Firm Despite Security Concern," *Washington Post*, August 14, 2011, www.washingtonpost.com
/politics/perry-welcomed-chinese-firm-despite-security-concern/2011/08/10
/gIQAAu80EJ_story.html.

111. "Gov. Perry Helps Cut Ribbon at Huawei Technologies' New U.S. Headquarters," YouTube video, 11:46, posted by Governor Perry, October 2, 2010, www.you
tube.com/watch?v=0eruWGDSYDg&ab_channel=GovernorPerry.

112. Governor Perry, "Gov. Perry Helps Cut Ribbon."

113. U.S. Department of Justice, "Chinese Telecommunications Conglomerate Huawei and Subsidiaries Charged in Racketeering Conspiracy and Conspiracy to Steal Trade Secrets," press release, February 13, 2020, www.justice.gov/opa/pr
/chinese-telecommunications-conglomerate-huawei-and-subsidiaries-charged
-racketeering.

114. *Motorola, Inc. v. Lemko Corporation et al.*, 08 CV 5427, 83-86 (N.D. Ill., 2010), https://
dig.abclocal.go.com/wls/documents/2019/060719-wls-motorola-huawei
-doc.pdf.

115. *Motorola, Inc.*, 08 CV at 86.

116. Henny Sender, "How Huawei Tried to Sell Itself to Motorola for $7.5Bn," *Financial Times*, February 27, 2019, www.ft.com/content/fa8e7ab4-3905-11e9-b856
-5404d3811663.

117. Nortel Networks Corporation, *2004 Annual Report*, n.d., x, https://beatriceco
.com/bti/porticus/bell/pdf/Nortel_annual_2004_en.pdf.

118. Nortel Networks Corporation, *2004 Annual Report*, xii.

119. John Kehoe, "How Chinese Hacking Felled Telecommunication Giant Nortel," *Australian Financial Review*, last modified May 28, 2014, www.afr.com/technology
/how-chinese-hacking-felled-telecommunication-giant-nortel-20140526-iux6a.

120. Siobhan Gorman, "Chinese Hackers Suspected in Long-Term Nortel Breach," *Wall Street Journal*, February 14, 2012, www.wsj.com/articles/SB10001424052970
2033635045771875022201577054.

121. Kehoe, "How Chinese Hacking Felled Telecommunication Giant Nortel."

122. Blackwell, "Did Huawei Bring Down Nortel?"; Mandiant Solutions, FireEye,

"APT1: Exposing One of China's Cyber Espionage Units," n.d., www.fireeye.com /content/dam/fireeye-www/services/pdfs/mandiant-apt1-report.pdf.

123. Ray Le Maistre, "Nortel & Huawei: Broadband Buddies," Light Reading, February 1, 2006, www.lightreading.com/broadband/nortel-and-huawei-broadband -buddies/d/d-id/622795.

124. Bruce Einhorn, "Nortel-Huawei, RIP," Bloomberg, June 14, 2006, www.bloomberg .com/news/articles/2006-06-13/nortel-huawei-rip?sref=VZPf2pAM.

125. James Bagnall, "Four-Year Tenure of Would-Be Saviour Couldn't Pull Nortel Out of Death Spiral," *Vancouver Sun*, November 4, 2009, www.pressreader.com /canada/vancouver-sun/20091104/282114927649044.

126. Jonathan Calof et al., *An Overview of the Demise of Nortel Networks and Key Lessons Learned: Systemic Effects in Environment, Resilience and Black-Cloud Formation* (Ottawa: Telfer School of Management, University of Ottawa, 2014), http://sites.telfer .uottawa.ca/nortelstudy/files/2014/02/nortel-summary-report-and-executive -summary.pdf.

127. John F. Tyson, *Adventures in Innovation: Inside the Rise and Fall of Nortel* (United States: Library and Archives Canada, 2014), 189, Kindle.

128. "Timeline: Key Dates in the History of Nortel," Reuters, January 14, 2009, www .reuters.com/article/us-nortel-timeline-sb/timeline-key-dates-in-the-history -of-nortel-idUSTRE50D3N120090115; *The Canadian Encyclopedia*, s.v. "Nortel," last modified January 4, 2018, www.thecanadianencyclopedia.ca/en/article /nortel.

129. James Bagnall, "Tech Vets Aim to Save Nortel, Build National Web Network; Ferchat Group Hopes $1B from Bankers Enough to Save Firm, Proposes Using Tax Credits to Help Fund Endeavor," *Ottawa Citizen*, May 30, 2009, www.press reader.com/canada/ottawa-citizen/20090530/281517927085416.

130. Bagnall, "Tech Vets Aim to Save Nortel"; Barrie McKenna, "The Ghost of Nortel Continues to Haunt Canada's Tech Sector," *Globe and Mail*, December 4, 2011, www.theglobeandmail.com/report-on-business/rob-commentary/the-ghost-of -nortel-continues-to-haunt-canadas-tech-sector/article1357909/.

131. Atkinson, "Who Lost Lucent?"

132. James Bagnall, "'Were We Prepared to Just Let Nortel Sink? The Answer Was No,'" *Vancouver Sun*, November 2, 2009, www.pressreader.com/canada/vancouver -sun/20091102/282166467255135.

133. Andy Greenberg, "The Deal That Could Have Saved Nortel," *Forbes*, January 14,

2009, www.forbes.com/2009/01/14/nortel-huawei-china-tech-wire-cx_ag_0114 nortel.html?sh=171aa966564f.

134. David Friend, "Nortel Bankruptcy: $7.3B in Remaining Assets to Be Split among Subsidiaries," CBC, May 12, 2015, www.cbc.ca/news/business/nortel -bankruptcy-7-3b-in-remaining-assets-to-be-split-among-subsidiaries-1.3071789.

135. Tom Hals, "Courts OK Nortel Patent Sale to Apple/RIM Group," Reuters, July 11, 2011, www.reuters.com/article/us-nortel-patents/courts-ok-nortel-patent-sale -to-apple-rim-group-idUSTRE76A51Y20110711.

136. Nathan Vanderklippe, "Huawei Founder Ren Zhengfei Denies Involvement with Nortel Collapse," *Globe and Mail*, July 2, 2019, www.theglobeandmail.com /world/article-huawei-founder-ren-zhengfei-denies-involvement-with-nortel -collapse/.

137. Claude Barfield, *Telecoms and the Huawei Conundrum: Chinese Foreign Direct Investment in the United States* (Washington, D.C.: American Enterprise Institute, 2011), 13, https://www.aei.org/wp-content/uploads/2011/11/-telecoms-and-the-huawei -conundrum-chinese-foreign-direct-investment-in-the-united-states_103528582 558.pdf; "Huawei Hires R&D Chief for US," Mobile World Live, November 24, 2010, www.mobileworldlive.com/latest-stories/huawei-hires-rd-chief-for-us.

138. John Paczkowski, "John Roese on Redefining Huawei and the Democratization of Smartphones," *All Things D* (blog), *Wall Street Journal*, October 20, 2011, http:// allthingsd.com/20111020/huaweis-john-roese-live-at-asiad/.

139. Gordon Corera, "GCHQ Chief Warns of Tech 'Moment of Reckoning,'" BBC, April 23, 2021, https://www.bbc.com/news/technology-56851558.

140. Francis Vachon, "Department of National Defence's New $1-Billion Facility Falls Short on Security," *Globe and Mail*, September 2, 2016, www.theglobeandmail .com/news/politics/department-of-national-defences-new-1-billion-facility-falls -short-on-security/article31685234/; David Pugliese, "The Mystery of the Lis-tening Devices at DND's Nortel Campus," *Ottawa Citizen*, October 18, 2016, https://ottawacitizen.com/news/national/defence-watch/the-mystery-of-the -listening-devices-at-dnds-nortel-campus.

141. "Nortel's Richardson Campus to Sell for More than $43 Million," *Dallas Morn-ing News*, May 24, 2011, www.dallasnews.com/business/real-estate/2011/05/24 /nortels-richardson-campus-to-sell-for-more-than-43-million/.

142. Brad Howarth, "Nortel Rides the Data Wave," *Australian Financial Review*, Oc-tober 27, 2000, www.afr.com/companies/nortel-rides-the-data-wave-20001027 -kb6yx.

### CHAPTER THREE    "WHEREVER THERE ARE PEOPLE"

1.  Andrew Van Dam, "Using the Best Data Possible, We Set Out to Find the Middle of Nowhere," *Washington Post*, February 20, 2018, www.washingtonpost.com /news/wonk/wp/2018/02/20/using-the-best-data-possible-we-set-out-to-find -the-middle-of-nowhere/.

2.  Jason Miller, "Ban on Chinese Products Starts Today Despite Confusion over Acquisition Rule," Federal News Network, August 13, 2020, https://federalnews network.com/acquisition-policy/2020/08/ban-on-chinese-products-starts -today-despite-confusion-over-acquisition-rule/.

3.  Yun Wen, *The Huawei Model: The Rise of China's Technology Giant* (Champaign, IL: University of Illinois Press, 2020), 36.

4.  Xi Le'a 喜樂阿, "Nongcun baowei chengshi: Yi bu shangye shi" 农村包围城市: 一部商业史 [Encircling the City from the Countryside: A Business History], Sohu, October 10, 2018, www.sohu.com/a/258532158_115207.

5.  Joan Helland et al., *Glasgow and Valley County* (Charleston, WV: Arcadia, 2010), back cover, https://books.google.com/books?id=uvlXpQ8hUBsC&pg=PA8#v= onepage&q=diamond&f=false.

6.  Susan Crawford, *Fiber: The Coming Tech Revolution—and Why America Might Miss It* (New Haven, CT: Yale University Press, 2018), 136, Kindle.

7.  DJ&A, P.C., "City of Glasgow, Montana: Growth Policy," October 30, 2013, 128, https://2ba70dec-0753-4999-8565-a5c84d9d967a.filesusr.com/ugd/ae3595 _5b0d2bb7ceb244288f31de5f0ba212ec.pdf.

8.  Federal Communications Commission, *Inquiry Concerning the Deployment of Advanced Telecommunications Capability to All Americans in a Reasonable and Timely Fashion, and Possible Steps to Accelerate Such Deployment Pursuant to Section 706 of the Telecommunications Act of 1996, CC Docket No. 98-146: Report*, FCC 99-005 (Washington, D.C.: Federal Communications Commission, 1999), 5, https://transition.fcc.gov /Bureaus/Common_Carrier/Reports/fcc99005-converted.pdf.

9.  Federal Communications Commission, *Inquiry Concerning the Deployment of Advanced Telecommunications Capability to All Americans in a Reasonable and Timely Fashion, and Possible Steps to Accelerate Such Deployment Pursuant to Section 706 of the Telecommunications Act of 1996, CC Docket No. 98-146: Second Report*, FCC 00-290 (Washington, D.C.: Federal Communications Commission, 2000), 87, https://transition.fcc.gov/Bureaus/Common_Carrier/Orders/2000/fcc00290 .pdf.

10. Federal Communications Commission, *Availability of Advanced Telecommunications*

*Capability in the United States, GN Docket No. 04-54: Fourth Report to Congress*, FCC 04-208 (Washington, D.C.: Federal Communications Commission, 2004), 5, www.fcc.gov/reports-research/reports/broadband-progress-reports/fourth -broadband-progress-report.

11. Bill Callahan, "More Digital Redlining? AT&T Home Broadband Deployment and Poverty in Detroit and Toledo," NDIA, September 6, 2017, www .digitalinclusion.org/blog/2017/09/06/more-digital-redlining-att-deployment -and-poverty-in-detroit-and-toledo/.

12. Federal Communications Commission, *Inquiry Concerning the Deployment of Advanced Telecommunications Capability to All Americans in a Reasonable and Timely Fashion, and Possible Steps to Accelerate Such Deployment Pursuant to Section 706 of the Telecommunications Act of 1996, as Amended by the Broadband Data Improvement Act, GN Docket No. 14-126: 2015 Broadband Progress Report and Notice of Inquiry on Immediate Action to Accelerate Deployment*, FCC 15-10 (Washington, D.C.: Federal Communications Commission, 2015), www.fcc.gov/reports-research/reports/broadband -progress-reports/2015-broadband-progress-report.

13. Tom Wheeler (former chairman, Federal Communications Commission), interview by author, March 2021.

14. Federal Communications Commission, *2015 Broadband Progress Report*, 111.

15. Ajit Pai, "Remarks of Ajit Pai, Chairman, Federal Communications Commission" (speech, Federal Communications Commission, Washington, D.C., January 24, 2017), www.fcc.gov/document/chairman-pai-remarks-federal-communi cations-commission.

16. Alex Marquardt and Michael Conte, "Huawei Connects Rural America. Could It Threaten the Country's Most Sensitive Military Sites?," CNN, last modified March 11, 2019, www.cnn.com/2019/03/11/politics/huawei-cell-towers -missile-silos/index.html.

17. Those without cellular connections can pay extra for a satellite link or forgo the real-time features and carry data from the machine to their computers on a USB drive.

18. Nemont Telephone Cooperative, Inc., email message to author, December 2020.

19. Tim Pierce, "High-Speed Internet? Bill Gives Tax Breaks to Companies That Install Fiber Optic Cables," *Missoula Current*, February 19, 2019, https://missoula current.com/business/2019/02/montana-high-speed-internet/.

20. Mike Rogers and C.A. Dutch Ruppersberger, *Investigative Report on the U.S. National Security Issues Posed by Chinese Telecommunications Companies Huawei and ZTE* (Washington, D.C.: Permanent Select Committee on Intelligence, U.S. House of Representatives, 2012), www.hsdl.org/?abstract&did=723367.

21. Huib Modderkolk, "Huawei Kon Alle Gesprekken van Mobiele KPN-Klanten Afluisteren, inclusief Die van de Premier" [Huawei Was Able to Eavesdrop on All of KPN Mobile's Customers' Calls, Including Those of the Prime Minister], *De Volkskrant*, April 17, 2021, https://www.volkskrant.nl/nieuws-achtergrond /huawei-kon-alle-gesprekken-van-mobiele-kpn-klanten-afluisteren-inclusief -die-van-de-premier~bd1aece1/; Morgan Meaker, "New Huawei Fears over Dutch Mobile Eavesdropping," *The Telegraph*, April 18, 2021, https://www.tele graph.co.uk/technology/2021/04/18/new-huawei-fears-dutch-mobile-eaves dropping/.

22. Cecilia Kang, "Huawei Ban Threatens Wireless in Rural Areas," *New York Times*, May 25, 2019, www.nytimes.com/2019/05/25/technology/huawei-rural-wire less-service.html.

23. Kang, "Huawei Ban Threatens Wireless."

24. Ren Zhengfei 任正非, "Xiong jiujiu qi angang kuaguo taipingyang" 雄赳赳气 昂昂跨过太平洋 [Gallantly and Valiantly Cross the Pacific], *Huawei Ren* 华为人 [Huawei People], January 18, 2001, http://app.huawei.com/paper/newspaper /newsBookCateInfo.do?method=showDigestInfo&infoId=13928&sortId=1.

25. Peter Nolan, *Re-balancing China: Essays on the Global Financial Crisis, Industrial Policy and International Relations* (London: Anthem Press, 2015), 117.

26. Cheng and Liu, *Truth of Huawei*, 69.

27. Li Jie 李杰, "Mosike bu xiangxin yanlei" 莫斯科不相信眼泪 [Moscow Does Not Believe in Tears], *Huawei Ren* 华为人 [Huawei People], November 5, 2002, http://app.huawei.com/paper/newspaper/newsBookCateInfo.do?method= showDigestInfo&infoId=13969&sortId=1.

28. Li, "Mosike bu xiangxin yanlei."

29. Yang Shaolong, *The Huawei Way: Lessons from an International Tech Giant on Driving Growth by Focusing on Never-Ending Innovation* (New York: McGraw-Hill Education, 2017), 188.

30. Yang, *Huawei Way*, 195–96.

31. William C. Kirby, Billy Chan, and John P. McHugh, *Huawei: A Global Tech Giant in the Crossfire of a Digital Cold War*, Harvard Business School Case 320-089 (Bos-

ton: Harvard Business School Publishing, 2020), www.hbs.edu/faculty/Pages
/item.aspx?num=57723.

32.  Ma Guangyi 马广义, "Dongbian richu xibian wangui" 东边日出西边晚归
[Setting Out with the Eastern Sunrise, Returning with the Western Sunset],
*Huawei Ren* 华为人 [Huawei People], November 30, 2005, http://app.huawei
.com/paper/newspaper/newsBookCateInfo.do?method=showDigestInfo&
infoId=13486&sortId=8.

33.  Peng Zhongyang 彭中阳, "Wo shi yi ge kuaile de xiao bing" 我是一个快乐的小
兵 [I'm a Happy Little Soldier], *Huawei Ren* 华为人 [Huawei People], January 20,
2009, http://app.huawei.com/paper/newspaper/newsBookCateInfo.do?method
=showDigestInfo&infoId=14144&sortId=1.

34.  Peng, "Wo shi yi ge kuaile de xiao bing."

35.  Wang Hong 汪宏, "Feizhou dalu shang de Huawei ren" 非洲大陆上的华为人
[Huawei People on the African Continent], *Huawei Ren* 华为人 [Huawei People],
June 12, 2000, http://app.huawei.com/paper/newspaper/newsBookCateInfo
.do?method=showDigestInfo&infoId=13841&sortId=1.

36.  *ZTE: A Threat to America's Small Businesses: Hearing before the Committee on Small
Business, United States House of Representatives*, 115th Cong. 7–8 (2018) (testimony
of Andy Keiser, visiting fellow, National Security Institute, Antonin Scalia Law
School, George Mason University), www.govinfo.gov/content/pkg/CHRG
-115hhrg30507/pdf/CHRG-115hhrg30507.pdf.

37.  Amy MacKinnon, "For Africa, Chinese-Built Internet Is Better Than No Internet at All," *Foreign Policy*, March 19, 2019, https://foreignpolicy.com/2019/03/19
/for-africa-chinese-built-internet-is-better-than-no-internet-at-all/.

38.  Ren Zhengfei 任正非, "Ren Zhengfei yu 2000–22 qi xueyuan jiaoliu jiyao" 任正
非2000–22期学员交流纪要 [Minutes of a Conversation between Ren Zhengfei
and Trainees from the Classes of 2000 to 2022], *Huawei Ren* 华为人 [Huawei Peo-
ple], September 8, 2000, http://app.huawei.com/paper/newspaper/newsBook
CateInfo.do?method=showDigestInfo&infoId=13873&sortId=1.

39.  Yang, *Huawei Way*, 191.

40.  Peng Gang 彭刚, "Bai niluohe pan de xingfu shenghuo" 白尼罗河畔的幸福生
活 [A Happy Life on the Shores of the White Nile], *Huawei Ren* 华为人 [Huawei
People], September 29, 2011, http://app.huawei.com/paper/newspaper/news
BookCateInfo.do?method=showDigestInfo&infoId=14213&sortId=13&
commentLanguage=1.

41.  "Is Corporate 'Wolf-Culture' Devouring China's Over-Worked Employees?,"

China Labour Bulletin, May 27, 2008, https://clb.org.hk/content/corporate-%
E2%80%9Cwolf-culture%E2%80%9D-devouring-china%E2%80%99s-over
-worked-employees.

42. Chen Hong, "Thousands of Huawei Staff 'Quit,'" *China Daily*, November 3, 2007,
www.chinadaily.com.cn/bizchina/2007-11/03/content_6228248.htm.

43. "Huawei gongsi juxing dongshihui zilü xuanyan xuanshi dahui" 华为公司举行
董事会自律宣言宣誓大会 [Huawei Holds Self-Discipline Oath Ceremony for
Its Board of Directors], *Huawei Ren* 华为人 [Huawei People], February 4, 2013,
http://app.huawei.com/paper/newspaper/newsBookCateInfo.do?method=
showDigestInfo&infoId=17479&sortId=8.

44. Ren Zhengfei, "Minutes of the Briefing on the Progress of Differentiated Ap-
praisals for Regions," Huawei Executive Office Speech No. [2015] 050, as cited
in Weiwei Huang, *Built on Value: The Huawei Philosophy of Finance Management* (Singapore: Palgrave Macmillan, 2019), 130, https://link.springer.com/content/pdf
/10.1007%2F978-981-13-7507-1_5.pdf.

45. Gilley, "Huawei's Fixed Line to Beijing."

46. "Russia and China 'Broke Iraq Embargo,'" BBC, December 19, 2002, http://
news.bbc.co.uk/2/hi/europe/2591351.stm.

47. Ellen Nakashima, Gerry Shih, and John Hudson, "Leaked Documents Reveal
Huawei's Secret Operations to Build North Korea's Wireless Network," *Washington Post*, July 22, 2019, www.washingtonpost.com/world/national-security/leaked
-documents-reveal-huaweis-secret-operations-to-build-north-koreas-wireless-net
work/2019/07/22/583430fe-8d12-11e9-adf3-f70f78c156e8_story.html.

48. Yi Mingjun 易明军, "Chuanyue zhandi" 穿越战地 [Traversing the Battlefield],
*Huawei Ren* 华为人 [Huawei People], January 15, 2004, http://app.huawei.com
/paper/newspaper/newsBookCateInfo.do?method=showDigestInfo&info
Id=13968&sortId=1.

49. "Huawei Wins Iraq Deal," Light Reading, July 23, 2007, www.lightreading.com
/huawei-wins-iraq-deal/d/d-id/644593.

50. "Zai digelisihe pan" 在底格里斯河畔 [On the Shores of the Tigris River], *Huawei Jiashi* 华为家事 [Huawei Family Matters] (blog), April 22, 2017.

51. Larry Wentz, Frank Kramer, and Stuart Starr, *Information and Communication Technologies for Reconstruction and Development* (Washington, D.C.: Center for Technology and National Security Policy, 2008), 18, www.aesanetwork.org/wp-content
/uploads/2018/02/Information-and-Communication-Technologies-for
-Reconstruction-and-Development-1.pdf.

52. Asian Development Bank, *Extended Annual Review Report* (Mandaluyong, Philippines: Asian Development Bank, 2011), 3, www.adb.org/sites/default/files /project-document/60266/42919-01-afg-xarr.pdf.

53. Lin Jincan 林进灿, "Afuhan gongzuo shenghuo shi lu" 阿富汗工作生活实录 [A Real Account of Life Working in Afghanistan], *Huawei Ren* 华为人 [Huawei People], September 28, 2010, http://app.huawei.com/paper/newspaper/news PaperPage.do?method=showSelNewsInfo&cateId=2101&pageId=2461&in foId=4522&sortId=1&commentLanguage=1&commentId=20009&search_result =2.

54. Amy Nordrum, "Afghan Wireless Launches First LTE Network in Afghanistan," *IEEE Spectrum*, June 1, 2017, https://spectrum.ieee.org/tech-talk/telecom/wire less/afghan-wireless-launches-first-4g-lte-network-in-afghanistan.

55. Jon B. Alterman, "Fighting but Not Winning," Center for Strategic and International Studies, November 25, 2019, www.csis.org/analysis/fighting-not-winning.

56. Thomas Donahue, "The Worst Possible Day: U.S. Telecommunications and Huawei," *PRISM* 8, no. 3 (2020): 17, https://ndupress.ndu.edu/Media/News /News-Article-View/Article/2053215/the-worst-possible-day-us-telecommun ications-and-huawei/.

57. Ren Zhengfei 任正非, "Ren Zhengfei guanyu zhen'ai shengming yu zhiye zeren de jianghua" 任正非关于珍爱生命与职业责任的讲话 [Ren Zhengfei's Lecture on Cherishing Life and Professional Responsibilities], *Huawei Ren* 华为人 [Huawei People], May 5, 2011, http://app.huawei.com/paper/newspaper/newsBook CateInfo.do?method=showDigestInfo&infoId=14240&sortId=13.

58. Lois Lonnquist, *Fifty Cents an Hour: The Builders and Boomtowns of the Fort Peck Dam* (Helena, MT: MtSky Press, 2006), loc. 1145 of 5005, Kindle.

59. Lonnquist, *Fifty Cents an Hour,* loc. 2755.

60. Lonnquist, *Fifty Cents an Hour,* loc. 2166.

61. Lonnquist, *Fifty Cents an Hour,* loc. 226.

62. Kristen Inbody, "Fort Peck Dam Puts Country Back to Work," *Great Falls Tribune,* March 3, 2017, www.greatfallstribune.com/story/life/my-montana/2014 /06/29/fort-peck-dam-puts-country-back-work/11559491/.

63. David Meyer, "MTA Official Defends 2nd Avenue Subway's $6B Price Tag," *New York Post,* September 16, 2019, https://nypost.com/2019/09/16/mta-official -defends-2nd-avenue-subways-6b-price-tag/.

64. Darryl Fears, "This Fish Lived in Peace for 70 Million Years. Then It Met the

Army Corps of Engineers," *Washington Post*, January 26, 2015, www.washington
post.com/news/energy-environment/wp/2015/01/26/after-70-million-years-a
-prehistoric-fish-is-vanishing-in-montana-heres-why/.

65.  Franklin D. Roosevelt, "Informal Remarks of the President" (speech, Fort Peck,
     MT, August 6, 1934), Franklin D. Roosevelt Presidential Library and Museum,
     Hyde Park, NY, www.fdrlibrary.marist.edu/_resources/images/msf/msf00746.

66.  Erin Blakemore, "These Women Taught Depression-Era Americans to Use Elec-
     tricity," History, last modified March 1, 2019, https://www.history.com/news
     /new-deal-great-depression-rural-electrification.

67.  *Missouri River (Fort Peck Dam), Mont.: Hearings before the Committee on Rivers and Har-
     bors, House of Representatives*, 75th Cong. 14 (1937) (Jerry J. O'Connell, Represen-
     tative from Montana), https://books.google.com/books?id=K55IAAAAMAAJ.

68.  Carl Kitchens and Price Fishback, "Flip the Switch: The Spatial Impact of the
     Rural Electrification Administration 1935–1940" (working paper, National Bu-
     reau of Economic Research, 2013), www.nber.org/papers/w19743.

69.  Carl Kitchens, "US Electrification in the 1930s," VoxEU, January 29, 2014,
     https://voxeu.org/article/us-electrification-1930s.

70.  Eugene Pike, interview by Merri Ann Hartse, n.p., circa November 1979, Rural
     Electrification Oral History Project, Archives and Special Collections, Mans-
     field Library, University of Montana, Missoula, MT, https://scholarworks.umt
     .edu/ruralelectrification_oralhistory/3/.

71.  Joshua Lewis and Edson Severnini, "Short- and Long-Run Impacts of Rural
     Electrification: Evidence from the Historical Rollout of the U.S. Power Grid,"
     *Journal of Development Economics* 143 (2020): 1, https://doi.org/10.1016/j.jdeveco
     .2019.102412.

72.  Michael W. Kahn, "FCC Chairman: Co-ops Key to Rural Broadband," Coop-
     erative, January 16, 2018, www.cooperative.com/news/Pages/ceo-close-up-fcc
     -broadband.aspx.

73.  Brad Smith and Carol Ann Browne, *Tools and Weapons: The Promise and the Peril of
     the Digital Age* (New York: Penguin, 2019), 156.

74.  Michael Bennet, "Bennet Urges FCC Chairman to Reconsider Proposal to Limit
     Resources for Program Essential to Bridging the Digital Divide between Rural
     and Urban Communities," press release, May 21, 2019, www.bennet.senate.gov
     /public/index.cfm/2019/5/bennet-urges-fcc-chairman-to-reconsider-proposal
     -to-limit-resources-for-program-essential-to-bridging-the-digital-divide-between
     -rural-and-urban-communities.

75. Federal Communications Commission, *Inquiry Concerning Deployment of Advanced Telecommunications Capability to All Americans in a Reasonable and Timely Fashion, GN Docket No. 18-238: 2019 Broadband Deployment Report*, FCC 19-44 (Washington, D.C.: Federal Communications Commission, 2019), 16, https://docs.fcc.gov /public/attachments/FCC-19-44A1.pdf.

76. Andrew Perrin, "Digital Gap between Rural and Nonrural America Persists," Pew Research Center, May 31, 2019, www.pewresearch.org/fact-tank/2019/05/31 /digital-gap-between-rural-and-nonrural-america-persists/.

77. Joan Engebretson, "USTelecom Measures Rural Broadband Gap: 65% of Rural Areas Have 25/3 Mbps vs. 98% of Non-Rural Areas," Telecompetitor, December 3, 2018, www.telecompetitor.com/ustelecom-measures-rural-broadband-gap-65 -of-rural-areas-have-25-3-mbps-vs-98-of-non-rural-areas/.

78. Dan Littmann et al., *Communications Infrastructure Upgrade: The Need for Deep Fiber* (Chicago: Deloitte, 2017), www2.deloitte.com/content/dam/Deloitte/us/Docu ments/technology-media-telecommunications/us-tmt-5GReady-the-need-for -deep-fiber-pov.pdf.

79. Elsa B. Kania (@EBKania), "Perhaps support and funding for online train- ing of workers in critical digital skillsets, such as cyber security and data sci- ence?," Twitter, April 29, 2020, 11:22 a.m., https://twitter.com/EBKania/status /1255532911639629830.

80. White House, "Fact Sheet: The American Jobs Plan," press release, March 31, 2021, https://www.whitehouse.gov/briefing-room/statements-releases/2021/03 /31/fact-sheet-the-american-jobs-plan/.

81. *5G Supply Chain Security: Threats and Solutions: Hearing before the S. Comm. on Commerce, Science, & Transportation*, 116th Cong. (2020) (statement of James A. Lewis, senior vice president and director, Technology Policy Program, Center for Strategic and International Studies), https://csis-website-prod.s3.amazonaws.com/s3fs -public/congressional_testimony/Jim%20Lewis%20Written%20Statement%20 3-4-20.pdf.

82. Federal Communications Commission, *Huawei Designation, PS Docket No. 19-351; ZTE Designation, PS Docket No. 19-352; Protecting against National Security Threats to the Communications Supply Chain through FCC Programs, WC Docket No. 18-89: Comments of Parallel Wireless—Innovators of Open 4G and 5G ORAN Network Solutions* (Washington, D.C.: Federal Communications Commission, 2020) (statement of Steve Papa, CEO, Parallel Wireless), https://ecfsapi.fcc.gov/file/1041345868634/FCC%20 Comments%20Supply%20Chain%20Security%20Parallel%20Wireless%20 April%2013.pdf.

83. Sean Kinney, "Is Open RAN Key to the 5G Future?," *RCRWireless News*, September 2020, 7, www.altiostar.com/wp-content/uploads/2020/10/RCR-Wireless-Is-Open-RAN-key-to-the-5G-Future.pdf.

84. Morning Consult, "Broadband Survey Results" (presentation, Internet Innovation Alliance, n.p., September 2, 2020), https://internetinnovation.org/wp-content/uploads/IIA-Broadband-Survey-Results-Registered-Voters-Final.pdf.

85. Crawford, *Fiber*, 210.

86. John Hendel, "Biden Infrastructure Plan Sparks Lobbying War over How to Fix America's Internet," *Politico*, April 21, 2021, https://www.politico.com/news/2021/04/21/biden-infrastructure-broadband-lobbying-484002.

87. Stu Woo, "The U.S. vs. China: The High Cost of the Technology Cold War," *Wall Street Journal*, October 22, 2020, www.wsj.com/articles/the-u-s-vs-china-the-high-cost-of-the-technology-cold-war-11603397438.

88. Kang, "Huawei Ban Threatens Wireless."

89. Gregg Hunter, correspondence with author, December 2020.

90. Jim Salter, "5G in Rural Areas Bridges a Gap That 4G Doesn't, Especially Low- and Mid-band," *Ars Technica*, September 14, 2020, https://arstechnica.com/features/2020/09/5g-03-rural/.

91. Jon Brodkin, "T-Mobile Touts 'Nationwide 5G' That Fails to Cover 130 Million Americans," *Ars Technica*, December 2, 2019, https://arstechnica.com/information-technology/2019/12/t-mobile-touts-nationwide-5g-that-fails-to-cover-130-million-americans/.

92. Ruopu Li, Kang Cheng, and Di Wu, "Challenges and Opportunities for Coping with the Smart Divide in Rural America," *Annals of the American Association of Geographers* 110, no. 2 (2020): 565, https://doi.org/10.1080/24694452.2019.1694402.

93. Kevin J. O'Brien, "An Optimist on 3G Despite Losing It All—Technology—International Herald Tribune," *New York Times*, July 30, 2006, www.nytimes.com/2006/07/30/technology/30iht-3Gschmid.2332154.html?searchResultPosition=131; Kevin J. O'Brien, "3G Cost Billions: Will It Ever Live Up to Its Hype?," *New York Times*, July 30, 2006, www.nytimes.com/2006/07/30/technology/30iht-3G.html?searchResultPosition=98.

94. Mark T. Esper, "As Prepared Remarks by Secretary of Defense Mark T. Esper at the Munich Security Conference" (speech, Munich Security Conference, Munich, February 15, 2020), www.defense.gov/Newsroom/Speeches/Speech

/Article/2085577/remarks-by-secretary-of-defense-mark-t-esper-at-the-munich -security-conference/.

95. Rob Schmitz, "U.S. Pressures Europe to Find Alternatives to Huawei," NPR, February 15, 2020, www.npr.org/2020/02/15/806366021/europe-pressures-u-s -to-back-low-cost-alternative-to-huawei.

96. Maximilian Mayer, "Europe's Digital Autonomy and Potentials of a U.S.- German Alignment toward China," American Institute for Contemporary German Studies, Johns Hopkins University, December 16, 2020, www.aicgs.org /2020/12/europes-digital-autonomy-and-potentials-of-a-u-s-german-alignment -toward-china/.

97. "Chinesischer Botschafter Ken Wu: 'Die Sicherheitsbedenken der USA gegen Huawei Sind Scheinheilig'" [Chinese Ambassador Wu Ken: 'U.S. Security Concerns About Huawei Are Hypocritical'], online video, 38:49, from live interview with *Handelsblatt*, posted by *Handelsblatt*, December 13, 2019, www .handelsblatt.com/video/live/handelsblatt-live-chinesischer-botschafter-ken-wu -die-sicherheitsbedenken-der-usa-gegen-huawei-sind-scheinheilig/25332882 .html?ticket=ST-1259683-3gjcruN7Ek1kqpedwqBg-ap1.

98. Heiko Maas, "Speech by Foreign Minister Heiko Maas on European Digital Sovereignty on the Occasion of the Opening of the Smart Country Convention of the German Association for Information Technology, Telecommunications and New Media (Bitkom)" (speech, Smart Country Convention, German Association for Information Technology, Telecommunications and New Media, Berlin, October 27, 2020), www.auswaertiges-amt.de/en/newsroom/news/maas -bitkom/2410398.

99. Elysée (Office of the President of France), "Il Est Temps pour l'Europe d'Avoir Sa Propre Souveraineté Technologique!" [It Is Time for Europe to Have Its Own Technological Sovereignty!], press release, December 9, 2020, www.elysee.fr /emmanuel-macron/2020/12/09/il-est-temps-pour-leurope-davoir-sa-propre -souverainete-technologique.

100. Anthony Boadle and Andrea Shalal, "U.S. Offers Brazil Telecoms Financing to Buy 5G Equipment from Huawei Rivals," Reuters, October 20, 2020, www .reuters.com/article/us-usa-brazil-trade/u-s-offers-brazil-telecoms-financing-to -buy-5g-equipment-from-huawei-rivals-idUSKBN2751TA.

101. "Brazilian Telecoms Snub U.S. Official over Huawei 5G Pressure: Source," Reuters, November 6, 2020, www.reuters.com/article/us-usa-brazil-5g/brazilian-tele coms-snub-u-s-official-over-huawei-5g-pressure-source-idUSKBN27M2YP.

## CHAPTER FOUR    FIVE HUNDRED BILLION EYES

1.  Opening words of George Orwell, *1984* (Boston: Houghton Mifflin Harcourt, 1977), 2: "It was a bright, cold day . . . "

2.  Lin Yijiang, "CCP Demands Cameras Installed in Rental Properties," *Bitter Winter*, April 8, 2019, https://bitterwinter.org/ccp-demands-cameras-installed-in -rental-properties/.

3.  Sheena Chestnut Greitens, "'Surveillance with Chinese Characteristics': The Development and Global Export of Chinese Policing Technology" (paper presented at the Princeton University IR Colloquium, Princeton, NJ, last modified September 30, 2019), http://ncgg.princeton.edu/IR%20Colloquium/Greitens Sept2019.pdf.

4.  Charles Rollet, "China Public Video Surveillance Guide: From Skynet to Sharp Eyes," IPVM, June 14, 2018, https://ipvm.com/reports/sharpeyes.

5.  Technically 1 for every 2.27 people; see Xiao Qiang, "The Road to Unfreedom: President Xi's Surveillance State," *Journal of Democracy* 30, no. 1 (2019): 53–67.

6.  "Zhejiang Dahua Technology Co., Ltd.," Yahoo! Finance, accessed February 1, 2021, https://finance.yahoo.com/quote/002236.SZ/key-statistics?p=002236 .SZ; "Hangzhou Hikvision Digital Technology Co., Ltd.," Yahoo! Finance, accessed February 1, 2021, https://finance.yahoo.com/quote/002415.SZ/key -statistics?p=002415.SZ; "CNY/USD - Chinese Yuan US Dollar," Investing, accessed February 1, 2021, www.investing.com/currencies/cny-usd-historical-data.

7.  Liza Lin and Newley Purnell, "A World with a Billion Cameras Watching You Is Just around the Corner," *Wall Street Journal*, December 6, 2019, www.wsj.com /articles/a-billion-surveillance-cameras-forecast-to-be-watching-within-two -years-11575565402.

8.  Greitens, "'Surveillance with Chinese Characteristics'"; see also Steven Feldstein, "The Global Expansion of AI Surveillance" (working paper, Carnegie Endowment for International Peace, 2019), https://carnegieendowment.org/2019 /09/17/global-expansion-of-ai-surveillance-pub-79847.

9.  Kai Strittmatter, *We Have Been Harmonized: Life in China's Surveillance State* (New York: HarperCollins, 2020), 7–8, Kindle.

10. See, for example, "Opinion: China Is Exporting Its Digital Authoritarianism," *Washington Post*, August 5, 2020, www.washingtonpost.com/opinions/china-is -exporting-its-digital-authoritarianism/2020/08/05/f14df896-d047-11ea-8c55 -61e7fa5e82ab_story.html.

11. Charles Rollet, correspondence with author, January 2021.

12. Jessica Chen Weiss, "Understanding and Rolling Back Digital Authoritarianism," War on the Rocks, February 17, 2020, https://warontherocks.com/2020/02/understanding-and-rolling-back-digital-authoritarianism/; Matthew Steven Erie and Thomas Streinz, "The Beijing Effect: China's 'Digital Silk Road' as Transnational Data Governance," *New York University Journal of International Law and Politics* (forthcoming), https://ssrn.com/abstract=3810256.

13. Steven Feldstein, correspondence with author, January 2021; see also Steven Feldstein, *The Rise of Digital Repression: How Technology Is Reshaping Power, Politics, and Resistance* (New York: Oxford University Press, 2021).

14. Walton, *China's Golden Shield*, 26.

15. National Development and Reform Commission et al., *Guanyu jiaqiang gonggong anquan shipin jiankong jianshe lianwang yingyong gongzuo de ruogan yijian* 关于加强公共安全视频监控建设联网应用工作的若干意见 [Several Opinions on Strengthening the Construction of Public Security Video Surveillance Network Applications], Fagai gaoji (2015) 996 hao 发改高技 (2015) 996号 [Development and Reform (2015) No. 996] (Beijing: National Development and Reform Commission, 2015), www.ndrc.gov.cn/xxgk/zcfb/tz/201505/t20150513_963825.html.

16. Jessica Batke and Mareike Ohlberg, "State of Surveillance: Government Documents Reveal New Evidence on China's Efforts to Monitor Its People," ChinaFile, October 30, 2020, www.chinafile.com/state-surveillance-china.

17. Zhang Zihan, "Beijing's Guardian Angels?," *Global Times*, October 10, 2012, www.globaltimes.cn/content/737491.shtml.

18. *Encyclopedia Britannica*, s.v. "Baojia," last modified August 31, 2006, www.britannica.com/topic/baojia.

19. Batke and Ohlberg, "State of Surveillance."

20. "Xueliang gongcheng bai yi ji shichang cheng anfang hangye xin lanhai" 雪亮工程百亿级市场 成安防行业新蓝海 [The Sharp Eyes Project's Ten-Billion Yuan Market Has Become the Security Industry's New "Blue Ocean"], *China Daily*, November 6, 2019, https://caijing.chinadaily.com.cn/a/201911/06/WS5dc23537a31099ab995ea387.html.

21. Paul Mozur and Aaron Krolik, "A Surveillance Net Blankets China's Cities, Giving Police Vast Powers," *New York Times*, December 17, 2019, www.nytimes.com/2019/12/17/technology/china-surveillance.html.

22. Yuan Yang and Nian Liu, "China Survey Shows High Concern over Facial Rec-

ognition Abuse," *Financial Times*, December 5, 2019, www.ft.com/content/7c 32c7a8-172e-11ea-9ee4-11f260415385.

23. Image of Guo Bing's text found in a video from *Xin jing bao* 新京报 [Beijing News], see "Zhongguo ren lian shibie di yi an" 中国人脸识别第一案 [The First Facial Recognition Case in China], Weibo, accessed July 22, 2020, https://s .weibo.com/weibo?q=%23%E4%B8%AD%E5%9B%BD%E4%BA%BA% E8%84%B8%E8%AF%86%E5%88%AB%E7%AC%AC%E4%B8%80%E 6%A1%88%23&sudaref=tineye.com&display=0&retcode=6102#_loginLayer _1595203062674.

24. Wu Shuaishuai 吴帅帅, "'Shua lian di yi an' hangzhou kaiting" '刷脸第一案' 杭州开庭 [The "First Facial Scanning Case" Trial Begins in Hangzhou], Xinhua, June 23, 2020, www.zj.xinhuanet.com/2020-06/23/c_1126149163.htm.

25. Du Qiongfang, "Park in Hangzhou Found Guilty of Breach of Contract for Using Visitor's Facial Recognition Information," *Global Times*, November 21, 2020, www.globaltimes.cn/content/1207570.shtml.

26. "Zheda faxue boshi jujue 'shua lian' ru yuan, qisu hangzhou yesheng dongwu shijie huo li'an" 浙大法学博士拒绝 '刷脸' 入园, 起诉杭州野生动物世界获立 案 [Zhejiang University Law School Doctoral Graduate Refuses "Facial Scanning" for Park Entry, Will File Lawsuit against Hangzhou Safari Park], *The Paper*, November 3, 2019, www.thepaper.cn/newsDetail_forward_4855453.

27. George Qi, Qianqian Li, and Darren Abernethy, "China Releases Draft Personal Information Protection Law," *National Law Review* 11, no. 21 (2021), www.natlaw review.com/article/china-releases-draft-personal-information-protection-law.

28. Qin Jianhang, Qian Tong, and Han Wei, "Cover Story: The Fight over China's Law to Protect Personal Data," Caixin Global, November 20, 2020, www .caixinglobal.com/2020-11-30/cover-story-the-fight-over-chinas-law-to-protect -personal-data-101633699.html.

29. "'Ren lian shibie di yi an' pan dongwuyuan shanchu yuangao zhaopian xinxi, yuangao cheng jiang jixu shangsu" '人脸识别第一案' 判动物园删除原告照片信 息, 原告称将继续上诉 [The "First Case Regarding Facial Recognition" Decrees That the Zoo Delete the Plaintiff's Photographic Information, Plaintiff Says He Will Continue to Appeal], Xinhua, November 21, 2020, www.xinhuanet.com /legal/2020-11/21/c_1126767913.htm.

30. "Urumqi Riots Three Years On—Crackdown on Uighurs Grows Bolder," Amnesty International, July 4, 2012, www.amnesty.org/en/press-releases/2012/07 /urumqi-riots-three-years-crackdown-uighurs-grows-bolder/; Austin Ramzy, "A

Year after Xinjiang Riots, Ethnic Tensions Remain," *Time*, July 5, 2010, http://content.time.com/time/world/article/0,8599,2001311,00.html.

31. Congressional-Executive Commission on China, "Chairs Urge Ambassador Branstad to Prioritize Mass Detention of Uyghurs, Including Family Members of Radio Free Asia Employees," press release, April 3, 2018, www.cecc.gov/media-center/press-releases/chairs-urge-ambassador-branstad-to-prioritize-mass-detention-of-uyghurs.

32. Bethany Allen-Ebrahimian, "Exposed: China's Operating Manuals for Mass Internment and Arrest by Algorithm," International Consortium of Investigative Journalists, November 24, 2019, www.icij.org/investigations/china-cables/exposed-chinas-operating-manuals-for-mass-internment-and-arrest-by-algorithm/.

33. Sophia Yan, "'One Minute Felt Like One Year': A Day in the Life of Inmates in the Xinjiang Internment Camps," *The Telegraph*, March 26, 2019, www.telegraph.co.uk/news/2019/03/26/dispatch-day-life-inmate-xinjiang-internment-camps/; "China: Free Xinjiang 'Political Education' Detainees," Human Rights Watch, September 10, 2017, www.hrw.org/news/2017/09/10/china-free-xinjiang-political-education-detainees#.

34. Orwell, *1984*, 211.

35. Austin Ramzy and Chris Buckley, "Leaked China Files Show Internment Camps Are Ruled by Secrecy and Spying," *New York Times*, November 24, 2019, www.nytimes.com/2019/11/24/world/asia/leak-chinas-internment-camps.html.

36. Paul Mozur and Nicole Perlroth, "China's Software Stalked Uighurs Earlier and More Widely, Researchers Learn," *New York Times*, last modified January 19, 2021, www.nytimes.com/2020/07/01/technology/china-uighurs-hackers-malware-hackers-smartphones.html?smid=em-share.

37. See "China: Minority Region Collects DNA from Millions," Human Rights Watch, December 13, 2017, www.hrw.org/news/2017/12/13/china-minority-region-collects-dna-millions; and Sui-Lee Wee, "China Uses DNA to Track Its People, with the Help of American Expertise," *New York Times*, February 21, 2019, www.nytimes.com/2019/02/21/business/china-xinjiang-uighur-dna-thermo-fisher.html.

38. Charles Rollet, "Hikvision Admits Minority Recognition, Now Claims Canceled," IPVM, July 23, 2020, https://ipvm.com/reports/hikvision-cancels; "Dahua Racist Uyghur Tracking Revealed," IPVM, November 4, 2020, https://ipvm.com/reports/dahua-uyghur; "Patenting Uyghur Tracking—Huawei, Megvii, More," IPVM, January 12, 2021, https://ipvm.com/reports/patents-uyghur.

39. Michael Wines, "To Protect an Ancient City, China Moves to Raze It," *New York Times*, May 27, 2009, www.nytimes.com/2009/05/28/world/asia/28kashgar .html.

40. Chris Buckley and Paul Mozur, "How China Uses High-Tech Surveillance to Subdue Minorities," *New York Times*, May 22, 2019, www.nytimes.com/2019/05/22 /world/asia/china-surveillance-xinjiang.html.

41. Gerry Shih, "Digital Police State Shackles Chinese Minority," Associated Press, December 17, 2017, https://apnews.com/1ec5143fe4764a1d8ea73ce4a3e2c570.

42. Bahram K. Sintash, "Demolishing Faith: The Destruction and Desecration of Uyghur Mosques and Shrines," Uyghur Human Rights Project (UHRP), October 2019, https://docs.uhrp.org/pdf/UHRP_report_Demolishing_Faith.pdf.

43. Rian Thum (@RianThum), "Last year, the Chinese government destroyed the central Uyghur graveyard and sacred shrine in Khotan. We can now see part of what they put in its place: a parking lot," Twitter, April 28, 2020, 10:42 a.m., https://twitter.com/RianThum/status/1255146071258349574?s=20.

44. Orwell, *1984*, 121.

45. Nathan Ruser et al., *Cultural Erasure: Tracing the Destruction of Uyghur and Islamic Spaces in Xinjiang*, Policy Brief Report no. 38 (Canberra: Australian Strategic Policy Institute, 2020), www.aspi.org.au/report/cultural-erasure.

46. Charles Rollet, "Hikvision Wins Chinese Government Forced Facial Recognition Project across 967 Mosques," IPVM, July 16, 2018, https://ipvm.com /reports/hik-mosques.

47. Charles Rollet, "Dahua and Hikvision Win over $1 Billion in Government-Backed Projects in Xinjiang," IPVM, April 23, 2018, https://ipvm.com/reports /xinjiang-dahua-hikvision.

48. See Jonathan E. Hillman and Maesea McCalpin, *Watching Huawei's "Safe Cities"* (Washington, D.C.: Center for Strategic and International Studies, 2019), www .csis.org/analysis/watching-huaweis-safe-cities; Greitens, "China's Surveillance State at Home and Abroad"; Sheena Chestnut Greitens, "The Global Impact of China's Surveillance Technology," in *The 2020-21 Wilson China Fellowship: Essays on the Rise of China and Its Implications*, ed. Abraham M. Denmark and Lucas Myers (Washington, D.C.: Woodrow Wilson International Center for Scholars, 2021), 129-52, https://www.wilsoncenter.org/2020-21-essay-collection.

49. "Hikvision North America 2017 Corporate Video," YouTube video, 2:10, posted by Hikvision USA, July 17, 2017, https://www.youtube.com/watch?v=fV4lZE y3KDg.

50. Hangzhou Hikvision Digital Technology Co., Ltd., *2019 Annual Report*, April 25, 2020, 14, www.hikvision.com/content/dam/hikvision/en/brochures/hikvision-financial-report/Hikvision%202019%20Annual%20Report.pdf.

51. Matthew Luce, "A Model Company: CETC Celebrates 10 Years of Civil-Military Integration," *China Brief* 12, no. 4 (2012): 10–13, https://jamestown.org/program/a-model-company-cetc-celebrates-10-years-of-civil-military-integration/.

52. "How Mass Surveillance Works in Xinjiang, China," Human Rights Watch, last modified May 2, 2019, www.hrw.org/video-photos/interactive/2019/05/02/china-how-mass-surveillance-works-xinjiang.

53. Ma Si, "CETC Speeds Reform Efforts," *China Daily*, last modified September 16, 2017, www.chinadaily.com.cn/china/fiveyearson/2017-09/16/content_32063151.htm.

54. Zhong dian hai kang jituan youxian gongsi 中电海康集团有限公司 [CETHIK Group Co., Ltd.], "Zhonggong zhong dian haikang jituan youxian gongsi di yi ci daibiao dahui longzhong zhaokai" 中共中电海康集团有限公司第一次代表大会隆重召开 [CETHIK Group Co., Ltd.'s First CCP Congress Was Held], press release, April 27, 2015, www.cethik.com/news_detail.aspx?c_kind=1&c_kind2=8&id=565.

55. "Hikvision Celebrates Xi Jinping Visit," YouTube video, 1:35, posted by IPVM, June 23, 2019, www.youtube.com/watch?v=i5zZQH4R0ZU.

56. John Honovich, "Hikvision Gets $3 Billion from Chinese Government Bank," IPVM, December 9, 2015, https://ipvm.com/reports/hikision-gets-%2431-billion-usd-financing-from-chinese-government-bank.

57. "We Visited Hikvision HQ," *a&s Adria*, December 25, 2018, www.asadria.com/en/we-visited-hikvision-hq/; for Western Digital information, see "WD Debuts Surveillance-Class Hard Drive Line," *SDM Magazine*, March 4, 2014, www.sdmmag.com/articles/90042-wd-debuts-surveillance-class-hard-drive-line.

58. Seagate, "Seagate Launches First Drive for AI-Enabled Surveillance," press release, October 28, 2017, www.seagate.com/news/news-archive/seagate-launches-first-drive-for-ai-enabled-surveillance-master-pr/.

59. Yukinori Hanada, "US Sanctions Blur Chinese Dominance in Security Cameras," *Nikkei Asia*, November 12, 2019, https://asia.nikkei.com/Economy/Trade-war/US-sanctions-blur-Chinese-dominance-in-security-cameras.

60. For the New York City apartments example, see "Hikvision's Custom-Tailored VMS Software Protects New York City Residents," *SDM Magazine*, November 3, 2014, www.sdmmag.com/articles/90628-hikvisions-custom-tailored-vms-soft

ware-protects-new-york-city-residents; for the Sunset Plaza Hotel example, see "Hikvision Provides 24-Hour Video Surveillance to Hollywood's Sunset Plaza Hotel," *SDM Magazine*, April 15, 2016, www.sdmmag.com/articles/92342-hik vision-provides-24-hour-video-surveillance-to-hollywoods-sunset-plaza-hotel.

61. "Memphis Police Department Combines Traditional and Unconventional Surveillance to Keep the City Safe," *SDM Magazine*, January 29, 2016, www.sdmmag .com/articles/92037-memphis-police-department-combines-traditional-and -unconventional-surveillance-to-keep-the-city-safe; "Hikvision and Eagle Eye Networks Provide Mobile Video Surveillance Solution," *SDM Magazine*, April 10, 2015, www.sdmmag.com/articles/91176-hikvision-and-eagle-eye-networks -provide-mobile-video-surveillance-solution; for the Colorado crime lab example, see "Hikvision Video Surveillance Secures Crime Lab in Colorado," *SDM Magazine*, April 4, 2016, www.sdmmag.com/articles/92248-hikvision-video -surveillance-secures-crime-lab-in-colorado; also see the original case study: Hikvision USA Inc., "Panoramic Surveillance Captures Fine Detail in Crime Lab," April 1, 2016, https://web.archive.org/web/20160615223003/http:/over seas.hikvision.com/ueditor/net/upload/2016-04-02/292a12ff-7fbb-4398-9e09 -c294ac527a6c.pdf.

62. Avi Asher-Schapiro, "Exclusive: Half London Councils Found Using Chinese Surveillance Tech Linked to Uighur Abuses," Reuters, February 18, 2021, www .reuters.com/article/us-britain-tech-china/exclusive-half-london-councils-found -using-chinese-surveillance-tech-linked-to-uighur-abuses-idUSKBN2AI0QJ.

63. Charu Kasturi, "How Chinese Security Cameras Are Compromising US Military Bases," OZY, July 23, 2019, www.ozy.com/the-new-and-the-next/how -chinese-security-cameras-are-compromising-us-military-bases/95665/.

64. John Honovich, "Ban of Dahua and Hikvision Is Now US Gov Law," IPVM, August 13, 2018, https://ipvm.com/reports/ban-law.

65. John Honovich, "Ezviz = Hikvision = Chinese Government," IPVM, January 8, 2016, https://ipvm.com/reports/ezviz-=-hikvision-=-chinese-government.

66. "EZVIZ," Amazon, accessed April 2020, www.amazon.com/stores/EZVIZ /page/D7A0ED48-0F3C-458E-9479-9F9FD0790D7F?ref_=ast_bln.

67. Cisco, "Digital Impact: How Technology Is Accelerating Global Problem Solving" (presentation, n.p., 2018), www.cisco.com/c/dam/assets/csr/pdf/Digital -Impact-Playbook.pdf.

68. "Mi Band," Xiaomi United States, accessed February 18, 2021, www.mi.com /global/miband/.

69. Daniel R. Deakin, "Xiaomi Mi Band Global Sales Top 13 Million Units for Q2 2020 as Pro and Lite Variant Rumors Still Linger for the Mi Band 5," NotebookCheck.net, September 23, 2020, www.notebookcheck.net/Xiaomi-Mi -Band-global-sales-top-13-million-units-for-Q2-2020-as-Pro-and-Lite-variant -rumors-still-linger-for-the-Mi-Band-5.495089.0.html.

70. Dan Strumpf, "U.S. Blacklisted China's Xiaomi Because of Award Given to Its Founder," *Wall Street Journal*, last modified March 5, 2021, www.wsj.com/amp /articles/u-s-blacklisted-chinas-xiaomi-because-of-award-given-to-its-founder -11614947281.

71. Laura DeNardis, *The Internet in Everything: Freedom and Security in a World with No Off Switch* (New Haven, CT: Yale University Press, 2020), 68, Kindle.

72. *Statement for the Record: Worldwide Threat Assessment of the US Intelligence Community: Senate Armed Services Committee*, 114th Cong. 1 (2016) (statement of James R. Clapper, former director of National Intelligence), www.armed-services.senate.gov /imo/media/doc/Clapper_02-09-16.pdf; DeNardis, *Internet in Everything*, 230.

73. "Inside the Infamous Mirai IoT Botnet: A Retrospective Analysis," *Cloudflare Blog*, Cloudflare, December 14, 2017, https://blog.cloudflare.com/inside-mirai -the-infamous-iot-botnet-a-retrospective-analysis/; Brian Karas, "Hacked Dahua Cameras Drive Massive Mirai Cyber Attack," IPVM, September 27, 2016, https://ipvm.com/reports/dahua-ddos.

74. James A. Lewis, "Securing the Information and Communications Technology and Services Supply Chain," Center for Strategic and International Studies, April 2, 2021, https://www.csis.org/analysis/securing-information-and -communications-technology-and-services-supply-chain.

75. EZVIZ, "EZVIZ Named as CES 2018 Innovation Awards Honoree," press release, January 9, 2018, www.ezvizlife.com/newsroom/ezviz-named-as-ces-2018 -innovation-awards-honoree/5.

76. EZVIZ, "Innovation Awards Honoree."

77. For the Minnesota schools example, see "Minn. School District Upgrades Video Surveillance System," *Campus Safety*, September 5, 2016, www.campussafety magazine.com/news/minn-_school_district_upgrades_video_surveillance _system/; for the Xinjiang camps example, see "Hikvision Cameras Covering Concentration Camps," IPVM, July 29, 2019, https://ipvm.com/reports/hik vision-bbc.

78. Hikvision Oceania, *Hikvision Face Recognition Solution—Powered by Artificial*

*Intelligence (AI)* (n.p.: Hikvision Oceania, n.d.), www.scribd.com/document/405 887979/Hikvision-Facial-Recognition-Oceania-1-1-pdf .

79.  "2MP Hikvision Facial Capture Recognition Camera Surveillance Face Recognition Software," Veley Security Ltd., accessed February 18, 2021, https:// veleysecurity.en.made-in-china.com/product/TNqxYiPoCIWO/China-2MP -Hikvision-Facial-Capture-Recognition-Camera-Surveillance-Face-Recognition -Software.html.

80.  National Institute of Standards and Technology, U.S. Department of Commerce, *Ongoing Face Recognition Vendor Test (FRVT) Part 3: Demographic Effects, Annex 8: False Match Rates with Matched Demographics Using Application Images*, NIST Interagency Report 8280 (Gaithersburg, MD: National Institute of Standards and Technology, 2019), https://pages.nist.gov/frvt/reports/demographics/annexes /annex_08.pdf.

81.  "What We Offer," DeepinMind Series, Hikvision, accessed February 18, 2021, www.hikvision.com/en/products/IP-Products/Network-Video-Recorders /DeepinMind-Series/.

82.  Ethan Ace, "Hikvision DeepInMind Tested Terribly," IPVM, February 15, 2018, https://ipvm.com/reports/deepinmind-test.

83.  Rob Kilpatrick, "Hikvision DeepinMind 2019 Test," IPVM, June 6, 2019, https:// ipvm.com/reports/deepinmind-retest.

84.  Drew Harwell, "Federal Study Confirms Racial Bias of Many Facial-Recognition Systems, Casts Doubt on Their Expanding Use," *Washington Post*, December 19, 2019, www.washingtonpost.com/technology/2019/12/19/federal -study-confirms-racial-bias-many-facial-recognition-systems-casts-doubt-their -expanding-use/.

85.  Kashmir Hill, "Another Arrest, and Jail Time, Due to a Bad Facial Recognition Match," *New York Times*, last modified January 6, 2021, www.nytimes.com /2020/12/29/technology/facial-recognition-misidentify-jail.html.

86.  Mara Hvistendahl, "How Oracle Sells Repression in China," *The Intercept*, February 18, 2021, https://theintercept.com/2021/02/18/oracle-china-police -surveillance/.

87.  Shoshana Zuboff, *The Age of Surveillance Capitalism: The Fight for a Human Future at the New Frontier of Power* (New York: PublicAffairs, 2018).

88.  "Ren Zhengfei's Roundtable with Media from Latin America and Spain," interview by Pablo Diaz, *Voices of Huawei* (blog), Huawei, December 11, 2019, www

.huawei.com/us/facts/voices-of-huawei/ren-zhengfeis-roundtable-with-media
-from-latin-america-and-spain.

89. Hoover Institution, Stanford University, "Q&A: Elizabeth Economy on the Biden Administration's China Challenge," press release, January 20, 2021, www .hoover.org/news/qa-elizabeth-economy-biden-administrations-china-challenge.

90. Charles Rollet, "Evidence of Hikvision's Involvement with Xinjiang IJOP and Re-Education Camps," IPVM, October 2, 2018, https://ipvm.com/reports /hikvision-xinjiang; Charles Rollet, "In China's Far West, Companies Cash In on Surveillance Program That Targets Muslims," *Foreign Policy*, June 13, 2018, https://foreignpolicy.com/2018/06/13/in-chinas-far-west-companies-cash-in -on-surveillance-program-that-targets-muslims/.

91. Marco Rubio, U.S. Senator for Florida, "ICYMI | Financial Times: US Funds Pull Out of Chinese Groups Involved in Xinjiang Detention," press release, March 28, 2019, www.rubio.senate.gov/public/index.cfm/2019/3/icymi -financial-times-us-funds-pull-out-of-chinese-groups-involved-in-xinjiang-detent ion; Hangzhou Hikvision Digital Technology Co., Ltd., *2018 Environmental, Social and Governance Report*, April 2019, www.hikvision.com/content/dam/hikvision /en/investor-relations/Hikvision%202018%20ESG%20Report.pdf.

92. Rachel Fixsen, "Denmark's AkademikerPension Bans Chinese Surveillance Kit Firm," Investment & Pensions Europe, November 24, 2020, www.ipe.com/news /denmarks-akademikerpension-bans-chinese-surveillance-kit-firm/10049183 .article.

93. Hikvision, *Advanced Security, Safer Society: Safe City Solution* (Hangzhou, China: Hikvision, n.d.), www.hikvision.com/content/dam/hikvision/en/brochures-download /vertical-solution-brochure/Safe-City-Solution-Brochure.pdf.

94. Joel Gehrke, "'It Improves Targeting': Americans under Threat from Chinese Facial Recognition Systems, Rubio Warns," *Washington Examiner*, August 27, 2019, www.washingtonexaminer.com/policy/defense-national-security/chinas- overseas-smart-city-surveillance-empire-could-trap-americans-lawmakers- warn.

95. Marco Rubio, U.S. Senator for Florida, "Rubio, Wyden Urge State Department to Issue Travel Advisories for Americans Traveling to Countries Using Chinese Surveillance," press release, August 1, 2019, www.rubio.senate.gov/public/index .cfm/2019/8/rubio-wyden-urge-state-department-to-issue-travel-advisories-for -americans-traveling-to-countries-using-chinese-surveillance.

96. Atha et al., *China's Smart Cities Development*, 3.

97. Helen Warrell and Nic Fildes, "UK Spies Warn Local Authorities over 'Smart City' Tech Risks," *Financial Times*, May 6, 2021, https://www.ft.com/content /46d35d62-0307-41d8-96a8-de9b52bf0ec3.

98. National Cyber Security Centre, GCHQ, *Connected Places: Cyber Security Principles* (London: National Cyber Security Centre, 2021), https://www.ncsc.gov.uk /collection/connected-places-security-principles.

99. Atha et al., *China's Smart Cities Development*, 60.

100. Jay Greene, "Microsoft Won't Sell Police Its Facial-Recognition Technology, Following Similar Moves by Amazon and IBM," *Washington Post*, June 11, 2020, www .washingtonpost.com/technology/2020/06/11/microsoft-facial-recognition/.

101. Huawei, "Network-Wide Intelligence, Opening and Sharing—Development Trend of Video Surveillance Technology and Service" (presentation, n.p., 2016), https://reconasia-production.s3.amazonaws.com/media/filer_public/aa/3d /aa3d5c68-e826-46c6-a2a5-bc8454d6a5ba/huawei_intelligent_video_surveillance _technology_and_service_development_trend_material.pdf.

102. ZTE, "Smart City: Road to Urban Digital Transformation" (presentation, techUK event on local digital connectivity, n.p., October 13, 2017), www.slide share.net/TechUK/zte-smart-city-solution-overview.

103. Sean Patton, "Hikvision, Dahua, and Uniview Falsify Test Reports to South Korea," IPVM, December 10, 2020, https://ipvm.com/reports/hikuaview-sk.

104. John Honovich and Charles Rollet, "Hikvision Impossible 30 People Simultaneously Fever Claim Dupes Baldwin, Alabama," IPVM, September 1, 2020, https://ipvm.com/reports/baldwin-30.

105. Sean Patton and Charles Rollet, "Alabama Schools Million Dollar Hikvision Fever Camera Deal," IPVM, August 11, 2020, https://ipvm.com/reports/alabama-hik.

106. Bent Flyvbjerg, "Introduction: The Iron Law of Megaproject Management," in *The Oxford Handbook of Megaproject Management*, ed. Bent Flyvbjerg (Oxford: Oxford University Press, 2017), 1–18, https://ti.org/pdfs/IronLawofMegaprojects .pdf.

107. "HUAWEI—Safe City Post Project Documentary," YouTube video, 7:57, posted by Xdynamix, November 14, 2017, https://www.youtube.com/watch?v=cmU JxdBlUYE&t=272s.

108. Prasso, "Huawei's Claims That It Makes Cities Safer Mostly Look Like Hype."

109. National Police Bureau, Ministry of Interior, Government of Pakistan, *Crimes*

*Reported by Type and Province* (Islamabad: National Police Bureau, n.d.), http://web
.archive.org/web/20191101090153/http:/www.pbs.gov.pk/sites/default/files
/tables/Crimes%20Reported%20by%20Type%20and%20Provinces%20s.pdf.

110. National Assembly of Pakistan, "It Is My Life Mission to Provide Job to Unem-
ployed Youth of Pakistan: Says Speaker NA," press release, September 15, 2018,
http://na.gov.pk/en/pressrelease_detail.php?id=3248.

111. Munawer Azeem, "Leaked Safe City Images Spark Concern among Citizens,"
*Dawn*, January 27, 2019, www.dawn.com/news/1459963.

112. Leo Kelion and Sajid Iqbal, "Huawei Wi-Fi Modules Were Pulled from Pakistan
CCTV System," BBC, April 8, 2019, www.bbc.com/news/technology-47856098.

113. Embassy of the People's Republic of China in the Islamic Republic of Pakistan,
"Statement of the Spokesperson from the Chinese Embassy in Pakistan," press
release, May 21, 2020, http://pk.chineseembassy.org/eng/zbgx/t1781421.htm.
Estimates range widely, with $62 billion often mentioned as an original target,
only a fraction of which has been delivered.

114. Michael Rubin, "Is Pakistan Nothing More than a Colony of China?," American Enterprise Institute, May 5, 2020, www.aei.org/op-eds/is-pakistan-nothing
-more-than-a-colony-of-china/; Fakhar Durrani, "Will Coronavirus Affect CPEC
and Pak Economy?," *The News International*, February 7, 2020, www.thenews.com
.pk/print/610253-will-coronavirus-affect-cpec-and-pak-economy.

115. "China-Pakistan Cross-Border Optical Fiber Cable Project: Special Report on
CPEC Projects (Transportation Infrastructure: Part 3)," Embassy of the People's
Republic of China in the Islamic Republic of Pakistan, October 1, 2018, http://
pk.chineseembassy.org/eng/zbgx/CPEC/t1627111.htm.

116. "Safe City: Kenya," online video, posted by Huawei, 2018, https://web.archive
.org/web/20200428034508/https:/e.huawei.com/en/videos/global/2018
/201804101038#.

117. Huawei, "Huawei Unveils Safe City Solution Experience Center at 2016 Mobile
World Congress," press release, February 23, 2016, www.huawei.com/us/press
-events/news/2016/2/unveils-safe-city-solution-experience-center.

118. "Crime Statistics," National Police Service, Government of Kenya, accessed February 27, 2021, www.nationalpolice.go.ke/crime-statistics.html.

119. Reuters, "Kenya Secures $666 Million"; Mark Anderson, "Kenya's Tech Entre-
preneurs Shun Konza 'Silicon Savannah,'" *The Guardian*, January 5, 2015, www
.theguardian.com/global-development/2015/jan/05/kenya-technology-entre
preneurs-konza-silicon-savannah.

120. "Konza Technology City Approved as Kenya's Vision 2030 Flagship Project," Konza Technopolis, October 18, 2019, www.konza.go.ke/timeline/konza-technology-city-approved-as-kenyas-vision-2030-flagship-project/; "Kenya Begins Construction of 'Silicon' City Konza," BBC, January 23, 2013, www.bbc.com/news/world-africa-21158928.

121. "Smart City," Konza Technopolis, accessed February 15, 2021, www.konza.go.ke/smart-city/.

122. Patrick Vidija, "Smart City: Development at Konza Takes Shape as 40% Sold Off," *The Star* (Kenya), February 2, 2021, www.the-star.co.ke/news/big-read/2021-02-02-smart-city-development-at-konza-takes-shape-as-40-sold-off/.

123. Vidija, "Smart City."

124. The Presidency, Republic of Kenya, "Press Statement: On April 27, 2019, in Statements and Speeches," press release, April 27, 2019, www.president.go.ke/2019/04/27/press-statement-2/.

125. Reuters, "Kenya Secures $666 Million"; Andrew Kitson and Kenny Liew, "China Doubles Down on Its Digital Silk Road," Reconnecting Asia, Center for Strategic and International Studies, November 14, 2019, https://reconnectingasia.csis.org/analysis/entries/china-doubles-down-its-digital-silk-road/; Sebastian Moss, "Huawei to Build Konza Data Center and Smart City in Kenya, with Chinese Concessional Loan," Data Center Dynamics, April 30, 2019, www.datacenterdynamics.com/en/news/huawei-build-konza-data-center-and-smart-city-kenya-chinese-concessional-loan/; "Konza Technopolis Board of Directors," Konza Technopolis, accessed March 18, 2021, www.konza.go.ke/eng-john-tanui/; "Eng. John Tanui, MBS: CEO, Konza Technopolis Development Authority," LinkedIn, accessed March 18, 2021, www.linkedin.com/in/johntanui/?originalSubdomain=ke.

126. "Kenyan Gov't, Chinese Firm Launch Construction of Major Power Transmission Project," Xinhua, November 15, 2019, www.xinhuanet.com/english/2019-11/15/c_138558244.htm; Liu Hongjie, "Chinese Company Empowers Kenya's Economic Transformation," *China Daily*, November 15, 2019, www.chinadaily.com.cn/a/201911/15/WS5dce9c50a310cf3e35577bc8_1.html; "Government Launches High Voltage Substation in Konza," YouTube video, 1:52, posted by KBC Channel 1, November 15, 2019, www.youtube.com/watch?v=_LzLbt0JutM&ab_channel=KBCChannel1; "Kenya: Chinese Firm to Build Konza Technopolis Power Line," *African Energy Newsletter*, November 21, 2019, www.africa-energy.com/article/kenya-chinese-firm-build-konza-technopolis-power-line.

127. Alibaba Cloud, "Alibaba Cloud Harnesses AI and Data Analytics Expertise to Advance China's Innovations in Urban Governance and Astronomy," press release, October 13, 2016, www.alibabacloud.com/press-room/alibaba-cloud -harnesses-ai-and-data-analytics-expertise-to-advance; "Alibaba Cloud's City Brain Solution Improves Urban Management in Hangzhou," *China Daily*, September 20, 2018, www.chinadaily.com.cn/a/201809/20/WS5ba3499ea310c4cc 775e7568.html.

128. "Alibaba Cloud Intelligence Brain," Alibaba Cloud, accessed February 27, 2021, www.alibabacloud.com/solutions/intelligence-brain/city; Liz Lee, "Alibaba to Take on Kuala Lumpur's Traffic in First Foreign Project," Reuters, January 29, 2018, www.reuters.com/article/us-alibaba-malaysia/alibaba-to-take-on-kuala -lumpurs-traffic-in-first-foreign-project-idUSKBN1FI0QV.

129. Jianfeng Zhang et al., "City Brain: Practice of Large-Scale Artificial Intelligence in the Real World," *IET Smart Cities* 1, no. 1 (2019): 28–37, https://doi.org /10.1049/iet-smc.2019.0034.

130. "You Can't Spell Attribution without AI," *Course Studies* (blog), Corsair's Publishing, April 28, 2019, https://course-studies.corsairs.network/you-cant-spell -attribution-without-ai-99c47327b6f4.

131. Min Wanli, "The Road to Digital Intelligence with Alibaba Cloud ET Brain," *Alibaba Cloud Community Blog*, Alibaba Cloud, October 12, 2018, www.alibaba cloud.com/blog/594066.

132. "Kuala Lumpur Traffic," TomTom, accessed February 1, 2020, www.tomtom .com/en_gb/traffic-index/kuala-lumpur-traffic/.

133. "Xi Calls for Making Major Cities 'Smarter,'" YouTube video, 1:30, posted by CCTV Video News Agency, April 1, 2020, www.youtube.com/watch?v=cJpsM WZDFD8&t=10s&ab_channel=CCTVVideoNewsAgency.

134. "Xinhua Headlines-Xi Focus: Xi Stresses Coordinating Epidemic Control, Economic Work, Achieving Development Goals," Xinhua, April 1, 2020, www.xin huanet.com/english/2020-04/01/c_138938742.htm.

135. Lee J, "Smart Cities with Not-So-Smart Security—Again!," DataBreaches.net, January 14, 2020, www.databreaches.net/smart-cities-with-not-so-smart-security -again/.

136. Zack Whittaker, "Security Lapse Exposed a Chinese Smart City Surveillance System," TechCrunch, May 3, 2019, https://techcrunch.com/2019/05/03/china -smart-city-exposed/.

137. See Philip Wen and Drew Hinshaw, "China Asserts Claim to Global Leadership,

Mask by Mask," *Wall Street Journal*, April 1, 2020, www.wsj.com/articles/china -asserts-claim-to-global-leadership-mask-by-mask-11585752077; Paul Mozur, Raymond Zhong, and Aaron Krolik, "In Coronavirus Fight, China Gives Citizens a Color Code, with Red Flags," *New York Times*, last modified August 7, 2020, www.nytimes.com/2020/03/01/business/china-coronavirus-surveillance.html.

138. Artificial Intelligence Industry Alliance, "AI Support for Coronavirus Control - AIIA Research Report," trans. Jeffrey Ding, accessed March 20, 2020, https:// docs.google.com/document/d/1XqlioXVv3t4czWp9_HIgX7KkuXtScbit _NU1nnqfi7Y/edit#heading=h.4sboxyupialu.

139. Ethan Ace and John Honovich, "Dahua Rigs Fever Cameras, Covers Up," IPVM, November 20, 2020, https://ipvm.com/reports/dahua-fever.

140. Yuan Yang, Nian Liu, and Sue-Lin Wong, "China, Coronavirus and Surveillance: The Messy Reality of Personal Data," *Financial Times*, April 2, 2020, www .ft.com/content/760142e6-740e-11ea-95fe-fcd274e920ca.

141. Raymond Zhong and Paul Mozur, "To Tame Coronavirus, Mao-Style Social Control Blankets China," *New York Times*, February 20, 2020, www.nytimes.com /2020/02/15/business/china-coronavirus-lockdown.html.

142. Jiefei Liu, "Founder of Alibaba Cloud Says Smart Cities Can't Solve Problems Caused by China's Rapid Urbanization," *TechNode* (blog), July 2, 2018, https:// technode.com/2018/07/02/techcrunch-city-brain/.

143. Chris Buckley, "Was That a Giant Cat? Leopards Escape, and a Zoo Keeps Silent (at First)," *New York Times*, May 10, 2021, https://www.nytimes.com/2021/05/10 /world/asia/china-zoo-leopards.html.

144. Atha et al., *China's Smart Cities Development*, 43–54.

145. Yuan Yang, "The Role of AI in China's Crackdown on Uighurs," *Financial Times*, December 11, 2019, www.ft.com/content/e47b33ce-1add-11ea-97df-cc63de1d73f4.

146. "China's Algorithms of Repression," Human Rights Watch, May 1, 2019, www .hrw.org/report/2019/05/01/chinas-algorithms-repression/reverse-engineering -xinjiang-police-mass.

147. Jennifer Pan, *Welfare for Autocrats* (New York: Oxford University Press, 2020), 174, Kindle.

148. Sarah Dai, "China Adds Huawei, Hikvision to Expanded 'National Team' Spearheading Country's AI Efforts," *South China Morning Post*, August 30, 2019, www.scmp.com/tech/big-tech/article/3024966/china-adds-huawei-hikvision -expanded-national-team-spearheading.

149. Hangzhou Hikvision Digital Technology Co., Ltd., *2019 Annual Report*.

150. Elizabeth Schulze, "40% of A.I. Start-Ups in Europe Have Almost Nothing to Do with A.I., Research Finds," CNBC, March 6, 2019, www.cnbc.com /2019/03/06/40-percent-of-ai-start-ups-in-europe-not-related-to-ai-mmc-report .html.

151. "Zhucheng shi tongchou liyong 'xueliang gongcheng' dazao 'san dapingtai'" 诸城市统筹利用 '雪亮工程' 打造 '三大平台' [Zhucheng City Integrates Applications from the "Sharp Eyes Project" in the Creation of the "Three Major Platforms"], Sohu, November 23, 2019, previously published on *People's Daily*, November 23, 2019, www.sohu.com/a/355605010_114731.

152. Reuters, "U.S. Says No Change in Its Genocide Determination for China's Xinjiang," March 9, 2021, www.reuters.com/article/us-china-usa-xinjiang/u-s-says -no-change-in-its-genocide-determination-for-chinas-xinjiang-idUSKBN2B1 2LG.

153. Strittmatter, *We Have Been Harmonized*, 194.

154. Pan, *Welfare for Autocrats*, 176.

## CHAPTER FIVE    A CREASE IN THE INTERNET

1.    "What Is BGP? | BGP Routing Explained," Cloudflare, accessed January 24, 2021, www.cloudflare.com/learning/security/glossary/what-is-bgp/.

2.    Paula Jabloner, "The Two-Napkin Protocol," *CHM Blog*, Computer History Museum, March 4, 2015, https://computerhistory.org/blog/the-two-napkin-protocol /?key=the-two-napkin-protocol.

3.    "World—Autonomous System Number Statistics—Sorted by Number," Regional Internet Registries Statistics, last modified January 18, 2021, www-public.imtbs -tsp.eu/~maigron/RIR_Stats/RIR_Delegations/World/ASN-ByNb.html.

4.    Doug Madory, "China Telecom's Internet Traffic Misdirection," *Internet Intelligence* (blog), Oracle, November 5, 2018, https://blogs.oracle.com/internetintelli gence/china-telecoms-internet-traffic-misdirection.

5.    Chris C. Demchak and Yuval Shavitt, "China's Maxim—Leave No Access Point Unexploited: The Hidden Story of China Telecom's BGP Hijacking," *Military Cyber Affairs* 3, no. 1 (2018): 1–5, https://doi.org/10.5038/2378-0789.3.1.1050.

6.    Doug Madory, "Large European Routing Leak Sends Traffic through China Telecom," *Internet Intelligence* (blog), Oracle, June 6, 2019, https://blogs.oracle .com/internetintelligence/large-european-routing-leak-sends-traffic-through

-china-telecom; Craig Timberg, "The Long Life of a Quick 'Fix': Internet Protocol from 1989 Leaves Data Vulnerable to Hijackers," *Washington Post,* May 31, 2015, www.washingtonpost.com/sf/business/2015/05/31/net-of-insecurity-part-2/.

7.  Rahul Hiran, Niklas Carlsson, and Phillipa Gill, "Characterizing Large-Scale Routing Anomalies: A Case Study of the China Telecom Incident," in *Passive and Active Measurement: 14th International Conference, PAM, 2013, Hong Kong, China, March 18–19, 2013, Proceedings* (Heidelberg: Springer, 2013), 229–38, https://doi .org/10.1007/978-3-642-36516-4_23.

8.  U.S.-China Economic and Security Review Commission, *2010 Report to Congress of the U.S.-China Economic and Security Review Commission* (Washington, D.C.: U.S. Government Printing Office, 2010), 243–44, www.uscc.gov/sites/default/files /annual_reports/2010-Report-to-Congress.pdf.

9.  Doug Madory, correspondence with author, January 2021; see also Doug Madory, "Visualizing Routing Incidents in 3D" (presentation, RIPE 80, virtual meeting, May 12–14, 2020), https://ripe80.ripe.net/presentations/14-3dleak_viz _madory_ripe.pdf.

10. "Cyber great power" can also be translated as "network great power." Yang Ting 杨婷, "Xi Jinping: Ba woguo cong wangluo daguo jianshe chengwei wangluo qiangguo" 习近平:把我国从网络大国建设成为网络强国 [Xi Jinping: Build China from a Major Cyber Country to a Cyber Great Power], Xinhua, February 27, 2014, www.xinhuanet.com//politics/2014-02/27/c_119538788.htm.

11. Pengxiong Zhu et al., "Characterizing Transnational Internet Performance and the Great Bottleneck of China," *Proceedings of the ACM on Measurement and Analysis of Computing Systems* 4, no. 13 (2020): 7, https://doi.org/10.1145/3379479.

12. Graham Webster and Katharin Tai, "Translation: China's New Security Reviews for Cloud Services," *Cybersecurity Initiative: Blog,* New America, July 23, 2019, www.newamerica.org/cybersecurity-initiative/digichina/blog/translation -chinas-new-security-reviews-cloud-services/.

13. "Azure China Playbook: Performance and Connectivity Considerations," Microsoft, last modified July 20, 2020, https://docs.microsoft.com/en-us/azure /china/concepts-performance-and-connectivity.

14. Kirtus G. Leyba, correspondence with author, January 2021.

15. Kirtus G. Leyba et al., "Borders and Gateways: Measuring and Analyzing National AS Chokepoints," in *Compass '19: Proceedings of the 2nd ACM SIGCAS Conference on Computing and Sustainable Societies* (New York: Association for Computing Machinery, 2019), 184–94, https://doi.org/10.1145/3314344.3332502.

16. Bill Marczak et al., "An Analysis of China's 'Great Cannon,'" in *FOCI '15: 5th USENIX Workshop on Free and Open Communications on the Internet* (Washington, D.C.: USENIX Association, 2015), www.usenix.org/system/files/conference /foci15/foci15-paper-marczak.pdf.

17. Zhu et al., "Great Bottleneck of China," 17.

18. Margaret E. Roberts, *Censored: Distraction and Diversion Inside China's Great Firewall* (Princeton, NJ: Princeton University Press, 2018).

19. David Bandurski, "A Brief Experiment in a More Open Chinese Web," *Tech-Stream* (blog), Brookings Institution, November 12, 2020, www.brookings.edu /techstream/a-brief-experiment-in-a-more-open-chinese-web/.

20. "China's Quiet Experiment Let Millions View Long-Banned Websites," Bloomberg, October 12, 2020, www.bloomberg.com/news/articles/2020-10-12/china -s-quiet-experiment-to-let-millions-roam-the-real-internet?sref=VZPf2pAM.

21. Zhu et al., "Great Bottleneck of China," 2.

22. China Telecom Global Ltd., "Unified Carrier Licence Telecommunications Ordinance (Chapter 106)," January 5, 2020, 2, www.chinatelecomglobal.com /files/Tariff_Notice_for_IP_Transit.pdf.

23. Robert Clark, "China Finally Embraces Full Internet Peering," Light Reading, March 2, 2020, www.lightreading.com/asia/china-finally-embraces-full -internet-peering/d/d-id/757892.

24. "Internet Way of Networking Use Case: Interconnection and Routing," Internet Society, September 9, 2020, www.internetsociety.org/resources/doc/2020 /internet-impact-assessment-toolkit/use-case-interconnection-and-routing/.

25. Hal Roberts et al., *Mapping Local Internet Control* (Cambridge, MA: Berkman Center for Internet & Society, Harvard University, 2011), https://cyber.harvard.edu /netmaps/mlic_20110513.pdf.

26. Rebecca MacKinnon, "Networked Authoritarianism in China and Beyond: Implications for Global Internet Freedom" (paper presented at Liberation Technology in Authoritarian Regimes, Stanford, CA, October 2010), 21, https:// rconversation.blogs.com/MacKinnon_Libtech.pdf.

27. MacKinnon, "Networked Authoritarianism," 21.

28. Ryan Fedasiuk, "A Different Kind of Army: The Militarization of China's Internet Trolls," *China Brief* 21, no. 7 (2021): 8, https://jamestown.org/program/a -different-kind-of-army-the-militarization-of-chinas-internet-trolls/.

29. Gary King, Jennifer Pan, and Margaret E. Roberts, "How the Chinese Gov-

ernment Fabricates Social Media Posts for Strategic Distraction, Not Engaged Argument," *American Political Science Review* 111, no. 13 (2017): 485, https://doi .org/10.1017/S0003055417000144.

30. Raymond Zhong et al., "Leaked Documents Show How China's Army of Paid Internet Trolls Helped Censor the Coronavirus," ProPublica, December 19, 2020, www.propublica.org/article/leaked-documents-show-how-chinas-army-of -paid-internet-trolls-helped-censor-the-coronavirus.

31. Marczak et al., "Analysis of China's 'Great Cannon,'" 1.

32. Internet Society, "Internet Way of Networking."

33. Blake Miller, "The Limits of Commercialized Censorship in China," SocArXiv (2019), https://doi.org/10.31235/osf.io/wn7pr.

34. Roberts, *Censored*, loc. 4144.

35. Yanfeng Zheng and Qinyu Wang, "Shadow of the Great Firewall: The Impact of Google Blockade on Innovation in China," *Strategic Management Journal* (forth-coming), http://dx.doi.org/10.2139/ssrn.3558289.

36. Paul Brodsky et al., *The State of the Network: 2021 Edition* (San Diego, CA: Pri-Metrica, 2021), https://www2.telegeography.com/hubfs/assets/Ebooks/state-of -the-network-2021.pdf.

37. Paul Mozur, "A Hong Kong Internet Provider Confirms It Censored a Website under the New Security Law," *New York Times*, last modified January 22, 2021, www.nytimes.com/live/2021/01/14/business/us-economy-coronavirus#a -hong-kong-internet-provider-confirms-it-censored-a-website-under-the-new -security-law.

38. Xi Jinping, "Remarks by H.E. Xi Jinping, President of the People's Republic of China, at the Opening Ceremony of the Second World Internet Conference" (speech, Second World Internet Conference, Wuzhen, China, December 16, 2015), www.fmprc.gov.cn/mfa_eng/wjdt_665385/zyjh_665391/t1327570.shtml.

39. Yali Liu, "Building CHN-IX: The First IXP in Mainland China," *APNIC Blog*, APNIC, April 22, 2016, https://blog.apnic.net/2016/04/22/building-chn-ix -first-ixp-mainland-china/.

40. "CHN-IX: Revamping China's Internet Infrastructure," ChinaCache, Janu-ary 25, 2019, https://en.chinacache.com/chn-ix-revamping-chinas-interent -infrastructure/.

41. Securities and Exchange Commission, *Form 20-F, ChinaCache International Hold-ings Ltd.: Annual and Transition Report of Foreign Private Issuers [Sections 13 or 15(d)]*

(Washington, D.C.: Securities and Exchange Commission, 2020), https://sec/
.report/Document/0001104659-20-041187/.

42. Securities and Exchange Commission, *Form 20-F, ChinaCache*, 7–11.

43. "CNIX," PeeringDB, accessed January 27, 2021, www.peeringdb.com/ix/1303.

44. According to PeeringDB, accessed January 25, 2021, https://www.peeringdb
.com/advanced_search?country__in=US&reftag=ix.

45. H. B. Acharya, Sambuddho Chakravarty, and Devashish Gosain, "Few Throats
to Choke: On the Current Structure of the Internet," in *2017 IEEE 42nd Conference on Local Computer Networks* (Los Alamitos, CA: IEEE, 2017), 339–46, https://
doi.org/10.1109/LCN.2017.78.

46. "The Top 500 Sites on the Web," Alexa, accessed January 25, 2021, www.alexa
.com/topsites.

47. "AS 4809," AS Rank, accessed January 25, 2021, https://asrank.caida.org/asns
/4809.

48. "AS 3356," AS Rank, accessed January 26, 2021, https://asrank.caida.org/asns
/3356.

49. Dave Allen, "Analysis by Oracle Internet Intelligence Highlights China's Unique
Approach to Connecting to the Global Internet," *Internet Intelligence* (blog), Oracle,
July 19, 2019, https://blogs.oracle.com/internetintelligence/analysis-by-oracle
-internet-intelligence-highlights-china%e2%80%99s-unique-approach-to-conn
ecting-to-the-global-internet.

50. Daniel R. Headrick and Pascal Griset, "Submarine Telegraph Cables: Business
and Politics, 1838–1939," *Business History Review* 75, no. 3 (2001): 553, https://doi
.org/10.2307/3116386.

51. "Unofficial USCBC Chart of Localization Targets by Sector Set in the MIIT
Made in China 2025 Key Technology Roadmap," U.S.-China Business Council, February 2, 2016, www.uschina.org/sites/default/files/2-2-16%20Sector%20
and%20Localization%20Targets%20for%20Made%20in%20China%202025
.pdf.

52. P. M. Kennedy, "Imperial Cable Communications and Strategy, 1870–1914,"
*The English Historical Review* 86, no. 341 (1971): 751, https://doi.org/10.1093/ehr
/LXXXVI.CCCXLI.728.

53. HMN Tech, "Huawei Marine Achieves over 100 Contracts," press release, January 21, 2020, www.hmntechnologies.com/enPressReleases/37319.jhtml; HMN

Tech, "Building the Backbone for Global Connectivity," press release, January 9, 2019, www.hmntechnologies.com/enPressReleases/37315.jhtml.

54. "Hannibal—Mediterranean | Telecoms: Global Marine Installs FOC Connecting Tunisia and Sicily," Global Marine, accessed January 25, 2021, https://global marine.co.uk/projects/hannibal-mediterranean/.

55. Zhang Hongxiang 张红祥, "Haishang 54 tian" 海上54天 [54 Days at Sea], *Huawei Ren* 华为人 [Huawei People], February 8, 2010, http://app.huawei.com /paper/newspaper/newsBookCateInfo.do?method=showDigestInfo&infoId =14233&sortId=1.

56. "The SGSCS System Represents HMN's First Repeater and Branching Unit Solution, Linking Trinidad, Guyana to Suriname in South America," Global Marine, November 2019, https://globalmarine.co.uk/wp-content/uploads/2019 /11/sgscs-case-study.pdf.

57. Bao Pengyun 鲍鹏云, "Cong ludi dao haiyang" 从陆地到海洋 [From the Land to the Sea], *Huawei Ren* 华为人 [Huawei People], May 30, 2011, http://app .huawei.com/paper/newspaper/newsBookCateInfo.do?method=showDigestInfo &infoId=14261&sortId=1.

58. Industry expert, interview by author, June 2020.

59. "Suriname Guyana Submarine Cable System (SGSCS)," HMN Tech, accessed January 25, 2021, www.hmntechnologies.com/enExperience/37690.jhtml.

60. Federal Communications Commission, *Improving Outage Reporting for Submarine Cables and Enhanced Submarine Cable Outage Data, GN Docket No. 15-206: Report and Order*, FCC 16-81 (Washington, D.C.: Federal Communications Commission, 2016), 52, https://docs.fcc.gov/public/attachments/FCC-16-81A1.pdf.

61. Stephen Malphrus, "Keynote Address" (speech, ROGUCCI Summit, Dubai, October 19, 2009).

62. "Hibernia Atlantic Selects Huawei Technologies USA," *Fiber Optics Weekly Update*, June 1, 2007, https://books.google.com/books?id=6Q3P9P77wcwC.

63. "Huawei Marine to Build Hibernia Atlantic's Project Express," Lightwave Online, January 17, 2012, www.lightwaveonline.com/network-design/article /16664889/huawei-marine-to-build-hibernia-altantics-project-express.

64. Lightwave Online, "Hibernia Atlantic's Project Express."

65. Jeremy Page, Kate O'Keeffe, and Rob Taylor, "America's Undersea Battle with China for Control of the Global Internet Grid," *Wall Street Journal*, March 12,

2019, www.wsj.com/articles/u-s-takes-on-chinas-huawei-in-undersea-battle-over-the-global-internet-grid-11552407466.

66. Tom McGregor, "China Breakthroughs: SAIL Ahead on South Atlantic Cable Network," CCTV, July 5, 2017, http://english.cctv.com/2017/07/05/ARTIT i0QntQhXqvZoN4dwobj170705.shtml.

67. HMN Tech, "South Atlantic Inter Link Connecting Cameroon to Brazil Fully Connected," press release, September 5, 2018, www.hmntechnologies.com/en PressReleases/37306.jhtml.

68. Doug Madory, email correspondence with author, December 20, 2020.

69. Jonathan E. Hillman, *The Emperor's New Road: China and the Project of the Century* (New Haven, CT: Yale University Press, 2020).

70. Nicole Starosielski, *The Undersea Network* (Durham, NC: Duke University Press, 2015), 41.

71. Iara Guimarães Altafin, "Especialistas apontam soluções para reduzir vulnerabilidade da internet" [Experts Point Out Solutions for Reducing Internet Vulnerability], Agência Senado, November 6, 2013, www12.senado.leg.br /noticias/materias/2013/11/06/especialistas-apontam-solucoes-para-reduzir-vulnerabilidade-da-internet.

72. "EllaLink: Connecting Europe to Latin America," Capacity Media, April 14, 2020, www.capacitymedia.com/articles/3825273/ellalink-connecting-europe-to-latin-america.

73. Jamal Shahid, "Army Seeks Fibre Optic Cables along CPEC," *Dawn*, January 25, 2017, www.dawn.com/news/1310593.

74. Hengtong Group, "PEACE Submarine Cable Project Perfectly Interpreting 'China Manufacturing Global Quality,'" press release, September 30, 2018, www .hengtonggroup.com/en/news/news-detail-510319.htm.

75. Khurram Husain, "Exclusive: CPEC Master Plan Revealed," *Dawn*, last modified June 21, 2017, www.dawn.com/news/1333101.

76. Farhan Bokhari and Kathrin Hille, "Pakistan Turns to China for Naval Base," *Financial Times*, May 22, 2011, www.ft.com/content/3914bd36-8467-11e0-afcb -00144feabdc0.

77. Andres Schipani, "Spying and Stability: Djibouti Thrives in 'Return to Cold War,'" *Financial Times*, May 11, 2021, https://www.ft.com/content/418b5250-f7 fa-4ad3-837f-871dd259ec87.

78. Abdi Latif Dahir, "Thanks to China, Africa's Largest Free Trade Zone Has Launched in Djibouti," *Quartz*, July 9, 2018, https://qz.com/africa/1323666/china-and-djibouti-have-launched-africas-biggest-free-trade-zone/.

79. Deborah Brautigam, Yufan Huang, and Kevin Acker, *Risky Business: New Data on Chinese Loans and Africa's Debt Problem* (Washington, D.C.: China-Africa Research Initiative, Paul H. Nitze School of Advanced International Studies, Johns Hopkins University, 2020), https://static1.squarespace.com/static/5652847de4b033f56d2bdc29/t/6033fadb7ba591794b0a9dff/1614019291794/BP+3+-+Brautigam%2C+Huang%2C+Acker+-+Chinese+Loans+African+Debt.pdf; Yufan Huang and Deborah Brautigam, "Putting a Dollar Amount on China's Loans to the Developing World," *The Diplomat*, June 24, 2020, https://thediplomat.com/2020/06/putting-a-dollar-amount-on-chinas-loans-to-the-developing-world/.

80. "Submarine Cable Map," TeleGeography and HMN Tech, accessed February 27, 2021, www.submarinecablemap.com/.

81. Michael Sechrist, *Cyberspace in Deep Water: Protecting Undersea Communication Cables by Creating an International Public-Private Partnership* (Cambridge, MA: Harvard Kennedy School of Government, 2010), www.belfercenter.org/sites/default/files/files/publication/PAE_final_draft_-_043010.pdf.

82. Ivan Seidenberg, "Keynote Address: Customer Partnership Conference," Defense Information Systems Agency Customer Partnership Conference, April 21, 2009, as cited in Sechrist, *Cyberspace in Deep Water*, 9.

83. Industry expert, interview by author, May 2020.

84. Takashi Kawakami, "Huawei to Sell Undersea Cable Unit to Deflect US Spy Claims," *Nikkei Asia*, June 4, 2019, https://asia.nikkei.com/Spotlight/Huawei-crackdown/Huawei-to-sell-undersea-cable-unit-to-deflect-US-spy-claims.

85. Hengtong Group, "Hengtong haiyang shang bang 2018 nian suzhoushi zhuan jing te xin shifan qiye mingdan" 亨通海洋上榜2018年苏州市专精特新示范企业名单 [Hengtong Marine Is on the 2018 Suzhou City List of Specialized and New Model Enterprises], press release, November 2, 2018, http://cn.hengtongmarine.com/index.php/news/newsInfo/22.html.

86. Headrick and Griset, "Submarine Telegraph Cables," 553.

87. See chapter 2 in Hillman, *The Emperor's New Road*.

88. Dave Allen, "Analysis by Oracle Internet Intelligence Highlights China's Unique Approach to Connecting to the Global Internet," *Internet Intelligence* (blog), Oracle,

July 19, 2019, https://blogs.oracle.com/internetintelligence/analysis-by-oracle
-internet-intelligence-highlights-china%e2%80%99s-unique-approach-to-conn
ecting-to-the-global-internet.

89. "Amazon Cloud Demands Massive On-the-Ground Infrastructure," *Seattle Times*,
last modified December 6, 2016, www.seattletimes.com/business/amazon
-cloud-demands-massive-on-the-ground-infrastructure/.

90. Canalys, "Global Cloud Services Market Q1 2020," press release, April 30, 2020,
https://www.canalys.com/newsroom/worldwide-cloud-infrastructure-services
-Q1-2020; Canalys, "Global Cloud Services Market Q2 2020," press release,
July 30, 2020, https://canalys.com/newsroom/worldwide-cloud-infrastructure
-services-Q2-2020; Canalys, "Global Cloud Infrastructure Market Q3 2020,"
press release, October 29, 2020, https://www.canalys.com/newsroom/world
wide-cloud-market-q320; Canalys, "Global Cloud Infrastructure Market Q4
2020," press release, February 2, 2021, https://www.canalys.com/newsroom
/global-cloud-market-q4-2020.

91. Raj Bala et al., "Gartner Magic Quadrant for Cloud Infrastructure as a Service,
Worldwide," Gartner, July 19, 2019, www.gartner.com/en/documents/3947472
/magic-quadrant-for-cloud-infrastructure-as-a-service-wor; Alibaba Group, "Alibaba Group Announces December Quarter 2020 Results," press release, February 2, 2021, www.alibabagroup.com/en/news/press_pdf/p210202.pdf.

92. Canalys, "Cloud Services Market Q1 2020"; Canalys, "Cloud Services Market
Q2 2020"; Canalys, "Cloud Infrastructure Market Q3 2020"; Canalys, "Cloud
Infrastructure Market Q4 2020."

93. ThousandEyes, Cisco Systems Inc., *Cloud Performance Benchmark: 2019–2020 Edition*
(San Francisco: Cisco Systems, Inc., 2020), 38, https://marketo-web.thousand
eyes.com/rs/thousandeyes/images/ThousandEyes-Cloud-Performance-Bench
mark-2019-2020-Edition.pdf.

94. Pei Li and Josh Horwitz, "In Cloud Clash with Alibaba, Underdog Tencent
Adopts More Aggressive Tactics," Reuters, July 2, 2020, www.reuters.com
/article/us-tencent-alibaba-cloud-focus/in-cloud-clash-with-alibaba-underdog
-tencent-adopts-more-aggressive-tactics-idUSKBN2433F9.

95. Josh Horwitz, "Alibaba to Invest $28 Billion in Cloud Services after Coronavirus
Boosted Demand," Reuters, April 19, 2020, www.reuters.com/article/us-china
-alibaba-cloud-investment/alibaba-to-invest-28-billion-in-cloud-services-after
-coronavirus-boosted-demand-idUSKBN22208E.

96. Pei Li, "Tencent to Invest $70 Billion in 'New Infrastructure,'" Reuters, May 26,

2020, www.reuters.com/article/us-tencent-cloud-investment/tencent-to-invest-70-billion-in-new-infrastructure-idUSKBN2320VB.

97. Nikki Sun, "Tencent's Plans for Indonesia Herald Wave of Asian Data Centres," *Financial Times*, April 18, 2021, https://www.ft.com/content/05a17586-5b08-4f2f-a228-f2c757c824b9.

98. Li Jingying 李菁瑛, "Zhongguo dianxin xuanbu weilai jiang ba yun jisuan fuwu zuowei zhuye" 中国电信宣布未来将把云计算服务作为主业 [China Telecom Announces That It Will Make Cloud Computing Services Its Main Business in the Future], Leifeng Wang 雷锋网 [Leifeng Net], November 9, 2020, www.leiphone.com/news/202011/9r5uwvX7I7YM0lzn.html.

99. Ding Yi, "Baidu Sets Out Its Ambitions for AI, Cloud Computing, Amid 'New Infrastructure' Push," Caixin Global, June 22, 2020, www.caixinglobal.com/2020-06-22/baidu-sets-out-its-ambitions-for-ai-cloud-computing-amid-new-infrastructure-push-101570657.html.

100. "30,000,000 American Depositary Shares: Representing 450,000,000 Ordinary Shares," Kingsoft Cloud Holdings Ltd., May 7, 2020, 35, https://ir.ksyun.com/static-files/29ac7d9f-935c-4540-a9a1-f8c66937a27e.

101. "Bringing the Digital World to Cape Verde," Huawei, accessed January 25, 2021, https://e.huawei.com/en/case-studies/global/2018/201807051343.

102. Jonathan E. Hillman and Maesea McCalpin, *Huawei's Cloud Strategy: Economic and Strategic Implications* (Washington, D.C.: Center for Strategic and International Studies, 2021), https://reconasia.csis.org/.

103. Kathrin Hille, Qianer Liu, and Kiran Stacey, "Huawei Focuses on Cloud Computing to Secure Its Survival," *Financial Times*, August 30, 2020, www.ft.com/content/209aa050-6e9c-4ba0-b83c-ac8df0bb4f86.

104. "Renzhengfei guanyu huawei yun de jianghua shifangle naxie zhongyao xinxi?" 任正非关于华为云的讲话释放了哪些重要信息? [What Important Information Did Ren Zhengfei's Speech on Huawei Cloud Reveal?], Tengxun wang 腾讯网 [Tencent Net], January 6, 2021, https://xw.qq.com/amphtml/20210106A0B7F500.

105. Zhang Erchi and Timmy Shen, "Huawei Deactivates AI and Cloud Business Group in Restructuring," Caixin Global, April 6, 2021, https://www.caixinglobal.com/2021-04-06/huawei-deactivates-ai-and-cloud-business-group-in-restructuring-101686317.html.

106. Huawei, "Bringing the Digital World to Cape Verde."

107. James Hamilton, "How Many Data Centers Needed World-Wide," *Perspectives*

(blog), April 2017, https://perspectives.mvdirona.com/2017/04/how-many-data
-centers-needed-world-wide/.

108. "Hyperscale Data Center Count Reaches 541 in Mid-2020; Another 176 in the
Pipeline," Synergy Research Group, July 7, 2020, www.srgresearch.com/articles
/hyperscale-data-center-count-reaches-541-mid-2020-another-176-pipeline.

109. Steve Dickinson, "China's New Cybersecurity Program: No Place to Hide,"
*China Law Blog*, Harris Bricken, September 30, 2019, https://harrisbricken.com
/chinalawblog/chinas-new-cybersecurity-program-no-place-to-hide/.

110. Eileen Yu, "Alibaba Points to Singapore in Response to Cloud Security Concerns," ZDNet, October 30, 2015, www.zdnet.com/article/alibaba-points-to
-singapore-in-response-to-cloud-security-concerns/.

111. "Alibaba Cloud Responses to CSA CAIQ v3.0.1," Alibaba Cloud, March 6,
2020, 3, https://video-intl.alicdn.com/video/ABC_CSA_CAIQ.pdf?spm=a
3c0i.87485.6110357070.3.119f72c9QdPSjJ&file=ABC_CSA_CAIQ.pdf.

112. Kevin Xu, "China's Cloud Ceiling," *Interconnected* (blog), October 15, 2020, https://
interconnected.blog/chinas-cloud-ceiling/.

113. International Data Corporation, email correspondence with author, April 2021.

114. Google, Temasek, and Bain & Company, *e-Conomy SEA 2020: At Full Velocity:
Resilient and Racing Ahead* (n.p.: Google, 2020), 29, https://storage.googleapis.com
/gweb-economy-sea.appspot.com/assets/pdf/e-Conomy_SEA_2020_Report
.pdf.

115. "Singapore," Submarine Cable Map, accessed January 26, 2021, www.submarine
cablemap.com/#/country/singapore.

116. Paul Brodsky et al., *The State of the Network: 2021 Edition* (San Diego, CA: Primet-
rica, Inc., 2021), https://www2.telegeography.com/hubfs/assets/Ebooks/state
-of-the-network-2021.pdf.

117. Sun, "Tencent's Plans for Indonesia"; Mercedes Ruehl, "US and Chinese Cloud
Companies Vie for Dominance in South-East Asia," *Financial Times*, May 19, 2020,
www.ft.com/content/1e2b9cd9-f82e-4d3b-a2d8-f20c08bdc3aa; James Hen-
derson, "Is Microsoft Building Data Centres in Indonesia?," Channel Asia, February 28, 2020, www.channelasia.tech/article/671441/microsoft-building-data
-centres-indonesia/.

118. Arpita Mukherjee et al., "COVID-19, Data Localisation and G20: Challenges,
Opportunities and Strategies for India" (working paper, Indian Council for Re-
search on International Economic Relations, 2020), 18, http://icrier.org/pdf
/Working_Paper_398.pdf.

119. Neil Munshi, "Africa's Cloud Computing Boom Creates Data Centre Gold Rush," *Financial Times,* March 2, 2020, www.ft.com/content/402a18c8-5a32-11ea -abe5-8e03987b7b20.

120. John Melick (former chairman, Djibouti Data Center), interview by author, July 13, 2020.

121. Russell Southwood, *Africa Interconnection Report: Analysis of Sub-Saharan Africa's Cloud & Data Centre Ecosystem* (n.p.: Balancing Act, 2020), 20, https://f.hubspotuser content00.net/hubfs/3076203/Africa%20Interconnection%20Report%202021 .pdf.

122. Southwood, *Africa Interconnection Report*, 14.

123. Toby Shapshak, "South Africa Is Now a Major Hub for Big Tech's Cloud Datacenters," *Quartz*, March 20, 2019, https://qz.com/africa/1576890/amazon -microsoft-huawei-building-south-africa-data-hubs/.

124. Steve Song, "Africa Telecoms Infrastructure in 2019," *Many Possibilities* (blog), January 3, 2020, https://manypossibilities.net/2020/01/africa-telecoms-infra structure-in-2019/.

125. Michael D. Francois, Chris George, and Jayne Stowell, "Introducing Equiano, a Subsea Cable from Portugal to South Africa," *Google Cloud Blog*, Google, June 28, 2019, https://cloud.google.com/blog/products/infrastructure/introducing -equiano-a-subsea-cable-from-portugal-to-south-africa.

126. "Meet the Partners," 2Africa, accessed January 25, 2021, www.2africacable .com/meet-the-partners.

127. Anne Edmundson et al., "Nation-State Hegemony in Internet Routing," in *Compass '18: Proceedings of the 1st ACM SIGCAS Conference on Computing and Sustainable Societies* (New York: Association for Computing Machinery, 2018), 1–11, https:// doi.org/10.1145/3209811.3211887.

128. Huawei Cloud, "Huawei Cloud Accelerates Digital Transformation in Brazil," press release, December 6, 2019, https://en.prnasia.com/releases/apac/huawei -cloud-accelerates-digital-transformation-in-brazil-267227.shtml.

129. "Alibaba Plans to Launch Cloud Services in Colombia," Latin America Business Stories, February 28, 2020, https://labsnews.com/en/news/business/alibaba -plans-to-launch-cloud-services-in-colombia/.

130. Ren Zhengfei, "Ren Zhengfei's Roundtable with Media from Latin America and Spain," interview by Pablo Diáz, *Voices of Huawei* (blog), Huawei, December 11, 2019, www.huawei.com/us/facts/voices-of-huawei/ren-zhengfeis-roundtable-with -media-from-latin-america-and-spain.

131. "Four Reasons Why Chile Is Becoming Latin America's Data Center Hub," *InvestChile Blog*, InvestChile, October 16, 2019, https://blog.investchile.gob.cl /four-reasons-why-chile-is-becoming-latin-americas-data-center-hub.

132. Josefina Dominguez Iino, "Huawei and Alibaba Join Amazon in Potentially In-stalling Regional Data Centers in Chile," LatamList, March 16, 2019, https:// latamlist.com/huawei-and-alibaba-join-amazon-in-potentially-installing -regional-data-centers-in-chile/.

133. "Fiber Optic Austral," HMN Tech, accessed January 27, 2021, www.hmntech nologies.com/enExperience/37709.jhtml.

134. Yohei Hirose and Naoyuki Toyama, "Chile Picks Japan's Trans-Pacific Cable Route in Snub to China," *Nikkei Asia*, July 29, 2020, https://asia.nikkei.com /Business/Telecommunication/Chile-picks-Japan-s-trans-Pacific-cable-route -in-snub-to-China.

135. "Huawei to Open 2nd Data Center in Chile," Xinhua, September 24, 2020. www.xinhuanet.com/english/2020-09/24/c_139393114.htm.

136. "Ren Zhengfei's Roundtable with Media from Latin America and Spain."

137. Federal Communications Commission, *China Mobile International (USA) Inc. Application for Global Facilities-Based and Global Resale International Telecommunications Authority Pursuant to Section 214 of the Communications Act of 1934, as Amended, ITC-214-20110901-00289: Memorandum Opinion and Order*, FCC 19-38 (Washington, D.C.: Federal Communications Commission, 2019), 20, https://licensing.fcc .gov/myibfs/download.do?attachment_key=1682030.

138. Federal Communications Commission, "FCC Denies China Mobile USA Ap-plication to Provide Telecommunications Services," press release, May 9, 2019, https://docs.fcc.gov/public/attachments/DOC-357372A1.pdf.

139. Kate O'Keeffe, "FCC Signals Likely Revocation of Four Chinese Telecom Firms' Licenses," *Wall Street Journal*, April 24, 2020, www.wsj.com/articles/fcc -signals-likely-revocation-of-four-chinese-telecom-firms-licenses-11587755961.

140. Kate O'Keeffe (@Kate_OKeeffe), "NEW: The FCC just gave 4 Chinese state-owned telecom operators 30 days to prove they're not Chinese state-owned telecom operators. In other words: expect imminent license revocations," Twitter, April 24, 2020, https://twitter.com/Kate_OKeeffe/status/1253768210387734528?s=20.

141. Jeanne Whalen and David J. Lynch, "Outgoing Trump Administration Bans Investments in Chinese Companies It Says Support China's Military," *Washington Post*, November 12, 2020, www.washingtonpost.com/technology/2020/11/12 /trump-bans-investment-china/.

142. Federal Communications Commission, "FCC Initiates Proceeding Regarding Revocation and Termination of China Telecom (Americas) Corporation's Authorizations," press release, December 10, 2020, https://docs.fcc.gov/public /attachments/DOC-368702A1.pdf; David Shepardson, "FCC Moves against Two Chinese Telecoms Firms Operating in U.S.," Reuters, March 17, 2021, www.reuters.com/article/us-usa-china-telecom-idUSKBN2B92FE.

143. Kevin Salvadori and Nico Roehrich, "Advancing Connectivity between the Asia-Pacific Region and North America," *Engineering Blog*, Facebook, March 28, 2021, https://engineering.fb.com/2021/03/28/connectivity/echo-bifrost/.

144. "Global Resources," China Mobile International, accessed January 27, 2021, www.cmi.chinamobile.com/en/pop; "Global Data Center Map," China Telecom Americas, accessed January 27, 2021, www.ctamericas.com/global-data -center-map/; "China Unicom Global Resource: PoPs," China Unicom, accessed January 27, 2021, https://network.chinaunicomglobal.com/#/resource/pops.

145. Demchak and Shavitt, "China's Maxim," 1.

146. Kieren McCarthy, "You Won't Guess Where European Mobile Data Was Rerouted for Two Hours. Oh. You Can. Yes, It Was China Telecom," *The Register*, June 10, 2019, www.theregister.com/2019/06/10/bgp_route_hijack_china_tele com/.

147. Markoff, "Internet Traffic Begins to Bypass the U.S."; National Security Agency, *Untangling the Web: A Guide to Internet Research*, NSA DOCID 4046925 (Washington, D.C.: National Security Agency, 2007), 487, www.nsa.gov/Portals/70/doc uments/news-features/declassified-documents/Untangling-the-Web.pdf.

148. Ted Hardie, "Thoughts on the Clean Network Program," Medium, August 5, 2020, https://medium.com/@ted.ietf/thoughts-on-the-clean-network-program -5f1c43764152.

149. "Network Operator Participants," MANRS, accessed January 25, 2021, www .manrs.org/isps/participants/.

150. Internet Society, "Internet Way of Networking."

151. Ge Yu (@Ge_Yu), "Thank you, @DougMadory, for championing this issue over the years," Twitter, December 11, 2020, https://twitter.com/Ge_Yu/status /1337433056421027840?s=20.

152. Richard Chirgwin, "Oracle 'Net-Watcher Agrees, China Telecom Is a Repeat Offender for Misdirecting Traffic," *The Register*, November 6, 2018, www.the register.com/2018/11/06/oracles_netwatchers_agree_china_telecom_is_a_repeat _bgp_offender/.

153. Participation among U.S. cloud and content providers is strong, however, with Amazon, Google, Facebook, and Microsoft on board. See MANRS, "Network Operator Participants" for a full list of participants.

## CHAPTER SIX    THE COMMANDING HEIGHTS

1.   "Blastoff! China Launches Beidou Navigation Satellite-3," YouTube video, 44:50, posted by VideoFromSpace, June 22, 2020, www.youtube.com/watch ?v=Hb04dOf4ZoQ&ab_channel=VideoFromSpace.

2.   European Global Navigation Satellite Systems Agency, *GSA GNSS Market Report: Editor's Special: GNSS and Newspace* (Luxembourg: Publications Office of the European Union, 2019), www.gsa.europa.eu/system/files/reports/market_report _issue_6_v2.pdf.

3.   David Hambling, "What Would the World Do without GPS?," BBC, October 4, 2020, www.bbc.com/future/article/20201002-would-the-world-cope-without-gps -satellite-navigation.

4.   Deng Xiaoci, "China Completes BDS Navigation System, Reduces Reliance on GPS," *Global Times*, June 23, 2020, www.globaltimes.cn/content/1192482 .shtml.

5.   Anatoly Zak, "Disaster at Xichang," *Air & Space Magazine*, February 2013, https:// www.airspacemag.com/history-of-flight/disaster-at-xichang-2873673/?page=1.

6.   Matt Ho, "Chinese Long March-3B Rocket Fails during Launch of Indonesian Satellite," *South China Morning Post*, April 10, 2020, www.scmp.com/news/china /science/article/3079407/chinese-long-march-3b-rocket-fails-during-launch -indonesian.

7.   Andrew Jones, "China Launches Final Satellite to Complete Beidou System, Booster Falls Downrange," *SpaceNews*, June 23, 2020, https://spacenews.com /china-launches-final-satellite-to-complete-beidou-system-booster-falls-down range/.

8.   Adam Mann, "SpaceX Now Dominates Rocket Flight, Bringing Big Benefits— and Risks—to NASA," *Science*, May 20, 2020, www.sciencemag.org/news /2020/05/spacex-now-dominates-rocket-flight-bringing-big-benefits-and-risks -nasa.

9.   Mike Wall, "SpaceX's Starship May Fly for Just $2 Million Per Mission, Elon Musk Says," Space, November 6, 2019, www.space.com/spacex-starship-flight -passenger-cost-elon-musk.html.

10. "'SoftBank World 2017' Day 1 Keynote Speech, Masayoshi Son," YouTube video, 2:12:15, posted by ソフトバンク [SoftBank], August 1, 2017, www.youtube.com /watch?v=z7kHvHKElQc.

11. "Fenfei zai xinshijide tiankong—Zhongyang junwei weiyuan, kongjun silingyuan xu qiliang da benbao jizhe wen" 奋飞在新世纪的天空—中央军委委员、空军司令员许其亮答本报记者问 [Flying Vigorously in the Sky of the New Century—Central Military Commission Member and Air Force Commander Xu Qiliang Answers Our Reporter's Questions], Sina, November 1, 2009, http://mil.news .sina.com.cn/2009-11-02/0625572165.html. Similar language was used in China's 2015 Defense White Paper: "Outer space has become a commanding height in international strategic competition. Countries concerned are developing their space forces and instruments, and the first signs of weaponization of outer space have appeared"; see State Council Information Office of the People's Republic of China, *China's Military Strategy* (Beijing: State Council Information Office, 2015), www.andrewerickson.com/wp-content/uploads/2019/07/China-Defense -White-Paper_2015_English-Chinese_Annotated.pdf.

12. Sina, "Fenfei zai xinshijide tiankong."

13. William Matthew, "To Military Planners, Space Is 'the Ultimate High Ground,'" *Air Force Times*, May 18, 1998.

14. "Chinese Navigation Exhibition Opens in Vienna," Xinhua, June 12, 2019, www.xinhuanet.com/english/2019-06/12/c_138134675.htm.

15. "50th Anniversary of the Launch of Dongfanghong 1, China's First Satellite," *South China Morning Post*, April 24, 2020, www.scmp.com/photos/3081412/50th -anniversary-launch-dongfanghong-1-chinas-first-satellite?page=6.

16. "Five Momerable [sic] Moments in China's Space Probe," *China Daily*, last modified April 23, 2016, www.chinadaily.com.cn/china/2016-04/23/content _24779035.htm.

17. Evan A. Feigenbaum, *China's Techno-Warriors: National Security and Strategic Competition from the Nuclear to the Information Age* (Redwood City, CA: Stanford University Press, 2003), 141.

18. Lei Ceyuan 雷册渊, "'863' Jihua, yige weida keji gongcheng de taiqian muhou" '863' 计划, 一个伟大科技工程的台前幕后 [The "863" Plan: The Public Face and behind the Scenes of a Great Technology Project], Sina, November 22, 2016, http://book.sina.com.cn/excerpt/rwws/2016-11-22/1610/doc-ifxxwrwh4 929717-p2.shtml.

19. Larry Greenemeier, "GPS and the World's First 'Space War,'" *Scientific American*,

February 8, 2016, www.scientificamerican.com/article/gps-and-the-world-s-first e-space-war/.

20. Dean Cheng, "Chinese Lessons from the Gulf War," in *Chinese Lessons from Other Peoples' Wars*, ed. Andrew Scobell, David Lai, and Roy Kamphausen (Carlisle, PA: Strategic Studies Institute, U.S. Army War College, 2011), 163, https://publications.armywarcollege.edu/pubs/2163.pdf.

21. Gao Yubiao 高宇标, chief ed., *Lianhe zhanyi xue jiaocheng* 联合战役学教程 [Joint Campaign Teaching Materials] (Beijing: Junshi kexue chubanshe 军事科学出版社 [Military Science Press], 2001), 54–57.

22. Minnie Chen, "'Unforgettable Humiliation' Led to Development of GPS Equivalent," *South China Morning Post*, November 13, 2009, www.scmp.com/article/698161/unforgettable-humiliation-led-development-gps-equivalent.

23. Select Committee on U.S. National Security and Military/Commercial Concerns with the People's Republic of China, U.S. House of Representatives, 105th Cong., *U.S. National Security and Military/Commercial Concerns with the People's Republic of China: Volume I*, Report 105-851 (Washington, D.C.: U.S. Government Printing Office, 1999), xvii–xix, https://china.usc.edu/sites/default/files/article/attachments/cox-report-1999-us-china-military-security.pdf.

24. Kevin Pollpeter, "China's Space Program: Making China Strong, Rich, and Respected," *Asia Policy* 27, no. 2 (2020): 12–18, https://doi.org/10.1353/asp.2020.0027.

25. Embassy of the People's Republic of China in the United States of America, "2003 Nian 10 yue 30 ri waijiaobu fayanren zai jizhe zhaodaihui shang da jizhe wen" 2003年10月30日外交部发言人在记者招待会上答记者问 [October 30, 2003: Foreign Ministry Spokesperson Answers Journalists' Questions at Press Conference], press release, October 30, 2003, www.china-embassy.org/chn/FYRTH/t39627.htm.

26. David Lague, "Special Report—In Satellite Tech Race, China Hitched a Ride from Europe," Reuters, December 22, 2013, www.reuters.com/article/breakout-beidou/special-report-in-satellite-tech-race-china-hitched-a-ride-from-europe-idUSL4N0JJ0J320131222.

27. "China's Beidou GPS-Substitute Opens to Public in Asia," BBC, December 27, 2012, www.bbc.com/news/technology-20852150.

28. Stephen Clark, "China Expands Reach of Beidou Navigation Network with Another Launch," Spaceflight Now, November 19, 2018, https://spaceflightnow

.com/2018/11/19/china-expands-reach-of-beidou-navigation-network-with -another-launch/.

29. State Council Information Office of the People's Republic of China, "China's BeiDou Navigation System Starts Global Service," press release, last modified December 28, 2018, http://english.scio.gov.cn/pressroom/2018-12/28/content _74320992.htm.

30. Kevin L. Pollpeter, Michael S. Chase, and Eric Heginbotham, *The Creation of the PLA Strategic Support Force and Its Implications for Chinese Military Space Operations*, RR-2058-AF (Santa Monica, CA: RAND, 2017), www.rand.org/pubs/research _reports/RR2058.html; John Costello and Joe McReynolds, *China's Strategic Support Force: A Force for a New Era*, China Strategic Perspectives No. 13 (Washington, D.C.: National Defense University Press, 2018), https://ndupress.ndu.edu/Portals /68/Documents/stratperspective/china/china-perspectives_13.pdf.

31. Costello and McReynolds, *China's Strategic Support Force.*

32. "Full Text of White Paper on China's Space Activities in 2016," State Council of the People's Republic of China, last modified December 28, 2016, http://english .www.gov.cn/archive/white_paper/2016/12/28/content_281475527159496 .htm.

33. Changfeng Yang, "Directions 2021: BDS Marches to New Era of Global Services," *GPS World*, December 8, 2020, www.gpsworld.com/directions-2021-bds -marches-to-new-era-of-global-services/.

34. Ryan Woo and Liangping Gao, "China Set to Complete Beidou Network Rivalling GPS in Global Navigation," Reuters, June 11, 2020, www.reuters.com /article/us-space-exploration-china-satellite/china-set-to-complete-Beidou -network-rivalling-gps-in-global-navigation-idUSKBN23J0I9.

35. Tsunashima, "China's Beidou Eclipses American GPS."

36. Minnie Chan, "Mainland China Deploys More Amphibious Weapons along Coast in Taiwan Mission," *South China Morning Post*, August 5, 2020, www.scmp .com/news/china/military/article/3096179/mainland-deploys-more-amphib ious-weapons-along-coast-long.

37. Huang Wei-ping, "PLA Drills Might Be a System Check," *Taipei Times*, September 19, 2020, www.taipeitimes.com/News/editorials/archives/2020/09 /19/2003743685.

38. Rob Miltersen, "Chinese Aerospace along the Belt and Road," China Aerospace Studies Institute, Air University, June 14, 2020, 9, www.airuniversity

.af.edu/Portals/10/CASI/documents/Chinese_Aerospace_Along_BR.pdf? ver=2020-06-26-085618-537.

39. "Saudi Shoura Council Wants Steps to Assess Public Agencies," *Arab News*, July 9, 2019, www.arabnews.com/node/1522921/saudi-arabia; Dana Goward, "BeiDou a Threat to the West, but Perhaps Not Individuals," *GPS World*, August 11, 2020, www.gpsworld.com/beidou-a-threat-to-the-west-but-perhaps-not -individuals/.

40. Quan Li and Min Ye, "China's Emerging Partnership Network: What, Who, Where, When and Why," *International Trade, Politics and Development* 3, no. 2 (2019): 66–67, https://doi.org/10.1108/ITPD-05-2019-0004.

41. Marcus Weisgerber, "Russian and Chinese Satellites Are Helping US Pilots Spy on Russia and China," *Defense One*, March 5, 2020, www.defenseone.com/tech nology/2020/03/russian-and-chinese-satellites-are-helping-us-pilots-spy-russia -and-china/163542/.

42. "BeiDou Headed Upwards of 1 Trillion This Decade. That's Yuan." *Inside GNSS*, May 26, 2021, https://insidegnss.com/beidou-headed-upwards-of-1-trillion -this-decade-thats-yuan/.

43. "Global Smartphone Market Share: By Quarter," Counterpoint Research, November 20, 2020, www.counterpointresearch.com/global-smartphone-share/; Abhilash Kumar, "Global Smartphone Market Shows Signs of Recovery in Q3, Xiaomi Reaches 3rd Place and Realme Grows Fastest at 132% QoQ," press release, October 30, 2020, www.counterpointresearch.com/global-smartphone-market -shows-signs-recovery-q3-realme-grows-fastest-132-qoq/.

44. Lukas Scroth, "The Drone Manufacturer Ranking 2020," Drone Industry Insights, October 6, 2020, https://droneii.com/the-drone-manufacturer-ranking -2020.

45. European Global Navigation Satellite Systems Agency, *GSA GNSS Market Report*, 6.

46. Fang Zuwang and Anniek Bao, "Late to Switch On, Apple Tunes into China's Homegrown Nav System," Caixin Global, October 15, 2020, www.caixinglobal .com/2020-10-15/late-to-switch-on-apple-tunes-into-chinas-homegrown-nav -system-101615153.html; "Qualcomm Collaborates with Samsung to Be First to Employ BeiDou for Location-Based Mobile Data," *GPS World*, November 22, 2013, www.gpsworld.com/qualcomm-collaborates-with-samsung-to-be-first-to -employ-beidou-for-location-based-mobile-data/.

47. European Global Navigation Satellite Systems Agency, *GSA GNSS Market Report*, 6.

48. Nikki Sun, "China's Geely Follows Tesla into Space with Own Satellite Network,"

*Nikkei Asia*, April 24, 2020, https://asia.nikkei.com/Business/China-tech/China -s-Geely-follows-Tesla-into-space-with-own-satellite-network.

49.   China Satellite Navigation Office, "Development of BeiDou Navigation Satellite System" (presentation, Krasnoyarsk, Russia, May 18, 2015), www.unoosa.org /documents/pdf/psa/activities/2015/RussiaGNSS/Presentations/5.pdf.

50.   State Council Information Office of the People's Republic of China, "Guo xin ban juxing beidou sanhao xitong tigong quanqiu fuwu yizhounian youguan qin-gkuang fabu hui" 国新办举行北斗三号系统提供全球服务一周年有关情况发布会 [State Council Information Office Holds Press Conference on Relevant Developments on the One-Year Anniversary of the Launch of Beidou-3's Global Services], press release, December 27, 2019, www.scio.gov.cn/xwfbh/xwbfbh /wqfbh/39595/42270/index.htm.

51.   European Global Navigation Satellite Systems Agency, *GSA GNSS Market Report*, 10.

52.   Stuart A. Thompson and Charlie Warzel, "8 Things to Know about Our Investigation into the Location Business," *New York Times*, December 19, 2019, www.nytimes.com/interactive/2019/12/19/opinion/nyt-cellphone-tracking -investigation.html.

53.   Liz Sly, Dan Lamothe, and Craig Timberg, "U.S. Military Reviewing Its Rules after Fitness Trackers Exposed Sensitive Data," *Washington Post*, January 29, 2018, www.washingtonpost.com/world/the-us-military-reviews-its-rules-as-new -details-of-us-soldiers-and-bases-emerge/2018/01/29/6310d518-050f-11e8-aa61 -f3391373867e_story.html.

54.   Liz Sly, "U.S. Soldiers Are Revealing Sensitive and Dangerous Information by Jogging," *Washington Post*, January 29, 2018, www.washingtonpost.com /world/a-map-showing-the-users-of-fitness-devices-lets-the-world-see-where-us -soldiers-are-and-what-they-are-doing/2018/01/28/86915662-0441-11e8-aa61-f 3391373867e_story.html.

55.   China-Arab States BDS/GNSS Center in AICTO, "Arab Region Beidou Cooperation on Satellite Navigation" (presentation, 13th Meeting of the International Committee on GNSS, Xi'an, China, November 7, 2018), www.unoosa.org/doc uments/pdf/icg/2018/icg13/wgb/wgb_22.pdf.

56.   "Second Edition China-Arab States BDS Cooperation Forum," China Arab-States BDS, accessed February 1, 2021, http://bds-aicto.org/.

57.   Test and Assessment Research Center of China Satellite Navigation Office and the Arab Information and Communication Technologies Organization, *China*

*-Arab Joint BDS Test & Evaluation Results* (n.p.: China Satellite Navigation Office, 2019),http://bds-aicto.org/wp-content/uploads/2019/04/China-Arab-Joint-BDS -Test-Evaluation-Results-ver6.0.pdf.

58.  Dr. Todd Humphreys (assistant professor, University of Texas at Austin), personal communication with author, August 2020.

59.  "U.S. Still Not Allowing GLONASS Stations," *GPS World*, October 31, 2014, www.gpsworld.com/us-still-not-allowing-glonass-stations/.

60.  Xiaochun Lu, "Update on BeiDou Navigation Satellite System and PNT System" (presentation, Stanford 2019 PNT Symposium, National Time Service Center, Chinese Academy of Sciences, October 19, 2019), http://web.stanford .edu/group/scpnt/pnt/PNT19/presentation_files/I10-Lu-Beidou_PNT_Up date.pdf. The company operating a third station in Australia announced in 2020 that it would not renew its contract with Chinese customers; see Jonathan Barrett, "Exclusive: China to Lose Access to Australian Space Tracking Station," Reuters, September 21, 2020, www.reuters.com/article/china-space-australia -exclusive/exclusive-china-to-lose-access-to-australian-space-tracking-station -idUSKCN26C0HB.

61.  Jordan Wilson, *China's Alternative to GPS and Its Implications for the United States* (Washington, D.C.: U.S.-China Economic and Security Review Commission, 2017),2,www.uscc.gov/sites/default/files/Research/Staff%20Report_China's %20Alternative%20to%20GPS%20and%20Implications%20for%20the%20 United%20States.pdf; Stephen Chen, "Thailand Is Beidou Navigation Network's First Overseas Client," *South China Morning Post*, April 4, 2013, www.scmp.com /news/china/article/1206567/thailand-beidou-navigation-networks-first-over seas-client.

62.  State Council Information Office of the People's Republic of China, "Beidou xi-tong yi fugai jin 30 ge 'yidai yilu' yanxian guojia" 北斗系统已覆盖近30个 "一带 一路" 沿线国家 [The Beidou System Covers Nearly 30 Countries along the "Belt and Road"], press release, December 16, 2017, http://www.scio.gov.cn/xwfbh /xwbfbh/wqfbh/35861/37517/xgbd37524/Document/1614255/1614255.htm.

63.  Dean Cheng, "How China Has Integrated Its Space Program into Its Broader Foreign Policy" (paper presented at 2020 CASI Conference, China Aerospace Studies Institute, Air University, n.p., September 2020), www.air university.af.edu/Portals/10/CASI/Conference-2020/CASI%20Conference %20China%20Space%20and%20Foreign%20Policy-%20Cheng.pdf?ver =tXD5KaN9JfGMNNf-oqH-Yw%3D%3D.

64.  Alan C. O'Connor et al., *Economic Benefits of the Global Positioning System (GPS)*, RTI

Report No. 0215471 (Research Triangle Park, NC: RTI International, 2019), www.rti.org/sites/default/files/gps_finalreport618.pdf?utm_campaign=SSES _SSES_ALL_Aware2019&utm_source=Press%20Release&utm_medium =Website&utm_content=GPSreport.

65. Nicholas Jackman, "Chinese Satellite Diplomacy: China's Strategic Weapon for Soft and Hard Power Gains" (master's thesis, Wright State University, 2018), https://corescholar.libraries.wright.edu/cgi/viewcontent.cgi?article=3064& context=etd_all; Vidya Sagar Reddy, *China's Design to Capture Regional SatCom Markets*, ORF Special Report no. 70 (New Delhi: Observer Research Foundation, 2018), www.orfonline.org/wp-content/uploads/2018/07/ORF_SpecialReport _70_China_SatCom.pdf; Julie Michelle Klinger, "China, Africa, and the Rest: Recent Trends in Space Science, Technology, and Satellite Development" (working paper, China-Africa Research Initiative, Paul H. Nitze School of Advanced International Studies, Johns Hopkins University, 2020), https://static1 .squarespace.com/static/5652847de4b033f56d2bdc29/t/5ecdb4ab6dad0e 25fa0feb06/1590539437793/WP+38+-+Klinger+-+China+Africa+Space +Satellites.pdf.

66. "Launch Record," China Great Wall Industry Corporation, last modified April 10, 2019, www.cgwic.com/Launchservice/LaunchRecord.html; "China to Launch Palapa-N1 Satellite Covering Indonesia and Surrounding Areas," China Aerospace Science and Technology Corporation, last modified April 2, 2020, http://english.spacechina.com/n16421/n17212/c2878985/content.html.

67. Craig Covault, "Sino Setback—Advanced Chinese Space Technology Initiative Is Off to a Disastrous Start," SpaceRef, December 3, 2006, www.spaceref.com /news/viewnews.html?id=1175.

68. U.S.-China Economic and Security Review Commission, *China's Proliferation Practices and Role in the North Korea Crisis: Hearing before the U.S.-China Economic and Security Review Commission* (Washington, D.C.: U.S. Government Printing Office, 2005), 55, www.uscc.gov/sites/default/files/transcripts/3.10.05ht.pdf.

69. "Company Profile," China Great Wall Industry Corporation, accessed March 18, 2021, www.cgwic.com/About/index.html; Jasper Helder et al., "International Trade Aspects of Outer Space Activities," in *Outer Space Law: Legal Policy and Practice*, ed. Yanal Abul Failat and Anél Ferreira-Syman (London: Globe Law and Business, 2017), 285–305, www.akingump.com/a/web/61872/aoiVR /outer-space-law-international-trade-aspects-of-outer-space-act.pdf.

70. Peter B. de Selding, "Winter Is Coming for Asian Satellite Operators as Capacity Outpaces Demand," *SpaceNews*, June 2, 2015, https://spacenews.com/winter-is -coming-for-asian-satellite-operators-as-capacity-outpaces-demand/.

71. Blaine Curcio, "Satellites for Nations: The Dawn of a New Era," West East Space, November 24, 2019, https://westeastspace.com/2019/11/24/satellites-for-nations -the-dawn-of-a-new-era/.

72. R. A. Boroffice, "The Nigerian Space Program: An Update," *African Skies* 12 (2008): 42, http://adsabs.harvard.edu/full/2008AfrSk..12...40B.

73. Boroffice, "Nigerian Space Program."

74. Peter B. de Selding, "China to Build and Launch Nigerian Telecom Satellite," *SpaceNews*, February 21, 2005, https://spacenews.com/china-build-and-launch -nigerian-telecom-satellite/.

75. De Selding, "China to Build."

76. Li Peng 李鹏, "Zhongguo jin chukou yinhang 2 yi meiyuan zhichi niriliya guo-jia 1 hao gongcheng" 中国进出口银行2亿美元支持尼日利亚国家1号工程 [The Export-Import Bank of China Provides $200 Million in Support of Nigeria's No. 1 National Project], Sina, January 14, 2006, http://finance.sina.com.cn /roll/20060114/1028496709.shtml; Klinger, "China, Africa, and the Rest"; Dai Adi 戴阿弟, "Zhongguo yu niriliya qianshu jianli zhanlüe huoban guanxi beiwan-glu" 中国与尼日利亚签署建立战略伙伴关系备忘录 [China and Nigeria Sign a Memorandum of Understanding on Establishing a Strategic Partnership], Sina, January 17, 2006, http://news.sina.com.cn/c/2006-01-17/10388006240s.shtml.

77. "China Launches Communications Satellite for Nigeria," *China Daily*, last modi-fied May 15, 2007, http://en.people.cn/200705/14/eng20070514_374236.html.

78. The Central People's Government of the People's Republic of China, "Niriliya tongxin weixing yi hao zai xichang fashe zhongxin chenggong fashe" 尼日利亚通信卫星一号在西昌发射中心成功发射 [NigComSat-1 Was Successfully Launched at Xichang Launch Center], press release, May 14, 2007, www.gov .cn/jrzg/2007-05/14/content_613077.htm.

79. "NigComSat-1R Becoming White Elephant Four Years after—Investigation," *Punch*, April 16, 2016, https://punchng.com/nigcomsat-1r-becoming-white -elephant-four-years-after-investigation/; "NigComSat: Nigeria's Satellite Com-pany Still Not Profitable 14 Years after Launch," International Centre for In-vestigative Reporting, March 20, 2020, www.icirnigeria.org/nigcomsat-nigerias -satellite-company-still-not-profitable-14-years-after-launch/.

80. Industry expert, correspondence with author, January 2021.

81. James Kwen, "Reps Begin Probe of Alleged N180.9M Insurance Breach," Busi-ness Day, August 18, 2020, https://businessday.ng/insurance/article/reps-begin -probe-of-alleged-n180-9m-insurance-breach/.

82. "Nigeria Agrees $550 Million Satellite Deal with China," Reuters, January 3, 2018, www.reuters.com/article/us-nigeria-satellite-china/nigeria-agrees-550 -million-satellite-deal-with-china-idUSKBN1ES1G0.

83. Emmanuel Elebeke, "Nigeria Wins Bid to Manage Belarus's Satellite for 15 Years," Vanguard, December 30, 2015, www.vanguardngr.com/2015/12/nigeria -wins-bid-to-manage-belaruss-satellite-for-15-years/.

84. "Belintersat 1 (ZX 15, ChinaSat 15)," Gunter's Space Page, accessed February 1, 2021, https://space.skyrocket.de/doc_sdat/belintersat-1.htm; "ChinaSat 15," China Satellite Communications Co., Ltd., last modified February 17, 2016, http://english.csat.spacechina.com/n931903/c1162059/content.html.

85. Everest Amaefule, "NigComSat, Belarus Sign Satellite Backup Deal," *Punch*, October 27, 2017, https://punchng.com/nigcomsat-belarus-sign-satellite-backup -deal/.

86. Tomasz Nowakowski, "China's Long March 3B Rocket Successfully Launches First Laotian Satellite," SpaceFlight Insider, November 22, 2015, www.space flightinsider.com/missions/commercial/chinas-long-march-3b-rocket-successfully -launches-first-laotian-satellite/; "Chinese, Lao Leaders Mark Successful Launch of Communication Satellite," China.org.cn, November 21, 2015, www.china.org .cn/world/Off_the_Wire/2015-11/21/content_37124112.htm.

87. Iulia-Diana Galeriu, "'Paper Satellites' and the Free Use of Outer Space," Glob-aLex, Hauser Global Law School Program, New York University School of Law, April 2018, www.nyulawglobal.org/globalex/Paper_satellites_free_use_outer _space1.html.

88. Peter B. de Selding, "Laos, with China's Aid, Enters Crowded Satellite Tele-com Field," *SpaceNews*, November 30, 2015, https://spacenews.com/laos-with -chinese-aid-is-latest-arrival-to-crowded-satellite-telecom-field/.

89. Caleb Henry, "Venezuela's Flagship Communications Satellite Out of Service and Tumbling," *SpaceNews*, March 23, 2020, https://spacenews.com/venezuelas -flagship-communications-satellite-out-of-service-and-tumbling/.

90. Reddy, *China's Design to Capture Regional SatCom Markets*; Thilanka Kanakarathna, "'SupremeSAT' Cost Rs 460Mn Obtained from CEB Funds: Champika," *Daily Mirror*, September 17, 2017, www.dailymirror.lk/article/-SupremeSAT-cost -Rs-mn-obtained-from-CEB-funds-Champika-136771.html.

91. Caleb Henry, "Cambodia to Buy Chinese Satellite as Relations Tighten on Belt and Road Initiative," *SpaceNews*, January 12, 2018, https://spacenews.com /cambodia-to-buy-chinese-satellite-as-relations-tighten-on-belt-and-road

-initiative/; "DR Congo's Planned Launch of CongoSat-1 Still a Mirage," Space in Africa, October 27, 2018, https://africanews.space/dr-congos-planned-launch -of-congosat-1-still-a-mirage/; "CongoSat 01," Gunter's Space Page, accessed February 1, 2021, https://space.skyrocket.de/doc_sdat/congosat-1.htm; "Nicaragua Plans to Have 2 Satellites in Orbit by 2017," Agencia EFE, November 18, 2015, www.efe.com/efe/english/technology/nicaragua-plans-to-have-2-satellites-in-or bit-by-2017/50000267-2767737; Ministry of Foreign Affairs of the People's Republic of China, "Joint Statement between the People's Republic of China and the Islamic Republic of Afghanistan," press release (communique), May 18, 2016, www.fmprc.gov.cn/mfa_eng/wjdt_665385/2649_665393/t1367681.shtml.

92. Maria Jose Haro Sly, "China and South American Region Eye Cooperation in Science and Technology," Global Times, January 16, 2020, https://www .globaltimes.cn/content/1177087.shtml; "Ecnec Approves Rs261Bn Development Projects," *Dawn*, January 7, 2020, www.dawn.com/news/1526768; "Inauguration: Prime Minister Lauds Success of PAKSAT-1R," *Express Tribune*, November 6, 2011, https://tribune.com.pk/story/288079/paksat-1r-pakistans -first-indigenously-made-satellite-inaugurated.

93. Curcio, "Satellites for Nations."

94. Richard Swinford and Bertrand Grau, "High Throughput Satellites: Delivering Future Capacity Needs," Arthur D. Little, 2015, www.adlittle.com/sites/default /files/viewpoints/ADL_High_Throughput_Satellites-Viewpoint.pdf; Rajesh Mehrotra, *Regulation of Global Broadband Satellite Communications GSR Advanced Copy*, (Geneva: International Telecommunication Union, 2011), www.itu.int/ITU-D /treg/Events/Seminars/GSR/GSR11/documents/BBReport_BroadbandSatellite Regulation-E.pdf.

95. "Alcomsat-1 Satellite Delivered to Algeria," China Great Wall Industry Corporation, April 2, 2018, www.cgwic.com/news/2018/0402.html; "Alcomsat-1 Successfully Positioned in Geostationary Orbit," Xinhua, December 19, 2017, www .xinhuanet.com/english/2017-12/19/c_136837590.htm.

96. "SpaceX Seattle 2015," YouTube video, 25:53, posted by Cliff O, January 17, 2015, www.youtube.com/watch?v=AHeZHyOnsm4&ab_channel=CliffO.

97. Jim Cashel, *The Great Connecting: The Emergence of Global Broadband and How That Changes Everything* (New York: Radius Book Group, 2019).

98. Michael Koziol, "SpaceX Confident about Its Starlink Constellation for Satellite Internet; Others, Not So Much," *IEEE Spectrum*, January 6, 2019, https:// spectrum.ieee.org/aerospace/satellites/spacex-confident-about-its-starlink -constellation-for-satellite-internet-others-not-so-much.

99. Israel Leyva-Mayorga et al., "LEO Small-Satellite Constellations for 5G and Beyond-5G Communications," *IEEE Access* 8 (2020), https://doi.org/10.1109 /ACCESS.2020.3029620.

100. Jeff Hecht, "Laser Links Will Link Small Satellites to Earth and Each Other," *Laser Focus World*, March 24, 2020, www.laserfocusworld.com/lasers-sources /article/14104017/laser-links-will-link-small-satellites-to-earth-and-each-other.

101. Sandra Erwin, "DARPA's Big Bet on Blackjack," *SpaceNews*, January 8, 2020, https://spacenews.com/darpas-big-bet-on-blackjack/.

102. Valerie Insinna, "Behind the Scenes of the US Air Force's Second Test of Its Game-Changing Battle Management System," *C4ISRNET*, September 4, 2020, www.c4isrnet.com/it-networks/2020/09/04/behind-the-scenes-of-the-us-air -forces-second-test-of-its-game-changing-battle-management-system/.

103. Gillian Rich, "SpaceX Starlink Impresses Air Force Weapons Buyer in Big Live-Fire Exercise," *Investor's Business Daily*, September 23, 2020, www.investors.com /news/spacex-starlink-impressed-air-force-in-big-live-fire-exercise/.

104. Cliff O, "SpaceX Seattle 2015."

105. Mark Handley, "Delay Is Not an Option: Low Latency Routing in Space," *Hot-Nets* 17, no. 1 (2018): 85–91, https://doi.org/10.1145/3286062.3286075.

106. Todd Cotts, "The Digital Divide: Solutions for Connecting the Forgotten 1 Billion," *Intelsat Blog*, Intelsat, November 4, 2019, www.intelsat.com/resources/blog /connecting-the-forgotten-1-billion.

107. Amazon, "Amazon Building Project Kuiper R&D Headquarters in Redmond, WA," press release, December 18, 2019, www.aboutamazon.com/news/company -news/amazon-building-project-kuiper-r-d-headquarters-in-redmond-wa.

108. Louise Matsakis, "Facebook Confirms It's Working on a New Internet Satellite," *Wired*, July 20, 2018, www.wired.com/story/facebook-confirms-its-working-on -new-internet-satellite/.

109. "Athena," Gunter's Space Page, accessed February 2, 2021, https://space.sky rocket.de/doc_sdat/athena_pointview.htm.

110. Devin Coldewey, "Facebook Permanently Grounds Its Aquila Solar-Powered Internet Plane," *TechCrunch*, June 26, 2018, https://techcrunch.com/2018/06/26 /facebook-permanently-grounds-its-aquila-solar-powered-internet-plane/.

111. Astro Teller, "How Project Loon's Smart Software Learned to Sail the Winds," *X, the moonshot factory* (blog), February 16, 2017, https://blog.x.company/how -project-loons-smart-software-learned-to-sail-the-winds-ec904e6d08c.

112. "Frequently Asked Questions," Loon, accessed February 1, 2021, https://loon
.com/faqs/; Paresh Dave, "Google Internet Balloon Spinoff Loon Still Looking
for Its Wings," Reuters, July 1, 2019, www.reuters.com/article/us-alphabet-loon
-focus/google-internet-balloon-spinoff-loon-still-looking-for-its-wings-idUS
KCN1TW1GN.

113. Salvatore Candido, "1 Million Hours of Stratospheric Flight," *Loon* (blog),
July 23, 2019, https://medium.com/loon-for-all/1-million-hours-of-stratospheric
-flight-f7af7ae728ac.

114. Abdi Latif Dahir, "A Bird? A Plane? No, It's a Google Balloon Beaming the
Internet," *New York Times*, July 7, 2020, www.nytimes.com/2020/07/07/world
/africa/google-loon-balloon-kenya.html.

115. Ben Geier, "How Google Could Make Billions from Balloons," *Fortune*, March 3,
2015, https://fortune.com/2015/03/03/google-loon/.

116. Steven Levy, "Alphabet Pops Loon's Balloons—but Won't Call It a Failure,"
*Wired*, January 21, 2021, www.wired.com/story/plaintext-alphabet-pops-loons
-balloons/.

117. Alastair Westgarth, "Saying Goodbye to Loon," *Loon* (blog), January 21, 2021,
https://medium.com/loon-for-all/loon-draft-c3fcebc11f3f.

118. Dave Mosher, "SpaceX May Shell Out Billions to Outsource Starlink
Satellite-Dish Production, an Industry Insider Says—and Lose Up to $2,000
on Each One It Sells," *Insider*, December 28, 2020, www.businessinsider.com
/spacex-starlink-satellite-dish-user-terminal-cost-stmelectronics-outsource
-manufacturer-2020-11.

119. "Elon Musk, Satellite 2020 Conference, Washington DC, March 9, 2020," You-
Tube video, 47:18, posted by Space Policy and Politics, March 24, 2020, www
.youtube.com/watch?v=ywPqLCc9zBU&ab_channel=SpacePolicyandPolitics.

120. Cliff O, "SpaceX Seattle 2015."

121. Ramish Zafar, "SpaceX Could Earn $30 Billion Annually from Starlink, 10x of
Sending ISS Supplies—Elon Musk," *Wccftech*, March 9, 2020, https://wccftech
.com/spacex-could-earn-30-billion-annually-from-starlink-10x-of-sending-iss
-supplies-elon-musk/.

122. u/Smoke-away, "Starlink Beta Terms of Service," *Reddit*, October 28, 2020,
www.reddit.com/r/Starlink/comments/jjti2k/starlink_beta_terms_of_service/.

123. Space Policy and Politics, "Elon Musk, Satellite 2020 Conference."

124. Caleb Henry, "LeoSat, Absent Investors, Shuts Down," *SpaceNews*, November 13, 2019, https://spacenews.com/leosat-absent-investors-shuts-down/.

125. Chris Daehnick et al., "Large LEO Satellite Constellations: Will It Be Different This Time?," McKinsey & Company, May 4, 2020, www.mckinsey.com /industries/aerospace-and-defense/our-insights/large-leo-satellite-constellations -will-it-be-different-this-time.

126. "News," Leptong Global Solutions, accessed February 1, 2021, https://lepton global.com/geo-meo-leo-satellites-why-geo-is-winning/.

127. Inigo del Portillo, Bruce G. Cameron, and Edward F. Crawley, "A Technical Comparison of Three Low Earth Orbit Satellite Constellation Systems to Provide Global Broadband" (presentation, 69th International Astronautical Congress 2018, Bremen, Germany, 2018), www.mit.edu/~portillo/files/Comparison-LEO -IAC-2018-slides.pdf.

128. Daehnick et al., "Large Leo Satellite Constellations"; "Focus: Kratos, The Looming HTS Gateway Crunch," *SatMagazine*, March 2018, www.satmagazine .com/story.php?number=856311740.

129. Michael Sheetz, "Morgan Stanley Expects SpaceX Will Be a $100 Billion Company Thanks to Starlink and Starship," CNBC, October 22, 2020, www.cnbc .com/2020/10/22/morgan-stanley-spacex-to-be-100-billion-company-due-to -starlink-starship.html.

130. State Council of the People's Republic of China, *Guowuyuan guanyu chuangxin zhongdian lingyu tou rongzi jizhi guli shehui touzi de zhidao yijian: Guo fa (2014) 60 hao* 国务院关于创新重点领域投融资机制鼓励社会投资的指导意见: 国发 (2014) 60号 [Guiding Opinions of the State Council on Innovating Investment and Financing Mechanisms in Key Fields to Encourage Social Investment: National Document (2014) No. 60], 000014349/2014-00142 (Beijing: State Council, 2014), www.gov.cn/zhengce/content/2014-11/26/content_9260.htm.

131. Blaine Curcio, "Best Frenemies Ever: CASC, CASIC, and the Aerospace Bridge," West East Space, June 17, 2019, https://westeastspace.com/2019/06/17/best -frenemies-ever/.

132. "Global 500: China Aerospace Science & Industry," *Fortune*, last modified August 10, 2020, https://fortune.com/company/china-aerospace-science-industry /global500/; "Global 500: China Aerospace Science & Technology," *Fortune*, last modified August 10, 2020, https://fortune.com/company/china-aerospace -science-technology/global500/.

133. Zhao Lei, "Testing at Smart Satellite Factory Now Underway," *China Daily*, January 18, 2021, http://epaper.chinadaily.com.cn/a/202101/18/WS6004c322a31099a2343534de.html.

134. Larry Press, "China Will Be a Formidable Satellite Internet Service Competitor," *CIS 471* (blog), January 28, 2020, https://cis471.blogspot.com/2020/01/china-will-be-formidable-satellite.html.

135. Blue Origin, "Blue Origin to Launch Telesat's Advanced Global LEO Satellite Constellation," press release, January 31, 2019, www.blueorigin.com/news/blue-origin-to-launch-telesats-advanced-global-leo-satellite-constellation; Caleb Henry, "Blue Origin Signs OneWeb as Second Customer for New Glenn Reusable Rocket," *SpaceNews*, March 8, 2017, https://spacenews.com/blue-origin-gets-oneweb-as-second-new-glenn-customer/.

136. Larry Press, "China on Its Way to Becoming a Formidable Satellite Internet Service Competitor," CircleID, January 29, 2020, www.circleid.com/posts/20200129_china_becoming_a_formidable_satellite_internet_service_competitor/.

137. Jacqueline Myrrhe, "5th CCAF—China (International) Commercial Aerospace Forum: Jointly Building an Industrial Ecology to Lead the Development of Commercial Aerospace," *Go Taikonauts!*, no. 28 (March 2020), www.go-taikonauts.com/images/newsletters_PDF/2019_CCAF-Wuhan_web.pdf.

138. China Aerospace Science and Industry Corporation, "Shangye hantian dachao qi yangfan qicheng kai xin pian—dang de shiba da yilai zhongguo hangtian ke gongshangye hangtian fazhan zongshu" 商业航天大潮起 扬帆启程开新篇—党的十八大以来中国航天科工商业航天发展综述 [The Tide of Commercial Aerospace Rises; Setting Sail on a New Chapter: A Summary of CASIC's Commercial Aerospace Development since the 18th Party Congress], press release, September 26, 2017, http://www.casic.com.cn/n12377419/n12378166/c12564106/content.html.

139. "China Launches Two Satellites for IoT Project," Xinhua, May 12, 2020, www.xinhuanet.com/english/2020-05/12/c_139051254.htm; Deng Xiaoci, "China Successfully Builds Laser Communication Links for New-Generation Space-Borne IoT Project," *Global Times*, August 13, 2020, www.globaltimes.cn/content/1197631.shtml.

140. Zhao Lei, "Solar-Driven Drone under Development," *China Daily*, March 18, 2019, www.chinadaily.com.cn/a/201903/18/WS5c8ecf35a3106c65c34ef0d0.html; "China to Fly Solar Drone to Near Space," *Asia Times*, March 18, 2019, https://asiatimes.com/2019/03/china-to-fly-solar-drone-to-near-space/.

141. China Aerospace Science and Industry Corporation Ltd., "Commercial Aerospace on the Cloud to Navigate China's Digital Economy—the 6th China (International) Commercial Aerospace Summit Forum Opened in Wuhan," press release, November 12, 2020, www.casic.com/n525220/c18355884/content.html; "A Chinese SpaceX? Aerospace Industry Eyes Commercial Market," China Space Report, September 16, 2016, https://chinaspacereport.wordpress.com/2016/09/16/a-chinese-spacex-aerospace-industry-eyes-commercial-market/; Chen Lan, Dr. William Carey, and Jacqueline Myrrhe, "Wuhan—China's Center of the Commercial Universe," *Go Taikonauts!*, no. 21 (April 2018), www.go-taikonauts.com/images/newsletters_PDF/2017_Wuhan_web.pdf; Tan Yuanbin 谭元斌 and Hu Zhe 胡喆, "Hangtian ke gong jituan 'wu yun yi che' gongcheng qude xilie zhongyao jinzhan" 航天科工集团'五云一车'工程取得系列重要进展 [CASIC's "Five Clouds and One Vehicle" Project Has Made a Series of Important Advancements], Xinhua, October 19, 2020, www.xinhuanet.com/fortune/2020-10/19/c_1126631246.htm; Zhang Su 张素, "Zhongguo hangtian ke gong jihua zai 2030 nian shifei 'kong tian feiji'" 中国航天科工计划在2030年试飞'空天飞机' [CASIC Plans to Flight-Test "Space Plane" in 2030], Xinhua, September 13, 2016, http://www.xinhuanet.com//politics/2016-09/13/c_129280259.htm.

142. "Guozi wei guanyu zujian zhongguo weixing wangluo jituan youxian gongsi de gonggao" 国资委关于组建中国卫星网络集团有限公司的公告 [State-Owned Assets Supervision and Administration Commission Announcement Regarding the Establishment of China Satellite Network Group Co., Ltd.], State-Owned Assets Supervision and Administration Commission of the State Council, April 29, 2021, http://www.sasac.gov.cn/n2588030/n2588924/c18286531/content.html.

143. Andrew Jones, "China Is Developing Plans for a 13,000-Satellite Megaconstellation," *SpaceNews*, April 21, 2021, https://spacenews.com/china-is-developing-plans-for-a-13000-satellite-communications-megaconstellation/; Blaine Curcio and Jean Deville, "#SpaceWatchGL Column: Dongfang Hour China Aerospace News Roundup 8," SpaceWatch.Global, March 14, 2021, https://spacewatch.global/2021/03/spacewatchgl-column-dongfang-hour-china-aerospace-news-roundup-8-14-march-2021/.

144. Blaine Curcio, correspondence with author, November 2020.

145. Irina Liu et al., *Evaluation of China's Commercial Space Sector*, IDA Document D-10873 (Washington, D.C.: Science & Technology Policy Institute, Institute for Defense Analyses, 2019), 75–76, www.ida.org/-/media/feature/publications/e/ev/evaluation-of-chinas-commercial-space-sector/d-10873.ashx.

146. OneWeb, "OneWeb Secures Global Spectrum Further Enabling Global Connectivity Services," press release, August 7, 2019, www.oneweb.world/media-center/oneweb-secures-global-spectrum-further-enabling-global-connectivity-services.

147. "Non-Geostationary Satellite Systems," International Telecommunication Union, last modified December 2019, www.itu.int/en/mediacentre/backgrounders/Pages/Non-geostationary-satellite-systems.aspx.

148. Peter B. de Selding, "OneWeb Bidders Include 2 from China, Eutelsat, with France and Other EU Nations, SpaceX, Amazon, Cerberus," Space Intel Report, May 6, 2020, www.spaceintelreport.com/oneweb-bidders-include-2-from-china-eutelsat-with-france-other-eu-nations-spacex-amazon-cerberus/.

149. Press, "China on Its Way."

150. Peter B. de Selding (cofounder, Space Intel Report), interview by author, December 2020.

151. Broadband Commission for Sustainable Development, *Connecting Africa through Broadband: A Strategy for Doubling Connectivity by 2021 and Reaching Universal Access by 2030* (n.p.: Broadband Commission for Sustainable Development, 2019), 121–26, www.broadbandcommission.org/Documents/working-groups/DigitalMoonshotforAfrica_Report.pdf.

152. Sharon Pian Chan, "The Birth and Demise of an Idea: Teledesic's 'Internet in the Sky,'" *Seattle Times*, October 7, 2002, https://archive.seattletimes.com/archive/?date=20021007&slug=teledesic070.

153. Richard Waters, "An Exclusive Interview with Bill Gates," *Financial Times*, November 1, 2013, www.ft.com/content/dacd1f84-41bf-11e3-b064-00144feabdc0.

154. Emily Chang and Sarah Frier, "Mark Zuckerberg Q&A: The Full Interview on Connecting the World," Bloomberg, February 19, 2015, www.bloomberg.com/news/articles/2015-02-19/mark-zuckerberg-q-a-the-full-interview-on-connecting-the-world?sref=VZPf2pAM.

155. Chang and Frier, "Mark Zuckerberg Q&A."

156. Amazon, "Email from Jeff Bezos to Employees," press release, February 2, 2021, www.aboutamazon.com/news/company-news/email-from-jeff-bezos-to-employees?utm_source=social&utm_medium=tw&utm_term=amznnews&utm_content=exec_chair&linkId=110535487.

157. "Blue's Mission: Building a Road," Blue Origin, accessed March 18, 2021, www.blueorigin.com/our-mission.

158. Larry Press, "Are Inter-Satellite Laser Links a Bug or a Feature of ISP Con-

stellations?" CircleID, April 3, 2019, www.circleid.com/posts/20190403_inter
_satellite_laser_links_bug_or_feature_of_isp_constellations/.

159. Caleb Henry, "Satcom Companies Willing to Partner with China to Gain Market Access," *SpaceNews,* June 29, 2018, https://spacenews.com/satcom-companies
-willing-to-partner-with-china-to-gain-market-access/.

160. Industry expert, interview by author, November 2020.

161. Cliff O, "SpaceX Seattle 2015."

## CHAPTER SEVEN   WINNING THE NETWORK WARS

1.  John F. Sargent, Jr., *Global Research and Development Expenditures: Fact Sheet*, CRS Report No. R44283 (Washington, D.C.: Congressional Research Service, 2020), 3, https://fas.org/sgp/crs/misc/R44283.pdf.

2.  Giuliana Viglione, "China Is Closing Gap with United States on Research Spending," *Nature,* January 15, 2020, www.nature.com/articles/d41586-020-00084-7.

3.  Ganesh Sitaraman, "A Grand Strategy of Resilience: American Power in the Age of Fragility," *Foreign Affairs*, September/October 2020, www.foreignaffairs.com
/articles/united-states/2020-08-11/grand-strategy-resilience.

4.  Melissa Flagg, *Global R&D and a New Era of Alliances* (Washington, D.C.: Center for Security and Emerging Technology, 2020), https://cset.georgetown.edu
/research/global-rd-and-a-new-era-of-alliances/; Sargent, *Global Research and Development Expenditures*; "International Macroeconomic Data Set," Economic Research Service, U.S. Department of Agriculture, last modified January 8, 2021, https://www.ers.usda.gov/data-products/international-macroeconomic-data
-set.aspx.

5.  Tim Pemberton, "The World in 2030," HSBC, October 2, 2018, www.mobile
news.hsbc.com/blog/the-world-in-2030/.

6.  Franklin D. Roosevelt, "Fireside Chat" (speech, Washington, D.C., December 29, 1940), The American Presidency Project, University of California, Santa Barbara, https://www.presidency.ucsb.edu/documents/fireside-chat-9.

7.  *U.S.-China: Winning the Economic Competition: Hearing before the Subcommittee on Economic Policy of the Committee on Banking, Housing, and Urban Affairs, U.S. Senate*, 116th Congress (2020) (statement of Martijn Rasser, senior fellow, Technology and National Security Program, Center for a New American Security), www
.banking.senate.gov/imo/media/doc/Rasser%20Testimony%207-22-20.pdf;
David Moschella and Robert D. Atkinson, "Competing with China: A Strategic

Framework," Information Technology and Innovation Foundation, August 31, 2020, https://itif.org/publications/2020/08/31/competing-china-strategic-frame work.

8.  Emiliano Alessandri, "World Order Re-Founded: The Idea of a Concert of De-mocracies," *The International Spectator* 43, no. 1 (2008): 73–90, https://doi.org /10.1080/03932720801892555.

9.  "About the CoD," Community of Democracies, accessed March 18, 2021, https:// community-democracies.org/values/organization/.

10. Thomas Carothers, *Is a League of Democracies a Good Idea?* (Washington, D.C.: Car-negie Endowment for International Peace, 2008), https://carnegieendowment .org/files/pb59_carothers_league_final.pdf.

11. Ivo H. Daalder and James Lindsay, "An Alliance of Democracies," *Washington Post*, May 23, 2004, www.washingtonpost.com/archive/opinions/2004/05/23 /an-alliance-of-democracies/73065856-4082-4d0f-a4b1-bdfca773d93d/; Rich-ard Perle, "Democracies of the World, Unite," *American Interest*, January 1, 2007, www.the-american-interest.com/2007/01/01/democracies-of-the-world-unite/; Anne-Marie Slaughter, John Ikenberry, and Philippe Sands, "The Global Gov-ernance Crisis," *The InterDependent*, United Nations Association of the USA, 2006, https://scholar.princeton.edu/sites/default/files/slaughter/files/interdependent .pdf.

12. John McCain, "McCain Remarks—Hoover Institution (May 1, 2007)" (speech, Hoover Institution, Stanford University, Stanford, CA, May 1, 2007), https:// www.hoover.org/sites/default/files/uploads/inline/docs/McCain_05-01-07 .pdf.

13. David Gordon and Ash Jain, "Forget the G-8. It's Time for the D-10," *Wall Street Journal*, June 16, 2013, www.wsj.com/articles/SB10001424127887324688404578 541262989391492; "D-10 Strategy Forum," Atlantic Council, accessed March 18, 2021, www.atlanticcouncil.org/programs/scowcroft-center-for-strategy-and -security/global-strategy-initiative/democratic-order-initiative/d-10-strategy -forum/.

14. David Rohde, "U.S. Embrace of Musharraf Irks Pakistanis," *New York Times*, February 29, 2008, www.nytimes.com/2008/02/29/world/asia/29pstan.html.

15. Elbridge Colby and Robert D. Kaplan, "The Ideology Delusion," *Foreign Affairs*, September 4, 2020, www.foreignaffairs.com/articles/united-states/2020-09-04 /ideology-delusion.

16. Charles A. Kupchan, "Minor League, Major Problems," *Foreign Affairs*, Novem-

ber/December 2008, www.foreignaffairs.com/articles/2008-11-01/minor-league-major-problems.

17. "Mapping the Future of U.S. China Policy," Center for Strategic and International Studies, accessed February 11, 2020, https://chinasurvey.csis.org/.

18. Dina Smeltz and Craig Kafura, "Do Republicans and Democrats Want a Cold War with China?," Chicago Council on Global Affairs, October 13, 2020, www.thechicagocouncil.org/publication/lcc/do-republicans-and-democrats-want-cold-war-china?utm_source=tw&utm_campaign=ccs&utm_medium=social&utm_term=china-brief-ccs20&utm_content=text.

19. Marietje Schaake, "How Democracies Can Claim Back Power in the Digital World," *MIT Technology Review*, September 29, 2020, www.technologyreview.com/2020/09/29/1009088/democracies-power-digital-social-media-governance-tech-companies-opinion/.

20. "Team," Inter-Parliamentary Alliance on China, accessed February 11, 2021, https://ipac.global/team/.

21. Latika Bourke, "MPs from Eight Countries Form New Global Coalition to Counter China," *Sydney Morning Herald*, June 5, 2020, www.smh.com.au/world/europe/mps-from-eight-countries-form-new-global-coalition-to-counter-china-20200604-p54zqj.html.

22. Robert S. Singh, "In Defense of a Concert of Liberal Democracies," *Whitehead Journal of Diplomacy and International Relations* 10, no. 1 (2009): 19–29, http://blogs.shu.edu/journalofdiplomacy/files/archives/03%20Singh.pdf.

23. Helen Warrell, Alan Beattie, and Demetri Sevastopulo, "UK Turns to 'Five Eyes' to Help Find Alternatives to Huawei," *Financial Times*, July 13, 2020, www.ft.com/content/795a85b1-621f-4144-bee0-153eb5235943.

24. Anthony R. Wells, *Between Five Eyes: 50 Years of Intelligence Sharing* (Philadelphia: Casemate Publishers, 2020), loc. 156 of 5424, Kindle.

25. Wells, *Between Five Eyes*, loc. 4189, Kindle.

26. Alan Beattie, "Five Eyes, 5G and America's Self-Sabotaging Trade Wars," *Financial Times*, July 16, 2020, www.ft.com/content/f0f782c4-bd3f-4c0f-83c1-4629a2c295dc.

27. Lucy Fisher, "Downing Street Plans New 5G Club of Democracies," *The Times*, May 29, 2020, www.thetimes.co.uk/article/downing-street-plans-new-5g-club-of-democracies-bfnd5wj57; Atlantic Council, "D-10 Strategy Forum."

28. Julie Smith et al., *Charting a Transatlantic Course to Address China* (Washington,

D.C.: Center for a New American Security and the German Marshall Fund of the United States, 2020), 18, https://s3.us-east-1.amazonaws.com/files.cnas .org/documents/CNAS-Report-Transatlantic-August-2020-final.pdf?mtime =20201019111640&focal=none.

29. Eric McGlinchey, associate professor at George Mason University, has used a different version of this comparison to describe the United States, Russia, and China in Central Asia; see Eric McGlinchey, *Central Asia's Autocrats: Geopolitically Stuck, Politically Free*, PONARS Eurasia Policy Memo No. 380 (Washington, D.C.: PO NARS Eurasia, 2015), www.ponarseurasia.org/new-policy-memo-central-asia-s -autocrats-geopolitically-stuck-politically-free/.

30. European Commission, *Joint Communication to the European Parliament, the European Council and the Council: A New EU-US Agenda for Global Change* (Brussels: European Commission, 2020), https://ec.europa.eu/info/sites/info/files/joint -communication-eu-us-agenda_en.pdf.

31. Noah Barkin, "Watching China in Europe – January 2021," German Marshall Fund of the United States, January 2021, https://sites-gmf.vuturevx.com /61/6509/january-2021/january-2021(1).asp?sid=584b91fc-5916-4605-9a57 -a6e6163b3aa3.

32. Jacob Poushter and Christine Huang, "Climate Change Still Seen as the Top Global Threat, but Cyberattacks a Rising Concern," Pew Research Center, February 10, 2019, www.pewresearch.org/global/2019/02/10/climate-change-still -seen-as-the-top-global-threat-but-cyberattacks-a-rising-concern/.

33. Richard Wike, Janell Fetterolf, and Mara Mordecai, "U.S. Image Plummets Internationally as Most Say Country Has Handled Coronavirus Badly," Pew Research Center, September 15, 2020, www.pewresearch.org/global/2020/09/15 /us-image-plummets-internationally-as-most-say-country-has-handled-corona virus-badly/.

34. Ivan Krastev and Mark Leonard, *The Crisis of American Power: How Europeans See Biden's America*, European Council on Foreign Relations, ECFR/363 (Berlin: European Council on Foreign Relations, 2021), https://ecfr.eu/publication/the -crisis-of-american-power-how-europeans-see-bidens-america/.

35. *China's Expanding Influence in Europe and Eurasia: Hearing before the Subcommittee on Europe, Eurasia, Energy, and the Environment of the Committee on Foreign Affairs, House of Representatives*, 116th Cong. 11 (2019) (statement of Philippe Le Corre, nonresident senior fellow, Carnegie Endowment for International Peace), https://www .govinfo.gov/content/pkg/CHRG-116hhrg36214/pdf/CHRG-116hhrg36214 .pdf.

36. European Commission, *Joint Communication to the European Parliament, the European Council and the Council: EU-China—A Strategic Outlook* (Strasbourg: European Commission, 2019), https://ec.europa.eu/commission/presscorner/detail/en/fs_19 _6498.

37. European Commission, "Secure 5G Networks: Commission Endorses EU Toolbox and Sets Out Next Steps," press release, January 29, 2020, https://ec.europa .eu/commission/presscorner/detail/en/ip_20_123.

38. Department for Digital, Culture, Media & Sport, National Cyber Security Centre and the Rt Hon Oliver Dowden CBE MP, "Huawei to Be Removed from UK 5G Networks by 2027," press release, July 14, 2020, www.gov.uk/government /news/huawei-to-be-removed-from-uk-5g-networks-by-2027.

39. Mathieu Rosemain and Gwénaëlle Barzic, "French Limits on Huawei 5G Equipment Amount to De Facto Ban by 2028," Reuters, July 22, 2020, www.reuters .com/article/us-france-huawei-5g-security-exclusive/exclusive-french-limits-on -huawei-5g-equipment-amount-to-de-facto-ban-by-2028-idUSKCN24N26R.

40. Laurens Cerulus, "Germany Falls in Line with EU on Huawei," *Politico*, April 23, 2021, https://www.politico.eu/article/germany-europe-huawei-5g-data-privacy -cybersecurity/.

41. Annabelle Timsit, "Who Will Win the Battle to Replace Huawei in Europe?," *Quartz*, October 30, 2020, https://qz.com/1920889/who-will-win-the-battle-to -replace-huawei-in-europe/; "Four European Countries Have Only Chinese Gear in 4G Networks, Researcher Says," Reuters, June 30, 2020, www.reuters .com/article/us-europe-telecoms-china/four-european-countries-have-only -chinese-gear-in-4g-networks-researcher-says-idUSKBN241187.

42. Stacie Hoffmann, Dominique Lazanski, and Emily Taylor, "Standardising the Splinternet: How China's Technical Standards Could Fragment the Internet," *Journal of Cyber Policy* 5, no. 2 (2020): 239–64, https://doi.org/10.1080/2373887 1.2020.1805482.

43. Nigel Cory and Robert D. Atkinson, "Why and How to Mount a Strong, Trilateral Response to China's Innovation Mercantilism," Information Technology and Innovation Foundation, January 2020, https://itif.org/publications/2020/01/13 /why-and-how-mount-strong-trilateral-response-chinas-innovation-mercantilism.

44. "Biography—Houlin Zhao," International Telecommunication Union (ITU), accessed March 18, 2021, www.itu.int/en/osg/Pages/biography-zhao.aspx.

45. See, for example, China's proposal for "New IP": Madhumita Murgia and Anna Gross, "Inside China's Controversial Mission to Reinvent the Internet," *Financial*

*Times*, March 27, 2020, www.ft.com/content/ba94c2bc-6e27-11ea-9bca-bf5039 95cd6f.

46. "Vote for 5G," Huawei, accessed November 1, 2020, www.huawei.eu/story/vote -5g/; Matina Stevis-Gridneff, "Blocked in U.S., Huawei Touts 'Shared Values' to Compete in Europe," *New York Times*, December 27, 2019, www.nytimes.com /2019/12/27/world/europe/huawei-EU-5G-Europe.html.

47. Schaake, "How Democracies Can Claim Back Power."

48. Alexandra de Hoope Scheffer et al., *Transatlantic Trends 2020: Transatlantic Opinion on Global Challenges before and after COVID-19* (Washington, D.C.: German Marshall Fund of the United States, 2020), www.gmfus.org/sites/default/files /TT20_Final.pdf; Smith et al., *Charting a Transatlantic Course to Address China*, 17.

49. Katja Bego and Markus Droemann, "A Vision for the Future Internet" (working paper, NGI Forward, Next Generation Internet, 2020), 20, www.ngi.eu /wp-content/uploads/sites/48/2020/10/Vision-for-the-future-internet-long -version-final-1.pdf.

50. Bego and Droemann, "Vision for the Future Internet," 26.

51. United Nations Conference on Trade and Development (UNCTAD), *Digital Economy Report 2019: Value Creation and Capture: Implications for Developing Countries*, UNCTAD/DER/2019 (New York: United Nations Publishing, 2019), 2, https:// unctad.org/system/files/official-document/der2019_en.pdf.

52. "DAX® (TR) EUR," Qontigo, last modified February 12, 2021, www.dax-indices .com/index-details?isin=DE0008469008.

53. "Top 100 Digital Companies: 2019 Ranking," *Forbes*, accessed February 1, 2021, www.forbes.com/top-digital-companies/list/#tab:rank.

54. European Commission, *Communication from the Commission to the European Parliament, the Council, the European Economic and Social Committee of the Regions: A European Strategy for Data* (Brussels: European Commission, 2020), https://ec.europa.eu /info/sites/info/files/communication-european-strategy-data-19feb2020_en.pdf.

55. European Commission, *Communication from the Commission to the European Parliament, the Council, the European Economic and Social Committee and the Committee of the Regions Empty: 2030 Digital Compass: The European Way for the Digital Decade*, COM/2021/118 (Brussels: European Commission, 2021), https://eur-lex.europa .eu/legal-content/en/TXT/?uri=CELEX%3A52021DC0118.

56. Adam Segal, "China's Vision for Cyber Sovereignty and the Global Governance of Cyberspace," in *An Emerging China-Centric Order: China's Vision for a New*

*World Order in Practice*, ed. Nadège Rolland, NBR Special Report no. 87 (Seattle, WA: The National Bureau of Asian Research, 2020), https://www.nbr.org/wp -content/uploads/pdfs/publications/sr87_aug2020.pdf.

57. Clarifying Lawful Overseas Use of Data or the CLOUD Act, H.R.4943, 115th Congress (2018), www.congress.gov/bill/115th-congress/house-bill/4943; "The Cloud Act," Electronic Privacy Information Center, accessed February 2, 2021, https://epic.org/privacy/cloud-act/; "The CLOUD Act and the European Union: Myths vs. Facts," BSA | The Software Alliance, February 2019, www.bsa.org /files/policy-filings/02282019CLOUDACTEUMythvsFact.pdf; U.S. Department of Justice, *Promoting Public Safety, Privacy, and the Rule of Law around the World: The Purpose and Impact of the CLOUD Act White Paper* (Washington, D.C.: U.S. Department of Justice, 2019), www.justice.gov/opa/press-release/file/1153446 /download.

58. Murray Scot Tanner, "Beijing's New National Intelligence Law: From Defense to Offense," *Lawfare* (blog), July 20, 2017, www.lawfareblog.com/beijings-new -national-intelligence-law-defense-offense; "China Passes Tough New Intelligence Law," Reuters, June 27, 2017, www.reuters.com/article/us-china -security-lawmaking/china-passes-tough-new-intelligence-law-idUSKBN19I1FW; Bonnie Girard, "The Real Danger of China's National Intelligence Law," *The Diplomat*, February 23, 2019, https://thediplomat.com/2019/02/the-real-danger -of-chinas-national-intelligence-law/; Arjun Kharpal, "Huawei Says It Would Never Hand Data to China's Government. Experts Say It Wouldn't Have a Choice," CNBC, March 5, 2019, www.cnbc.com/2019/03/05/huawei-would -have-to-give-data-to-china-government-if-asked-experts.html.

59. "European Cloud Network to Start in Late 2020," Euractiv, November 5, 2019, www.euractiv.com/section/digital/news/european-cloud-network-to-start-in -late-2020/.

60. Phillip Grüll and Samuel Stolton, "Altmaier Charts Gaia-X as the Beginning of a 'European Data Ecosystem,'" Euractiv, June 5, 2020, www.euractiv.com /section/data-protection/news/altmaier-charts-gaia-x-as-the-beginning-of-a -european-data-ecosystem/.

61. Melissa Heikkilä and Janosch Delcker, "EU Shoots for €10B 'Industrial Cloud' to Rival US," *Politico*, October 15, 2020, www.politico.eu/article/eu-pledges-e10 -billion-to-power-up-industrial-cloud-sector/.

62. Federal Ministry for Economic Affairs and Energy, Federal Government of Germany, *GAIA-X: The European Project Kicks Off the Next Phase* (Berlin: Federal Ministry for Economic Affairs and Energy, 2020), www.bmwi.de/Redaktion

/EN/Publikationen/gaia-x-the-european-project-kicks-of-the-next-phase.pdf?
__blob=publicationFile&v=7.

63. Liam Tung, "Meet GAIA-X: This Is Europe's Bid to Get Cloud Independence
from US and China Giants," ZDNet, June 8, 2020, www.zdnet.com/article
/meet-gaia-x-this-is-europes-bid-to-get-cloud-independence-from-us-and-china
-giants/; Silvia Amaro, "Meet Gaia X—Europe's Answer to the Power of U.S.
and Chinese Cloud Giants," CNBC, July 16, 2020, www.cnbc.com/2020/07/17
/gaia-x-europes-answer-to-us-and-chinese-tech-giants-power.html.

64. "Frequently Asked Questions about the GAIA-X Project: Common Digital Infrastructure for Europe," Federal Government of Germany, October 1, 2020,
www.bundesregierung.de/breg-en/service/gaia-x-1795070; GAIA-X, "List of
New Members to the GAIA-X AISBL," press release, March 29, 2021, https://
www.data-infrastructure.eu/GAIAX/Redaktion/EN/Downloads/gaia-press
-release-march-31-list-en.pdf?__blob=publicationFile&v=3.

65. Daphne Leprince-Ringuet, "Europe's Cloud Computing Project Needs to Hurry
Up, If It Wants to Catch Its Giant Rivals," ZDNet, November 12, 2020, www
.zdnet.com/article/europes-cloud-computing-project-needs-to-hurry-up-if-it
-wants-to-catch-its-giant-rivals/; "Microsoft Announced as a Member of GA-
IA-X," *Microsoft Corporate Blogs*, Microsoft, November 26, 2020, https://blogs
.microsoft.com/eupolicy/2020/11/26/microsoft-announced-as-a-member-of
-gaia-x/; Max Peterson, "What's Next for Europe's Data Revolution? AWS
Joins the GAIA-X Initiative," *AWS Public Sector Blog*, Amazon, November 19,
2020, https://aws.amazon.com/blogs/publicsector/what-next-europes-data-rev
olution-aws-joins-gaia-x-initiative/; Catherine Stupp, "European Cloud-
Computing Initiative Limits U.S. Companies' Role," *Wall Street Journal*, November
23, 2020, www.wsj.com/articles/european-cloud-computing-initiative-limits-u
-s-companies-role-11606127402.

66. European Union, *Declaration: Building the Next Generation Cloud for Businesses and the
Public Sector in the EU* (n.p.: European Union, 2020), https://ec.europa.eu/news
room/dae/document.cfm?doc_id=70089.

67. Canalys, "Global Cloud Infrastructure Market Q4 2020."

68. Henry Farrell and Abraham L. Newman, *Of Privacy and Power: The Transatlantic
Struggle over Freedom and Security* (Princeton, NJ: Princeton University Press, 2019),
loc. 3538 of 6092, Kindle.

69. Annegret Kramp-Karrenbauer, "Speech by Federal Minister of Defense Annegret Kramp-Karrenbauer on the Occasion of the Presentation of the Steuben
Schurz Media Award" (speech, Steuben Schurz Society, Frankfurt, Germany,

October 23, 2020), https://nato.diplo.de/blob/2409698/75266e6a100b6e3589
5f431c3ae66c6d/20201023-rede-akk-medienpreis-data.pdf.

70. Institute for Health Metrics and Evaluation, "The Lancet: World Population
   Likely to Shrink after Mid-Century, Forecasting Major Shifts in Global Population and Economic Power," press release, July 14, 2020, previously published
   by *The Lancet*, www.healthdata.org/news-release/lancet-world-population-likely
   -shrink-after-mid-century-forecasting-major-shifts-global.

71. "Countries," Freedom House, accessed March 2, 2021, https://freedomhouse
   .org/countries/freedom-net/scores; Stein E. Vollset et al., "Fertility, Mortality,
   Migration, and Population Scenarios for 195 Countries and Territories from
   2017 to 2100: A Forecasting Analysis for the Global Burden of Disease Study,"
   *The Lancet* 396, no. 10258 (2020): 1285–1306, https://doi.org/10.1016/S0140-67
   36(20)30677-2.

72. Ruchir Sharma, "Technology Will Save Emerging Markets from Sluggish
   Growth," *Financial Times*, April 11, 2021, https://www.ft.com/content/2356928b
   -d909-4a1d-b108-7b60983e3d22.

73. UNCTAD, *Digital Economy Report 2019*, iv.

74. UNCTAD, *Digital Economy Report 2019*, 12.

75. UNCTAD, *Digital Economy Report 2019*, 13.

76. UNCTAD, *Digital Economy Report 2019*, 8.

77. Homi Kharas and Kristofer Hamel, "A Global Tipping Point: Half of the
   World Is Now Middle Class or Wealthier," *Future Development* (blog), Brookings Institution, September 27, 2018, www.brookings.edu/blog/future-develop
   ment/2018/09/27/a-global-tipping-point-half-the-world-is-now-middle-class
   -or-wealthier/.

78. Data provided by Homi Kharas and Meagan Dooley, October 2020. Also see
   Homi Kharas and Meagan Dooley, "China's Influence on the Global Middle Class," Brookings Institution, October 2020, https://www.brookings.edu
   /research/chinas-influence-on-the-global-middle-class/.

79. Data provided by Homi Kharas and Meagan Dooley, October 2020.

80. Noshir Kaka et al., *Digital India: Technology to Transform a Connected Nation* (n.p.: Mc-
   Kinsey & Company, 2019), 1, www.mckinsey.com/~/media/McKinsey/Business
   %20Functions/McKinsey%20Digital/Our%20Insights/Digital%20India%20
   Technology%20to%20transform%20a%20connected%20nation/MGI-Digital
   -India-Report-April-2019.pdf.

81. "India 5G Activities Updates," GSMA, September 3, 2019, www.gsma.com/asia -pacific/resources/india-5g-updates/.

82. This includes the G-7 (Canada, France, Germany, Italy, Japan, the United Kingdom, and the United States).

83. Data provided by Washington University's Institute for Health Metrics and Evaluation, October 2020.

84. William Mauldin and Rajesh Roy, "Pompeo Touts U.S.-India Defense Deal, with an Eye on China," *Wall Street Journal*, October 27, 2020, www.wsj.com/articles /pompeo-touts-u-s-india-defense-deal-with-an-eye-on-china-11603791947; "India Says to Sign Military Agreement with U.S. on Sharing of Satellite Data," Reuters, October 26, 2020, www.reuters.com/article/us-india-usa-defence-idUS KBN27B1QY; Sanjeev Miglani, "India, U.S., Japan and Australia Kick Off Large Naval Drills," Reuters, November 3, 2020, www.reuters.com/article/us -india-navy-drills-idUSKBN27J11Z.

85. White House, "Fact Sheet: Quad Summit," press release, March 12, 2021, www .whitehouse.gov/briefing-room/statements-releases/2021/03/12/fact-sheet -quad-summit/.

86. Evan A. Feigenbaum and James Schwemlein, "How Biden Can Make the Quad Endure," Carnegie Endowment for International Peace, March 11, 2021, https:// carnegieendowment.org/2021/03/11/how-biden-can-make-quad-endure -pub-84046.

87. Tanvi Madan, *Fateful Triangle: How China Shaped US-India Relations during the Cold War* (Washington D.C.: Brookings Institution Press, 2020).

88. George W. Bush, "President Discusses Strong U.S.-India Partnership in New Delhi, India" (speech, Purana Qila, New Delhi, India, March 3, 2006), https:// georgewbush-whitehouse.archives.gov/news/releases/2006/03/20060303-5. html; "Bush, India's Singh Sign Civil Nuclear Cooperation Agreement," U.S. Department of State (archive), March 2, 2006, https://web.archive.org/web/200 60306172637/http://usinfo.state.gov/sa/Archive/2006/Mar/02-806725.html.

89. "Secretary Michael R. Pompeo with Rahul Shivshankar of Times Now," U.S. Department of State (archive), October 27, 2020, http://web.archive.org/web /20201102040052/www.state.gov/secretary-michael-r-pompeo-with-rahul-shiv shankar-of-times-now/.

90. Office of the U.S. Trade Representative, *2021 National Trade Estimate Report on Foreign Trade Barriers* (Washington, D.C.: Office of the U.S. Trade Representative, 2021), 248, https://ustr.gov/sites/default/files/files/reports/2021/2021NTE.pdf.

91. Han Lin 韩琳, "Zhongguo xiwang yu yindu jianli zhengchang de guojia guanxi yin tai zhanlüe buzu wei ju" 中国希望与印度建立正常的国家关系印太战略不足为惧 [China Hopes to Establish Normal State-to-State Relations with India, the Indo-Pacific Strategy Should Not Be Feared], Zhongguo wang 中国网 [China Net], July 14, 2020, http://fangtan.china.com.cn/2020-07/14/content_76270833.htm.

92. Office of the United States Trade Representative, *2021 National Trade Estimate Report*; Office of Economic Adviser, Department for Promotion of Industry and Internal Trade, Ministry of Commerce & Industry, Government of India, *Key Economic Indicators* (New Delhi: Ministry of Commerce & Industry, last modified 2021), https://eaindustry.nic.in/Key_Economic_Indicators/Key_Macro_Economic_Indicators.pdf; Russell A. Green, *Can "Make in India" Make Jobs? The Challenges of Manufacturing Growth and High-Quality Job Creation in India* (Houston, TX: James A. Baker III Institute for Public Policy, Rice University, 2014), www.bakerinstitute.org/media/files/files/9b2bf0a2/Econ-pub-MakeInIndia-121514.pdf; M. Suresh Babu, "Why 'Make in India' Has Failed," *The Hindu*, January 20, 2020, www.thehindu.com/opinion/op-ed/why-make-in-india-has-failed/article30601269.ece.

93. Munish Sharma, *The Road to 5G: Technology, Politics and Beyond*, IDSA Monograph Series No. 65 (New Delhi: Institute for Defence Studies and Analyses, 2019), 116, https://idsa.in/system/files/monograph/monograph-65.pdf; "Merchandise Trade Matrix—Imports of Individual Economies in Thousands of United States Dollars, Annual," UNCTADstat, UNCTAD, accessed February 2, 2021, https://unctadstat.unctad.org/wds/TableViewer/tableView.aspx?ReportId=195167.

94. Mukherjee et al., "COVID-19, Data Localisation and G20: Challenges, Opportunities and Strategies for India."

95. Harsh V. Pant and Aarshi Tirkey, "The 5G Question and India's Conundrum," *Orbis* 64, no. 4 (2020): 571–88, https://doi.org/10.1016/j.orbis.2020.08.006.

96. Ding Yi, "Xiaomi Still Top Dog in Indian Smartphone Market Despite Tensions," Caixin Global, August 10, 2020, www.caixinglobal.com/2020-08-10/xiaomi-still-top-dog-in-indian-smartphone-market-despite-tensions-101590849.html.

97. Sharma, *Road to 5G*.

98. Ajey Lele and Kritika Roy, *Analysing China's Digital and Space Belt and Road Initiative*, IDSA Occasional Paper No. 54/55 (New Delhi: Institute for Defence Studies and Analyses, 2019), 57, https://idsa.in/system/files/opaper/china-digital-bri-op55.pdf.

99. Ministry of Communications, Government of India, "Telecom Department Gives Go-Ahead for 5G Technology and Spectrum Trials," press release, May 4, 2021, https://pib.gov.in/PressReleasePage.aspx?PRID=1715927.

100. "India Doesn't Name Huawei among Participants in 5G Trials," Reuters, May 4, 2021, https://www.reuters.com/technology/india-doesnt-name-huawei-among -participants-5g-trials-2021-05-04/.

101. Nisha Holla, "Democratising Technology for the Next Six Billion," *Digital Frontiers* (blog), Observer Research Foundation, October 19, 2020, www.orfonline .org/expert-speak/democratising-technology-next-six-billion/.

102. Mukherjee et al., "COVID-19, Data Localisation and G20," 3.

103. Arindrajit Basu and Justin Sherman, "Key Global Takeaways from India's Revised Personal Data Protection Bill," *Lawfare* (blog), January 23, 2020, www.law fareblog.com/key-global-takeaways-indias-revised-personal-data-protection-bill.

104. "Freedom on the Net 2020: India," Freedom House, accessed February 1, 2021, https://freedomhouse.org/country/india/freedom-net/2020.

105. Sonia Faleiro, "How India Became the World's Leader in Internet Shutdowns," *MIT Technology Review*, August 19, 2020, www.technologyreview.com/2020 /08/19/1006359/india-internet-shutdowns-blackouts-pandemic-kashmir/.

106. Adrian Shahbaz and Allie Funk, *Freedom on the Net 2020: The Pandemic's Digital Shadow* (Washington, D.C.: Freedom House, 2020), https://freedomhouse .org/sites/default/files/2020-10/10122020_FOTN2020_Complete_Report _FINAL.pdf.

107. James Dobbins, "Why Russia Should Not Rejoin the G7," *The RAND Blog*, RAND, June 13, 2018, www.rand.org/blog/2018/06/why-russia-should-not -rejoin-the-g-7.html.

108. Robert K. Knake, *Weaponizing Digital Trade—Creating a Digital Trade Zone to Promote Online Freedom and Cybersecurity*, Council Special Report No. 88 (New York: Council on Foreign Relations, 2020), 11, https://cdn.cfr.org/sites/default/files /report_pdf/weaponizing-digital-trade_csr_combined_final.pdf.

109. These products can include U.S. and other non-Chinese components, but they are assembled in China; see James Rogers et al., *Breaking the China Supply Chain: How the "Five Eyes" Can Decouple from Strategic Dependency* (London: The Henry Jackson Society, 2020), 26, https://henryjacksonsociety.org/wp-content/uploads /2020/05/Breaking-the-China-Chain.pdf.

110. Mukherjee et al., "COVID-19, Data Localisation and G20," 39.

111. Roosevelt, "Fireside Chat."

112. Jens Stoltenberg, "Keynote Speech by NATO Secretary General Jens Stoltenberg at the Global Security 2020 (GLOBSEC) Bratislava Forum" (speech, Global Security 2020 Bratislava Forum, Bratislava, Slovakia, October 7, 2020), www.nato.int/cps/en/natohq/opinions_178605.htm.

113. James Stavridis and Dave Weinstein, "NATO's Real Spending Emergency Is in Cyberspace," Bloomberg, July 18, 2018, www.bloomberg.com/opinion/articles/2018-07-18/nato-s-real-spending-emergency-is-in-cyberspace.

114. Safa Shahwan Edwards, Will Loomis, and Simon Handler, "Supersize Cyber," Atlantic Council, October 14, 2020. www.atlanticcouncil.org/content-series/nato20-2020/supersize-cyber/.

115. Lindsay Gorman, "NATO Should Count Spending on Secure 5G towards Its 2% Goals," *Defense One*, December 3, 2019, www.defenseone.com/ideas/2019/12/nato-should-count-secure-5g-spending-towards-its-2-goals/161648/.

116. Stoltenberg, "Keynote Speech by NATO Secretary General."

117. "The Defense Business Board's 2015 Study on How the Pentagon Could Save $125 Billion," *Washington Post*, January 22, 2015, http://apps.washingtonpost.com/g/documents/investigations/the-defense-business-boards-2015-study-on-how-the-pentagon-could-save-125-billion/2236/; "Pentagon Buried Study That Found $125 Billion in Wasteful Spending: Washington Post," Reuters, December 5, 2016, www.reuters.com/article/us-usa-defense-waste/pentagon-buried-study-that-found-125-billion-in-wasteful-spending-washington-post-idUSKBN13V08B; Lawrence J. Korb, "The Pentagon's Fiscal Year 2021 Budget More than Meets U.S. National Security Needs," Center for American Progress, May 6, 2020, www.americanprogress.org/issues/security/reports/2020/05/06/484620/pentagons-fiscal-year-2021-budget-meets-u-s-national-security-needs/.

118. Jessica Tuchman Mathews, "America's Indefensible Defense Budget," Carnegie Endowment for International Peace, June 27, 2019, https://carnegieendowment.org/2019/06/27/america-s-indefensible-defense-budget-pub-79394; "Foreign Commercial Service," American Foreign Service Association, accessed February 15, 2021, www.afsa.org/foreign-commercial-service.

119. American Foreign Service Association, correspondence with author, March 2019.

120. "Global Diplomacy Index," Lowy Institute, accessed February 1, 2021, https://globaldiplomacyindex.lowyinstitute.org/.

121. "Forecasting Infrastructure Investment Needs and Gaps," Global Infrastructure Outlook, accessed February 1, 2021, https://outlook.gihub.org/.

122. Nirav Patel, "US Should Offer a Digital Highway Initiative for Asia," *Strait Times*, February 8, 2018, www.straitstimes.com/opinion/us-should-offer-a-digital -highway-initiative-for-asia.

123. Tim Hwang, *Shaping the Terrain of AI Competition* (Washington, D.C.: Center for Security and Emerging Technology, 2020), 19, https://cset.georgetown.edu /research/shaping-the-terrain-of-ai-competition/.

124. Eric Schmidt et al., *Asymmetric Competition: A Strategy for China and Technology* (n.p.: China Strategy Group, 2020), https://assets.documentcloud.org/documents/2046 3382/final-memo-china-strategy-group-axios-1.pdf.

125. China Task Force, U.S. House of Representatives, 116th Cong., *China Task Force Report* (Washington, D.C.: U.S. House of Representatives, 2020), 27, https:// gop-foreignaffairs.house.gov/wp-content/uploads/2020/09/CHINA-TASK -FORCE-REPORT-FINAL-9.30.20.pdf.

126. Stu Woo, "U.S. to Offer Loans to Lure Developing Countries Away from Chinese Telecom Gear," *Wall Street Journal*, October 18, 2020, www.wsj.com /articles/u-s-to-offer-loans-to-lure-developing-countries-away-from-chinese -telecom-gear-11603036800.

127. Agatha Kratz, Allen Feng, and Logan Wright, "New Data on the Debt Trap Question," Rhodium Group, April 29 2019, https://rhg.com/research/new -data-on-the-debt-trap-question/; Agatha Kratz, Matthew Mingey, and Drew D'Alelio, *Seeking Relief: China's Overseas Debt after COVID-19* (New York: Rhodium Group, 2020), https://rhg.com/research/seeking-relief/.

128. Angus Grigg, "Huawei Data Centre Built to Spy on PNG," *Australian Financial Review*, August 11, 2020, www.afr.com/companies/telecommunications/huawei -data-centre-built-to-spy-on-png-20200810-p55k7w.

129. Huawei Cyber Security Evaluation Centre Oversight Board, *Annual Report 2019: A Report to the National Security Adviser of the United Kingdom* (London: Cabinet Office, 2019), https://assets.publishing.service.gov.uk/government/uploads/system /uploads/attachment_data/file/790270/HCSEC_OversightBoardReport-2019. pdf; Lily Hay Newman, "Huawei's Problem Isn't Chinese Backdoors. It's Buggy Software," *Wired*, March 28, 2019, www.wired.com/story/huawei-threat-isnt -backdoors-its-bugs/; Kate O'Keeffe and Dustin Volz, "Huawei Telecom Gear Much More Vulnerable to Hackers than Rivals' Equipment, Report Says," *Wall Street Journal*, June 25, 2019, www.wsj.com/articles/huawei-telecom-gear-much -more-vulnerable-to-hackers-than-rivals-equipment-report-says-11561501573.

130. Herb Lin, "Huawei and Managing 5G Risk," *Lawfare* (blog), April 3, 2019, www .lawfareblog.com/huawei-and-managing-5g-risk; Carisa Nietsche and Martijn

Rasser, "Washington's Anti-Huawei Tactics Need a Reboot in Europe," *Foreign Policy*, April 30, 2020, https://foreignpolicy.com/2020/04/30/huawei-5g -europe-united-states-china/.

131. Amy Webb, *The Big Nine: How the Tech Titans and Their Thinking Machines Could Warp Humanity* (New York: PublicAffairs), 208, Kindle.

132. Thomas, *Dragon Bytes*, 35.

133. Thomas Donahue, "The Worst Possible Day: U.S. Telecommunications and Huawei," *PRISM* 8, no. 3 (2020), https://ndupress.ndu.edu/Media/News/News -Article-View/Article/2053215/the-worst-possible-day-us-telecommunications -and-huawei/.

134. National Intelligence Council, *Global Trends 2040: A More Contested World*, NIC 2021- 02339 (Washington, D.C.: National Intelligence Council, 2021), 102, https:// www.odni.gov/files/ODNI/documents/assessments/GlobalTrends_2040.pdf.

135. As cited in Thomas, *Dragon Bytes*, 45.

136. Shen Weiguang, "Checking Information Warfare-Epoch Mission of Intellectual Military," *People's Liberation Army Daily*, February 2, 1999, as quoted and cited in Thomas, *Dragon Bytes*, 13.

137. James A. Lewis, "A Necessary Contest: An Overview of U.S. Cyber Capabilities," *Asia Policy* 15, no. 2 (2020): 92, https://doi.org/10.1353/asp.2020.0016.

138. Ryan Hass, "China Is Not Ten Feet Tall," *Foreign Affairs*, March 3, 2021, www .foreignaffairs.com/articles/china/2021-03-03/china-not-ten-feet-tall.

139. Ryan Hass, *Stronger: Adapting America's China Strategy in an Age of Competitive Interdependence* (New Haven, CT: Yale University Press, 2021).

140. Michael Beckley, *Unrivaled: Why America Will Remain the World's Sole Superpower* (Ithaca, NY: Cornell University Press, 2018).

141. Reagan, "Triumph of Freedom."

# INDEX

# ABOUT THE AUTHOR

Jonathan E. Hillman is a senior fellow at the Center for Strategic and International Studies (CSIS) and director of the Reconnecting Asia Project, one of the most extensive open-source databases tracking China's Belt and Road Initiative. Prior to joining CSIS, he served as a policy advisor at the Office of the U.S. Trade Representative and worked as a researcher at the Belfer Center for Science and International Affairs, the Council on Foreign Relations, and in Kyrgyzstan as a Fulbright scholar. A graduate of the Harvard Kennedy School and Brown University, he has written for the *Washington Post* and the *Wall Street Journal*, among other outlets, and received the 2019 Bracken Bower Prize from the *Financial Times*.